Sweet Violence

Sweet

VIOLENCE

THE IDEA OF THE TRAGIC

TERRY EAGLETON

Blackwell
Publishing

350 Main Street, Malden, MA 02148-5018, USA
108 Cowley Road, Oxford OX4 1JF, UK
550 Swanston Street, Carlton South, Victoria 3053, Australia
Kurfürstendamm 57, 10707 Berlin, Germany

First published 2003 by Blackwell Publishers Ltd, a Blackwell
Publishing company

Library of Congress Cataloging-in-Publication Data has been applied for.

ISBN 0-631-23359-8 (hbk); ISBN 0-631-23360-1 (pbk)

A catalogue record for this title is available from the British Library.

Set in 10/12^1/$_2$pt Meridien
by SNP Best-set Typesetter Ltd, Hong Kong
Printed and bound in the United Kingdom by T.J. International,
Padstow, Cornwall

For further information on
Blackwell Publishing, visit our website:
http://www.blackwellpublishing.com

In memory of Herbert McCabe

Contents

Acknowledgements

Terry Collits, Peter Dews, Franco Moretti and Tony Nuttall were all kind enough to read all or some of this book in manuscript and made some invaluable suggestions to improve it. I am also deeply grateful to my editor Andrew McNeillie, whose friendship, loyalty and wise counsel over so many years have been a precious gift to me.

Introduction

Tragedy is an unfashionable subject these days, which is one good reason for writing about it. It smacks of virile warriors and immolated virgins, cosmic fatality and stoical acquiescence. There is an ontological depth and high seriousness about the genre which grates on the postmodern sensibility, with its unbearable lightness of being. As an aristocrat among art forms, its tone is too solemn and portentous for a streetwise, sceptical culture. Indeed, the term hardly scrapes into the postmodern lexicon. For some feminists, tragic art is far too enamoured of sacrifice, false heroics and a very male nobility of spirit, a kind of high-brow version of ripping yarns for boys. For leftists in general, it has an unsavoury aura of gods, myths and blood cults, metaphysical guilt and inexorable destiny.

The odd leftist who does write about tragedy today usually takes for granted a highly reactionary version of the form, which he or she then proceeds to reject. This is a marvellously labour-saving manoeuvre. It is rather like assuming that all non-Marxist philosophy denies the existence of a material world, thus saving oneself the tedium of having to read it. Jonathan Dollimore seems to assume that tragedy is invariably about fatalism, resignation and inevitability,[1] while Francis Barker speaks disapprovingly of tragedy's 'celebration of sovereign presence in the form of lost plenitude'.[2] Barker sees tragedy as inherently unhistorical, a quality which is truer of his own view of it than of the thing itself. Both he and Dollimore essentialize the form; it is just that while others have done so affirmatively, they do so negatively. Barker, rather grudgingly, ends his excellent study by acknowledging that 'The situation in which we who inhabit a seemingly common earth do not all do so with the same space, validity and pleasure may properly be described as tragic'. Indeed so; in fact, if this does not merit the title, it is hard to see what does. But Barker nevertheless feels constrained to enter an instant caveat: 'But not [tragedy] defined as an inescapable and irremediable given, an unrelievable historicism, or a mysterious condition'.[3] No, to be sure; but why have we allowed our political antagonists to monopolize the definition of the form to the point where, like Barker, we are wary of using the term at all? And this, unbelievably, in an age when more men and women have been killed or deliberately allowed to die than ever before in history.[4] A recent estimate of the twentieth century's 'megadeaths' is 187 million, the equivalent of more than one in ten of the world population in 1900. Yet tragedy remains a word of which the left is distinctly nervous.

If some postmodernism is rather too shallow for tragedy, some post-structuralism takes it altogether too seriously. A recent collection of essays entitled *Philosophy and Tragedy*,[5] a volume of admirable power, range and intricacy, has scarcely a critical word to breathe of such classical tragic notions as fate and heroism, gods and essences, Dionysian frenzy, the ennobling role of suffering, the character of the Absolute, the need to sacrifice the individual to the whole, the transcendent nature of tragic affirmation, and other such high-minded platitudes of traditional tragic theory. The role of poststructuralism, it would seem, is to reinterpret the concept rather than to change it. For all its undoubted depth of insight, the volume's implicit politics of tragedy are entirely acceptable to those scholars who would reach for their timeless Sophoclean wisdom at the faintest mention of the floating signifier. From one end to another, the collection scarcely has a word to say of tragedy as human distress and despair, breakdown and wretchedness. As we shall see later, it runs the persuasive thesis that in the modern epoch tragedy has been a continuation of philosophy by other means; but it does not seem aware that its own lofty theoreticist disdain for the historical represents the less alluring side of this complicity between the two.

Not that the present book is itself an historical study of tragedy.[6] It is, rather, a political one. The two terms are not synonymous. Indeed, I am almost tempted to say that they are today in some danger of actually becoming opposites. I have argued elsewhere, though hardly to much effect, that to historicize is by no means an inherently radical move.[7] Much historicism, from Edmund Burke to Michael Oakshott, has been politically conservative. The left is deluded if it believes that it has a monopoly on historically contextualizing. To historicize is indeed vital; but there is in vogue today a brand of left-historicism which seems more indebted to capitalist ideology than to socialist theory. In a world of short-term contracts, just-in-time deliveries, ceaseless downsizings and remodellings, overnight shifts of fashion and capital investment, multiple careers and multipurpose production, such theorists seem to imagine, astonishingly, that the main enemy is the naturalized, static and unchanging. Whereas the truth is that for millions of harassed workers around the globe, not many of them academics, a respite from dynamism, metamorphosis and multiple identities would come as a blessed release.

A faith in plurality, plasticity, dismantling, destabilizing, the power of endless self-invention – all this, while undoubtedly radical in some contexts, also smacks of a distinctively Western culture and an advanced capitalist world. Indeed, it smacks more specifically of a particular corner of Western culture – the United States – in which ideologies of self-fashioning, along with a strenuously self-affirmative moulding of Nature, have always gripped the imagination more compellingly than in the more sceptical, self-doubting, deterministic cultures of Europe. It is just that, in a later stage of capitalist production, we are now confronted with the singular spectacle of self-fashioning without a subject. An openness to cultural 'otherness' comes pre-wrapped in ideas of the protean, provisional and performative which may strike some of the cultural others in question as distinctly foreign goods. But it is scarcely surprising that those most sensitive to cultural difference should unwittingly project the ideologies of their own piece of the world on humanity at large. It is, after all, what their rulers have been up to for rather a long time.

At its starkest, then, it is a choice between suffocating under history in Lisbon and stifling for lack of it in Los Angeles. In what sense, however, is this rather upbeat brand of historicism at risk of becoming the opposite of radical politics rather than its intellectual ally? Simply because it is embarrassed by much that such a politics must address: age-old structures of power which are still obdurately in place; doctrines which seem to have all the intransigence of a tornado; deep-seated desires and resistances which are not easily amenable to change. If the more callow sort of historicism is right, how come we have not long since reinvented ourselves out of such dreary continuities? Moreover, those who insist with suspicious stridency on the malleability of things, and for whom 'dynamic' is as unequivocally positive a term as 'static' is unambiguously negative, tend to forget that there are kinds of change which are deeply unpleasant and undesirable, just as there are forms of permanence and continuity which are to be affirmed and admired. Capitalism may be justly upbraided for many defects, but lack of dynamism is hardly one of them. One thinks of Walter Benjamin's wise dictum that revolution is not a runaway train but the application of the emergency brake. It is capitalism which is anarchic, extravagant, out of hand, and socialism which is temperate, earth-bound and realistic. This is at least one reason why an anarchic, extravagant poststructuralism has been rather wary of it. Anyway, if it is indeed the case that human subjects are always historically constituted, then here at least is one vitally important non-historical truth.

Most of the left-historicism of our day is reductionist. It does not recognize that history is striated with respect to rates of change. If there is the speedy temporality of the 'conjuncture', there is also the *longue durée* of a mode of production, which sometimes seems to shift no more perceptibly than the planet itself, and somewhere in between the two the medium-range time of, say, the political state. A particular historical event – a strike, for example – may involve all three. To attend only to the first of them, as Francis Mulhern has argued, is to reduce history to change.[8] But there is also much in the human record which does not change, or which alters only very gradually, which is one reason why radical politics are in business. Most of any present is made up of the past. History, as Mulhern insists, is for the most part continuity. It belongs to its complex material weight that it cannot be perpetually refashioned. And even when we do manage to transform it, its weight may still be found resting like a nightmare on the brains of the living.

This is a recipe for sober realism, not for political despair. Materialism is concerned with the sudden shock of political conjunctures, dramatic shifts in the balance of political forces. Who would have expected, only a few years before the event, that the Soviet bloc would be overthrown almost overnight, and with a minimum of violence? But a genuine materialism, as opposed to an historicist relativism or idealism, is also attentive to those aspects of our existence which are permanent structures of our species-being. It is concerned with the creaturely, ecological dimensions of our existence, not only with cultural value and historical agency. And among these is the reality of suffering. As Theodor Adorno famously remarked, 'The One and All that keeps rolling on to this day – with occasional breathing spells – would teleologically be the absolute of suffering'.[9]

There is no occasion here for the predictable culturalist or historicist riposte that such suffering is always contextually specific. How could the man who lived through the genocide of his own people have failed to notice this? It is as though someone were to point out the curiousness of the fact that everyone at the party is wearing thick green goggles, only to be witheringly informed that they are wearing them for quite different reasons. The point that Adorno is making is not that torture and affliction are non-contextual, but that they crop up with such alarming regularity in so *many* contexts, from the neolithic age to NATO. Is not this fact, 'unhistorical' though it is, worthy of note? Is not its transhistoricality precisely the point? If some on the left are instinctively alarmed by the thought of the transhistorical, it is partly because they fail to grasp the fact that *longues durées* are quite as much part of human history as pastoral verse or parliaments, and partly because the only alternative they can imagine to historical change is the timeless essence. Why their imaginations are so gripped by idealism in this respect is a different question. They will not allow that materialism itself offers some rather more plausible alternatives to this contingency/essentialism couplet because they are fearful of a reductive biologism. But they appear quite unfearful of a reductive historicism. Nor do they seem to recognize that the distinction between change and permanence is not the same as the contrast between culture and nature. It is proving rather more feasible in our age to alter certain genetic structures than it is to tamper with capitalism or patriarchy.

Radicals are suspicious of the transhistorical because it suggests there are things which cannot be changed, hence fostering a political fatalism. There are indeed good grounds for suspicion here. But the truth is that there *are* things which cannot be changed, as well as some which are highly unlikely to change, and in some cases this is a matter to celebrate rather than lament. It is reassuring that not ritually slaughtering all those over the age of forty seems to be a reasonably permanent feature of human cultures. There are other situations which cannot be changed, but to no particular detriment. And there are some which cannot be changed much to our chagrin. Tragedy deals in the cut-and-thrust of historical conjunctures, but since there are aspects of suffering which are also rooted in our species-being, it also has an eye to these more natural, material facts of human nature. As the Italian philosopher Sebastiano Timpanaro points out, phenomena such as love, ageing, disease, fear of one's own death and sorrow for the death of others, the brevity and frailty of human existence, the contrast between the weakness of humanity and the apparent infinity of the cosmos: these are recurrent features of human cultures, however variously they may be represented.[10] However left-historicism may suspect that universals are governing-class conspiracies, the fact is that we die anyway. It is, to be sure, a consoling thought for pluralists that we meet our end in such a richly diverse series of ways, that our modes of exiting from existence are so splendidly heterogeneous, that there is no drearily essentialist 'death' but a diffuse range of cultural styles of expiring. Indeed, perhaps we should speak of death as a way of being 'challenged', a mode of being which is neither inferior nor superior to breathing or love-making, simply different. Perhaps the dead are not really dead, just differently capacitated. But we die anyway.

Cultural continuities, Timpanaro points out, 'have been rendered possible by the fact that man as a biological being has remained essentially unchanged from the beginnings of civilization to the present; and those sentiments and representations which are closest to the biological facts of human existence have changed little'.[11] However culturalists may wince at this cheek-by-jowl consorting of 'sentiments and representations' with 'biological facts', it is surely true that to ask, say, why we feel sympathy for Philoctetes is a pseudo-problem bred by a bogus historicism. We feel sympathy for Philoctetes because he is in agonizing pain from his pus-swollen foot. There is no use in pretending that his foot is a realm of impenetrable otherness which our modern-day notions can grasp only at the cost of brutally colonizing the past. There is nothing hermeneutically opaque about Philoctetes's hobbling and bellowing. There is, to be sure, a great deal about the art form in which he figures which is profoundly obscure to us. We are, for example, bemused and mildly scandalized by Antigone's declaration that she would not have broken the law for a husband or a son, as opposed to a brother. It is not the kind of thing a good liberal would say. But as far as his agony goes, we understand Philoctetes in much the same way as we understand the afflictions of those around us. It is not that such a response is 'unhistorical'; it is rather that human history includes the history of the body, which in respect of physical suffering has probably changed little over the centuries. No doubt this is why the body in pain, despite a few splendidly perceptive accounts of it, has scarcely been the most popular of topics in a body-oriented academia, hardly able to compete with the sexual, disciplined or carnivalesque body. It confirms much less readily a certain case about historical pliability. And the suffering body is largely a passive one, which does not suit a certain ideology of self-fashioning. It is of no particular consolation to the victims of torture to be told that their anguish is culturally constructed, as it is, perhaps, to be told that one's lowly place in the hierarchies of gender or ethnicity is a changeable historical affair.

The current preoccupation with the body grew up in part as a reaction against a rationalist, objectivist outlook. This is ironic, since the human body is what gives us an objective world. It is what objectivity is rooted in. There is, to be sure, a whole galaxy of cultural worlds, all claiming some sort of objective status; but they are possible only within the matrix formed by the 'species-body' as such. There could not be a cultural world in which people regularly toasted one another's achievements in large doses of sulphuric acid, one in which there were no social relations whatsoever, or one in which there was no concept of something being the case. Even if such worlds could come into being, which they could not, they would quickly pass out of it again. This, perhaps, is what Ludwig Wittgenstein has in mind when he comments cryptically in the *Philosophical Investigations* that if a lion could speak, we would not be able to understand what he said. Even if we could, we would not be able to pick an argument with him over what was the case, since what is the case for a lion is not what is the case for us.

For all that we venerate ferrets and respect the ontological autonomy of weasels, speciesism must hold epistemologically, if not morally; whereas the concept of objectivity means that we can always argue with each other over what is the case. Because we share a form of material body, in other words, conflict is built into our existence, as it is not built into our relations with badgers. The body is itself a kind of sign, in which we are present rather as the meaning is present in a word; but it also sets the outer boundaries to signification as such. Historicism is right to insist that the world given us by our species-being is by no means always the most significant or exciting. The universal can be supremely trivial. It is not the fact that Orestes has to sleep or that Cordelia has knees which claims our attention. But it is illogical to deny the significance of the species-body altogether while making rhetorical claims about materialism.

Historicism is mistaken to believe that what belongs to our species-being must invariably be politically retrograde or irrelevant. It can indeed be this; but one would expect such devotees of cultural relativity to be a little less inflexibly universalist in their opinions. It is true that there is much about our species-being which is passive, constrained and inert. But this may be a source of radical politics, not an obstacle to it. Our passivity, for example, is closely bound up with our frailty and vulnerability, in which any authentic politics must be anchored. Tragedy can be among other things a symbolic coming to terms with our finitude and fragility, without which any political project is likely to founder. But this weakness is also a source of power, since it is where some of our needs take root. If these needs are rebuffed, then they have behind them a force rather more intractable than the purely cultural. The champions of the protean fail to appreciate that intractability is sometimes just what we need. If we can successfully confront death-dealing, oppressive forces, it is not because history is mere cultural clay in our hands, or (a more vulgarized version of the same ideology) because when there's a will there's a way. It is because the impulse to freedom from oppression, however that goal is culturally framed, seems as obdurate and implacable as the drive to material survival. Which is by no means to say that it is everywhere evident or that it will always triumph.

I have touched on several senses in which some aspects of tragedy cut against the grain of cultural left orthodoxy. It is not that these aspects define the form in general, which, as I seek to show, is not totalizable as a whole. And there are elements in the form which run directly counter to these concerns. But I am interested in this book in how some tragic art highlights what is perishable, constricted, fragile and slow-moving about us, as a rebuke to culturalist or historicist hubris. It stresses how we are acted upon rather than robustly enterprising, as well as what meagre space for manoeuvre we often have available. This recognition, indeed, is the positive side of a mystified belief in destiny. What for some suggests fatalism or pessimism means for others the kind of sober realism which is the only sure foundation of an effective ethics or politics. Only by grasping our constraints can we act constructively.

The aspects of tragedy I have in mind take with the utmost serious-ness the lethal as well as life-giving inheritances of which the present is partly made up, and which an amnesiac postmodernism has conveniently suppressed. If we cannot fashion ourselves as we choose, as Henrik Ibsen knew, it is because of the burden of history under which we stagger, not only because of the restrictions of the present. This truth is perhaps least understood in those societies with the least history. But it is a universal one, even so. And where tragedy is concerned, the question of univer-sality cannot be side-stepped by a glib particularism. In one sense, to be sure, all tragedies are specific: there are tragedies of particular peoples and genders, of nations and social groups. There is the destruction of the English handloom weavers, the long degradation of African-American slavery, the day-by-day indignities of women, not to speak of those hole-in-the-corner calamities of obscure individual lives which lack even the dignity of a collective political title. And none of these experiences is abstractly exchangeable with the others. They have no shared essence, other than the fact of suffering. But suffering is a mightily powerful language to share in common, one in which many diverse life-forms can strike up a dialogue. It is a communality of meaning. It is a sign of how far many so-called radicals today have drifted from socialism, if they were ever anywhere near it in the first place, that for them all talk of com-munality is an insidious mystification. They do not seem to have noticed that difference, diversity and destabilization are the *dernier cri* of the transnational corporations. But a community of suffering is not the same thing as team spirit, chauvinism, homogeneity, organic unity or a des-potically normative consensus. For such a community, injury, division and antagonism are the currency you share in common.

Tragedy disconcerts some on the cultural left by its embarrassingly portentous 'depth'. Indeed, some readers will no doubt find this book rather too metaphysical for their taste, with its talk of the demonic and the Satanic, its unfashionable use of theological jargon to throw light on political realities. The political left's silence about religion is curious, given that in terms of compass, appeal and longevity, it is far and away the most important symbolic form which humanity has ever known. Even sport pales in comparison with it, not to speak of art. Yet those eager to study popular culture pass embarrassedly over this global, longest-lasting, most supremely effective mode of it, while those leftists who take seriously, say, Spinozist rationalism or Schellingian idealism dismiss it in the crudest of gestures as mere false consciousness. One of the few exceptions is the suggestive body of historical work on the relations between capitalism and Protestantism. As for postmodernists, it is rather odd that they should be so respectfully attuned to other cultures, yet such stereotypical Western liberals in their indifference to the religious beliefs which often bulk so large in them. Intellectuals who pride themselves on an informed understanding of, say, Aboriginal cosmology are quite unashamed to display the most red-necked, reductively caricaturing of responses when it comes to Christianity. Those accustomed to discussing almost any other question with admirable dispassionateness can become extravagantly irrational on this one.

In one sense, this is entirely understandable. Religion, and perhaps Christianity in particular, has wreaked untold havoc in human affairs. Bigotry, false consolation, brutal authoritarianism, sexual oppression: these are only a handful of the characteristics for which it stands condemned at the tribunal of history. Its role, with some honourable exceptions, has been to consecrate pillage and canonize injustice. In many of its aspects, religion today represents one of the most odious forms of political reaction on the planet, a blight on human freedom and a buttress of the rich and powerful. But there are also theological ideas which can be politically illuminating, and this book is among other things an exploration of them. So it is perhaps worth alluding at the very beginning to what I argue at the very end – that even if it is not exactly a metaphysical, theological or foundational discourse that the cultural left stands in need of, it would certainly profit it to broaden its theoretical sights and extend the narrow, repetitive circuit of preoccupations in which it is currently caught. Those preoccupations should by no means be abandoned, simply deepened in resonance. This study is among other things a contribution to that end.

Chapter 1

A Theory in Ruins

In everyday language, the word 'tragedy' means something like 'very sad'. We speak of the tragic car crash of the young woman at the busy crossroads, just as the ancient Greeks used the same epithet for a drama about the slaying of a king at a similar place. Indeed, it may well turn out that 'very sad' is also about the best we can do when it comes to the more exalted realm of tragic art.

But surely tragedy involves more than this. Is it not a matter of fate and catastrophe, of calamitous reversals of fortunes, flawed, high-born heroes and vindictive gods, pollution and purgation, deplorable endings, cosmic order and its transgression, a suffering which chastens and trans-figures? In any case, isn't this to mistake the tragic for the pathetic? Tragedy may be poignant, but it is supposed to have something fearful about it too, some horrific quality which shocks and stuns. It is traumatic as well as sorrowful. And doesn't the tragic differ from the pathetic in being cleansing, bracing, life-affirming? Susanne K. Langer speaks of the 'sad but non-tragic character of the French classical drama'[1] – non-tragic in her view because such drama deals in misfortune rather than destiny, lacks any rich realization of individual personality, and is rather too enamoured of the rational. Racine and Corneille, she suggests, write 'heroic comedies' rather than tragedies, which will no doubt come as a surprise to anyone who has sat through *Andromache* or *Polyeucte*. The French must have a strange sense of humour.

Tragedy, some will claim, is surely a *technical* term, whereas 'very sad' is plainly not. One can, in fact, use the word in both senses together, as in a sentence like 'What is really tragic about Beckett is that tragedy (heroic resistance, exultant self-affirmation, dignified endurance, the peace which comes from knowing that one's actions are predestined, and the like) is no longer possible'. And one can call something very sad – the peaceful, predictable death of an elderly person, for example – without feeling the need to dub it tragic. One can also be sad over nothing in particular, in the manner of Freud's melancholia, but it is hard to be tragic over nothing in particular. 'Tragic' is a more transitive term than 'sad'. Moreover, 'tragic' is a strong word, like 'scum' or 'squalid', whereas 'sad' is embarrassingly feeble. Geoffrey Brereton notes that it is hard to come up with a synonym of 'tragic',[2] a truth stumbled on by a fellow-student of mine at Cambridge, who realized that a suitably withering utterance of the word 'Tragic!' could effortlessly trump almost any other comment, however witty, acerbic or impassioned. The problem is how not to rob the word of this peculiar charge while not being jealously exclusive about it either.

'Tragic' and 'very sad' are indeed different notions; but this is not because the former is technical while the latter is drawn from ordinary language. 'Sad but not tragic' is not the same kind of distinction as 'erratic but not psychotic', 'cocky but not megalomaniac' or 'flabby but not obese'. The long-standing spouse of the expired elderly person might well feel the event as tragic, even though it is neither shocking, fearful, catastrophic, decreed by destiny or the upshot of some hubristic transgression of divine law. 'Tragic' here means something like 'very *very* sad' for the spouse, and just sad or very sad for everyone else. R. P. Draper tells us that 'there is an immense difference between the educated and uneducated intuitions of the meaning (of tragedy)',[3] but it does not follow, as he seems to imagine, that 'educated' intuitions are always the most reliable. One might still protest that tragedy involves more than just sorrow, and in a sense one would be right. But so does sorrow. Sorrow implies value. We do not usually grieve over the fading of a bruise, or feel the scattering of a raindrop to be a melancholic matter. These are not destructions of what we rate as especially valuable.

This is why there are difficulties with Paul Allen's definition of tragedy as 'a story with an unhappy ending that is memorably and upliftingly moving rather than simply sad'.[4] We shall see later that not all tragedies in fact end unhappily; but it is also hard to know what 'simply sad' means. Can a work be sad but not moving? Perhaps 'upliftingly' moving makes the difference; but it is not clear that *Blasted*, *Endgame* or *A Farewell to Arms* are exactly that, which is no doubt why conservative commentators would refuse them the title of tragedy in the first place. But they would probably confer it on *Titus Andronicus*, *The Jew of Malta* or *Antonio's Revenge*, whose edifying effects are almost as questionable. And Aristotle says nothing of edification. For one kind of traditionalist, Auschwitz is not tragic because it lacks a note of affirmation. But how far is the invigorating quality of a good tragedy that of any successful work of art? And are we enthralled by the sadness, or despite it? Doesn't sadness in any case depend on a sense of human

2

value which tempers it, so that 'simple sadness' is a somewhat spurious entity?

The truth is that no definition of tragedy more elaborate than 'very sad' has ever worked. It would, to be sure, be false to conclude from this that works or events we call tragedies have nothing significant in common. Nominalism is not the only alternative to essentialism, whatever post-modern theory may consider. On the one hand, there are full-blooded essentialists such as Paul Ricoeur, who believes that 'it is by grasping the essence [of tragedy] in the Greek phenomenon that we can understand all other tragedy as analogous to Greek tragedy'.[5] For Ricoeur, one assumes, *A Streetcar Named Desire* is best illuminated by the *Agamemnon*. On the other hand, there are nominalists such as Leo Aylen, who declares that there is no such thing as tragedy: 'There are only plays, some of which have always been called tragedies, some of which have usually been called tragedies'.[6] But this, as with most nominalism, simply pushes the question back a stage: *why* have these plays always or usually been called tragedies? Why have some of them not been called pastoral or pantomime instead? Raymond Williams notes that 'tragedy is . . . not a single and permanent kind of fact, but a series of experiences and conventions and institutions'.[7] But though this is true enough, it fails to answer the question of why we use the same term of *Medea* and *Macbeth*, the murder of a teenager and a mining disaster.

In fact, tragedy would seem exemplary of Wittgenstein's 'family resem-blances', constituted as it is by a *combinatoire* of overlapping features rather than by a set of invariant forms or contents. There is no need to languish in the grip of a binary opposition and suppose that because the members of a class lack a common essence, they have nothing in common at all. As early as 1908, the American scholar Ashley Thorndike warned his colleagues in his work *Tragedy* that no definition of tragedy was possible beyond the egregiously uninformative 'all plays presenting painful or destructive actions', but few seem to have taken his point. Aristotle's description of tragedy in the *Poetics* in fact makes little refer-ence to destruction, death or calamity; indeed he speaks at one point of a 'tragedy of suffering', almost as though this might be just one species of the genre. The *Poetics* is well into its argument before it begins to use words like 'misfortune'. As an early instance of reception theory, the work defines tragedy rather through its effects, working back from these to what might structurally best achieve them. A wicked person passing from misery to prosperity, for example, cannot be tragic because the process cannot inspire either pity or fear. This leaves open the question of what one calls a work which is structured to arouse pity and fear but in fact doesn't. Is a comedy which fails to arouse the faintest flicker of amusement a poor comedy or not a comedy at all?

The more laconic one's definition, the less chance it has of inadvertently passing over whole swathes of tragic experience. Schopenhauer claims that 'the presentation of a great misfortune is alone essential to [tragedy]',[8] and such cautiousness is well justified. It is a pity, then, that he goes on to claim that resignation and renunciation are of the essence of the form, a case which forces him to downgrade the ancient Greeks and implausibly upgrade some more stoically minded moderns. Samuel Johnson, no doubt equally eager to sidestep a whole range of thorny issues, defines tragedy in his dictionary as 'a dramatic representation of serious actions', which for all its studied vagueness comes close, as we shall see in a moment, to how the medievals understood the matter. 'Serious', for all its apparent lack of exactness, is a key component of the whole conception, from Aristotle to Geoffrey Chaucer. The former makes what he calls *spoudaios* central to the whole business. Indeed, it is still central as late as Pierre Corneille's *Discours de l'utilité et des parties du poème dramatique*, which describes tragedy as *'illustre, extraordinaire, sérieuse'*. Horace remarks in 'On the Art of Poetry' that 'tragedy scorns to babble trivialities'.[9] For a long time, tragedy really means nothing much more than a drama of high seriousness concerning the misfortunes of the mighty. It makes no necessary allusion to fate, purgation, moral flaws, the gods, and the rest of the impedimenta which conservative critics tend to assume are indispensable to it. As F. L. Lucas puts it: tragedy for the ancients means serious drama, for the middle ages a story with an unhappy ending, and for moderns a drama with an unhappy ending.[10] It is hard to get more imprecise than that.

John Orr claims that 'the essential tragic experience is that of irreparable human loss', though he rather tarnishes the impressive terseness of this by going on to develop a more elaborate theory of tragedy as alienation.[11] Richard Kuhns speaks with airy anachronism of the conflict between the private, sexual and psychological on the one hand, and the public, political and obligatory on the other, as being central to all tragedy, including the ancient Greeks.[12] It is not clear in what sense the sexual or psychological were 'private' for classical antiquity. The *Oxford English Dictionary* gives for tragedy 'extreme distress or sorrow', though ironically it goes on to illustrate this definition with the sentence 'the shooting was a tragic accident', which for some classical tragic theory would be an oxymoron. Tragedies, on this traditional view, cannot be accidental.

The *OED* also gives 'pity or sorrow' for 'pathos', thus bringing it close to the common sense of tragedy. There are, however, grammatical differences between the two terms. For the informal meaning of 'pathetic', the *OED* offers 'his ball control was pathetic', which one could hardly

4

replace with 'his ball control was tragic' even in the lower ranks of the football league. We say that someone looked sad but not, without a slight sense of strain, that she looked tragic, since the former term tends to denote a response and the latter a condition. But Walter Kaufmann, in one of the most perceptive modern studies of tragedy, refuses to distinguish between the tragic and the merely pitiful, and doubts that the ancient Greeks or Shakespeare did either.[13] He does, however, suggest that for the classical view suffering has to be 'philosophically' interesting to qualify as tragic, which would no doubt rule out such philosophically trivial matters as having your feet chopped off or your eyeballs gouged out.

For all these grim caveats, critics have persisted in their hunt for the Holy Grail of a faultless definition of the subject. Kenneth Burke's definition of tragedy in *A Grammar of Motives*, like Francis Fergusson's in his immensely influential *The Idea of a Theater*, involves an essential moment of tragic recognition or *anagnorisis*,[14] but while this may be true of Oedipus, it holds only doubtfully for Othello and hardly at all for Arthur Miller's Willy Loman. In the case of Phaedra, no such recognition is needed because everything has been intolerably clear from the outset. David Hume, by contrast, believes that an individual 'is the more worthy of compassion the less sensible he is of his miserable condition', finding something peculiarly poignant about a wretchedness which seemed unaware of itself.[15] Georg Simmel observes that 'in general we call a relationship tragic – in contrast to merely sad or extrinsically destructive – when the destructive forces directed against some being spring from the deepest levels of that very being'.[16] We shall have occasion to revisit this insistence on the immanent, ironic or dialectical nature of the tragic, in contrast with the purely extrinsic or accidental; but it is worth remarking now that, like every other general formula in the field, it holds only for some tragedy and not for the rest. The downfall of Goethe's Faust, or Pentheus in Euripides's *The Bacchae*, may be sprung in just this way, but it is hard to argue a similar case about the death of Shakespeare's Cordelia or Tolstoy's Anna Karenina.

A. C. Bradley holds that a tragedy is 'any spiritual conflict involving spiritual waste',[17] while in a brave but imprudent flourish, Oscar Mandel offers as an all-inclusive definition of the form a situation in which 'a protagonist who would command our earnest good will is impelled in a given world by a purpose, or undertakes an action, of a certain seriousness and magnitude; and by that very purpose or action, subject to that same given world, necessarily and inevitably meets with grave spiritual or physical suffering'.[18] This, for all its White House bureaucratese and judicious sub-clausal hedging, falsely assumes with Simmel and others that tragedy is always immanent or ironic, staking too much on what the Greeks call *peripeteia*. It also throws in for good measure an emphasis on necessity which, as we shall see later, is equally unwarranted. Aristotle, for example, is for the most part silent on the question. Leo Aylen believes that tragedy is largely about death, while generously conceding that some tragedies are not. In an insight of positively Kantian intricacy, he informs us that in the face of death, 'Certain things become much less important, others much more'.[19] For Geoffrey Brereton, 'a tragedy is a final and impressive disaster due to an unforeseen or unrealized failure involving people who command respect and sympathy'.[20] This suggests that we do not find tragic those for whom we have limited sympathies, a common but debatable proposition of tragic theory. It also implies rather oddly that some disasters are unimpressive.

In *The Case for Tragedy*, a riposte to the death-of-tragedy school, Mark Harris defines the form rather maladroitly as 'the projection of personal and collective values which are potentially or actually put in jeopardy by the course of the dramatic action'.[21] This tells us remarkably little, though the title of the book tells us rather more. It is revealing that critics like Harris should feel the need to claim, in defensive, mildly anxious tones, that tragedy can indeed still thrive in contemporary conditions, as though it would be an unquestionable loss if it could not. It might well prove a loss, but one cannot merely assume the fact. For some, this would be rather like insisting that it is indeed still possible to be cruel and rapacious in the modern era, despite the cynics who would demean the age by denying it. John Holloway tells us with laborious unhelpfulness that 'every tragedy or near-tragedy is a serious play, in which the characters, including the protagonist, are likely to speak earnestly about the world, or about how it works, or about how they would like it to do so'.[22] It is not easy to see on this view how a tragedy differs from a congress on global warming. Walter Kerr offers us 'an investigation into the possibilities of human *freedom*' as his particular tragic essence, a view which may have rather more to do with American ideology and rather less with Büchner or Lorca than he suspects.[23] One threat to such freedom is the dogmatism which proposes it as the central *topos* of all tragedy. Tragedy, in Schlegelian fashion, allows us to pursue 'that longing for the infinite which is inherent in our being', and occurs 'when man uses his freedom without reservation'.[24] Its opposite begins to sound less like comedy than the Soviet Union.

Kerr is forced by his libertarian definition to dismiss as non-tragic works which do not affirm freedom, and where destruction is not part of an evolutionary process leading to new life. Since he can find precious little of this in the modern period, he ends up denying the possibility of modern tragedy altogether. The modern epoch lacks finality and determinacy, both tragic prerequisites, and freedom has been undermined by both Darwinian and Freudian determinism. Gripped by a Western ideology of untrammelled liberty, along with a remorseless American upbeatness, Kerr sees tragedy as springing from 'a fiercely optimistic society', in need of 'arrogance', robustness and certainty.[25] Tragedy, in short, begins to sound a little like the US Marine corps. But tragic Man, self-confident, unquestioning and spontaneous, has now been subverted by various squalid determinisms; and in denying freedom, we have despatched tragedy along with it. Kerr is apparently in no doubt that tragedy is a thoroughly excellent thing, an injuriousness which must be endured if human progress is to thrive. The form, however, may be less extinct than playing possum: in a final rousing burst of New World hopefulness, Kerr suggests that the apparent demise of tragic art may itself be simply a stage in its evolution. We can thus look gleefully forward to more mayhem, misery and massacres on the stages of the future.

Dorothea Krook, who stands somewhere on the far right wing of tragic theory, holds that tragedy portrays an action of universal import involving a hero of some considerable stature who is flawed, who comes to grief on account of this deficiency, so that the play ends badly, and in doing so shows something of the power of the gods or destiny, while revealing human suffering to be part of a meaningful pattern.[26] Here, perhaps, is what we might call the popular conception of tragedy, if such a thing exists. Or if not exactly popular, then popular-academic. It is thus all the more unfortunate that, as we shall see, hardly a word of this definition holds generally true. It constrains Krook to conclude along with George Steiner that Ibsen, for example, does not write authentic tragedies, just as Mandel, absurdly, manoeuvres himself into denying tragic status to *Romeo and Juliet* and the plays of Webster and Tourneur.

I. A. Richards, who considers tragedy to be the greatest, rarest thing in literature, also believes that most Greek tragedy, and Elizabethan tragedy apart from Shakespeare, is 'pseudo-tragedy'.[27] Other critics rule out works in which the protagonist's downfall is accidental, or in which she deserves her doom, or in which she is merely a victim. It is rather like defining a vacuum cleaner in a way which unaccountably omits the Hoover. If one comes up with a supposedly universal definition of tragedy which turns out to cover only five or six plays, the simplest option is to proclaim that other so-called tragedies are bogus specimens of the genre. Samuel Johnson, on the other hand, doubted that what Shakespeare wrote was strictly tragedy, but thought the plays none the worse for that.

7

Another difficulty with defining tragedy is that, like 'nature' or 'culture', the term floats ambiguously between the descriptive and the normative. For most commentators, as we shall see in the next chapter, tragedy is not only a matter of value but, strangely, the supreme mode of it. But the word can also just mean a lot of blood, death and destruction, regardless of its moral connotations and without involving much complex interiority. In early modern times it could simply be a synonym of death or ruin, as in Thomas Kyd's 'I'll there begin their endless tragedy' (*The Spanish Tragedy*, Act 4, sc. 5). In this sense of the word, you can tell whether something is tragic just by looking at it, as you can tell whether a parrot is dead by prodding it. Even with the sound turned all the way down, one would know in this sense of the term that a television play was a tragedy. If the body-count, as at the close of *The Spanish Tragedy*, hovers around nine, exactly a third of the play's total cast, then the spectacle is as indubitably tragic as one with an enormous number of belly laughs is incontrovertibly comic. Marlowe's *Tamburlaine*, a play which seems quite non-tragic in outlook and sensibility, qualifies as a tragedy because of its bloodiness, even though the first part is not tragic at all and was written with no sense that it would have a sequel. Something of the same goes for Middleton's *Women Beware Women*, with its concluding havoc, or Marston's morbid, brutal and sadistic *Antonio's Revenge*. Aristotle thought epic could be tragic; but though it trades in death and destruction, it doesn't use them as the occasion for a reflection on justice, fate and suffering in general, in the manner of a Sophocles. It is thus tragic in the descriptive rather than normative sense.

Or think of the splendid extravaganzas of Seneca – *Thyestes*, *Medea*, *Phaedra* and the rest – with their bombast and carnage, their vision of the world as vile, bloody and chaotic and of men and women as betraying a bottomless capacity for cruelty. In this theatre of the grotesque, action takes precedence over meaning, rather as it does when comedy tilts over into farce. It is what Northrop Frye dubs 'low mimetic tragedy'.[28] For this vein of art, tragedy can just mean something sombre and sorrowful; it need not satisfy such normative demands as that the suffering be largely unmerited, preordained, non-contingently caused, inflicted on a pre-eminent figure, partly his or her responsibility, revelatory of divine order, exultantly life-affirming, conducive to dignity and self-knowledge and so on. Someone who clung to the normative sense of the word could always exclaim 'I don't regard *that* as tragic!' no matter how much blood was being spilt and torment inflicted. From the normative standpoint, only certain kinds of death, strife, suffering and destruction, treated in certain ways, qualify for the accolade of tragedy. Tragedy here is more a matter of response than of occurrence. And it is true that almost nobody views destruction as inherently negative, that only the blander sort of liberal regards conflict as intrinsically undesirable, and that most people do not consider death to be *ipso facto* calamitous. For Aristotle and most other critics, the death of a villain would not be tragic, whereas for a certain strain of existentialist philosophy death is tragic as such, regardless of its cause, mode, subject or effect. All the same, 'normative' or 'moral' tragedy often betrays a certain sensationalist subtext, an aura of violence or exoticism, of sweetly heightened sensations and covert erotic pleasures, which links it reluctantly to its melodramatic sibling. As with most high-toned phenomena, it conceals some rather less reputable roots.

Even so, there is one significant contrast between 'descriptive' and 'normative' tragedy. The former type of art tends to be sombre, gloomy, even at times nihilistic, and this, for its more normative counterpart, is exactly what tragedy cannot allow. It is a curious irony that for much traditional tragic theory, wretchedness and despondency threaten to subvert tragedy rather than enhance it. The more cheerless the drama, the less tragic its status. This is because tragedy must embody value; but it is odd, even so, that an art form which portrays human anguish and affliction should have been so often brandished as a weapon to combat a typically 'modern' pessimism and passivity. Tragedy for a great many commentators is all about cheering us up.

A further problem of definition springs from the fact that 'tragedy' can have a triple meaning. Like comedy, it can refer at once to works of art, real-life events and world-views or structures of feeling. You can be comic without being optimistic, or comic but not funny, like Dante's best-known work. As far as the art/life distinction goes, we do, after all, inherit the concept of tragedy from a social order which made less of a hard-and-fast distinction between the poetic and the historical than we do, and had no conception of the autonomously aesthetic. Indeed, it was a civilization which once based a territorial claim on a verse from the *Iliad*. The modern age, by contrast, distinguishes more sharply between art and life, as well as between artefacts and ways of seeing. We would not generally speak of a poem as a tragedy, despite the writings of Milton, Mandelstam and Akhmatova, though we might speak of one as embodying a tragic world-view. For some death-of-tragedy theorists, we are now 'post-tragic' exactly because we are post-ideological, bereft of all synoptic vision. Tragic art, on this theory, presupposes a tragic vision – a bleak view of the world, an absolute faith for which you are prepared to die, or at least a dominant ideology to be heroically resisted. Like almost every other general view of tragedy, this one identifies the entire mode with one kind of action, and then proceeds to write off whatever fails to conform to it.

For obituarists of tragedy like George Steiner, only tragic world-views can finally sustain legitimately tragic works of art.[29] If the modern epoch has witnessed the death of tragedy, it is among other things because its two dominant *Weltanschauungen*, Marxism and Christianity, are judged by Steiner (mistakenly, as we shall see) to be inhospitable to tragic insight. Raymond Williams, in contrast, sees the twentieth century as under the sway of three essentially tragic ideologies: Marxism, Freudianism and existentialism.[30] Art and world-views, however, do not sit so neatly together as Steiner imagines. Aeschylus's general vision, unlike perhaps that of his two great colleagues, would not seem to be particularly tragic, to say nothing of the sentimental optimism which underlies the staggeringly popular tragic dramas of Voltaire, or the finest theatre-pieces of a Dryden. Scott, Edgeworth and George Eliot all bear witness to specific tragedies, while being for the most part progressivist in their general outlook. Scott, chronicler of the tragic downfall of Scottish clan society, is also a zealot of moderation, the *via media* and a more civilized future.

For Murray Krieger, by contrast, the problem is the reverse: we lack a tragic art because there is too much of a tragic outlook abroad, not too little. The role of tragic art in our time is to contain and defuse an otherwise perilously overweening tragic vision. A 'demoniac' world-view, existing in churlish defiance of all rational, ethical and civic order, currently lacks a tragic art which might discipline and absorb it. The taming of tragedy, the recuperation of the Dionysian by the Apollonian, the holding of the tragic and the civic in precarious tension, has become less feasible in our anarchic times, and this is a potent source of political anxiety.[31] If social disaffection is to be managed, so Krieger's case implies, it must be sublimated; but since such disaffection also undermines the civic forms of such sublimation, tragedy is unable to repair tragedy, and we remain caught in a vicious circle.

There is also the question of whether tragedy is always an *event*. The word has resonances of cataclysm and disaster, and one dictionary definition speaks of a 'great and sudden misfortune'; Geoffrey Brereton thinks that it has to involve 'unexpected and striking circumstances', which would rule out a great many deaths.[32] But it may also describe a more chronic, less ostentatious sort of condition than Brereton supposes. Tragedy as a matter of being knocked abruptly sideways evidently lends itself to effective theatre; indeed, such theatre enters interestingly into the very description of the mode, in the shape of sudden reversals, ironic backfirings, condensed, crisis-ridden action, a stringent economy of passion and the like. But there are steady-state as well as big-bang tragedies, in the form of the sheer dreary persistence of certain hopeless, obscure conditions, like a dull bruise in the flesh. One thinks of the exacting Kantian duty which impels the heroine of James's *Portrait of a Lady* to return to her profoundly unlovable husband, or the desolate vistas of time stretching before the jilted Catherine Sloper at the end of *Washington Square*.

These less eye-catching, spectacular brands of tragedy, which George Eliot considered at least as excruciating as the more manifest forms of torment, are perhaps more appropriate to the novel than to the stage. But there is also, say, the love-lorn pathos of the raddled, alcoholic Blanche DuBois at the end of Tennessee Williams's *A Streetcar Named Desire*, or Lavinia Mannon at the close of Eugene O'Neill's *Mourning Becomes Electra*, whose problem is precisely that they will linger futilely on. If all of these examples are of women, it is doubtless because for them tragedy is typically less heroic crisis than inveterate condition, a blighted existence rather than a bungled action. There are those, in other words, for whom, as Walter Benjamin soberly reminds us, history constitutes one long emergency, for whom the exceptional (high tragedy) is the quotidian norm. As early as Euripides, so Adrian Poole comments, 'crisis is permanent'.[33] Emile Zola writes in *Nana* of 'the tragic climaxes of everyday life', and such extremities may be less tolerable precisely because they are routinely predictable, rather than abrupt, incalculable irruptions from some other world.

Alasdair MacIntyre once compared the wranglings of the modern age over moral questions to someone seeking forlornly to decipher fragments of writing inherited from some previous epoch and now almost wholly devoid of context.[34] Much the same can be said of the various laborious medieval attempts to reconstruct the idea of tragedy, given the absence at the time of Aristotle's *Poetics*.[35] Most medieval authors considered tragedy to be an obsolete genre, just as death-of-tragedy ideologues do today, and very few regarded themselves as making an addition to it. There was considerable, sometimes comic, confusion over what tragedy was all about. There were times when all the medieval era seemed to know was that it was an especially serious form – Ovid remarks in his *Tristia* that it surpasses every other form of writing in its solemnity – along with the fact that it concerned the misfortunes of the high and mighty. Theophrastus had defined tragedy as representing the fortunes of heroes, and this high-life emphasis is a constant factor in medieval accounts, often more important than notions of fate, downfall, transgression, innocence, irreparable injury and the like.

The grammarian Placidus writes around the turn of the sixth century of tragedy as 'a genre of poetry in which poets describe the grievous fall of kings and unheard of crimes, or the affairs of the gods, in high-sounding words'.[36] 'High-sounding' could make tragedy sound akin to bombast, and this appears to have been one widespread meaning of the term. Thomas Aquinas seems to use it in this sense. This partly pejorative meaning survives at least as late as Goethe's *Wilhelm Meister*, in which Wilhelm speaks of tragedy as 'representing high social station and nobility of character by a certain stiffness and affectation'.[37] Aquinas also appears to have thought that tragedy meant 'speech about war', whereas comedy was speech about civic affairs. Averroes, by contrast, seems to think the word synonymous with 'praise' – the praise of suffering virtue. That he was also a commentator on Aristotle's *Poetics* suggests a certain tragicomic failure of communication between antiquity and its aftermath, as though Marx had imagined that by 'dialectic' Hegel had meant a regional form of speech.

Dante seems to have thought tragedy neither invariably dramatic nor especially concerned with sorrow and disaster. Instead, he too defined it in terms of its high seriousness – of noble verse forms, elevated construction, excellent vocabulary and profundity of substance. The *Aeneid* he considered a tragic work of art, even though it contains more triumph than catastrophe and shifts from the latter to the former rather than (as Aristotle prescribes) vice versa. 'Horrific crimes of the great' would be a summary slogan of much medieval usage, rather as it would be of much of the tabloid press today. Tragedy was really a kind of exposé of ruling-class corruption, for the ideological purpose of rendering the lives of high-living villains abominable to the populace; and its stress, unlike that of Aristotle, falls accordingly on deserved rather than unmerited disgrace. 'Imposing persons, great fears, and disastrous endings' is the nutshell definition of the Roman commentator Donatus.[38] This tradition survives as late as George Puttenham's *The Art of English Poesie* (1589), for which tragic art deals in the lust, infamy and licentiousness of the powerful, who are punished for their sins for the moral edification of the audience. It teaches the mutability of fortune, and God's assured vengeance on wicked lives. There is no question here of an iron fate, of Aristotle's tolerably virtuous hero, of a pitiful identification with him, of the good suffering excessively, or of the moral dubiousness of the higher powers. Tragedy dealt in sorrowful matters and great iniquities, and among the Romans sometimes took the form of a danced or pantomimed performance, in which both Nero and St Augustine are said to have taken part.

In the sixth century an apparently eccentric meaning of the word 'tragedy' springs up with Boethius, who uses it in the context of Christ's Incarnation to denote a kind of fall or come-down. He speaks of Christ's assuming flesh as 'a tremendous tragedy', no doubt in the Pauline sense of a *kenosis* or self-emptying rather than any sort of disaster. Boethius's quaint use of the word is true to the classical theological view that the

Incarnation involves a loss or self-estrangement on God's part as well as a fullness of presence. Hegel will later see Spirit's process of self-objectification in much the same tragic light. Perhaps such maverick uses of the word resulted in part from what was now its near-indecipherability. The medievals knew that the word 'tragedy' derived from 'goat', and that (since Horace says so) a goat was the prize for which ancient tragedians competed. It is not clear whether they were aware that there is no word for tragedy in any language other than ancient Greek, all other uses being adopted from this; and it does not seem to have occurred to them that, as Gerald Else suggests, the word 'tragedian' might originally have been a joke at the expense of the dramatists, meaning 'goat-bard'.[39] Some of them speculated with bizarre implausibility that the prize in question was a goat because of the filth of the artistic subject-matter, while others believed that a goat was actually sacrificed to the tragic poets, or that the word came from goatskin footwear which the actors wore in recital. A fourteenth-century commentator, Francesco da Buti, ingeniously speculated that the goat was a symbol of tragedy because it looks princely from the front, with its imposing horns and beard, but has a filthy, naked rear-end. We shall see later, in investigating the ambivalence of the tragic scapegoat, that this idea is not quite as fanciful as it sounds.

Medieval scholars were heirs to a tradition that tragedy evolved from prosperity to adversity, an emphasis which can be found in Chaucer's *Monk's Tale*. But this lineage said nothing *à la* Aristotle about the moral status of the tragic protagonist, as indeed Chaucer does not. John of Garland distils the received medieval wisdom around 1220 with his comment that tragedy is written in a grave style, sets forth shameful and criminal deeds, and begins in joy but ends in tears. But tragedy in medieval society could occasionally mean a complaint or song of lamentation (as in 'the tragedy of his miseries'), and this game of Chinese whispers from ancients to medievals reaches its surreal consummation with the fourteenth-century English scholar John Arderne, who calls the Bible a tragedy, probably meaning no more than a serious sort of book. In a final grotesque twist of misprision, Arderne recommends the scriptures and other so-called tragedies as a source of humorous tales.

In the twelfth century, Otto of Freising employs the term 'tragedy' of an account of real-life disaster, probably one of the earliest such uses, remarking of the report in question that it was 'written miserably and excellently in the manner of a tragedy'.[40] This conjunction of misery and excellence says much about a familiar paradox of the form, rather as one might commend a horror movie by stressing how disgusting it is. Otto's comment, however, implies that the real-life usage is derivative from the artistic. William of Malmesbury also gives the word a real-life meaning in an account of the shipwreck and death of William the Conqueror's son, though perhaps with the theatrical sense of the term also in mind. Thomas Kyd, as we have seen, uses the word in *The Spanish Tragedy* to mean actual ruin, though the play draws several times on the artistic sense of the term as well. Indeed, Kyd's drama merges real-life and theatrical tragedy in its very structure, as Hieronimo uses a stage play to pursue his actual revenge, all of which is in turn given a choric framing. 'Tragedy', then, would appear to evolve in a three-step process from describing a play or piece of writing to denoting an account of historical adversity, and from there to designating historical adversities themselves. In the best Wildean fashion, tragedy begins as art, which life then imitates. And the earlier real-life uses of the word still retain a resonance of its origins in stage or story, which can later drop out altogether. The word thus progresses from art, to life with an echo of art, to life.

For most people today, tragedy means an actual occurrence, not a work of art. Indeed, some of those who nowadays use the word of actual events are probably unaware that it has an artistic sense at all; so that whereas some conservative critics claim that it is unintelligible to speak of real life as tragic, some of their fellow citizens who freely use the word of famines and drug overdoses might be puzzled to hear it used of a film or novel. Even so, when the *OED* speaks of tragedy as 'an unhappy or fatal event or series of events in real life; a dreadful calamity or disaster', it is careful to note that this is a merely *figurative* employment of the word, dating from no earlier than the sixteenth century. So real-life tragedy is a metaphorical derivation from the actual artistic thing, a view which converts an historical development into an ontological priority. For a host of exponents of tragic theory, there can be no more shameful naivety than confusing tragedy in art with tragedy in life, despite Freud's teaching that the most tumultuous crisis of our early lives is scripted by an ancient tragic drama. Indeed, for a good many critics, there can be no real-life tragedy at all. This is one major reason why 'tragedy' cannot mean 'very sad', since the former is an aesthetic term and the latter an everyday one. 'In real life there are no tragedies', declares W. McNeile Dixon, who as a cloistered academic might perhaps have been speaking for himself.[41]

But he certainly speaks for a whole raft of commentators. Even the radical Franco Moretti denies that the tragic exists in historical life, and reserves the term 'tragedy' only for representations of that existence.[42] One reason for this restriction of the term is plain enough. If tragic art for conservative theorists is a supremely affirmative affair, and if this is not wholly on account of its artistic form, then they can avoid the embarrassment of having to extol real-life cataclysms as equally positive by the barefaced but simple device of refusing to define them as tragic at all. It is not that one is being hard-hearted, so the argument goes; it is just that tragedy is a technical affair, quite different from run-of-the-mill calamity. Those who dissent from this proposition are then regarded as mildly obtuse, like someone who accuses a surgeon of sadism for extracting a diseased lung. All-out nuclear warfare would not be tragic, but a certain way of representing it in art might well be. Behind this apparently lunatic notion, which only the remarkably well-educated could conceivably have hatched, lie a series of false assumptions: that real life is shapeless, and art alone is orderly; that only in art can the value released by destruction be revealed; that real-life suffering is passive, ugly and undignified, whereas affliction in art has an heroic splendour of resistance; that art has a gratifying inevitability lacking in life.

In his *Experiments in Criticism*, C. S. Lewis writes in witheringly patrician style of the 'uninterestingness of (real-life) grief', an 'uncouth mixture of agony and littleness' which is bereft of 'grandeur or finality' and strikes one merely as 'dull and depressing'.[43] Lewis's writings on the premature death of his wife do not seem to view the event as dull and uninteresting, though other people's real lives are perhaps more uncouth than one's own. A. C. Bradley agrees with Lewis's case: 'A tale, for example, of a man slowly worn to death by disease, poverty, little cares, sordid vices, petty persecutions, however piteous or dreadful it might be, would not be tragic in the Shakespearian sense'.[44] Lewis and Bradley have the enthusiastic support of Ulrich Simon, who gravely informs us that 'disablement, genetic malformation, crippling diseases, may torment the victims and destroy their families, but they are not tragic'.[45] No doubt this judgement would come as a blessed relief to the diseased and disabled, as one cross less for them to bear. It seems an odd note to strike in a work about Christianity. Simon proceeds to list other palpably non-tragic events such as floods, earthquakes which wipe out whole communities, genocide or the battle of the Somme. The Holocaust was not tragic, but rather the death of tragedy. Tragedy must be more than mere victimage; it must involve a courageous resistance to one's fate, of the kind we witness in the great tragic works of art.

There was, of course, heroic resistance to Nazism on the part of some Jews. And plenty of people battle bravely against floods, disease, disablement, genocide and the like. Along with many other commentators on tragedy, Simon makes the curious assumption that such resistance flourishes only in art; that without it there is no revelation of value; and that without such value there is no tragedy. Tragedy is held to be about the response to an event, not just the event itself; but this surely cannot mark the difference between art and life, since the distinction is as hard

15

to draw in the one case as in the other. The argument, anyway, seems to be that Heinrich von Kleist's drama *Penthesilea* is tragic, while the fact that Kleist blew his brains out at the age of thirty-four in a suicide pact with a cancer victim is not. (Ever resourceful in planning for his future, Kleist had previously joined the French army in the hope of being killed during Napoleon's projected invasion of England.) The discrepancy between art and life here begins to assume grotesque proportions, as though someone were to claim that a three-hour monologue delivered in a nasal monotone would be tedious in real life but enchanting on stage.

As Raymond Williams sardonically observes, in a book devoted to refuting this fallacy: 'War, revolution, poverty, hunger; men reduced to objects and killed from lists; persecution and torture; the many kinds of contemporary martyrdom; however close and insistent the facts, we are not to be moved, in a context of tragedy. Tragedy, we know, is about something else.'[46] Williams rightly recognizes that the quarrel is not really about kinds of suffering; it is about traditional tragic theory's mandarin disdain for modernity and the common life. It is not 'real life', but a certain post-classical, post-aristocratic species of it, which is the true target of the Bradleys, Lewises and Steiners. What is at stake is the war against modern vulgarity, of which the nobility of tragic art is the antithesis. As Geoffrey Brereton puts the point: 'The death of a great man in an air-crash qualifies for tragedy unequivocally; if he is killed in a sports-car, the tragic quality becomes more dubious; if by falling off a bicycle, the whole conception is endangered.'[47] Perhaps this takes the metaphor of the tragic fall a little too literally.

The theory of tragedy is full of such absurdities. Few artistic forms have inspired such extraordinarily pious waffle. H. A. Mason writes that 'the Hero becomes a candidate for Tragedy only when we are struck by some analogy between his relation to the whole world of his play and the relation of the Soul of Man to all that it is surrounded by in the Universe'.[48] It is hard to see how this is true of *Cat On A Hot Tin Roof*. John S. Smart holds that tragedy raises fundamental questions about our place in the cosmic order, which is hardly the case with *Rosmersholm*.[49] In *Tragedy Is Not Enough*, a by no means imperceptive study, Karl Jaspers writes that 'Tragedy shows man as he is transformed at the edge of doom. Like Cassandra, the tragic hero comprehends the tragic atmosphere. Through his questions he relates himself to destiny. In struggle he becomes aware of that power for which he stands, that power which is not yet everything. He experiences his guilt and puts questions to it. He asks for the nature of truth and in full consciousness acts out the meaning of victory and of defeat.'[50] It may well be that poor translation has a hand in this chain of flat-footed platitudes, but it is, even so, depressingly typical of a certain vein of commentary on the subject. Maud Bodkin, who does not even have the excuse of being in translation, informs us that 'Hamlet, though he dies, is immortal, because he is the representative and creature of the immortal life of the race'.[51] Tragedy, another critic instructs us, has 'the power to suggest something illimitable, to place life against a background of eternity, and to make the reader feel the presence of problems which he cannot solve'.[52] It is indeed uplifting to feel that one's problems are insoluble, not least for those of a masochistic turn of mind.

The discrepancy between tragedy as art and tragedy as life is an ironic one. For most pieces of tragic art behave exactly as though tragedy were indeed a matter of actual experience, rather than some purely aesthetic phenomenon. As with any art or piece of language, there is that immanent in them which points beyond them. The deconstruction of art and life is known as art. While tragic theory insists for the most part upon one version of tragedy, tragic practice tends to illustrate another; and this incongruity, which runs back to Aristotle's *Poetics*, is deep-seated and persistent enough to suggest that it constitutes a cultural problem or intellectual contradiction in its own right. Raymond Williams wryly observes that some modern theory of tragedy perversely denies that actual tragedy is possible 'after almost a century of important and continuous and insistent tragic art',[53] while Roland Galle remarks on the Owl-of-Minerva-like irony by which philosophical speculation on tragedy in the nineteenth century, in the heyday of Hegel, Schelling, Schlegel, Schopenhauer and Nietzsche, flourishes at a point when the form itself seems to be temporarily exhausted.[54] Those who can, create; those who can't, philosophize.

Indeed, one might claim that philosophy here is a continuation of tragedy by other means. The two ideas are even linked in popular consciousness, tragedy signifying the unavoidable and philosophy signifying fatalism ('she was surprisingly philosophical about losing her husband to a lap dancer'). Just as artistic modernism was later to migrate into avant-garde cultural theory, so from Hegel to Nietzsche tragedy is displaced into theoretical speculation. It now becomes a cultural signifier, a theodicy, a majestic Idea, a fertile source of ultimate value or form of counter-Enlightenment, an artistic resolution of philosophical dualities, rather than in the first place a matter of ordeal and affliction. An age of revolution, which the visionary youth of the era feel belongs to them in particular, has little time for such dispiriting realities; and since tragedy therefore becomes less and less possible on stage, it is free as a concept to take up home in reflections on the Dionysian or the Absolute, in the necessity of sacrifice, the conflict between Nature and culture or the self-estrangement of Spirit, where it becomes the sign of a vitalism or humanism which has little enough to do with human misfortune.

That tragic art and tragic theory should be so dissonant should come as no surprise. The antithesis between them, according to Nietzsche's *The Birth of Tragedy*, runs back as far as Socrates. For Nietzsche, it was philosophy, with its vainglorious universalist claims, which spelt the ruin of the local, unreflective pieties and rituals by which the roots of ancient tragic art were nourished. For Walter Benjamin, it is the serene, unshowy death of Socrates, a distinctly non-sublime parody of a tragic death, which marks the death of tragedy as such.[55] For Nietzsche, myth and tragedy have been liquidated by an unholy alliance of rationalism (Euripides and Socrates), psychological realism, naturalism, everyday life, dialectics, historical optimism, ethics and rational inquiry. The death of tragedy was the first great victory of this contemptible enlightenment, and Nietzsche's mission will be to proclaim the death of this death. From this early *Aufklärung* onwards, so Nietzsche considers, a slave mentality lethal to tragic art is brought gradually to birth. Socrates's belief that the world should be intelligible – what Nietzsche scornfully calls his 'instinct-dissolving influence' – strikes at the root of the Dionysian mysteries. It is no wonder that Socrates himself is said to have shunned the public performance of tragedy. Knowledge in the long aftermath of tragic theatre is no longer mythical or mystical but coupled to the grovelling English values of virtue and morality, happiness and self-transparency. As we witness the detestable emergence of 'theoretical man', the exultant aesthetic spectator yields ground to the joyless academic eunuch, with his pathetic illusion that thought can penetrate and even correct Being. For Nietzsche, however, the world is essentially unreadable, and 'tragic knowledge', which needs art to render tolerable its appalling insights, involves a grasp of the world's meaninglessness. It also involves a sense of the limits of knowledge, frontiers to which Kant and Schopenhauer have recalled us in philosophy; but from this scepticism may spring a rebirth of tragic culture, in which myth will once more flourish and wisdom will come to oust science. It is little wonder, then, that tragedy and philosophy should be at daggers drawn, given that the former signifies an irreducible mystery or opacity in human affairs which is impenetrable to anything as lowly as cognition. Tragedy, in this sense of the term, is counter-Enlightenment.[56]

One of the most sophisticated recent studies of the topic, Michelle Gellrich's deconstructive *Tragedy and Theory*, regards this discrepancy between practice and philosophy as a kind of de Manian resistance to theory on the part of the embattled artefacts themselves. 'Tragic plays',

she comments, 'rather than bearing out the salient principles of traditional dramatic theory, resist them and withstand the modes of understanding that they make possible'.[57] Gellrich reads the philosophy of
tragedy as seeking to repress and exclude the conflicts which tragic practice reveals, neutralizing its moral outrage, defusing its tendencies to
social dissolution, and resisting its more adversarial aspects.[58] This overlooks the fact that some theory of tragedy (Schopenhauer, say) is considerably more dissident than some practice of it (Claudel, for example);
but Gellrich is right to see much tragic theory as being, in a fairly rigorous sense of the word, ideology, defusing the disruptiveness of its subject-
matter with its anodyne appeals to virtue, rationality and social harmony.
The theory of tragedy, with its bland moral didacticism, plays Apollo, as
it were, to the Dionysus of the practice. *Poesis* for Aristotle, Gellrich
argues, involves rendering meaningful the random or accidental – so
that the very artistry of plot betrays what Gellrich, in her mildly con-
spiratorial post-structuralist way, perceives as a kind of repressive
making-intelligible of the subversive and unpredictable. By virtue of the
art form itself, a certain deceptive necessity is introduced into the world,
while history itself remains bound to randomness and contingency.
Gellrich would thus position tragic art in the Aristotelian schema somewhere between science and history, miming the necessity of the former
but without its mathematical rigour. Much the same place, poised
ambiguously between science and ideology, will be assigned to art by
Louis Althusser some centuries later.[59]

Radical French theory, though this time in a Foucaultian rather than
Derridean vein, also informs Timothy Reiss's erudite, adventurous *Tragedy
and Truth*. Tragedy for Reiss inaugurates a new order of discourse by
marking the limits of an existent regime of knowledge, articulating the
absent significations at its heart. It shows up what is necessary for a
certain social or legal order to exist, and thus, in sketching its outer
horizon of meaning, the points where it trembles into silence and non-
signification, acts as a kind of transcendental phenomenon. If this makes
the form sound subversive, doing to discourse something of what for
Pierre Macherey literature does to ideology,[60] the subversion proves
short-lived. For the function of the tragic is also to reduce this elusive
silence to regulated knowledge, so that tragedy becomes 'the art of overcoming unmeaning'.[61] Like Gellrich, Reiss harbours a post-structuralist
suspicion of systematized articulate knowledge, which in typically indiscriminate fashion he sees as oppressive. It does not seem to occur to
either exponent of this abstractly formalist judgement that some kinds
of ordered knowledge can be emancipatory, just as some forms of
non-meaning can be violent and repressive.

19

Just as Gellrich risks falling into too sharp an opposition between tragic art (disruptive, hence to be commended) and tragic theory (regulatory, hence to be resisted), so Reiss contrasts the tragic as the absence, excess or impossibility of meaning with a tragic knowledge which tames and naturalizes this perilously destabilizing force, reducing it to a stable order of reference, representation and rationality. Tragedy acts out the chaos at the core of a socio-discursive order, but also recuperates for knowledge the 'inexpressible' which eludes that order. Our response to it, then, is 'at once the fear of a lack of all order and the pleasure at seeing such lack overcome',[62] a rather more dialectical formulation than Gellrich's which nonetheless casts in new conceptual garb a fairly traditional sort of paradox. Indeed, both critics recycle the Apollonian/Dionysian opposition into the idiom of post-structuralism, and predictably come down emphatically in favour of the latter. The ancient Greeks, by contrast, knew enough to fear and loathe the Dionysian as well as to venerate it. But Reiss, at least, complicates Gellrich's too-stark antithesis by seeing both order and disorder, reason and the inexpressible, in tragic art itself, as a form which 'brings about rationality by showing what can be termed the irrational within that rationality'.[63] By combining a Machereyan notion of art as highlighting the limits of intelligibility with a rather more Foucaultian emphasis on regulation and containment, Reiss seeks to show tragedy as both ideological and counter-ideological, as 'enclosing' the inexpressible but also 'performing' it.

The idea of the inexpressible, of a meaning which slips through the net of signification as a mere trace of madness and chaos, is simply the reverse of a notion of meaning as rationalized and regulated. Such pessimism needs such mysticism as its necessary complement. The only alternative to conceptual tyranny is conceptual indeterminacy, and for Reiss tragedy see-saws perpetually between the two. It is a suggestive case, but one which entails some curious consequences. For one thing, it lands up embarrassingly cheek-by-jowl with the right-wing death-of-tragedy thesis. For Nietzsche, as for such latter-day custodians of the classical tradition as George Steiner, tragedy has died because fate, the gods, heroism, mythology and a proper appreciation of the darkness of human hearts have ruinously yielded in our own time to chance, contingency, democracy, rationality, religious disenchantment and a callow progressivism. Reiss does not of course subscribe to this right-wing syndrome; but like his mentor Michel Foucault, he is enough of a Nietzschean to be allergic to ideas of rationality and social progress, as well as to court a certain philosophical pessimism. For him, modern tragedy has become 'analytical', defusing the inexpressible in a form of discourse which supports social order. This is not, to be sure, quite why Steiner, Krieger and their confrères regard tragedy as having exhaled its last breath with the death of Racine; but it is not light-years removed from it either.

Reiss's case carries another conservative corollary. His aversion to representation as insidiously stabilizing (an oddly universalizing doctrine for a post-structuralist) means that he cannot look with much enthusiasm on the idea of tragedy as a real-life phenomenon. For one thing, the very concept of 'real life' is bound to appear epistemologically naive to a post-structuralist. So whereas some conservative critics plump for art rather than life, Reiss opts for discourse rather than experience. For another thing, since real-life reference is one way in which the fluidities of discourse are oppressively disciplined, tragedy should not be concerned with much other than itself. Once again, the most provocatively avant-garde theory comes full circle to rejoin the most doggedly traditionalist.

For both Gellrich and Reiss, tragic theory and tragic practice are locked in a contradictory relationship, like warring marriage partners who need one another but are constantly at loggerheads. But it may also be that tragedy and its theory have been so out of kilter simply because they have different preoccupations. The philosophy of art always comes furnished with its own agenda, rather than obediently reflecting its object; and this has been strikingly true in the case of tragedy. It is with the onset of the modern epoch that the idea of tragedy begins to outgrow its humble incarnations in this or that closet drama or stage performance to become a full-blown philosophy in its own right. If tragedy matters to modernity, it is as much as a theodicy,[64] a metaphysical humanism, a critique of Enlightenment, a displaced form of religion or a political nostalgia as it is a question of the slaying at the crossroads, the stench of the Furies or the monster rising from the sea. Tragedy, as Raymond Williams remarks, often 'attracts the fundamental beliefs and tensions of a period, and tragic theory is interesting mainly in this sense, that through it the shape and set of a particular culture is often deeply realized'.[65] What is at stake, as Williams shrewdly points out, is the culture from which the theory itself springs, at least as much as the culture which gave birth to the tragic art itself.

The traditionalist conception of tragedy turns on a number of distinctions – between fate and chance, free will and destiny, inner flaw and outer circumstance, the noble and the ignoble, blindness and insight, historical and universal, the alterable and the inevitable, the truly tragic and the merely piteous, heroic defiance and ignominious inertia – which for the most part no longer have much force for us. Some conservative critics have thus decided that tragedy is no longer possible, while some radicals have concluded that it is no longer desirable. Both camps agree that tragedy really *does* hinge on these dichotomies; it is just that the former regrets their passing while the latter rejoices in it. Otherwise, left and right are at one in their understanding of tragedy; it is just that the left rejects it while the right endorses it. But this need not be the only meaning of tragedy, and the left should not airily ditch the notion as antiquated and elitist. For there are other understandings of it, not least of those aspects of tragedy which seem most alien and obsolete, which as we shall see are surprisingly close to contemporary radical concerns.

Chapter 2

The Value of Agony

We have seen that Ovid thought tragedy the most solemn and elevated of all literary kinds,[1] while Juliette Brioche observes in a flash of Hegelian profundity that 'when we learn to understand that tragedy is a treasure in disguise, then we will begin to understand life'.[2] Rarely has an art form been so fulsomely complimented. Aristotle believed it superior to epic and probably to comedy, while John Milton claims it in his preface to *Samson Agonistes* as 'the gravest, moralest, and most profitable' of literary forms. Jean Racine speaks of tragedy's 'majestic sadness'. Hegel sees Sophocles's *Antigone* not just as the finest tragedy ever written, but as history's pre-eminent work of art. 'With Hegel', as one critic remarks, 'tragedy becomes synonymous with excellence',[3] so that there is now the same sort of logical problem about what to call a second-rate tragedy as there is over bad literature for those for whom literature means 'fine writing'.

Philippe Lacoue-Labarthe sees the sublime as the generalization of the Greek tragic experience to the whole of art.[4] For much post-Hegelian opinion, tragedy is the very measure of depth and maturity, of tempered experience and reflective wisdom, in contrast with the callowness of the comic. It is not obvious how well such a judgement emerges from a comparison of Philip Massinger's *The Roman Actor* with Ben Jonson's *Volpone*, or Charles Lamb's *John Woodvil* with J. M. Synge's *The Playboy of the Western World*. In his Cambridge lectures on the English novel, Raymond Williams resisted the conventional view that George Eliot's later novels, by virtue of their wryly resigned wisdom, their ironic sense of the unbudgeability of things, are therefore necessarily more mature and realistic than the earlier, more buoyant and 'pastoral' fiction.

This high opinion of tragedy is not one commonly shared by publishers and publicity agents. It is remarkable how often a gloomy literary work drives the blurb-writers to nervously apologetic language. 'The story, despite its bleakness, culminates not in despair but in a strange spiritual tranquillity'; 'The novel's dark vision is relieved by brilliant flashes of sardonic humour': time and again, tragedy or pessimism must be massaged or softened at the edges by the literary industry for public consumption, on the deeply questionable assumption that the public do not reap sadistic enjoyment from such tales of woe. There is something offensive and disconcerting, even to the calloused modern sensibility, about works which abandon all hope. The Penguin Chekhov nervously reassures its readers that 'each play contains at least one character who expresses Chekhov's hopes for a brighter future', which Samuel Beckett might have described as a reasonable percentage.[5]

In the second part of the nineteenth century, a clear ideological imperative lay behind this censure of glumness, to which Thomas Hardy, for one, fell victim. Like atheism and determinism, pessimism was socially disruptive, breeding cynicism, fatalism and dissent, whereas the role of art was to edify. So it is that Matthew Arnold guiltily leaves his tragedy *Empedocles on Etna* out of the 1853 edition of his poems, as too desolate, enervating a work for an age of ideological anxiety and smouldering popular rebellion. Though he approves of tragedy, he can see no justification for the kind of suffering which finds no vent in action, 'mental distress' unrelieved by hope or resistance.[6] His action has an august precedent: Plato recommends in *The Republic* that 'poets (should) stop giving their present gloomy account of the after-life, which is both untrue and unsuitable to produce a fighting spirit'.[7] W. B. Yeats follows suit, omitting the poetry of the First World War from his *Oxford Book of Modern Verse*. 'I have rejected these poems', he declares, 'for the same reason that made Arnold withdraw his *Empedocles on Etna* from circulation; passive suffering is not a theme for poetry. In all the great tragedies, tragedy is a joy to the man who dies; in Greece the tragic chorus danced.'[8] Yeats obediently repeats what by this time is the sheerest literary cliché: tragedy is more about ecstasy than agony. But since he has just been referring to the military bravery of the war poets, it is hard to see why he should see the suffering they record as passive. The late Victorian author W. E. Henley observes that it irks the public 'to grapple with problems capable of none save a tragic solution'.[9] Earlier in the nineteenth century, the great anti-tragic ideologist is William Wordsworth, with his fearfulness of fissures in time and lofty sublimations of sorrow.

The modern world, then, would seem both to commend tragedy and to live in fear of its despondency. The contradiction, however, is only apparent. For critics of tragedy are at one in their belief that despondent is the very last thing that it is. Indeed, one of them upbraids Voltaire's *Candide*, a work with more than its fair share of grotesque mishaps, for being untragic because too sceptical of providence.[10] Ibsen, Dorothea

Krook informs us, is not really tragic because, lacking a sense of redemption, he 'never escaped the limits of a profoundly pessimistic view of life ... Ibsen in his blindness remains, tragically, as incapable of writing tragedy as any romantic lady novelist in hers'.[11] It is not clear what the word 'tragically' is doing in that sentence, since being incapable of writing tragedy would not in fact qualify as in the least tragic on Krook's preternaturally stringent criteria.

The effect of tragedy, anyway, is to leave us 'liberated, restored, and exhilarated'.[12] Nothing is said of compassion or distress. Despair, dejection, misery, melancholia: all the states which the dim-witted populace associates with the tragic are regarded in this rarefied aesthetic view as actual obstacles to it. Tragedy begins accordingly to sound just the thing to lift one's spirits after a bankruptcy or bereavement, a tonic solution to one's ills. In this liberal-humanist caricaturing of tragedy's undoubtedly creative powers, the fact that it deals in blasted hopes and broken lives is quickly forgotten. An educational board in South Africa recently recommended the banning of *Hamlet* from schools on the grounds that it was 'not optimistic or uplifting'. Neither, for that matter, is most writing which deals with the history of apartheid.

The critic D. D. Raphael believes that tragedy 'shows the sublimity of human effort',[13] while the playwright Eugene O'Neill proclaims that 'the tragedy of Man is perhaps the only significant thing about him ... the individual life is made significant just by the struggle'.[14] For Nietzsche, tragedy is less a condition to be repaired than a state to be aspired to: 'Only dare to be tragic beings', he exhorts his readers in *The Birth of Tragedy*. Richard Wagner saw in the ancient Greek theatre a chance to forge the soul of the German nation: the Greek drama 'was the nation itself ... that communed with itself, and, within the space of a few hours, feasted its eyes with its own noblest essence'.[15] For the classicist Gilbert Murray, tragedy 'attests the triumph of the human soul over suffering and disaster',[16] a case which Macbeth might have found intriguing. Joseph Addison thought tragic art the noblest production of human nature. I. A. Richards, who considers tragedy to be 'the most general, all-accepting, all-ordering experience known', finds its value in its courage to dispense with subterfuges and illusions. The mind, instead, 'stands uncomforted, unintimidated, alone and self-reliant'.[17] The Spanish philosopher Miguel de Unamuno, in a work laced with pseudo-profound banalities, exclaims: 'Yes, we must learn to weep! Perhaps that is the supreme wisdom'. Unamuno wants to weep because he knows that he must die, even though, so he plangently informs us, 'I want to live for ever and ever and ever'.[18] It is not, perhaps, the century's most subtle philosophical pronouncement.

Even a figure as bohemian as Antonin Artaud takes a depressingly conventional line on the value of tragedy, writing that tragic theatre 'collectively reveals their dark powers and hidden strength to men, urging them to take a nobler, more heroic stance in the face of destiny than they would have assumed without it'.[19] Once again, tragedy is really a superior way of cheering yourself up. The paradox of tragedy as a supremely positive mode is encapsulated by Christopher Caudwell's comment that 'tragedy is not in itself tragic; it is beautiful, tender and satisfying – in the Aristotelian sense cathartic'.[20] The form is not melancholic, even if the content is. Lear, on this view, is redeemed not by Cordelia, but by the very splendour and integrity of the verse which unflinchingly records his disintegration. Perhaps the form satisfies our desire for immortality, lending us a sense of being indestructible as long as this magnificent poetry pulses on.

Tragedy can indeed be precious. No doubt we should hesitate before clamouring to live in a non-tragic society, since it may have discarded its sense of the tragic along with its sense of value. If there is no need for redemption, this may simply mean there is nothing worthwhile enough to be redeemed. Tragedy needs meaning and value if only to violate them. It disrupts the symmetry of our moral universe with its excess and inequity, but its power depends on a faith in that even-handedness. Otherwise words like 'excess' and 'inequity' would have no meaning. It makes no sense to claim that things are going badly if there could be no conception of their going well. To this extent, the tragic can be a negative image of utopia: it reminds us of what we cherish in the act of seeing it destroyed. It is perhaps pressing the point rather far to agree with W. MacNeile Dixon's hard-nosed Spinozist proposal that 'if evil vanished from the world much good, the most precious, would assuredly go with it, and the best in us rust unused'.[21] It is hard to see that we need torture and infanticide around the place to cajole us into virtue. But as long as we continue to describe as tragic a human calamity, as opposed to the withering of a daisy or the loss of a tooth, we have preserved some measure of human value.

As the philosopher William James inquires: 'Doesn't the very "seriousness" that we attribute to life mean that ineluctable noes and losses form part of it, that there are genuine sacrifices somewhere, and that something permanently drastic and bitter always remains at the bottom of the cup?' Life without such losses, he maintains, would be neither serious nor valuable; it isn't, he remarks, as if it's all 'yes yes in the universe'.[22] Tragedy can show us how value is released in the act of destruction itself, so that, as with the ecstatically burst grape of Keats's 'Ode to Melancholy', we savour the opulence of a thing in the very moment of its ruin. And this, if Freud is to be credited, is no more than a raising to consciousness of how we address ourselves to the world in any case, grasping objects as we do under the sign of their potential absence. It is not only that tragic figures reveal value by strenuously defying their doom (some do and some do not), but that the very fact of their passing recalls us to their inestimability, estranges for a moment our too taken-for-granted sense of their uniqueness. The richness which dies along with a single human being is beyond our fathoming, though tragedy may furnish a hint of it.

There are other senses in which tragedy can be affirmative. Raymond Williams has remarked on the modern age's sceptical response to those final moments of Elizabethan and Jacobean tragedy when life is restored and a Malcolm or Fortinbras comes marching on stage. For us, bred in a cynical era, these are mere perfunctory gestures or ideological necessities, dramatic tidyings-up or dollops of false comfort. The typical modernist text draws to its close without any such reassuring resolution; but as Williams points out, 'to conclude that there is no solution is also an answer'.[23] For us, what grips the imagination is the death of the hero; but Williams is right to insist that 'the ordinary tragic action is what happens *through* the hero'.[24] The renewal of life, the restoring and reaffirming of common meanings, is not necessarily a cynically recuperative gesture. Nor need it involve pushing the hero's agony off-stage. It also represents a political hope and a sense of continuing collective life, a capacity for faith even at the darkest of historical moments, which transcends any mere individualist fixation on the protagonist. Tragedy, Williams claims, is the whole of this action, not some abstractable part of it which happens to engage a morose modern sensibility more than the rest. He thus plucks political relevance from a tragic affirmation which, in less historically sensitive hands, can lapse into mere callousness or euphoria.

It is remarkable, in fact, what unguarded hyperboles tumble from the pen of commentators apparently insensitive to the paradox of the truth that destruction may also be creation. How can an art form which trades in human despair and desolation represent the deepest human value? If the commentators are generally agreed that it does, they are far from being at one in their reasons for this. A. C. Bradley sees tragedy as teaching that Man 'may be wretched and he may be awful, but he is not small'.[25] It is surely not obvious that it is better to be big and miserable rather than small and content. With a robust essentialism which might disconcert some of her devotees, Virginia Woolf declares in *The Common Reader* that 'the stable, the permanent, the original human being is to be found' in ancient Greek tragedy.[26] It is as though critics compete with each other in bestowing the most extravagant plaudits on the art form, as in some rather unsavoury game of seeing who can pluck the greatest triumphs from human destitution and despair. F. W. J. Schelling comes near to winning hands down, maintaining as he does in the *Philosophy of Art* that 'only within the maximum of suffering can that principle be revealed in which there is no suffering, just as everywhere things are revealed only by their opposites'.[27] One is still waiting for British politicians to turn to Schelling as a rationale for dismantling the public health service. As Franco Moretti puts it, it is 'as though it were argued that in strangling Desdemona, Othello paid tribute to her importance'.[28]

The poet Friedrich Hölderlin, in his essay 'The Ground for Empedocles', speaks of the whole as being able to feel itself only through the suffering and splitting-off of one its constituent parts. As long as reality remains undifferentiated, we cannot be sensible of it with any intensity.[29] It seems an implausible apologia for the death of a child. Tragedy for Hölderlin reveals the incarnate presence of the gods in humanity; yet for this presence to be felt in all its logocentric immediacy, its sign or medium – the tragic hero himself – must be annihilated. Human suffering is thus once more philosophically legitimated. In tragedy, asserts T. R. Henn, 'there is implicit, not only the possibility of redemption, but the spiritual assertion that man is splendid in his ashes, and can transcend his nature'.[30] It is hard to see that the victims of Bosnia or Cambodia are particularly splendid in their ashes; and if Henn is reserving the triumph for art rather than life, then it is difficult to see its relevance to the latter. W. MacNeile Dixon is convinced that tragedy 'presents the worst and excites in us the best', offering us heroes who are triumphant in defeat.[31] The end of tragedy, F. L. Lucas enthuses, is 'so to portray life that its tears become a joy for ever.'[32] It is not clear just how this is to be distinguished from a high-flown sadism. Yet what if tragedy can fulfil its role of lending a glamorous aura to suffering only at the price of a palpable lack of truth-to-life, which then undercuts its ideological impact?

Oliver Taplin, rather less rhapsodically, sees the value of tragedy as lying in the shape and significance it imparts to suffering, in contrast to the often meaningless, amorphous tragic events of everyday life. Tragedy 'gives the hurtful twists of life a shape and meaning which are persuasive, which can be lived with'.[33] But not all real-life tragedies are meaningless or disordered. The flowers reverently placed by mourners on the spot of some appalling catastrophe – a shooting at a school, a fire in a nightclub – are sometimes accompanied by a card inscribed with the single, bewildered word 'Why?' But the answer, it must bluntly be confessed, is often all too obvious: a psychotic youth neglected by harassed social services, a space packed too full of bodies for the sake of profit, a bridge left unrepaired for lack of funds. Not all tragedies, to be sure, are so readily explicable, and to be told that the child is dying of leukaemia is in one important sense not to have answered the question 'Why?' about its death. The query is more metaphysical than empirical. But the philosophical sense of tragedy as a divine mystery opaque to any mere human reasoning can be too quickly extended to historical disasters, in a way which then conveniently relieves those responsible of blame. It is commonplace, for example, to speak of war as 'meaningless', as though it were some surreal *acte gratuit* without rhyme or reason. On the contrary, war is all too rational, at least in one somewhat shrivelled sense of the term. In *Heart of Darkness*, Joseph Conrad famously portrays a ship firing its guns pointlessly into an African river bank, as though imperialism were merely some grotesque aberration or absurdist theatre rather than the hard-headed, systematic, sordidly explicable business that it is.

If tragedy ennobles suffering, then it edifies only at the cost of the truth, since most real-life suffering is not in fact ennobling. And nothing convinces like the truth. But if it tells the truth, then it is hard to see how it can fulfil its function of justifying the ways of God to men. Like Adorno's modernist work of art, then, it is caught on the hop between being beautiful but false and truthful but ugly. But not all tragic art persuades us that suffering is purposive. This is not the sentiment which most audiences derive from *Philoctetes* or *King Lear* – though Walter Stein, a sensitive analyst of the latter play, reads it as disclosing 'an order in which there is meaning – even (perhaps even especially) in affliction and heartbreak and death'.[34] Lear, Stein remarks, has at least learned to live – though one might question just how much use this is to him.

Walter Kerr is a good deal more emphatic: in his view, we come away from *Lear* 'not filled with disgust but filled instead with an inexpressible satisfaction; we acknowledge that Necessity is somehow just in its own way'.[35] This is hardly an opinion shared by the old man himself, or probably for that matter by his creator. That unobtrusive 'somehow' is being forced to do an inordinate amount of work. The doctrine of *catharsis* suggests that there is indeed something edifying and enjoyable about the experience of tragedy, but 'inexpressible satisfaction', with Cordelia dead in her father's arms, borders on the positively sadistic. A great many readers of *King Lear*, and not just the notoriously disgusted Samuel Johnson, find nothing whatsoever just in the action it portrays, which is not to say that they leave the theatre depressed and disgruntled. They may be edified by the play's art, but that is a different matter. Here, as so often in the discussion of tragedy, a theoretical dogma – tragic art must always be uplifting – seizes the reins from actual practice.

Even if suffering appears shapely on stage, this may come as scant comfort to its real-life victims. A forlorn clutch of critics, such as Walter Kaufmann in his splendidly acute, acerbic *Tragedy and Philosophy*, written at the height of the Vietnam war, see the value of tragic art as lying in its 'refusal to let any comfort, faith, or joy deafen our ears to the tortured cries of our brethren'.[36] Yet even the shrewd, humane Kaufmann falls prey to an excessively sanguine view of tragic suffering, which allows us to 'see how countless agonies belong to one great pattern'.[37] Amélie Oksenberg Rorty thinks rather similarly that tragedy brings us to recognize that 'however apparently fragmented, ill-shaped and even terrible our lives may seem to us in the living, they form a single activity, a patterned, structured whole'.[38] But it is far from obvious that any human life forms a single activity or belongs to a larger pattern, or that the fact that it does can bring any particular comfort to the afflicted. Is this really true of Euripides's *The Children of Heracles* or Büchner's *Woyzeck*? And even if it were, how exactly would it console us to know that our anguish was both generally shared and symmetrically ordered? It might well prove more tolerable to see it as a purely random, personal affair. Anyway, why should we need tragedy to teach us this lesson, rather than deriving it from some more benign, less shattering source?

Besides, there are tragic thinkers like Albert Camus who seek to wrest value from the very pointlessness of the world, which is not to be confused with some Conradian attempt to disown the chaos of reality for some ideologically convenient fiction of order. For Camus, revolt means refusing to accept an absurd world and dying defiantly unreconciled with it, which is the reverse of one traditional tragic case. In an early version of postmodern 'subversion', the system can be bucked if not broken, disrupted by a steadfast refusal. The suicide, by contrast, sells out to necessity. The critic Jan Kott regards suicide as justified only as a protest against the world's injustice – but not if the gods do not exist, since then there is nobody to protest to. Suicide also implies a kind of power; and one reason why there is none of it in the work of Samuel Beckett is doubtless because there is no such power either.

Kaufmann, rather extraordinarily, seems to think that there is solace in the thought that suffering is general, not just peculiar to oneself, and that 'fates worse than ours can be experienced as exhilarating'.[39] It may be that the thought of someone else being decapitated is unusually comforting, but this is not much consolation when trying to come to terms with a bereavement. Anyway, how far does the sheer act of understanding our plight justify or redeem it? It is no justification of torture to claim that through it we come to appreciate our vulnerability, or recognize our place in the great scheme of things. John Jones, however, maintains that 'in both Aeschylus and Sophocles, the moment when a man perceives the operation of the powers that are destroying him is one of solemn religio-tragic exaltation – not because the individual is "saved" thereby, but because Necessity and Fate and the ways of Zeus have been exposed for human consciousness in a flash of perfect clarity: a demonstration which is also a sufficient vindication.'[40]

It is that last phrase which betrays the glibness of the point. If the ways of necessity are scandalously unjust (and some Greek tragedy harbours just such a suspicion), why should clarifying them mean validating them? Isn't it a donnish error to stake so much, in the midst of so much carnage and desolation, on understanding alone? Plenty of tragic protagonists understand all too well the plottings and prejudices which have brought them low, without imagining that this is sufficient recompense for losing their sanity or eyesight or sexual partners. R. P. Draper claims that tragedy shows suffering in a way which 'modulates initial protest into final acceptance . . . the result is an intuition of the meaning of suffering on a level which is, however, inaccessible to reason as such'.[41] If critics like Draper really have discovered the meaning of suffering, however intuitively, then it would be considerate of them to share the news with the rest of us as speedily as possible, if indeed it can be put into anything as workaday as words.

Not all tragedies portray suffering as ennobling. Amory Blaine of F. Scott Fitzgerald's *This Side of Paradise* reflects that 'all tragedy has that strain of the grotesque and squalid – so useless, futile' (ch. 2). Sophocles forces us to listen to the agonized bellows of Heracles and Philoctetes, squeezing every drop of theatre he can out of their raw, pointless, unbearable pain. In the case of Heracles, this happens to a son of Zeus himself, one who has loyally served the gods and is now reduced to 'a thing that cannot crawl, a piece of nothing'. And all this, in an extra sadistic twist of the knife, stems not from some cosmic pattern but from the sheerest blunder: Heracles's wife gives him an anointed shirt to keep him faithful, which accomplishes that aim superbly by corroding his flesh. The drama ends with his son Hyllus accusing the gods of gazing down stony-faced and unmoved on such atrocities. Neither Heracles nor Philoctetes bear their pain with a shred of stoicism, yet they are tragic figures for all that.

Tragedy is commonly supposed to teach wisdom through suffering, as the Chorus chants in Aeschylus's *Agamemnon*. Yet nobody in the *Oresteia* really learns from their suffering, least of all Agamemnon himself. It is by no means unequivocally true, as George Steiner asserts in *The Death of Tragedy*, that 'man is ennobled by the vengeful spite or injustice of the gods. It does not make him innocent, but it hallows him as if he had

31

passed through fire'.[42] If tragedy discloses the deepest human value, then it is hard to see how it is not necessary to human existence, in which case one risks ending up heartlessly endorsing the indefensible. But if the values which tragedy cherishes – freedom, courage, realism, modesty, dignity, endurance, resistance and the like – are not a monopoly of the mode, it is difficult to see why such anguish is so desirable. George Eliot reminds us in 'Janet's Repentance' in *Scenes From Clerical Life* that the thought of a man's death 'hallows him anew' for us – as though his life, she adds dryly, were not sacred as well. We do not need death to foster our sense of value. Joseph Wood Krutch claims in *The Modern Temper* that tragedy is a way of contemplating life without pain, a form which exploits suffering to wring joy out of existence. In Krutch's unpleasantly effervescent rhetoric, it is no less than the solution to the problem of existence, a spirit which reconciles us to life. Even Nietzsche was rarely as bland about the business as this, though his compatriot Friedrich Hebbel, with an airy callousness comparable to Krutch's, sees suffering and sacrifice as supremely positive forms of self-realization, indeed of apotheosis. The eponymous heroine of his drama *Judith* achieves reconciliation through sacrifice, converting her tragedy into a kind of triumph.[43]

Even the radical Georg Büchner, one of whose characters exclaims in *Danton's Death* that 'The tiniest spasm of pain, be it in a single atom, and divine creation is utterly torn asunder' (Act 3, sc. 1), is also reported to have remarked on his deathbed that we have not too much pain but too little, for through pain we could enter into God. As a high cliché of Romanticism, these are not quite the kind of words to expire with. Friedrich Schiller, in his essay 'Das Pathethische' of 1793, sees tragedy as a form of heroic resistance to suffering through which Freedom and Reason make their presence felt, raising the tragic hero to the status of the Kantian sublime. Like sublimity for Kant, tragedy for Schiller demonstrates the sway of the supersensible over the sensible, of dignity over pain and autonomy over pathos, as the protagonist shakes himself free from the compulsive forces of Nature and exultantly affirms his absolute freedom of will in the face of a drearily prosaic necessity. Far from being avoided, tragedy sounds like the kind of experience to be eagerly courted.

As with many idealist descriptions of tragedy, it is difficult to see quite what is *tragic* about this triumphalism. In all such conceptions, the tragic hero would seem in peril of winning his victories on the cheap, confronting a Nature which is clay in his hands and which, for all its apparent recalcitrance, is secretly of one substance with his own indomitable spirit. For Schlegel, in somewhat more stoical vein, the preciousness of tragedy lies in its affirmation of the free spirit, of a sense of dignity and supernatural order in the face of a forbidding destiny. Tragic fate cannot be overthrown; but it throws us back upon our own resources, so that we can pluck some virtue from this dire determinism.

Shelley, as idiosyncratic as always, values tragedy for just the opposite reason, arguing in his *Defence of Poetry* that it divests crime of half its horror by showing it as the fatal consequence of the unfathomable agencies of Nature. Tragedy, in short, can be seen as a critique of bourgeois self-determination, since we need no longer see error as the creation of our choice. The classical scholar E. R. Dodds finds the value of Sophocles's *King Oedipus* in the fact that Oedipus, despite being 'subjectively innocent', accepts responsibility for all his actions, including those which are 'objectively most horrible'.[44] It is true that the ancient Greeks did not enforce our own occasionally simplistic distinctions between guilt and innocence, agency and determination. As Hegel comments in his lectures on aesthetics, they did not divorce their purely subjective self-consciousness from what was objectively the case. It is also true, and bemusing to a modern, that the Oedipus of *King Oedipus* never once summons his subjective lack of guilt in his self-defence. It would not occur to him to imagine that an incestuous parricide could be spared from pollution simply on account of his ignorance. Even so, it is surely perverse to find a drama's deepest value in the fact that its hero accepts responsibility for what is palpably not his fault. Perhaps there is a hint here of the public-school ethic of sportingly taking someone else's punishment for them. Oedipus is certainly a sacrificial scapegoat, who will finally come to assume the burden of the community's sins; but in *Oedipus at Colonus* he rightly considers himself ill-treated by the heavens, and appeals to his ignorance as the ground of his innocence.

For other critics, tragedy is precious because it confronts us with the worst, and shows us able to survive it. The violence of tragedy, according to Roy Morrell, is aimed at 'complicating and strengthening the psyche by means of shocks from the outside: not, of course, violent and disorganized shocks, but mild, provocative, reorganizing ones'. One wonders if the death of Cordelia or Medea's butchery of her own children qualifies as mild, provocative and reorganizing.[45] 'There is consolation', remarks Jonathan Lear, 'in realizing that one has experienced the worst, that there is nothing further to fear, and yet the world remains a rational, meaningful place in which a person can conduct himself with dignity. Even in tragedy, perhaps especially in tragedy, the fundamental goodness of man and world are reaffirmed.'[46]

Does the world really still appear a rational, meaningful, dignified place after the tragic crisis has lashed itself quiet in Seneca or Euripides,

Webster or Marston, Strindberg or O'Neill? Or is its force not precisely to call Lear's rationalist complacency into question? Another Lear is forced to confront the worst in the death of his daughter, while Edgar murmurs consolingly that 'The worse is not, / So long as we can say "This is the worst"'. But the comment, however kindly intended, is devastatingly ambiguous. Charitably interpreted, it can mean 'While there's still language there's still hope, since simply to give tongue to the unspeakable is by that token to transcend it'. In tragedy, observes Roland Barthes, 'one never dies because one is always talking'.[47] And if there were no such articulate intelligence, the worst would not be the worst because there would be no one to name and know it. But Edgar's implication is almost certainly 'As long as we can still speak, there's likely to be worse to come, which we will be forced to suffer but not have the strength to name'. The observation yields some comfort, but of a fearfully cold kind.

It may well be that confronting the worst is a potent source of value. In Edward Bond's *Lear*, it will turn Cordelia into a freedom fighter. What almost all the critics fail to point out, however, is that it would be better to learn the truth without having to face the worst in the first place. It may be, as modernity suspects, that common-or-garden consciousness is now so ineluctably false consciousness that only such a violent passage through hell will return it, purged and demystified, to true cognition. Breaking through to the truth is both ebullient and exacting, demanding a painful self-transformation. This is certainly true of Lear; but it is, so to speak, tragic that there need be such tragedy. It is not, *pace* Caudwell, that tragedy is non-tragic, but that it is tragic. Suffering may well evoke such admirable values as dignity, courage and endurance, but it would be pleasant if one could stumble upon some less excruciating method of exercising them. It is this simple fact, astonishingly, which scarcely a single commentator on tragedy pauses to register. Nor do they tend to note that a good deal of human suffering, including much of it on stage or in print, reveals no such redemptive qualities, and could hardly be expected to.

The New Testament is a relevant document here. Although Jesus is very often to be found curing the sick, he at no point exhorts them to be reconciled to their suffering. On the contrary, he seems to regard such sickness as an evil, depriving its victims of an abundance of life and cutting them off damagingly from community with others. He would no doubt have shared the mythological opinion of his age that suffering could be the work of evil spirits. There is no sanitizing pretence that such disabilities constitute a 'challenge', an 'opportunity' or an enriching difference. On the contrary, they are rightly seen as a curse, and Jesus's battle against them is presented as an integral part of his redemptive mission, not as some mere outward sign of an inward healing. Jesus plainly does not welcome his own impending torture and death, even though he seems impelled by an obscure conviction that such failure will prove the only way in which his mission will succeed. In the carefully staged Gethsemene scene, however, he is clearly presented as panicking, terror-stricken at the thought of what he must undergo and urgently pressing his Father to spare him such torment. He does not sound like a man for whom resurrection is just round the corner. One must be prepared to lay down one's life for others, while praying devoutly that one is never called upon to do anything so thoroughly disagreeable.

If Jesus finally submits willingly to death, it is only because he seems to see it as unavoidable. We do not know why he felt this way, and no doubt neither did he. But it appeared the only path left open to him, given the way of the world and what we may speculate was his disappointment over the relative lack of impact of his mission in Galilee. It was probably not as effective, for example, as his mentor John the Baptist's, at least as far as crowd-pulling went. And for him to have felt this way about his death is to say that his crucifixion is tragic. Since he was not, as far as we can judge, insane, it is not what he would have chosen had the decision been his own, which he did not consider it was. His death is a sacrifice precisely on this account. Sacrifice is not a matter of relinquishing what you find worthless, but of freely surrendering what you esteem for the benefit of others. It is this which marks the difference between the suicide and the martyr. Proust writes in his *Three Dialogues* that 'to be an artist is to fail, as no other dare fail . . . failure is his world and the shrink from it desertion'.[48] Unlike most critics of tragedy, he is speaking not of affirmation *in* defeat but of the affirmation *of* defeat, rather as Samuel Beckett writes of a 'fidelity to failure' as the mark of his vocation. It is this solidarity with failure which the virile Nietzsche, in his campaign for Dionysus against the Crucified, scorns as so much chicken-hearted submissiveness.

All this is somewhat remote from Jeanette King's judgement that 'the tragic view of life affirms both the inevitability of suffering and evil, and their irrelevance'.[49] It is hard to see how anyone could regard evil as *irrelevant*, as opposed to, say, remediable, non-existent or erotically alluring. Neither does all tragedy – *Iphigenia in Aulis*, for example, or *Othello* or *When We Dead Awaken* – claim that suffering is ineluctable. We must be careful here to distinguish two different cases. One is the Boy Scout theory of tragedy, which regards suffering as inherently valuable because through it we are toughened and matured. It was this view of the world that Prince Andrew was expounding when he remarked that being shot at as a pilot during the Falklands war was 'terribly character-building'.

Leo Aylen writes with theological illiteracy that a Christian 'has to welcome the suffering that comes to him, when he can no longer prevent it, to welcome physical disability, moral disintegration, and death'.[50] One has a grotesque vision of pious believers rejoicing in their coronaries and cancers, locked in hand-to-hand combat with saints struggling fervently to cure them. Even so, there is much to be said for the opinion that in confronting death, one may learn something of how to live. If we have the resources to encounter our own deaths without undue terror, then we probably have some of the resources to live well too; and tragedy grants us opportunities for such an encounter in imaginative and thus non-injurious terms. In any case, living in the perpetual knowledge of death, which both St Paul and Martin Heidegger recommend as one constituent of an authentic human existence, allows us to sit loose to life and thus relish it more fully. By relativizing life in carnivalesque style, death relaxes our neurotic grip upon it and sets us free for a deeper enjoyment. Such detachment is the reverse of indifference.

But there is a difference between the belief that suffering is precious in itself, and the view that, though pain is generally to be avoided as an evil, there are kinds of affliction in which loss and gain go curiously together. It is around this aporetic point, at which dispossession begins to blur into power, blindness into insight and victimage into victory, that a good deal of tragedy turns. So does much revolutionary politics. But it does not follow that you have to burn someone alive to get the best out of them. Nor should one mistake this blending of loss and gain for some kind of teleology, as so many commentators do. On this view, suffering is no more than a way-station or essential passage to victory, rather as dental surgery is an unpleasant but unavoidable step towards oral health. Indeed, Harold Schweizer perceptively points out that the very word 'suffering' suggests narrative and temporality, and hence the possibility of a positive conclusion.[51] Tragic theory becomes a kind of secular theodicy. If heaven is now a less credible way of justifying suffering, humanism may serve instead. Several critics speak of 'evil' as the chief concern of tragedy, though there are in fact fairly few tragedies in which evil in the metaphysical sense bulks large.

Walter Kerr, for whom tragedy is a more optimistic mode than comedy, sees the spiritual evolution of humanity as necessarily involving destruction. For man to become 'more than man', the creature as we know him must be dismantled. Tragedy concerns the human quest for godlike status, in the teeth of all despicable desire for security – the tragic hero as spiritual entrepreneur, so to speak, a compound of Faust and Henry Ford, flouting the craven complacency of the pettty-bourgeois suburbs. In this majestically unfurling teleology, a good many men and women will be crushed and discarded, rather like the lower biological species in the course of evolution; but 'even the failed and abandoned have been participants in a forward journey',[52] and will no doubt reap the consolations of knowing as much as they selflessly expire in order to clear the way for more robust spiritual types than themselves. Henry Kelly comments that 'the best-expressed tragedies have given us much solace and comfort',[53] but one may doubt that it was this kind of cruel consolation which he has in mind. Certainly Walter Kaufmann does so, when he repudiates this brutal teleology by reminding us that the Holocaust was not justified by the founding of the state of Israel.

The irony, however, is that once suffering is conceived in this instrumental or consequentialist way, it ceases to be redemptive, rather as a gift ceases to be truly a gift when one is thinking of a return. This is another reason why Jesus's crucifixion is genuinely tragic. If his death was a mere device for rising again in glory, a kind of *reculer pour mieux sauter*, then it was no more than a cheap conjuring trick. It was because his death seemed to him a cul-de-sac, as his despairing scriptural quotation on the cross would suggest, that it could be fruitful. (Two of the evangelists, Luke and John, embarrassedly omit the quotation, no doubt because it is not done for deities to despair.) The truth is that Jesus was a miserable failure, and his probable expectation that he would return to earth in the lifetime of his followers seems to have been a little too optimistic. However, only by accepting the worst for what it is, not as a convenient springboard for leaping beyond it, can one hope to surpass it. Only by accepting this as the last word about the human condition can it cease to be the last word. Jesus was left only with a forlorn faith in what he called his Father, despite the fact that this power seemed now to have abandoned him. But it was precisely this bereftness, savoured to the last bitter drop, which in a classically tragic rhythm could then become the source of renewed life. It is the political meaning of this rhythm which matters. The destitute condition of humanity, if it was to be fully restored, had to be lived all the way through, pressed to the extreme limit of a descent into the hell of meaninglessness and desolation, rather than disavowed, patched up or short-circuited. Only by being 'made sin' in the Pauline phrase, turned into some monstrous, outcast symbol of inhumanity, can the scapegoat go all the way through that condition to emerge somewhere on the other side. As Pascal comments: 'The Incarnation shows man the greatness of his wretchedness through the greatness of the remedy required'.[54]

Jesus's engagingly human reluctance to die contrasts with that of a character like Corneille's Polyeucte, who puts his life recklessly on the line with all the zealous imprudence of the neophyte. Polyeucte 'pines for death' and accounts the world as nothing, eagerly looking forward to the eternal bliss of the martyr and ignoring his friend Nearchus's warning that God himself feared to die. The play is described by its author as a Christian tragedy, but Polyeucte's death, rather like Socrates's, is hardly tragic for himself, however much it may be for his audience. He is in danger of doing what Thomas in *Murder in the Cathedral* calls 'the right thing for the wrong reason', embracing martyrdom in order to enjoy its spiritual benefits. Polyeucte actually wants to die, whereas a genuine martyr has no such rash desire. There is not much merit in relinquishing a world which strikes you as fairly worthless in the first place. Eliot's renunciation of the world in *Ash Wednesday* would be rather more convincing if, as with Yeats's *Sailing to Byzantium*, the life being so austerely abjured was portrayed with a little more sensuous relish.

Even so, the anti-instrumentalists should not be allowed to have it all their own way. There can be no politics without calculating the likely consequences of one's actions. An instrumental rationality, one attentive to the uses of objects, is at least an alternative to the fetishism of them, as Francis Bacon recognized. It is also a rather less privileged posture than the aestheticism for which actions and objects are gloriously autotelic, soiled by anything as lowly as a goal. Those who dismiss teleologies out of hand need to guard against such elitism. There is a difference between the vulgar instrumentalism for which any means will do to secure an end, and the intentional practice for which the use of an object must be governed by its specific properties. In the economic sphere, it is the difference between exchange-value and use-value. Just as in the sphere of use-value there is an internal bond between the inherent properties of an object and the ends for which it is mobilized, so should there be in the realm of historical practice. And this means neither abandoning intentionality, even if necessary of a grand-narrative sort, nor allowing some sublime *telos* to ride roughshod over the particularity of the present.

Consequentialism, which judges actions wholly in terms of their effects, is a microcosmic equivalent of this cosmic fable; but its opposite need not be some austerely deontological disowning of results, as with the moral autotelism of a Kant, for whom we ought to be good because it is good to be so. One need not remain trapped in the quasi-Buddhist paradox for which, as for T. S. Eliot's *Four Quartets*, action is fruitful only if one ceases to think of the fruits of action. It is possible, after all, to foresee and calculate consequences without acting wholly for the sake of them. One can will a just society without willing the disruption it would no doubt entail, while still accepting such disruption as an inevitable corollary of one's desire. And this is a classically tragic scenario. Rather like Oedipus, one does not will what is injurious, while nevertheless accepting some responsibility for it. This is by no means a condition confined to the political left. Anyone who approves of the Allies' engagement in the Second World War, or accepts that capitalism involves unemployment, is placed in this moral position. Tragedy differs from the more brittle forms of teleology in that the injurious remains injurious; it is not magically transmuted into good by its instrumental value. The 'exchange-value' of the action, the renewed life to which it may lead, is not allowed to cancel its 'use-value'.

It is thus a mistake to believe with George Steiner that Christianity is inherently anti-tragic. Steiner makes the same mistake about Marxism, for much the same reasons. Because these are both ultimately hopeful world-views they can have no truck with the tragic, which for Steiner is all about ill-starred endings. There are, in fact, pessimistic brands of Marxism, and most interesting Marxists, including Marx himself in some of his moods, have been anti-determinists for whom no particular historical outcome is guaranteed. Christianity, which supposedly champions individual freedom against Marxist predestinarianism, is in one sense a far more full-blooded form of determinism: socialism may not arrive, but there is no possibility that the kingdom of heaven will fail to show up eventually, its advent being in rather less fallible hands than the coming of the workers' state. The proletariat may falter, but providence will not.

Steiner's view is a popular one among theorists of tragedy. Una Ellis-Fermor sees tragedy as finely balanced between religious and non-religious values, in an equilibrium which endorses neither; for her as for I. A. Richards, the experience is simply annulled by any hint of a compensatory heaven.[55] Chu Kwang-Tsien declares that 'Christianity is in every sense antagonistic to the spirit of tragedy',[56] while other critics find an absence of tragedy in the Bible because figures like Job present no heroic resistance to their fate. It is the old macho notion that self-respecting tragic protagonists must put up a bit of a fight, give destiny a run for its money. Job is also considered non-tragic because his story ends well; but then so does the *Oresteia*, and in one sense the narrative of Oedipus. Oscar Mandel, by contrast, finds in Christ a tragic instance of the innocent figure brought low.[57] Northrop Frye maintains that 'the sense of tragedy as a prelude to comedy seems almost inseparable from anything explicitly Christian'.[58] But the fact that something needs to be broken in order to be repaired is scarcely a sanguine way of seeing, whatever one's faith that the breaking may finally prove fruitful.

Both Marxism and Christianity take the common life seriously, yet trust to its potential transformation. Indeed, Charles Taylor has argued that a belief in the value of the ordinary is an early Christian invention.[59] This is a classic formula for tragedy, as against a Platonism which disdains the empirical world or a pragmatism which believes it to be in tolerably good shape. If the common life is flawed but trivial, or important but in fine fettle, tragedy on a major scale need not ensue. It is the tragic which both Marxism and Christianity seek to redeem, but they can do so only by installing themselves at the heart of it. Marxism is an immanent critique of class society, not simply a utopian alternative to it; and resurrection for Christianity involves a crucifixion and descent into hell. Otherwise what is reclaimed in both cases would not be *this* condition, in all its deadlock and despair. Reclamation is necessary exactly where it seems least possible. Anywhere less drastic would not be in need of it. As Walter Stein comments with a slight mixing of metaphor: 'tragedy must be fully tragic, not only to come into its own, but, equally, if it is to provide proportionate soil for news of resurrection'.[60]

In confronting the worst yet hoping for the best, both creeds are considerably more sombre than liberal idealism, seeing sin or exploitation as the definitive condition of history; but both are also a good deal more buoyant than pragmatism or conservatism, confident that men and women are both worthy and capable of much more than is currently apparent. Kierkegaard writes in *The Sickness Unto Death* of Christianity setting up sin so firmly that it seems impossible to remove it, but then wanting to do just that.[61] One knows that one is a realist, then, when the idealists accuse you of apocalyptic gloom and the conservatives upbraid you for dewy-eyed optimism. The latter crime is perhaps these days the more heinous. If Samuel Johnson edited out some of the horror of *King Lear*, a Peter Brook production of the play cut out the passage in which Cordelia appears as a symbol of redemption. The late modern age finds something incorrigibly naive about hope. It is considerably more embarrassed by it than it is by adolescent shouts of apocalypse. And it is right to be so, when hope betrays the reality of suffering. But conservatives and postmodernists dislike the notion because it suggests the possibility of social progress, whereas some liberals and reformists disdain it because it suggests that there is something deeply enough awry to warrant it. There is a kind of tragedy that is gloomier than the conservatives and more hopeful than the progressives. And these two viewpoints have a common source.

Chapter 3

From Hegel to Beckett

The most renowned tragic teleology is that of Hegel. There is a sense in which one could call his *Phenomenology of Spirit* a tragic text, insisting as it does that philosophy means 'looking the negative in the face, and tarrying with it'.[1] To come into its own, *Geist* must first lose itself, undergo discord and dismemberment, thus rehearsing in a modern key the ancient rhythms of sacrifice. And this confrontation with loss is not just a ruse or a feint, as indeed the verb 'tarry' is meant to suggest. Only through the *via negativa* of self-division, through a whole-hearted surrender of itself to its opposite, can Spirit finally triumph. Dialectic, according to Rodolphe Gasché, is structurally tragic,[2] while Peter Szondi sees it as both tragic and the means of transcending tragedy.[3] Death, Hegel remarks in the *Phenomenology*, is of all things the most dreadful, and to hold to it requires the greatest strength. The life of Spirit is what refuses to shrink from this shattering encounter with the Real, but steadfastly maintains itself within this deathly sundering.

This, as Miguel de Beistegui observes, is 'a tragic conception of truth',[4] one which presents *Geist* itself as a tragic hero. The motor of history for Hegel is negativity, and negativity is ultimately death. Behind the synthetic power of Reason lurks the frightful phantasmagoria which he calls the 'night of the world', a realm of chaos and psychosis, of severed heads and mangled limbs. But it is through being torn apart in this way that Spirit will rise to eternal life. Like many a tragic narrative, then, this one will end well. What is tragic here and now will be recuperated as non-tragic in the great *telos* of Reason. But this does not abolish its pain. There is genuinely tragic conflict, for example, at the early master-and-slave stage of *Geist*'s tortuous progress, as two consciousnesses struggling for what Hegel calls 'pure prestige' war to the death, each seeking to win the acknowledgement of the other without conceding such recognition in return.

Truth undoubtedly exists, but the path to it is error. You must now recount an ironic tale of how truth emerges from its opposite, how it includes within itself all the zigzags, fissures, false starts and blind alleys involved in its unfolding. Only in retrospect will you come to recognize that what seemed at the time sheer error, accident or pointless deviation was all the while stealthily adding up to a luminously coherent text, rather as Oedipus can look back on his previously benighted self and recognize that his life forms an intelligible whole, however devoutly he may wish that it did not. We live forward tragically, but think back comically. And since Spirit can know itself only by losing track of itself, falling into the profane realm of objectification in order to return to itself, there is now a tragic structure to epistemology itself.

Indeed, for Hegel, philosophy itself is the result of a tragic condition. With growing social complexity and a deepening division of labour, society has now become unrepresentable by the sensuous image, and can be captured only by the concept. If we could still feel its unity intuitively, there would be no need for the likes of Hegel. Spurning icons, however, is anyway suitable to the dignity of a rational being. The senses are what we share in common with the other animals, so that while a crocodile can feel cold like ourselves, it cannot rise to the uncarnal majesty of the notion of freedom. We have the edge over it there. Hegel shares Kant's austerely iconoclastic belief that the truths of Reason are beyond our creaturely reach and could only be degraded by representation. To be equal to them, as well as to see them without the distortions of passion, we must leave the body behind us. Social totality can now be reflected only inside the head of Hegel, not in a pantheon of statues or set of religious icons. It can no more be perceptually portrayed than one could sketch a square triangle. Art must therefore make way for philosophy, which will restore totality to us in conceptual form; but the conditions which make this necessary – the fragmentation of social life, the loss of spontaneous social unity – belong to a tragic fable. And though the discursiveness of philosophy is part of its capacious power, it dispels the phenomenal immediacy of the art work. Philosophy springs from rupture and discord, and its task is to redeem the very divisive conditions which brought it to birth. It is a self-consuming artefact.

Far from being a catastrophe, tragic art for Hegel is supremely affirmative. It is the finest working model we have of how Spirit, once pitched into contention with itself, restores its own unity through negation. When powers which are just but one-sided detach themselves from the universal, promoting themselves as absolute and autonomous, tragedy is on hand to annul their presumptuous claims and resolve them back into the whole. Ethical substance, as Hegel puts it, is restored in the downfall of the individual which disturbs its repose. Having been riven into tragic opposition, *Geist* now recovers its self-identity and rolls serenely on its way. The fulfilment we reap from tragic art is the deep satisfaction of bearing witness to this transcendence. Sophoclean Fate becomes Hegelian Reason. 'Mere' pity and terror are outweighed by an exultant knowledge of eternal justice. The world is rational, even if, curiously, it is through violent destruction that we come to appreciate the fact.

For Hegel as for Schlegel, tragedy ends with a sublime indifference to the colliding forces it has set loose. These powers, in being gathered into the higher order of the Absolute, are at once defeated and victorious. With Schopenhauer, this lordly indifference will reappear rather less consolingly as the malevolent Will. Perhaps we post-Freudians can detect in this delight in the indestructibility of both Reason and Will the fantasy of the ego confronted with its own demise. Adversity and affliction in Hegel's eyes are not the final point: what matters is the victory of Reason, which adversity highlights by contrast with itself. As he remarks in *The Philosophy of Fine Art*, 'the necessity of all that particular individuals experience is able (in tragedy) to appear in complete concord with reason'.[5] It is unlikely that Marlowe's Edward the Second, who dies with a redhot poker thrust up his anus, would rush to endorse this view. A. C. Bradley, a devout Hegelian himself, astutely points out that to reveal suffering as rational does nothing to diminish it.[6] There is little sense in Hegel of tragic art as piteous and harrowing. Indeed, his aesthetic could be seen as much as a defence against the tragic as an exploration of it. In exalting the tragic, his language also diminishes it.

As far as Marlowe goes, it is true that Hegel has in mind ancient rather than modern tragedy. But even here his reflections are far too conditioned by *Antigone*, as Aristotle's are by *King Oedipus*. It is remarkable how many general theories of tragedy have been spun out of a mere two or three texts. A number of ancient tragedies, not least those of the iconoclastic Euripides, could be summoned to bear testimony against him. The characters of modern tragedy, in Hegel's view, are more individual personalities than embodiments of world-historical forces, motivated more by subjective states than conflicts of ethical substance; so that strife, as with Hamlet, becomes internalized, and the dramatic action must lean too heavily on sheer extraneous accident. Ancient characters, by contrast, are monumentally self-identical: as the bearers of an 'essential' individuality, they are merely, magnificently what they are. Tragedy here is immanent rather than accidental, flowing from the inner logic of action rather than from commonplace contingency. As Hegel puts it in *The Phenomenology of Spirit*, the characters of tragedy are artists, free from individual idiosyncrasies and the accidents of circumstance, giving utterance to their inner essence rather than to the empirical selfhood of everyday life.[7] It is with Hegel above all that tragedy first becomes 'essentialized', reified to a spiritual absolute which presides impassively over a degraded everyday existence. It is the great philosopher of modernity who hands the adversaries of that epoch a vital poetic weapon in their campaign against the half-literate prose of its daily life.

Hegelian Spirit, with its customary cunning, knows that it can enter into its own only through conflict and negation. In this it is different from Abraham in Søren Kierkegaard's *Fear and Trembling*, who knows that it is impossible to slay Isaac and have him restored to him, but who refuses to back down from the impossible in that unthinkable paradox known to Kierkegaard as faith. Like the Lacanian analysand on the road to recovery, Abraham refuses to give up on his desire for the impossible, holding fast to the finite even as he resigns himself to the fact that nothing on earth will satisfy his longing. As the work comments: 'it is great to give up one's desire, but greater still to stick to it after having given it up'.[8] Abraham's way is not that of Schopenhaurian renunciation, but neither is it that of Hegelian affirmation. It is because Abraham clings so tenaciously to the impossible that it comes to pass in reality, as God stays his hand and rescues his son.

From the standpoint of Hegelian teleology, Abraham's action is simply unintelligible. For Hegel as for Kant, the ethical involves relating one's particularity to the universal. For Kant, this involves overriding one's individual desires in the name of moral duty; if virtue does not feel unpleasant, it is unlikely to be virtue. For Hegel, such sharing in the Absolute is what brings the individual to its finest flourishing. But in both cases the structure is one of sacrifice, as the particular is subordinated to the well-being of the whole. Abraham's sacrifice, by contrast, is not of this rational, universalist kind, but a scandal and stumbling-block to all such tragic teleology. But nor is it a mere *acte gratuit* or piece of absurdism, since Abraham trusts that it will have a profitable consequence, namely the restoration of Isaac.

Abraham also knows, however, that this is logically impossible, and his action is not undertaken in the name of any universal *telos*. He is prepared to slaughter his own son even though it does nothing for the well-being of humanity at large, and certainly no good to himself. In this, he differs from the classical tragic hero, who sacrifices himself for the state or nation or to appease the irascible gods, and who in doing so evokes the admiring pity of his fellows. But nobody, Kierkegaard comments, weeps for Abraham, whose deed one approaches rather with a 'holy terror'. The classical tragic action may prove fruitful in the lives of others, which is part of what can make tragedy valuable. Abraham's intended deed is more deeply tragic precisely because it will be fruitless; yet it is through his acceptance of this in faith that God brings him through to a felicitous conclusion. He is, as Kierkegaard observes, 'great with that power which is powerlessness'.[9]

The tragic hero renounces his particularity in order to express the universal, translating himself into that august sphere. As Kierkegaard remarks, he 'gives up what is certain for what is still more certain',[10] whereas Abraham goes one further and relinquishes the universal as well as his own desire, enduring all the affliction of the tragic hero, abandoning everything, bringing his joy in the world to nothing, without any sure guarantee of a return. The tragic hero, Kierkegaard writes, is the one 'who so to speak makes a clear and elegant edition of himself, as immaculate as possible, and readable for all', whereas he who has faith 'renounces the universal in order to become the particular', thus becoming illegible to others.[11] That which is uniquely, irreducibly itself is bound to defeat the concept, which is ineluctably general. The typical tragic hero, by contrast, remains steadfastly within the domain of the ethical, so that his fate, however unenviable, is at least intelligible, and thus on the same plane as the non-tragic. Neither Brutus nor Agamemnon, Kierkegaard remarks, could have breathed 'it won't happen' when staring destiny in the eye, as Abraham does.

The figure of faith like Abraham by-passes the mediation of the ethical, in which all particulars are indifferently interchangeable, and establishes instead a direct relationship with the absolute which pitches him beyond the frontiers of ethical discourse or rational comprehension. The 'Other' for him is by no means identical with the symbolic order. He is a living affront to the Hegelian dialectic, defiantly elevating the particular over the universal, daring to embrace what for Kierkegaard is the most terrifying risk of all, existing as an individual. This, which for Kierkegaard is the only authentic heroism, means recognizing that, *pace* the equivalences of the ethical or political spheres, one is absolutely incommensurable with any other individual, and so infinitely opaque to them. The reality of others is only ever a 'possibility' for us, and all believers are 'incognitos'. It is the ruin of any rational politics. Individuality is the claim of infinity upon the finite, the mind-shaking mystery that God has fashioned this irreplaceably specific self from all eternity, that all eternity is at stake in one's sheer irreducible self-identity.

The Kierkegaardian 'suspension of the ethical' characterizes the figure of faith, not the figure of tragedy. Yet as we shall see a little later, it is exactly this stubborn fidelity to some absolute claim on one's being, regardless of the social or moral consequences, which for Jacques Lacan is most typical of the tragic protagonist. Antigone's conduct is no more socially conformist or ethically prudent than Christ's crucifixion. Faith, Kierkegaard sees, cannot be translated into ethical discourse without an opaque remainder. There are times when faith will be folly to the wise, as when we refuse to launch a military assault on an enemy even when we have political justice on our side, and when the result of our refusal might be his attacking us. But there is also a savage parody of the suspension of the ethical, which is the elitism of evil. It is the aficionados of evil who believe that they exist not simply beyond good, but beyond the ethical domain as such. If such connoisseurs of chaos have scant respect for virtue, they are equally contemptuous of anything as drearily petty bourgeois as immorality.

For a lineage of modern thinkers from Hegel and Baudelaire to Nietzsche, Dostoevsky, Yeats, Claudel, Mauriac and T. S. Eliot, tragedy represents a privileged mode of cognition, a spiritual experience reserved for the metaphysically minded few. It is, in effect, an ersatz form of religion for a secular age, countering its vulgarity with a higher wisdom. George Steiner, in a sentence tremulous with pathos, remarks that 'at the touch of Hume and Voltaire the noble or hideous visitations which had haunted the mind since Agamemnon's blood cried out for vengeance, disappeared altogether or took tawdry refuge among the gaslights of melodrama'.[12] No doubt Steiner is just as sceptical of the scriptural God as Hume and Voltaire ever were, but the spirit of religion must nevertheless be salvaged as a bulwark against a faithless modernity. One does not personally believe in God, but it would be a fine thing if everyone else did. Tragic insight is incomparably superior to the workaday domain of ethics, rationality, fellow-feeling and the like. Ida Arnold in Graham Greene's *Brighton Rock*, with her suburban platitudes and busybody moralizing, is in one sense by no means as admirable as the damned Pinkie, who exactly because of his wickedness is as much on terms with salvation and perdition as a saint. Better to rule in hell than serve tea in suburbia.

The Jesuitical Naphta of Thomas Mann's *The Magic Mountain* claims that God and the devil are at one in being hostile to life, which is to say 'bourgeoisiedom', reason and virtue. Adrian Leverkühn of Mann's *Doctor Faustus* speaks of swinging between towering flights and abysmal desolation in a manner incomprehensible to the moderate bourgeoisie. His music reveals 'the substantial identity of the most blest with the most accurst'. Good and evil are alike in their glamorous extremity. The devil in *Doctor Faustus* sniffily contrasts the exclusivist mysteries of religion with the banality of the petty bourgeoisie, declaring that he is now the sole custodian of theology. He means that evil is all that survives of metaphysics in the modern world. Plato comments in *The Republic* that really spectacular wickedness usually springs from vigorous, gifted characters, not petty ones. In medieval Christianity, writes Jean-François Lyotard, 'a narrow complicity is established between the sinner and the confessor, the witch and the exorcist, sex and sainthood'.[13]

The problem with T. S. Eliot's Hollow Men, along with most of the dingy inhabitants of *The Waste Land*, is that they are too shallow even to be damned. If they could muster some really eye-catching depravity, they might stand a slim chance of salvation. At least then there would be something to redeem. But humankind for Eliot cannot bear very much reality, and erects its shabby suburban virtues as a defence against the holy terror of the divine. Evil, announces Pascal in the *Pensées*, is easy, whereas good is almost unique. But there is, he goes on to add, a certain brand of evil which is as rare as true goodness, 'and this particular evil is often on that account passed off as good. Indeed it takes as much extraordinary greatness of soul to attain such evil, as to attain good'.[14] Anyone can aspire to common-or-garden wickedness, but it takes a real virtuoso to be damned. It is likely that the kind of evil Pascal has in mind is what we know as the demonic, which we shall be investigating a little later.

The doctrine that the saintly and the Satanic are mirror images of each other sails close to the heresy of Gnosticism, the deconstructive belief that God himself is doubled, containing both good and evil in his own unsearchable being. For a few plucky souls, the path of debauchery, of drinking the foul dregs of human experience in truculent Baudelairean fashion, is therefore as valid an approach to him as the road of sanctity. There is a fine line between this conscious wallowing of degradation, so that you might pass right through it and out again into the sphere of divinity, and a familiar kind of tragic action, in which you are forced through hell willy-nilly but thereby struggle through to a deeper kind of existence. Gnosticism is a grisly parody of this kind of tragedy, a state in which you will your own ruin in order to have carnal knowledge of the ultimate, indifferent as it is to such simple-minded polarities as good and evil.

Dostoevsky's Ivan Karamazov, an atheist who writes articles on theology, is one such member of the elite company of the damned. Ivan needs to believe in God in order to reject him, and in this sense resembles the devil, who has excellent reason for knowing that God exists. Dimitry, Ivan's degenerate brother, sings praises to God from the depths of his debauchery. As one character in the novel comments of him: 'The experience of ultimate degradation is as vital to such unruly, dissolute natures as the experience of sheer goodness' (Part 4, Book 12, ch. 6). You can be aglow with the perfection of the Madonna, the novel observes, and still not renounce Sodom. Even the saintly Alyosha has the corrupt blood of the Karamazovs in his veins. And the holy-fool, all-things-are-blessed philosophy of his mentor Father Zosima may be just the reverse side of Ivan's libertine belief that in the absence of God all things are permitted. Like many an atheist, Ivan is merely an inverted metaphysician, whose negative relationship with divinity is quite as intimate as Alyosha's more positive one. Like Bendrix in Graham Greene's *The End of the Affair*, he hates God as though he existed. Raskolnikov of *Crime and Punishment* kills half-senselessly in order to prove his membership of a spiritual elect beyond good and evil. He ends up regretting not the crime itself but its lack of aesthetic purity, the fact that he bungles the business in a way beneath the dignity of a classical tragic protagonist.

One can trace this tragic elitism in the downward curve of T. S. Eliot's drama. Just as Brecht believed that a theatre audience should be, so to speak, horizontally divided, so Eliot believed that it should be vertically stratified, ranked into the more and less *cognoscenti* by levels of meaning within the play itself. The play, like the audience, will contain a select few who understand what is spiritually afoot; a rather larger band of characters who fumble towards some dim sense of the action's significance; and an outer circle of suburbanite groundlings, beyond both salvation and damnation, who haven't a clue what is going on. It is as though a few of the characters on stage are aware that they are speaking in blank verse, whereas the rest are not; indeed, Eliot's brand of blank verse is discreetly low-profiled enough to permit this distinction. *Murder in the Cathedral*, the Agatha Christie-like title of which conceals high spiritual drama beneath waggish sensationalism, pulling in the plebs only to impishly bamboozle them, can connect these levels by its liturgical form, as meanings filter down from Thomas himself to arrive in obscured but still pregnant form in the choric speech of the Women of Canterbury. Thomas's martyrdom, although only dimly apprehended by this assortment of spiritually middle-brow folk, will nevertheless fructify in their own lives, and perhaps also in the lives of the audience-cum-congregation.

By the time of *The Family Reunion*, however, the ritual form – Greek this time, rather than Christian – seems consciously ironic, mischievously designed in Old Possum style to expose rather than bridge the gap between those who are spiritually in the know and those who are not. By having the Furies stage an appearance at the drawing-room window, Eliot throws up his hands in mock despair at the very notion of inserting metaphysical meaning into the waste land of high society. As with Ibsen, all the key events are therefore pushed off-stage, alluded to rather than dramatically represented, incongruously at odds with the world in which men and women sip sherry or take a stroll through the shrubbery.

But it is an incongruity which Eliot seems to relish as well as lament. The plays take a perverse delight in disconnection. The toings-and-froings we observe on stage are no more than an inferior objective correlative of some altogether more arcane drama of sin, guilt and salvation which the theatrical action is really too brittle to sustain, and which runs its course in some other place entirely, not least in that foreign country known as the past.

The stage business of *The Family Reunion* is deliberately attenuated so that spiritual values may be illuminated by contrast with it; but the tactic undercuts itself, leaving those values with nowhere to realize themselves, and so emptying them of content. This is to be regretted, but it is also a deliberate device. It is as though the action takes place on one level and the meaning on another – or, in the language of *Four Quartets*, as though we had the experience but missed the meaning. Indeed, as far as Harry's guilt-ridden past goes it hardly matters much what actually happened, or whether anything actually happened at all. Empirical occurrences are for shopkeepers, not the spiritual elect, and Eliot was never greatly enthralled by actuality. This nonchalant way with action, disconcerting enough in a dramatist, is already foreshadowed in *Murder in the Cathedral* in the deliberate downplaying of the actual murder of Thomas, which is relegated to a sub-clause in a stage direction, in contrast to the portentous connotations clustered around it. What matters in Eliot is not action, and not even the consciousness of it, which is invariably false consciousness, but those meanings which act themselves out on a different stage altogether, that of the spirit or the unconscious. The point of the dramatic form is not to fuse action and meaning, but to provide the space in which they ostentatiously fail to intersect.

Four Quartets is caught within much the same duality as the drama, as its flatter, more profane discourse is thrust up cheek-by-jowl against a more cryptic, *symboliste* language only for the two registers to cancel each other out. Perhaps truth can be discerned only in the way these various dismally inadequate idioms bounce off one another, glimpsed fitfully in the incongruous gaps between them. This, however, is a problem for a poem so preoccupied with the Incarnation, the intersection of time and eternity at the still point of the turning world. The poem's language stiffly withholds any special value from that world, which appears hardly less sterile and contemptible than it was in *The Waste Land*, at the very moment that its theology insists on secular history as the theatre of divine redemption.[15] Only through time is time conquered. It is as though the Incarnation makes all the difference and no difference at all. The poem is a performative contradiction, its form at odds with its content. Whatever Eliot's theology, the poetry remains resolutely anti-incarnational, ascetically suspicious of creaturely life, as indeed does the *Quartets'* anti-logocentric language, the word which can never capture the full presence of the Word.

The Family Reunion, for all its wry defeatism, can still depict Harry's redemption as more than just a private affair. It involves Mary and Agatha too, though each of them must find her own lonely path to salvation. There is no longer a collective action, though connections can still be established; there is still a Chorus, even if what it registers is largely its incomprehension. In *The Cocktail Party*, however, Eliot's Olympian division of the spiritual sheep from the secular goats achieves its final grisly parody. It is now as if his own dramatic forms are busy sending themselves up, as banality and intensity constantly thwart each other and set metaphysical speeches are archly interrupted by the telephone. The redemptive figure is now the psychiatrist Reilly, member of a secular priesthood for which Eliot's Tory-Anglican disdain is not hard to imagine. But though this is a genteel joke in one sense, it is deadly serious in another: in the spiritually shrivelled world of West End cocktail parties, psychiatric truth is probably the nearest one can approach to religious revelation. Human kind cannot bear very much reality. There is no point in trying to force spiritual meanings on those for whom such exalted discourse is about as meaningful as the sound of a cricket rubbing its legs together.

The attempt to bridge the gap between sacred and secular is accordingly abandoned, with a defeatism which can pass itself off as a wryly tolerant wisdom. Reilly acts as a frail link between the two realms, extricating Celia from the world and returning Edward and Lavinia to its dreary social routines enlivened by rather more insight than before. And other characters are allowed to glimpse something of the meaning of the central spiritual drama, perhaps more so indeed than in *The Family Reunion*. But the fact that most of these boneheaded socialites can summon a little spiritual insight when pushed is also a covert apologia for their anaemic social world. Each world – that of metaphysics and that of Martinis – is necessary in its own way, but mixing them too vigorously only creates bemusement. In *The Family Reunion* there was at least a real conflict between different levels of perception; now it is as though these levels have been separated out and each of them endorsed in its own right. Ordinary life is a bad joke, but so is Celia's martyrdom; secular history is devoid of grace, but must be accepted as the best most of us can manage. A few lonely visionaries will abjure the world, but it is better for the rest of us to conform to it. One should accept the Order of Merit and pursue a pin-striped existence in London clubland, while inwardly renouncing the whole futile business.

Redemption is thus carefully quarantined from the arena it was supposed to transfigure, a move which in turn seals off that domain of empty-headed privilege from any very searching criticism. Indeed, it is now as if transcendence is being as much sent up by triviality as vice versa. How else can one account for the vein of wearily self-debunking black humour which runs throughout the play, as the saintly Celia is crucified near an African ant hill and Alex talks breezily of cooking monkeys? Martyrdom still takes place, but a long way from the West End, and it will bear no fruit there. The device of the Guardians parodies the detective story and satirizes a shallow country-house existence; but it seems equally to send up the spiritual issues themselves, so that it is the vacuity of these transcendent matters, as well as the inanity of upper-class living, which these cardboard figures bring into focus. The transcendence rises above meaning, while the inanity falls below it. In both cases, the result is a blank. If social existence is death-in-life, martyrdom is life-in-death; but there seems as little to be resurrected from it as there does from drawing-room chit chat.

Kierkegaard, though far too Protestant for Eliot's taste, shares something of this tragic elitism, as his remarks on the demonic in chapter 3 of *The Concept of Anxiety* would suggest. 'There are very few people', he remarks in *The Sickness Unto Death*, 'who live their lives to any degree at all in the category of spirit.'[16] 'Very few' is a pet phrase of Eliot's prose, one which seems to give its author an almost physical *frisson*. Though Kierkegaard's work succeeds in doing the well-nigh impossible, raising Protestantism to the dignity of a universal philosophy, it remains in the end the preserve of the elect. Tragedy is an antidote to the self-righteous petty-bourgeois ethics of the Ida Arnolds, a case of *Vernunft* as opposed to *Verstand*. Yet Kierkegaard steals a march on his elitist colleagues by relegating tragedy itself to the merely ethical realm, outranking it with a faith which is absurd and impenetrable to the populace at large. Those unable to bear what he calls this 'martyrdom of unintelligibility' are the humanists and civic moralists, with their 'foolish concern for others' weal and woe which is honoured under the name of sympathy, but which is really nothing but vanity'.[17] If tragedy holds itself aloof from commonplace human sympathies, cultivating altogether more elevated passions, faith is even more supercilious about them. Like sin, it is the rock on which all sheerly ethical life is shipwrecked.

Most individuals, Kierkegaard remarks in *The Sickness Unto Death*, are so far from faith as to be almost as far from despair as well. Or at least from knowing they are in despair – for despair in Kierkegaard's eyes is the most common condition there is, even if false consciousness prevents the ruck of humanity from being aware of it. To be capable of despair is both our doom and our edge over the unreflective beasts. Stoats and wombats may have their problems, but being plunged into eternal despondency is not among them. Our capacity for despair is both infinite merit and absolute ruin, a sickness which it is the greatest ill-fortune never to have contracted. For we can arrive at the truth, tragically, only by way of negativity, and when one is brought to the verge of utter ruin only God remains as a possibility. The believer, then, rather like Abraham, is one who is caught in an absolute impasse, and can only trust that God will somehow pluck new life from this plight. He or she lives the contradiction of an irreparable undoing which God will nevertheless redeem. Tragedy can indeed be transcended, but only by going all the way through it in the act of confronting one's despair. And this is an act beyond the reach of all but a spiritual coterie.

Granted his belief that the human condition is critical, Kierkegaard could certainly be called a tragic thinker. Faith is not a steady state but an existential struggle, pinning together antinomies in the sheer sweated labour of living which no mere dialectical reason could hope to synthesize. Socratic irony does well to preserve a certain respectful distance between human and divine knowledge, drawing a line between the two somewhat in the manner of a Kant or Schopenhauer. Yet such Socratic irony is also a denial of sin in the name of ignorance, and thus anti-tragic in all the wrong ways. Despair has its most cherished dwelling-place at the very heart of happiness, rather as for *The Concept of Anxiety* there is a nameless dread of nothingness at the core of all immediacy. And the unique portion of eternity known as oneself can always be irredeemably lost. As Theodor Adorno puts it: 'For Kierkegaard, the tragic is the finite that comes into conflict with the infinite and, measured according to it, is judged by the measure of the infinite'.[18] And before the infinite, as every good Protestant knows, we are always in the wrong.

Hegel is the great Enlightenment theorist of tragedy, seeking to rescue its depth, seriousness and intensity from sentimentalist dilutions, but striving at the same time to reconcile it with Enlightenment Reason. The great counter-Enlightenment tragic philosopher is then Friedrich Nietzsche, who shares Kiekegaard's contempt for rationalism from a pagan rather than Protestant standpoint.[19] Yet tragedy for Nietzsche is a sort of theodicy or apologia for evil just as it is for Hegel. For him, too, tragic art is a containment of tragic breakdown, as the soothing balm of the Apollonian is applied to the primordial wound of the Dionysian. If Hegel's non-tragic theory of tragedy is an unconscious defence against irreparable ruin, Nietzsche argues out loud for just this position. For him, tragedy is the supreme critique of modernity, which is one reason why the subject looms so large in an age undistinguished for its actual tragic art. It is a question of myth versus science, 'life' against morality, music versus discourse, eternity rather than progress, the ravishment of suffering in the teeth of a callow humanitarianism, heroism rather than mediocrity, the aesthetic at war with the ethico-political, the barbaric against the civic and cultural, Dionysian madness *contra* Apollonian social order. It is a syndrome which has re-emerged in our own time in the shape of some postmodern theorizing, much of which has been Nietzschean without fully knowing it.

Nietzsche opposes a bloodless historicism, which strips the past of its ungovernable vitality, in the name of a creative amnesia or a recovery of the past through myth. This represents an anti-tragic reversal of Marx's 'nightmare of history': we will shake off the traumatizing burden of the past by forgetting whatever impedes heroic action in the present, or by remembering only what we can use. The present turns the tables on the archaic, exploiting its primal energies rather than allowing itself to be crushed to death under its unbearable weight. It is this latter condition which Henrik Ibsen will later see as the paradigm of tragedy. Yet for Nietzsche, forgetfulness is tragic too – but tragedy this time as a celebration of mutability, a scandalous affirmation of what is cruel, barbarous and bestial in humanity, an ecstatic yea-saying to life's sheer obdurate imperishability. Mutability, the evanescence of human life, has traditionally been a *topos* of grief, on the curious assumption that what is unchanging or eternal is necessarily to be commended. It is one of Nietzsche's many original strokes that he dares to query this doctrine and inquire what is so wrong with the fleeting, the transitory, the fugitive.

For Nietzsche, as for such later acolytes as Joseph Conrad, we can act purposively only through certain salutary myths which by masking the obscene chaos of existence, lend the self a life-sustaining illusion of purpose. Freud took the point in his own way, as indeed did Louis Althusser, whose theory of ideology as 'imaginary' is not altogether remote from this doctrine. It is a tragic tenet of modernity, behind which the shadow of Nietzsche looms large, that we can act historically only out of amnesia, self-oblivion, self-violence or repression. Otherwise we are doomed to the destiny of a Hamlet. Yet tragedy is both the home of such redemptive illusions and a shattering revelation of the holy terrors they disguise. Tragic Man is he who is brave enough to endorse the beauty and necessity of illusion, in the teeth of the Platonists who would peer peremptorily behind it, but also he who risks gazing into the abyss of the Real and dancing on its edge without being turned to stone, reading what the scholars decorously call history as a squalid genealogy of blood, toil and terror.

For Nietzsche as for Walter Benjamin, every document of civilization is simultaneously a record of barbarism; it is just that Nietzsche was rather less disapproving of the barbarism, though he by no means endorsed it entirely. Tragedy is a way of living permanently with the horror which the Kurtz of Conrad's *Heart of Darkness* can give voice to only at the moment of death. And 'culture' is Nietzsche's scathingly dismissive name for the opiates we take in order to numb ourselves to these terrors. In place of the man of culture, then, he will mischievously offer us the satyr, those mocking, aboriginal, libidinal creatures of Nature who are eternally the same, who have seen civilizations come and go and who will finally see them off.

Formally speaking, Nietzsche's tragic affirmation is not altogether different from Hegel's. If Hegel regards tragedy with Apollonian satisfaction as reinforcing the sovereignty of Reason, Nietzsche sees it with Dionysian delight as exulting in the indestructibility of life, which the sacrifice of the individual simply enhances. The tragic hero, as he remarks with his customary grisly relish in *The Birth of Tragedy*, is 'negated for our pleasure'. And since for this early essay individuality is the very source of evil and suffering, the Dionysian fury which tears individuals apart is to be applauded. Individuals in tragedy, in any case, are merely masks of the god himself. As the high priest of Dionysus, Nietzsche finds in tragic art a frenzy, chaos, excess and horror which takes pleasure in both creating and destroying – the domain, we might say, of *Thanatos* or the death drive, where we can reap sadistic *jouissance* from misery and carnage secure in the consolation that this eternal flux of strife, savagery and rebirth will never pass away. 'We believe in eternal life' is tragedy's exultant cry, in a pagan parody of Christian faith. Transience, at least, is here to stay.

Meanwhile we, the spectators, identify with this blissful, terrible profligacy, assured that the belligerence and brutality of existence is inevitable if so many teeming life-forms are to be brought exuberantly to birth. Our response to this ambivalent process thus matches its own sadomasochism. We feel a medley of pleasure and pain, fear and compassion, rapture and repulsion, which for Nietzsche are the tainted sources of tragic pleasure. We shudder at the protagonist's torments yet delight to see him destroyed, rejoice in pure appearance but also in its negation. Why, Nietzsche inquires, would suffering be so often represented in so many forms if it were not a source of intense fulfilment? We are not to moralize our sadism away but frankly to affirm it, in what Raymond Williams sternly calls 'a brutal rationalization of suffering'.[20] We are pierced by the agonies of the dying at the very moment that we sense at work in their dissolution the immortality of the life-force itself, and are consoled by the thought (as a later Nietzschean, W. B. Yeats, was to feel comforted) that everything will return an infinity of times in this mighty aesthetic spectacle of death, dismemberment and rebirth.

It is this imperishable force which the later post-Schopenhaurian Nietzsche will dub Will to Power, though in doing so he discards the appearance/reality model of his early essay on tragedy. In the phenomenalism of the later writings, the Will is at one with its perpetually changing 'appearances' rather than a *noumenon* behind or beneath them, affirming itself in a sublime, tail-chasing aesthetic game in which beings contend ceaselessly with each other for dominion. The *Übermensch* is the one who dares to will this groundlessness without shedding his blitheness and serenity, and to will it moreover in its unending, obscenely meaningless recurrence. One cannot really speak of this ceaseless cosmic play as either tragic or comic, since Will to Power simply is what it is, the source of all values but beyond valuation itself. Since it constitutes everything there is, from the wavering of a snail's horns to the flourishing of the political state, there could be no vantage-point outside it from which to pass judgement on it as either positive or negative. Nietzsche thus dismantles the opposition between comedy and tragedy, combining a Strindbergian spectacle of ferocious global warfare with a cheerful Joycean equipoise in the face of this strife-racked universe. Tragedy perceives a frightful abyss where the stout burghers see a foundation; but an unfounded world is also a self-founding one, with all the blissful pointlessness of a stupendous work of art. And the doctrine of eternal recurrence – the truth that nothing can ever be irreparably sunk in this ceaseless cosmic recycling – is both the ultimate horror and an escape from absolute loss.

The Dionysian is a Janus-faced realm, whatever the simple-minded affirmations of some later sub-Nietzschean thought. One thinks, for example, of D. H. Lawrence's execrable novel *The Plumed Serpent*. Those modern-day critics who celebrate madness, transgression, desire and disruption from the Apollonian comfort of their armchairs forget, as Nietzsche does not, how malignant such forces can be. The bliss of Dionysus is laced with the anguish of division, as we desire to be at one with Nature but also to tear ourselves from its orgiastic embrace. Dionysus is at once the principle of unity and individuation, identity and difference, breaching boundaries in the name of communal bliss yet also, as the god of progress and evolution, summoning us to autonomous existence. In tragedy this whole conflictive process, simply to be rendered bearable, is then framed, distanced and sublimated in the domain of the Apollonian, with its rational knowledge, moderating limits, formal pleasures and beautiful unities. One kind of pleasure thus redoubles another.

At the very moment that the Real of the Dionysian threatens to trau-
matize us, rendering us unfit for action, the Apollonian or symbolic order
casts its enchanting veil of illusion over this abhorrent abyss, reshaping
its unspeakable horror as the aesthetic sublime. Each dimension will then
play into the other, as dream-world and intoxication merge and begin
to speak each other's language, beauty or the Apollonian rescuing the
Dionysian from pure amorphousness, and the Dionysian redeeming
the Apollonian from the dead-end of sheer vacuous form. Tragedy
is Dionysian impulse discharging itself in Apollonian imagery. It is, for
all its mythological panache, a conventional enough aesthetic opposition.
It is also one which can be dismantled. Form is a fending off of
the lethal sublimity of Dionysus, but its contained stillness is itself an
image of death. In this sense, it shares in the very forces it strives to
contain, as the ego for Freud is itself an organ of the unconscious.
And the Dionysian is both life instincts and death drive. For both philosophers, *Eros* and *Thanatos* can be found on both sides of the chasm which
separates them.

Tragic art, then, is the sworn foe of science, political progress, revolutionary optimism and ethical culture. It is also the enemy of *mimesis*, since
the role of art is to transfigure rather than reflect. Nietzsche is thus one
source of the view that tragedy is too precious to be abandoned to real
life. It is a victory over the workaday world, not an illumination of it. For
him as for Yeats, only a slavish, ignoble art needs to leech on reality. The
myth of Faust has lain bare the limits of rational or Socratic knowledge,
and a freshly flourishing tragic culture will replace this rationalism with
the more fertile cognitions of myth. Tragedy has no truck with ethics:
instead, it offers us an aestheticized version of sacrifice, of death-in-life
and life through death, which is as implacably amoral as the old fertility
cults. It is this world of wounded gods and life-enhancing heroes which
will provide a vibrant alternative to Christianity and secular humanism
alike, disfigured as they are by their sickly obsession with guilt, sin, pity
and altruism.

In its reckless bravura, its spendthrift way with life-forms, its haughty
refusal of petty-bourgeois timidity, its relish of the hard, sinewy and well-
tempered, its aversion to the stink of humanitarianism, tragedy, whose
god Dionysus is the Anti-Christ, is a virile aristocratic rebuke to a femi-
nine, Christian, democratic age of equality and odious compassion. It can
confess what is pitiless and rapacious in humanity without lapsing into
some despicable culture of shame and self-laceration. Yet if tragedy is a
riposte to social optimism, it is also a response to modern pessimism, as
the Will, drunk with an overwhelming abundance of life and high spirits,

rejoices in its own indissolubility in the very act of squandering its highest types.

Human existence, for both Schopenhauer and the early Nietzsche, is an arena of atrocious pain. But whereas Schopenhauer draws from this the Sophoclean lesson that it would be far better not to have been born, indeed thinks this blatantly obvious for the toiling masses of history, Nietzsche's flight from woe is not through non-existence but tragic metamorphosis. For him as for Rilke, 'happiness . . . is the fruit of so radical an acceptance of suffering that abundant delight springs from its very affirmation'.[21] Just as Rilke proclaims in his eighth sonnet to Orpheus that 'Only in the realm of Praise may lamentation move', so his forebear joyfully wills the world's existence along with its inevitable sorrow. In bursting the grape, you must like John Keats reckon the ruin of pleasure into the savouring of it.

It is a dangerous ethic in all cases. Nietzsche quotes Cardanus as insisting that one should seek out as much pain as possible in order to deepen the joy which springs from its transcendence,[22] while Rilke also speaks of heightening the agony of existence so as to increase the bliss of its transformation. Neither writer pauses to note that plenty of people have no need to multiply their torments, since they can confidently rely on others to do it for them. Yet there is a difference. For Rilke, what redeems Nature is humanity, 'der Verklarer des Daseins'; for Nietzsche, humanity is the problem, not the solution. It is an ephemeral invention which post-dates his beloved Greeks, and by refashioning a tragic culture we may hope finally to be shot of it. The death of God does not herald the birth of humanity, since that notion is itself tied securely to the Almighty's throne. It is rather a call to travel beyond humanity itself, that pitiful, admirable product of guilt and self-loathing, towards that tragedy on the far side of the tragic which is the *Übermensch*.

Tragedy is not just about things ending badly. There are not many tragedies, whatever George Steiner cavalierly asserts in *The Death of Tragedy*, in which destruction is literally the last word. Tragedy can also mean that one must be hauled through hell to have any chance of freedom or fulfilment. And if W. B. Yeats is right that nothing can be sole or whole that has not been rent, then tragedy of a kind is endemic to the human condition. But this is to claim that truth and justice demand a radical remaking, not that they can never prevail. Tragedy can be an index of the outrageous price we have sometimes to pay for them, not of their illusoriness. To claim that this is *tragic* is to insist that it would be far better were it not so. It is the antithesis of the barracks-room view that suffering makes a man of you. It is a measure of how catastrophic things are with us that change must be bought at so steep a cost. Only by some bruising encounter with the Real, to cast the case in Lacanian terms – a confrontation which we cannot survive undamaged, and which will leave its lethal scars silently imprinted on our existence – can we hope for genuine emancipation.

It is no wonder that, faced with this Hobson's choice, most of us opt for an Eliotic evasion of tragedy, the living and partly living of the sub-urban Hollow Men or the women of Canterbury, clinging affectionately to our false consciousness since we are understandably terrified of such death-dealing truth. Only the Ibsenite heroes and Sartrian existentialists of this world can go the whole hog in this respect, defiantly embracing authenticity whatever its cost in human wreckage. Not one of Chekhov's plays, by contrast, is labelled a tragedy, even though two of them end with suicides. Most of us, like the lawyer Alfieri at the end of Arthur Miller's *A View From The Bridge*, deliberately opt to settle for half, as Alfieri warily admires the hero Eddie Carbone's tragic intransigence, his refusal to back down or be less than purely himself, while sombrely doubting that this is any recipe for a thriving civic existence.

Not all tragedy is about breaking and renewal. It may end simply in waste or rancour, despair or defiance. But there is a lineage of art for which tragedy is not a question of happiness, but of the conditions which might be necessary for its flourishing. Meanwhile we, the readers or spec-tators, live on, having been vicariously granted our own muffled, cun-ningly modulated encounter with the Real through the medium of the tragic action, deriving some meagre resources from those deaths for our own lives. Tragedy, after all, is only fiction, and thus a tolerable way for the timorous like ourselves to live with the recognition that the good life involves moving in the shadow of death. Otherwise, fearfully trauma-tized by the Real Thing, we would scarcely be able to survive at all. In Christian theology, this ritual or symbolic sharing in death, shielded by signification from its actual horror, is known as the eucharist.

The finest formulation of this tension between the need for a radical remaking, and the rebarbative cost of it, is Raymond Williams's concept of tragedy as revolution. Williams's view of tragedy belongs to what Northrop Frye, in his mildly pathological categorizing of the world, calls the fourth phase of ironic tragedy, made up of those who mimimize the importance of ritual and fate, provide social and psychological motives for the tragic action, and regard much tragic wretchedness as avoidable and superfluous.[23] The present study, then, is glad to join Williams in his allotted mythological niche. In *Modern Tragedy*, a coded riposte to George Steiner's *Death of Tragedy*, Williams views the long global

58

revolution for justice, democracy and political independence as at once to be affirmed, and as inescapably bearing with it a heavy burden of bloodshed and destruction. 'The tragic action', he comments, 'is not the confirmation of disorder, but its experience, its comprehension and its resolution. In our own time, this action is general, and its common name is revolution.'[24]

Yet at the same time, Williams adds, we see the struggle to end alienation producing its own kinds of alienation. Here, then, is the typical tragic dilemma for the modern age – that we can neither discard the values of justice and democracy, nor brush aside their appalling historical cost in the name of some triumphalist teleology. There is no tragedy in this sense (though there may well be in others) for the conservative or liberal, the former of whom may be less than zealous about such questions as social justice, while the latter appears to believe that it can be realized without major upheaval. Tragedy and revolution have been opposed ideas both for the custodians of spiritual supremacism and for the advocates of political change. The latter can see in the idea of tragedy little but defeatism and determinism, while the former can find in the notion of revolution nothing but a barbarous vandalism. Yet since the French Revolution, so Williams insists, the two ideas have in fact become indissolubly united. One might note, too, that one of the most poignant tragedies of our time is the fact that socialism has proved least possible where it is most necessary.

The idea of revolution, Williams writes, 'is born in pity and terror: in the perception of a radical disorder in which the humanity of some men is denied and by that fact the idea of humanity itself is denied'. But if it is thus tragic in its origins, 'it is equally tragic in its action, in that it is not against gods or inanimate things that its impulse struggles, nor against mere institutions and social forms, but against other men . . . What is properly called utopianism, or revolutionary romanticism, is the suppression or dilution of this quite inevitable fact.'[25] The tragic contradiction is clear: the practice of revolution may itself give the lie to the very humanity in whose name it is conducted. Yet neither, in the name of justice, can it be denied or disavowed. Williams identifies Boris Pasternak's *Dr Zhivago*, in the teeth of its liberal interpreters, as embodying a tragic action in just this sense, recording as it does 'not simply the killing, to make way for a new order, but the loss of the reality of life while a new life is being made'.[26]

Williams commits himself to the cause of political change, then, but in fear and trembling. 'I do not mean', he writes, 'that the liberation cancels the terror; I mean only that they are connected, and that this connection is tragic.'[27] What *Modern Tragedy* does here, remarkably, is to translate one of the most ancient of tragic idioms – the idea of sacrifice – into the most pressingly contemporary of terms. For sacrifice, like revolution, concerns the demand to yield up what you see as unutterably precious – in Abraham's case, his son – in the name of some even greater value; and there is never any telling whether the bargain will prove worth it. It is this moment of crisis or aporia, when you cannot not choose yet cannot do so without unbearable loss, which Williams rightly terms tragic. In ancient cults of sacrifice, value stemmed from the expiatory, life-renewing potential of death and destruction. To translate the cultic into the political is not to trade human lives for the prize of a more just social order, but to trust that some forms of anguish will finally bear fruit in a more peaceable, fulfilled society, as Walter Benjamin hoped that the dispossessed would be retrospectively vindicated on Judgement Day. But that trust must come with a cry of outrage that attaining such a goal, given the corrupt, predatory nature of political systems, should ever need to involve such pain in the first place. This conception of tragic sacrifice differs from that of the literary anthropologists, for whom tragedy is the ritual by which the individual's submission to the social whole strengthens its corporate life.[28]

'Things being at the worst, begin to mend', remarks Bosola in John Webster's *The Duchess of Malfi*. There are several ways in which confronting the worst can be redemptive. Since realism is the foundation of all ethical and political virtue, it is only by taking the full measure of calamity that we can redress it. Realism in our kind of world implies radicalism, not pragmatism. And only by recognizing how dire our situation is might we be moved to repair it in the first place. Moreover, if it is not the worst that we transform, there can be no true reparation. Perhaps, in addition, we can muster the will to alter such situations only when we have nothing very precious left to lose – when most alternatives are likely to prove more palatable than the status quo. The political dissensions that matter, then, are between those for whom our condition is indeed calamitous, and those who regard this as lurid leftist hyperbole or apocalyptic alarmism. Or, to put it in Walter Benjamin's terms, those liberals or conservatives for whom revolution is a runaway train, and those radicals for whom it is the application of the emergency brake.

Finally, since the one thing which cannot get worse is the worst, it can offer us a negative image of transcendence. In weighing how drastic things are with us, we take the measure of their potential remedy. So it is that Walter Benjamin finds his utopia or kingdom of God not in the triumphant consummation of history but among its very ruins, as the detritus of baffled hopes and broken bodies which piles up before our horror-stricken eyes to darken the sky becomes itself a warning sign of how no ultimate hope can be placed in evolutionism, historicism or secular time, thus for Benjamin turning our eyes instead to the Messiah who by tinkering a little with the cosmos here and there will succeed in transfiguring everything at a stroke. If history is so unremittingly bleak, then no salvation can spring from within it, only from beyond its frontiers; and this would mean nothing less than the redemption of history itself, rather than just this or that portion of it. There are those of us non-Messianic types, however, for whom the redemption of one or two portions of it would do perfectly well.

It is not quite true, then, as Karl Jaspers claims, that 'when man faces the tragic, he liberates himself from it'.[29] It is rather that the liberation is part of the tragedy; but it would be better if the whole action had not been necessary in the first place. Jaspers is writing in Nazi Germany, and his words accordingly command respect; in the midst of that misery, he recognizes that failure and breakdown are in some sense where human reality reveals itself most significantly. But he, too, overvalues the tragic, not least in his comment that 'without [such] a metaphysical basis [in tragedy], we have only misery, grief, misfortune, mishap, and failure'.[30] It is the word 'only' which is most disconcerting. Tragedy for Jaspers, as for the early Georg Lukács, is a spiritual refuge from the drearily empirical: by bringing to realization 'the highest possibilities of man . . . it makes truth a part of us by cleansing us of all that in our everyday experience is petty, bewildering, and trivial'.[31] It is as though such menial forms as the novel can be left to cope with quotidian life, while tragedy occupies the place of transcendence increasingly vacated by more orthodox versions of the sacred. 'There is no tragedy without transcendence', Jaspers insists,[32] but that transcendence would seem at times more of a flight from an insufferable reality than a depth within it. If Jaspers has good historical reason for such escapism, other theorists of tragedy, in less turbulent political conditions, can be less easily exculpated.

One such thinker is the pre-Marxist Georg Lukács, whose effusions on the subject outrank most others in their exuberance. Tragedy for the idealist Lukács of *Soul and Form* represents the highest form of anthropology, a realization of pure being. In a kind of tragic version of phenomenology, it is in such momentous crises that we are granted the privilege of a pure experience of selfhood, shorn of empirical or psychological trivia. An austere, absolute, unforgiving form, tragedy 'expresses the becoming-timeless of time';[33] it represents, in Heideggerian style, authentic Being itself, sublimely untainted by temporal existence. It all sounds more than enough to give a theatre director a headache. Tragedy is the 'becoming-real of the concrete, essential nature of man',[34] the high point of human existence, a perfect fulfilment of human longing which involves mystical ecstasy and an oceanic unity of being. This is not quite the kind of thing one finds in *Shadow of a Gunman* or *All My Sons*. It is not easy to see the tormenting of the Duchess of Malfi as the high point of human existence, or detect an oceanic unity of being in *Gorboduc*. In any case, Lukács assumes in Hegelian fashion that the Absolute, which tragedy is supposed to mirror, is bound to be majestic. But a character in Tennessee Williams's *Suddenly Last Summer*, admittedly not the kind of drama one can imagine Lukács perusing with any great relish, glimpses the absolute truth of a cruel God in the spectacle of torn flesh and plundered bodies.

There are critics like Jonathan Dollimore who find the value of tragedy in its 'subversive knowledge of political domination,'[35] or like Adrian Poole, for whom all tragedy challenges the *doxa* of everyday life.[36] There are also conservatives who think it precious because it helps to sustain social order, breaching it only to see it the more durably restored. If society can withstand even this shaking of the foundations, then it must be resilient indeed. Comedy might then be seen as wryly unmasking the fragility of such social order, the arbitrariness of its conventions and capriciousness of its identities. A luminary of the conservative camp is René Girard, who sees the role of tragedy in functionalist spirit as being to 'protect the community against its own violence', ritually expelling internal conflicts.[37] By contrast, there are those like Timothy Reiss who also see tragedy as having conservative functions at times, but regard this as a reason to criticize rather than commend it. Other observers applaud the form on liberal pluralist grounds, finding in faintly tautological terms that tragic poets 'insist on the one-sidedness of all uncompromising faiths'.[38] Adrian Poole's thoughtful study of the subject claims that 'tragedy affirms with savage jubilation that man's state is diverse, fluid and unfounded'.[39] In interrogating convention and celebrating diversity, posing questions to which there can be no satisfactory answers, its menace and promise 'lie in this recognition of the sheer potentiality of all the selves we might be, and of all the worlds we might make together or destroy together'.[40]

Aeschylus, in short, begins to sound for all the world like a latter-day liberal or postmodernist. And tragedy itself certainly sounds like a highly attractive proposition. But for one thing it is not true that all tragedy promotes the doctrines of fluidity, diversity or anti-foundationalism in the manner of the multiculturally minded transnational corporations. A good deal of tragedy is about being trapped in irresolvable dilemmas, coerced into action by dully compulsive forces. Some tragic art affirms diversity, while some charts the dismal constraints of human existence, its dingy, monotonously repetitive dimensions, the alarming narrowness of our scope for free decision. It cannot be recruited to the cause of some dogmatic American voluntarism, a cracker-barrel pioneer ideology in glamorous new guise for which the world is plastically, perpetually open and the self an exhilarating series of self-inventions. *Ghosts* or *Le Cid* are not obvious testimony to such bogus liberty. And even if tragedy does occasionally affirm such notions, it is not clear that it is wise to do so. Fluidity and unfoundedness are not usually as pleasant for migrants as they are for professors. Not all diversity is by any means positive. Those liberals who relish questions which rebuff conclusive answers might change their tune when asked whether white supremacism can be justified. Such questions in fact receive gratifyingly definitive, even absolute responses from liberals, to their enduring credit. Does tragedy's challenge to our conventional wisdom include a challenge to the liberal belief in fluidity and diversity? Or are these values immune from interrogation?

There have been other reasons for rating tragedy so highly. Jean Anouilh's Chorus in his *Antigone* sees tragedy as peculiarly restful, precisely because its action is predestined and there is nothing to be done. Hope and illusion have no part in it, which brings one a certain stoical serenity. Others, by contrast, have seen it in Promethean style as dramatizing humanity's heroic resistance to destiny or oppression. Shelley remarks in his preface to *The Cenci* that Beatrice should not have taken revenge for being outraged by her father Count Cenci, but it is the fact that she does which makes her a tragic figure. For Albert Camus in *The Rebel*, every act of rebellion implies a tragic value, which is what distinguishes the rebel from the nihilist. Rebellion, Camus comments, says a yes as well as a no, an ambivalence which Jacques Derrida has occasionally affirmed of deconstruction. Yet Cordelia, or Euripides's *Women of Troy*, not to speak of a whole gallery of other tragic characters, hardly put up much robust resistance to their fate. Women have often been less well placed to do so, as the case of Richardson's Clarissa would testify.

Alternatively, you can see the value of tragedy as a kind of aesthetic analogue of the scene of analysis, in which recounting a narrative of being possessed by forces as relentless as the Furies reaches its climax in a cure which mirrors the moment of tragic recognition or illumination. Tragic art involves the plotting of suffering, not simply a raw cry of pain. And while this very *mise-en-scène* may endow suffering with a spurious shapeliness, lending it an intelligibility which seems to betray the ragged incoherence of the thing itself, it is hard to see how we could even use words like 'tragic' outside some such social or moral contextualizing, in life as much as in art. Tidying up the tragic may thus be part of the price we pay for articulating it. But such articulation is also a way of trying to transcend it, as Bertolt Brecht's Philosopher suggests in *The Messingkauf Dialogues*: 'Lamentation by means of sounds, or better still words, is a vast liberation, because it means that the sufferer is beginning to produce something. He's already mixing his sorrow with an account of the blows he's received; he's already making something out of the utterly devastating. Observation has set in.'[41]

Despite Georg Lukács's assertion in *Soul and Form* that loneliness is of the essence of tragedy, we should recall that even solitude is a social condition. Like any other state of affairs, we can identify it only by using concepts drawn from a public language. To know that I am isolated, I must have a sign-system which links me in principle to others. Since there could be no meaning which was in principle mine alone, absolute solitude would be a state of hellish unintelligibility. It would be the death of experience, not just an extreme case of it. And even if nothing is in a sense more tragic than a torment utterly without point, reference, parallel, cause or context, we still could not *say* that it is tragic, since we could get no conceptual toe-hold in such circumstances.

Perhaps this is one reason why the world of Beckett, along with history after Auschwitz, have been seen as post-tragic. There can be no more tragedy, so the hypothesis runs, because a monstrous excess of the stuff has finally obliterated our sense of the value by which it might be measured. We have supped too full of horrors, and even 'tragedy' is a shallow signifier for events which beggar representation. There can be no icons of such catastrophes, to which the only appropriate response would be screaming or silence. If major tragedy belongs to periods of transition, in which we can measure our decline by reference to a still usable past, we are now too remote from such a past even to recall it. It is as though alienation is now so total that it cancels all the way through and leaves everything apparently as it was, having also alienated the criteria by which we could judge our condition to be abnormal. On one jaded postmodern view, there is no more alienation because there is really nothing left to alienate, no interiority to be confiscated or estranged.

In this sense, pessimism pushed to an extreme limit returns us to where we were. We cannot call our situation tragic if it is tragic all the way through. For classical realism, conflicts can be resolved; for modernism, there is still redemption, but it is now barely possible; for postmodernism, there is nothing any longer to be redeemed. Or at least, so the post-tragic case runs, disaster is now too casual and commonplace for us to portray it in ways which imply an alternative. How can there be tragedy when we have forgotten that things could ever be different? It would be like being astounded at the fact that one had nostrils, or scandalized by the crashing of a wave. If boredom and brutality are just the way things are, then (so the case goes) they may be pitiable but scarcely tragic, any more than one could speak of the colour of the grass as tragic. Anyway, if human beings are in fragments, then they are not even coherent enough to be the bearers of tragic meaning, like those Beckettian characters whose suffering cannot be without respite since they cannot even remember what happened to them yesterday.

It is not clear, however, why all this is not also true of some epochs of high tragedy, which were bloodstained enough. Nor is it clear how one can use terms such as 'evil' of Auschwitz without implying a sense of value. If we can still find it shocking that the extreme is now routine, then it cannot be as routine as all that. Raymond Williams points out in *Modern Tragedy* that if some people built concentration camps, others gave their lives to destroy them. There has been no great political crime in our time which has not provoked selfless resistance. Samuel Beckett himself opposed the Nazis as a resistance fighter. And the period in which value is supposed to have evaporated without trace witnessed the most successful emancipatory movement of modern times, the anti-colonial struggle.

Besides, if life is meaningless, then as the existentialists were not slow to see, it presents a temptingly blank slate on which to inscribe one's own values rather than slavishly conform to those of God, Nature or social convention. Perhaps it is simply a metaphysical hangover to expect the world to be the kind of thing which could be meaningful in the first place, and so to find its apparent senselessness somehow lamentable. 'Isn't there some meaning?' asks Masha in Chekhov's *Three Sisters*, to which Toozenbach dryly responds: 'Look out of there, it's snowing. What's the meaning of that?'(Act 2). It is not a deficiency of the snow that it does not 'have' a meaning, meaning not being a property of a thing like a certain weight or texture. The world of Samuel Beckett, in which things appear at once enigmatic and baldly self-identical, seems less a place which once had a meaning which has now haemorrhaged away than one which calls that whole rather peculiar way of looking into question. Maybe what we call nihilism is just the wish that things had meaning in the sense that fish have gills, and the fury that they do not.

Perhaps what the death-of-tragedy advocates really mean is that a certain *kind* of value – immanent, heroic, sacred, foundational – is no longer much in vogue. From so Olympian a vantage-point, merely human value looks like no value at all. The sceptic and the absolutist are akin in holding that values must be incontestable or nothing. If Beckett is anti-tragic, it is perhaps less because tragedy is now too customary to catch our eye than because the word signifies a kind of writing which is no longer possible. Tragedy is too highbrow, portentous a term for the deflation and debunkery of Beckett's work. His farce and bathos may spell the ruin of hope, but they also undercut the terrorism of noble ideals, maintaining a pact with ordinariness which is a negative version of solidarity. They represent the grisly underside of the carnivalesque. The dispossessed know that what matters is scraping by, the unglamorous persistence of the body, and in Beckett, who hails from a society which is no stranger to such destitution, this is at once a humdrum and critical business. His characters are too busy fussing over their pathetic clutch of knick-knacks or keeping their heads biologically above water to lose much sleep over the meaning of life. There is no such unitary phenomenon to have meaning in the first place, or for that matter to lack it.

Beckett's refusal of such daunting, high-toned words as tragedy (*Waiting for Godot* is described as a tragi-comedy) belongs with an underdog suspicion of ideology. The ideology in question is not only that of Literature, against which the scrupulous meanness of Beckett's work calculatedly sets its face, but more or less the one we have been investigating in the various theorists of tragedy. Yet the writing of this man so chary of grand propositions is so self-consciously about 'the human condition', so much the kind of thing that the suburban theatregoer expects from his evening out, so well-stocked with self-flaunting symbols and pseudo-philosophical one-liners, that one wonders whether this, like Wilde's insouciantly well-made plays, is not in itself a roguish irony at the theatregoer's expense. Beckett retains the scale of the classical humanist vision while resolutely emptying it of its affirmative content.

In a literary manner not unfamiliar in Ireland,[42] Beckett's work is at once 'philosophical' and allergic to the pretentiousness of all that, mercilessly debunking it with a flash of farce, a mocking aside or the blunt obtrusiveness of the body. In a venerable Irish tradition, he combines surreal imagination, black humour and conceptual precision. Much of the value of his writing lies in its remorseless demystification of what conventionally passes for value. The merciless onslaught on the pretensions of Literature, the sardonic refusal of idealist morphine even when in atrocious pain, the compact with failure which undermines the braggadocio of achievement, the puristic horror of deceit which nevertheless knows itself to be unavoidably mystified: all this represents not the absence of value, but of a particular conception of it. What troubles humanism about Beckett is not the sweeping scenarios of despair, which are the kind of thing one expects from modern art and are in any case simply the obverse of affirmation, but the kind of things which worry it about Brecht too: his apparent lack of affect, his mechanizing and externalizing of the psyche, his seeming indifference to human difference, his scepticism of narrative, the impassive tone which seems not to register just how grotesque his scenarios are, his distressing downbeatness, his embarrassing knack of falling short of the grandeur of tragedy, his refusal not just of splendidly vigorous characters but of 'character' as such. There have accordingly been more than a few attempts to retrieve Beckett from the valuelessness of sheer gloom, which miss the point that it is here, among other places, that the value of his work can be found. For gloom implies value quite as much as grandeur does.

Beckett's world, then, is populated by those who fall below the tragic, those who fluff their big moment, fail to rise to their dramatic occasions, cannot quite summon up the rhetoric to ham successfully and are too drained and depleted to engage in colourful theatrical combat. It is not just that epic actions are a thing of the past, but that action itself is over. For these ontologically famished figures, getting the simplest action off the ground is as baffling a business as carrying out some high-risk, exquisitely intricate technical operation. At least Phaedra and Hedda Gabler are up to their roles, carry them off with brio and panache, whereas these puppets and pedants bungle even that, muff even that amount of meaning. In these parched, starved landscapes, men and women can no longer rise to significance, let alone sublimity. Striking tragic postures is just another way of passing the time, along with sucking stones or pulling on your trousers. We have finally stumbled upon a solution to tragedy, but it is known not as redemption but the absurd, a realm in which nothing stays still long enough to merit tragic status.

If tragic heroes meet with a fall, Beckett's figures fail to rise to a height from which a fall would be possible. Existence has all the dull compulsion of destiny with nothing of its purpose. In such a world, even malevolence would be a meaning. What also makes these writings only doubtfully tragic is their indeterminacy, as the products of an author who observed that his favourite word was 'perhaps'. Tragedy would seem a determinate kind of condition, like envy or lumbago, but nothing in Beckett's world is as stable as that. The puzzle of his world is how things can be at once so capricious and so persistently painful. If everything in this universe seems gratuitous, this must also include the texts themselves, which in a contingent world seem constantly struck by the fact that they do anything as indecently emphatic as existing.

But the view that everything is hypothetical is itself a hypothesis, and under risk of self-contradiction must calculate this truth into its reckoning. How can those bereft of certainty be sure that they are, if there can be no certainty? Godot's absence may have plunged everything into ambiguity, but that must logically mean that there is no assurance that he will not come. If the world is indeterminate, then this must also apply to our knowledge of it, in which case its indeterminacy is uncertain. Not even misery can be absolute in a world without absolutes, even if it is the absence of absolutes which makes life so miserable in the first place. In such a universe there can be no absolute salvation, but no absolute need for it either, which is some meagre consolation. If everything is opaque and obscure, how can we be sure that this world of freaks and cripples is not, viewed from some other perspective, teetering on the brink of transfiguration? There is something funny as well as menacing about absurdity, which like comedy in general detaches us from too intense an investment in a specific way of seeing just enough to allow us to contemplate the dim possibility of another.

Beckett's indeterminacies are not the cloudy, portentous immensities of a Conrad, but the products of an Irish scholastic with a monkish devotion to exactitude and a Joycean obsession with categories. What is striking about his work is not the swell of some monstrous chaos which laps at the edges of speech, but its crazedly clear-minded attempt to eff the ineffable, its exquisite sculpting of sheer vacancy, the fastidious exactness with which it plucks ever more slender nuances from what are only hints and velleities in the first place. He has a Protestant animus against the superfluous and ornamental. Each of his sentences has an air of being free-wheeling, reminding us like his transparently gratuitous narratives that it might very well not have existed, while appearing at the same time rigorous and meticulous. There must still be a trace of truth in the world, since otherwise why would one be driven to specify so punctiliously one's doubts about its existence?

What may make us think Beckett's work non-tragic, then, is less a matter of value than a question of ambiguity. If the world is such that nothing about it can be conclusively determined, then 'tragedy' is just as partial, provisional a description of it as any other, and Beckettian scepticism becomes among other things a salutary safeguard against the baneful absolutism which he himself witnessed in the Second World War. This is even more so if there is no such unitary thing as 'the world' in the first place to be an appropriate object of judgement. But it is not a question of value having leaked away – partly because it has not, partly because even if Beckett did indeed portray this kind of post-tragic world, there is still a sense in which we could exclaim of it: how tragic! Perhaps the ultimate tragedy is to have lost the capacity to identify one's condition as such, which has been true of a whole lineage of tragic protagonists. It did not start with modernism.

To this extent, the 'post-tragic' no more leaves tragedy definitively behind it than post-structuralism simply jettisons structuralism. It may be that Beckett adumbrates a future in which the concept will indeed cease to have meaning; but in the meanwhile it lives on in the grief which springs from knowing that we can no longer even bestow a dignified title on our wretchedness, view it as part of some predestined order, or discern in its very terror the shadow of transcendence. Without a sense of value, such sorrow would be meaningless. And as long as there is value, there can be tragedy.

As far as being able to name our situation goes, it may not be true that the moment of recognition is always the most vital. If, as some believe, one transcends the tragic in the act of articulating it, then those who have lost the power to name their condition, or who never had it in the first place, may well be considered the most lamentable of all. There are tragedies of false consciousness as well as of transformative insight, as Ibsen, Chekhov and Arthur Miller are aware. Perhaps Othello goes to his death cocooned in just this kind of grandiose self-deception, his suicide, in F. R. Leavis's sceptical phrase, 'a superb *coup de théâtre*'.[43] What tragedy in the technical sense might demand – a crisis of recognition, a spectacular about-turn of consciousness – may prove less tragic in the common-or-garden sense of the word than such self-delusion, just as what tragic theory might require by way of fate and necessity may prove less tragic in the popular sense of the term than catastrophes which could have been prevented. In this sense as in others, the aesthetic and every-day senses of the word are constantly at loggerheads. On one fairly plausible reading of Aristotle's *Poetics*, for example, the death of a princess would be tragic (though not, as it happens, in a car accident), but the crushing to death of a hundred plebeian football fans would not. And – though Aristotle is in two minds about this – critical situations which are resolved happily may be technically speaking more tragic than those which are not.

To have lost the power to articulate one's condition belongs with what Jean-François Lyotard sees as the tragedy of the Holocaust. The extermination camps, he writes, condemned their victims to an abjection which 'was first and foremost the severing of communication'.[44] It is hard to accept that this was their major crime, but Lyotard's point remains suggestive. Acts of communication, he argues, always carry with them a tacit appeal: Deliver me from my abandonment, allow me to belong to you, acknowledge my humanity as a speaking being. *Amnestos* means one who is cut off from speech. Language works as a sign of recognition as well as a pragmatic affair, and it was this which the people of the death camps were denied. Their destiny was to have no destiny, to mean nothing, not to be speakable to, not even to be enemies. They were refuse and vermin, treated more like garbage than like animals.

This ultimate form of abjection, so Lyotard considers, cannot be articulated by its survivors because it is a case of being cut off from speech, of lacking language to excess. In this sense, the Holocaust does not simply beggar description because of its horror, but because this horror involved the deliberate conversion of meaning to absurdity – the fact that, if the Nazis had had their way, their victims would be men and women about whom, like the snow in *Three Sisters*, there would simply be nothing to say. But in this respect the Nazis did not have their way, for these are people of whom we do speak, and who have meaning for us. As long as this is the case – and it may not always be so – we may speak of the Holocaust as a tragedy.

Not all those who have pronounced on tragedy have been quite so blithe as some of the views we have recorded. One such dissenting voice is that of Roland Barthes, who argues that 'tragedy is only a way of assembling human misfortune, of subsuming it, and thus of justifying it by putting it in the form of a necessity, of a kind of wisdom, or of a purification. To reject this regeneration and to seek the technical means of not succumbing perfidiously (nothing is more insidious than tragedy) is today a necessary undertaking.'[45] Like many a left-wing critic, Barthes sets up a traditionalist view of tragedy only to knock it briskly over; but his scepticism, amidst so much piety and rhetorical reverence, is nonetheless therapeutic. John Snyder in his *Prospects of Power* questions the life-enhancing power of tragedy ('A tragic sufferer always loses'),[46] though he later claims that the audience's experience is one of communal strengthening, which sounds life-enhancing enough. And Nietzsche insists in *The Birth of Tragedy* that high culture is a spiritualization of cruelty, a point which the celebrants of tragedy might well bear in mind.

But it is Arthur Schopenhauer who is perhaps the most heretical commentator of all. If Hegel and Nietzsche cast a somewhat casual eye on tragic suffering, Schopenhauer, perhaps the gloomiest philosopher who ever lived,[47] is acutely conscious of it. Tragedy presents 'the unspeakable pain, the wretchedness and misery of mankind, the scornful mastery of chance, and the irretrievable fall of the just and innocent'.[48] There is, despite this, value in the form; but it is the value of being allowed to pierce through the illusory *principium individuationis*, surrender one's egoism, and for a precious moment see things as they really are, which is to say as nothing more reputable than the fleeting product of the voracious Will. To be granted this insight into the Real is to learn how to abandon the world as so much dross and debris, renouncing the will to live in a nirvanic moment of self-immolation and turning one's face contemptuously from the charnel house of history towards an existence of a wholly different kind, one which is as yet inconceivable to us. There is wisdom in tragedy for Schopenhauer, but no affirmation.

Hegel argues that the principles of freedom and individual self-determination are essential to the flourishing of tragedy. This is an odd view for him to take, since it is doubtful that the ancient Greeks whom he so admired shared his own notion of self-determination. Susanne K. Langer, who believes that tragedy shows 'the rhythm of man's life at its highest powers in the limits of his unique, earth-bound career', sees it as a 'mature' art form which requires the development of individuality – a development 'which some religions and some cultures – even high cultures – do not possess . . . Tragedy can arise and flourish only when people are aware of individual life as an end in itself, and as a measure of other things.'[49] The message is clear: potential tragedians should first of all ensure that they are not denizens of Sarawak or the Kalahari desert. Only Western cultures need apply.

And it is true for the most part that only Western cultures have. Tragic art is on the whole a Western affair, though it has resonances in some Eastern cultures. In China, there is no exact equivalent of tragedy in the sense of the downfall of a valued individual. But there is traditionally the vision of a universal harmony governed by a power whose dispositions are often inscrutable, but which may be justified as validating the order of human society. To rebel against this power is to invite retribution from the heavens; and the concept of *ming* represents an idea of destiny. Some of this is not far from classical Western conceptions. China also absorbed the Indian doctrine of *karma*, with its belief in punishments or rewards for individual actions; but in traditional Indian literature there is no tragedy, in the sense that literary works are not permitted to include or end with the death of the protagonist. This is clearly prescribed by literary and dramaturgical theory in the Sanskrit tradition, and was adhered to in artistic practice. Epics in which the hero meets his death can be attributed to Muslim influence.

On the other hand, there is much that might be called tragic in great Indian epics like the *Mahabharata* and the *Ramayana*, and a sense of tragedy pervades a major branch of Hindu theism in the notion of *viraha bhakti* or doomed love. In the classical culture of Japan, the centrepiece of the theatrical programme presented by Noh and Bunraku is a drama of dissidence and conflict: violent jealousy, a woman's unrequited love, a noble warrior facing battle. The dramatic themes of Bunraku or puppet theatre very often centre on the idea of *migawari* or the sacrifice of the self for another. Much of the philosophical stage-setting, however, would seem different from Western tragedy.[50]

But tragedy is not always to be found on stage or in libraries. Quite apart from real-life tragedies, which are common to all human cultures, it may be that some motifs of Western tragedy, not least the need for a

71

painful transformation of the self if a richer life is to flourish, find their resonance in some pre-modern societies in cult, ritual and religion, in the death and rebirth of the soul or in arduous rites of passage from one condition to another. Yet there is a vital point here. If tragic art really does bear witness to the highest of human values, as so many of its advocates insist, then this carries one generally overlooked implication: that societies in which such art is either marginal or unknown are incapable of rising to what is most precious. As often in the West, a generous-spirited humanism has its darker, more disreputable roots.

Yet it is questionable whether tragedy, for all its astonishing wealth and depth, is indeed the custodian of supreme value. For one thing, many of the values it embodies can be found in other cultural forms. Tragic art does not enjoy a monopoly of courage and dignity, freedom and wisdom. For another thing, there are less glamorous, more prosaic kinds of value – compassion, tolerance, humour, humility, forgiveness – which are arguably as precious. The stages of Racine and Beckett, Frenchman and honorary Frenchman, are alike in their stripped, static qualities, their stark economies of word and gesture; but it is an open question which world is the more humane. Tolerance, humility and the like do not bulk large among the high heroic virtues; but they are no doubt all the more worthwhile for that. There is a kind of inhumane humanism, much given to praise of the dauntless human spirit and distinctly indifferent to common-or-garden compassion, which a good deal of tragic theory exemplifies.

Tragedy of this kind – what the doggedly down-to-earth Montaigne describes as 'transcending humours (which) affright me as much, as steepy, high and inaccessible places'[51] – is in thrall to the superego, with its implacable high-mindedness and intolerance of weakness, its aristocratic absolutism and demand for ascetic self-renunciation. This conception of the tragic betrays the brutality of a certain vein of humanism, which in its eagerness to affirm the human must at all costs deny its fragility. No doubt we should cherish the values of truth, beauty, selflessness, unflinching commitment, uncommon courage and the rest. But we should not be too downcast if people fail to live up to these noble notions, or terrorize them with such ideals in ways which make their weaknesses painful to them and erode their self-esteem. Such tragic idealism can be violent and merciless in its demands, and though we may admire it, it is generally from a safe distance. It has cut loose from that larger plebeian wisdom which knows when not to ask too much of others.

Such wisdom is far from cynicism, which is often no more than disenchanted idealism. It is, indeed, the very stuff of a certain strain of comedy, with its ironic debunking and all-inclusive acceptance. Such an art concedes that all ideals have clay feet and rejoices in imperfection. As Christopher Norris writes of William Empson's 'complex words', they are redolent of 'a down-to-earth quality of human scepticism which . . . permits (us) to build up a trust in human nature on a shared knowledge of its needs and attendant weaknesses'.[52] Blaise Pascal, a touch more cynically, argues that 'the power of kings is founded on the reason and the folly of the people, but especially on their folly. The greatest and most important thing in the world is founded on weakness. This is a remarkably sure foundation, for nothing is surer than that the people will be weak.'[53] There are, however, more positive ways of viewing the power of weakness, as we shall see. In Simon Critchley's view, 'comedy is the eruption of materiality into the spiritual purity of tragic action and desire'.[54] Tragedy, he argues, 'is insufficiently tragic because it is too heroic. Only comedy is truly tragic. Comedy is tragic by not being a tragedy.'[55] Comedy, in short, confronts us with our finitude without terrorizing us with it. But so, one might claim, do *King Oedipus* and *King Lear*. 'They told me I was everything', Lear says, '–'tis a lie: I am not ague-proof.' By and large, it is tragic *theory* which has struck heroic postures, not tragic practice. It is Hegel and Hölderlin, not Ben Jonson and Edward Bond, who are entranced by an ideal of purity.

Empson, whose concept of pastoral promotes such wry wisdom against the clenched high-mindedness of some tragedy, reminds us that 'the most refined desires are inherent in the plainest, and would be false if they weren't'.[56] It is a wisdom shared in different ways by Swift, Freud and Bakhtin. Herman Melville remarks in *Moby-Dick* that 'even the highest earthly felicities ever have a certain unsignifying pettiness lurking in them' (ch. 106). Every signifying system has a residue of non-signification within it, but this excremental left-over is part of what makes it work. Such a bathetic movement from the highest felicity to the mundane detail marks the New Testament's staging of Christ's Second Coming, which opens in suitably grandiose, apocalyptic style, with some reach-me-down scriptural imagery of the Messiah sweeping in on clouds of glory, and then bumps calculatedly down to the real issues of salvation, the question of whether you fed the hungry or cared for the sick. Salvation is a disappointingly humdrum affair. Even the end of the world proves bathetic. The finest kinds of tragedy share this carnivalesque consciousness of the poor forked creature, and are thus critiques of heroism as well as examples of it.

It is not, of course, simply a question of being *anti*-heroic, which would be no more than the obverse of the same way of seeing. John Osborne's Jimmy Porter is a notably heroic anti-hero, full of cosmic self-importance, lavish theatrical gestures and brutally domineering monologues. If it is sometimes necessary to affirm the commonplace against the heroic, it is equally important to see that the heroic often *is* commonplace, a truth which simple anti-heroism misses. Words like 'heroism' are probably too tainted by their patrician, patriarchal history to be of much further use, and to reject them means a drastic rewriting of history. The pharaohs did not build the pyramids. Nelson did not win the battle of Trafalgar. Hitler did not invade Poland. Yet such high-flown notions still stand in need of a modern translation. Vision, courage, dedication, loyalty, selflessness and endurance are not simply to be derided as quasi-feudal affairs in some burst of bogus populism, least of all as exclusively male ones. Without them, no deep-seated transformation of society would be conceivable. It is just that they are so much hot air unless they are somehow firmly rooted in the commonplace. The point is not to abandon notions of power, a liberal privilege if ever there was one, or transfer them intact from one agent to another, but to transform them. By portraying Jesus as riding into Jerusalem on a donkey, the New Testament transforms the very meaning of kingship, burlesquing the received images of it in a carnivalesque reversal. As Slavoj Žižek writes: 'There is a certain passage from *tragique* to *moque-comique* at the very heart of the Christian enterprise: Christ is emphatically *not* the figure of a dignified heroic Master.'[57] In the Judaic tradition, the idea of a crucified Messiah would be a kind of sick joke, along the lines of a squeamish mobster or a paralytically shy politician.

Early bourgeois society was shrewder in this respect than some present-day radicalism. It saw that the point was not to ditch the heroic but to appropriate it. John Milton, Richard Steele and Samuel Richardson are all co-labourers in an audacious project to empty heroism of its pagan, macho, militarist, aristocratic contents and fill it instead with the benevolent, self-effacing, long-suffering virtues of the Christian gentleman. If the Satan of *Paradise Lost* is an icon of the wrong sort of heroism, all pomp, bravura and flashy power, the Christ of *Paradise Regained* is an image of what Milton dubs 'the better fortitude' of the true kind of hero.[58] The Christ of that poem dreamed as a child of growing up to become a traditional military hero, but now rejects despotic force for what his author regards as a finer kind of valour. For Steele and Richardson, the barbarous *hauteur* of a clapped-out heroism must yield to the meek, pacific values of a new social order, epitomized for Richardson in the monumentally tedious figure of Sir Charles Grandison, a kind of Jesus Christ in knee-breeches. The death of the classical hero does not spell the death of tragedy, as *Clarissa* attests.

Tragedy, as classically conceived, belongs with an ethics of crisis and confrontation – of revelations, momentous turning-points, dramatic disclosures and existential moments of truth, all of which turn their face aloofly from anything as drearily prosaic as everyday virtue. Yet if Aristotle is the theorist of tragedy, he is also the founder of so-called virtue ethics, for which moral values are embedded in habitual ways of life. The solitary splendour of a later kind of tragic hero is implicitly denied by this sociable, quotidian ethics, which refuses to isolate actions, however earth-shaking, from their practical contexts. Christianity encompasses both the moment of spiritual crisis or *metanoia* – the decisive transformation of being which is faith – and a similar insistence on the good life as everyday practice. Tragedy may concern states of emergency; but we should recall Walter Benjamin's point that such states are routine for the dispossessed, and that the fact that everything just carries on as normal *is* the crisis.[59] Whether crisis and the commonplace are opposed depends largely on where you happen to be standing.

Karl Jaspers, who is hardly innocent of rhapsodizing about tragedy, recognizes even so that it can radiate a spurious glamour which lures us 'into an exalting realm of grandeur', becoming 'the privilege of the exalted few'. For all its aura of majesty, it can actually narrow our awareness, sweeping aside petty miseries in the name of a 'pseudo-seriousness'.[60] Since he himself does precisely this elsewhere in his study of the subject, he has little need to labour the point. Tragedy, he believes, can be a mask to conceal the unheroic reality of everyday life, lending 'a cheap aura of heroism to a life lived in comfort and security'.[61] At times, one might claim, it has been a vicarious form of spiritual aristocratism for those sedate suburban animals who enjoy all the benefits of modernity while chafing at its vulgarities. It is surely too vital a notion to be surrendered to such victims of *mauvaise foi* without a struggle.

Chapter 4

Heroes

Let us look more closely at the portrait of tragedy sketched by Dorothea Krook in her *Elements of Tragedy*, taking it as an exemplary (if doubtless extreme) statement of a traditionalist case. Tragic art for Krook must arise out of what she calls the fundamental human condition, and involve a protagonist who shows some fighting spirit. The sufferings of a passive victim may be harrowing and pitiable, but they are not tragic. The hero must be representative of humanity as a whole, but at the same time elevated above his fellows. His suffering must be expiatory, must be conscious rather than blind, and must be accepted by both him and ourselves as necessary. This is so even if his transgression, like Oedipus's, is unconscious; the fact remains that cosmic order has been disrupted, and must be restored whatever the cost in human agony. Even if the tragedy is not the hero's fault, he is still representative of a depraved humanity, and to this extent deserves to be chastised. What may seem brutal and unjust by human standards, then, makes complete sense by cosmic ones. Indeed, Krook even appears to defend the death of Cordelia in this light. In this way, tragedy reaffirms the supremacy of the moral order and the dignity of the human spirit, as propitiatory suffering plus redemptive knowledge reinforces the moral law. Through his courage and endurance, the hero converts the mystery of suffering into intelligibility, redeems it and achieves reconciliation. Our faith in the human condition is accordingly fortified and reaffirmed.

It would be difficult to make tragic art sound more thoroughly unpleasant. If this really is what tragedy is about, then it may be an agreeable pursuit for a sadist but scarcely for those with less exotic tastes. It is a square-jawed, masculinist ideal of tragedy, replete with pugnacious, public-spirited heroes who take their punishment like a man even when they are not guilty. But even Krook has implicitly to confess that this is not in fact what all tragedy is about. Shakespeare's tragedies, she tells us, are much the same as the ancient Greeks, the only difference being that in the former there are 'no gods, prophets, or oracles to pronounce the doom to be objectively necessary and inescapable'.[1] This would indeed seem quite a difference. But her description does not hold true for a good many Greek tragedies either. Let us proceed to unravel it strand by strand, beginning with the fortunes and misfortunes of the tragic hero.

Aristotle says nothing of a tragic hero. Nor did the ancient Greeks in general employ the term. Aristotle mentions tragic protagonists, but the tragic action does not necessarily centre upon them. It is not the subject which holds the action together, in a kind of dramatic Kantianism. Characters for Aristotle, in what not so long ago might have been dubbed 'theoretical anti-humanism', are a kind of ethical colouring on the action rather than its nub. They are its bearers and supports rather than its sources. In a kind of anti-humanist thought experiment, one could imagine the possibility of an action without them, rather as an artist might draw without colour. In fact Aristotle maintains that dramatic actions without characters are fairly common. Nothing could be less akin to the realist cult of complex, credible, well-rounded characters. Tragedy is the imitation of an action, not of human beings. By and large, it is events which are tragic, not people. The classicist Bruno Snell, who maintains that 'tragedy is not so much interested in events . . . but in human beings', is almost certainly mistaken when it comes to the Greeks.[2] John Jones, in a valuable critique of the modern humanizing, psychologizing and individualizing of Aristotle's doctrines, thinks that the celebrated tragic flaw or *hamartia* is more of a bungling or missing-of-the-mark in the action itself than some moral defect, an objective blunder or error more than a state of the soul.[3] It is an opinion endorsed by Humphrey House in his study of Aristotle's *Poetics*.[4] For Hegel, it is just the fact that drama is a matter of action which makes it the most graphic image of that ceaseless objectification of human spirit which is *Geist*. As a practical incarnation of contradictions, it is the most ontologically privileged form of art.

Classical antiquity did not share the modern conception of the human personality, and drew less of a hard-and-fast line than we do between an individual and her actions. In this respect at least, Jean-Paul Sartre has something in common with Sophocles. Bernard Knox points out that most of Aeschylus's dramas have collective titles, while Euripides does not typically focus upon individuals.[5] Northrop Frye maintains that the isolation of the tragic hero epitomizes his condition, whereas comedy is collective;[6] but this is another high cliché of traditionalist commentary, since a fair number of tragic heroes are no more isolated than their comic counterparts. It is not isolation which catches the eye about Romeo, Egmont or Mother Courage. The protagonist of the *Oresteia* is not so much any of its individual figures, who are hardly intricate personalities in the first place, than the *oikos* or house of Atreus itself. H. D. F. Kitto also believes that 'the modern critic [of Greek tragedy] is tempted to see personal relations and therefore character-drawing which in fact are not there'.[7] The change of fortune which characterizes tragedy, so Jones argues, is again more a quality of the action than of the protagonist. Aristotle is somewhat casual about whether such reversal is from prosperity to adversity or vice versa, so that in Jones's view the tragic focus is on mutability rather than misfortune, the fact of change rather than the direction of it. One might claim rather that for Aristotle any sort of shift of fortune will do which evokes in us pity and fear. A change from adversity to prosperity is ruled out simply because it fails to do this. It is as though it would be ruled in if it could. What matters is the audience response to the narrative, not the fortunes or misfortunes of a protagonist as an end in themselves.

If tragedy for Aristotle involves the elevation of action over character, then his aesthetics are interestingly in tune with his ethics. This may not seem so at first sight. Unlike deontology, which looks to universal principles, and utilitarianism, which considers consequences, virtue ethics of an Aristotelian kind place the moral evaluation of action in the context of character. A good action, so Rosalind Hursthouse argues, is one which a virtuous person would typically perform.[8] But the *Poetics*, as we have seen, is only secondarily concerned with character, a notion which seems to Aristotle almost as irrelevant for the success of the dramatic performance as is the psychological disposition of a vicar for the success of the performative act of marrying or burying you. However, Aristotle makes it clear in the *Ethics* that the purpose of living is an end which is a kind of activity, not a quality. Ethics revolves on *praxis*, just as tragedy does. The word 'drama' means 'a thing done'.

In a remarkably perceptive essay, Aryeh Kosman sees the *Poetics* as relating to the *Ethics* in their concern with the alarming frailty of virtue and the vulnerability of the happiness which we seek through its cultivation. Virtue is indeed the only sure path to well-being, as the *Ethics* insists; but in a violent, unjust world it is absolutely no guarantee of it, as tragedy soberly reminds us. Tragedy is thus 'the recognition of a strain of insouciant refractoriness to human agency that is woven into the very fabric of action itself, a recognition of the inability of agents to guarantee their well-being and happiness even when they attempt, *correctly*, to found that well-being and happiness on the cultivation of moral virtue and deliberation'.[9] There is that within action which runs against the grain of its intentionality, disrupting the economy by which it is governed. Martha Nussbaum places this point in the context of a disagreement between Plato and Aristotle. Plato, like Socrates, claims that the truly virtuous person cannot come to harm, whereas the more realistically minded Aristotle, rather like Henry Fielding, sees that virtue helps you against being injured but doesn't prevent it.[10] Indeed, if to be virtuous is to be wet behind the ears *à la* Fielding's Parson Adams, it mightily facilitates it. Socrates, who doubts that much in human affairs is serious, incarnates the anti-tragic spirit of a certain stoicism, while Plato's faith that the serenity of the virtuous is impregnable is loftily indifferent to the empirical changes of fortune which tragedy exemplifies. Aristotle, by contrast, holds that someone under torture or swept up in some dramatic down-turn of fortune simply cannot be contented, however good-living they are. This, incidentally, raises the question of whether we can be self-deceived about feeling content. What do we say if someone under torture sincerely declares that he is happy? Tell him that he is wrong? Or that he should strive, if not now then a little later, to distinguish masochism from true happiness?

In another sense, however, Aristotle's ethics and poetics are not wholly compatible. Aristotle may have been the first to write a treatise on tragedy, but though his own philosophy as a whole is laced with arguably tragic elements, it is not really much concerned with human breakdown or failure. Perhaps this is one reason why the *Poetics*, in its dry, scrappy, lecture-note style, conveys notoriously little sense of the actual experience of tragedy. The work betrays no hint that anything even mildly unpleasant ever happened to its author. Aristotle holds that happiness or well-being consists in realizing one's powers by the practice of virtue. Virtue is about enjoyment, not deprivation. This is not the conventional wisdom of the modern age: as Georg Büchner's Lacroix remarks to Danton in *Danton's Death*, 'What's more, Danton, we're "full of vice", as Robespierre puts it, in other words we enjoy life, and the people are "virtuous", in other words they *don't* enjoy life' (Act 1, sc. 5). The good life is one lived to the full, while the bad one is crippled and deficient. Being human is something you have to get good at, like playing the trombone or tolerating bores, and the vicious are those who have never got the hang of it. They are tenderfoots in the art of living, as botching and cack-handed as a dog waltzing on its hindlegs. The virtuous, by contrast, are those who are successful in the business of living, and what Christians call saints are the virtuosi, the George Bests or Pavarottis of the moral domain.

This is many ways an admirable ethic. It is certainly an advance on hedonism, asceticism, utilitarianism or the fetish of duty. But Aristotle, living in a grossly unjust slave society, does not see that for human well-being to be possible all-round, a radical transformation of our powers is also demanded. And this involves more than extending them to currently excluded groups, as liberals or social democrats hold. It involves, rather, the tragic rhythm of death and regeneration – of relinquishing a form of life which is inherently exploitative so that another, more just one may be brought to birth. It is not that the end of happiness must be abandoned for that of sacrifice, *eudaimonia* forsaken for ascesis. It is rather that the full achievement of the former tragically entails the latter – that the breaking and remaking of human powers may prove essential to their general flourishing. And this is a deeply misfortunate condition.

Aristotle is naturally silent on this question, just as he is silent on the tragic hero. And this reflects ancient tragic practice. There is no real tragic protagonist in Euripides's *Andromache*, a drama in which Andromache herself disappears half-way through, and it is hard to name the hero or heroine of *The Suppliant Women*. A number of tragedies have more than one central tragic figure: Euripides's *The Bacchae*, for example, which can boast Pentheus but also his mother Agauë, who tears him to pieces while rapt in Dionysian ecstasy. E. F. Watling in his edition of Sophocles's plays asks himself whether the *Women of Trachis* should really have been called *Deianeira* or *Heracles*, searching anxiously for his single tragic protagonist.[11] Not all tragic protagonists have tragic flaws (Oedipus, Agamemnon, Orestes, Antigone, Iphigenia, Kyd's Hieronimo, Tamburlaine, Desdemona, probably Macbeth), and not all of them are morally speaking our sort of people, as Aristotle suggests they should be. Not many women are likely to let loose a delighted cry of recognition at the first entry of Medea or Clytemnestra. Nor are they likely to find themselves reflected in Kunigunde, the villainess of Kleist's *Ordeal by Fire*. The eighteenth-century critic Thomas Rymer argues that women don't pity Seneca's Phaedra because she is in no way akin to them; nor are they moved to fear her, as they do not believe that they themselves could be so wicked.[12] Paradoxically, then, the most lurid tragic actions may be the feeblest in their effect.

But neither are all tragic protagonists, as Aristotle also considered, morally reputable. Some of them can be distinctly unprepossessing, like the loutish, opinionated Bazarov, the philistine nihilist of Turgenev's *Fathers and Sons*, who dies of typhus in a way which, contrary to some classical tragic theory, is wholly accidental and quite unrelated to the previous action. Another unprincipled Russian character, Puskhin's Eugene Onegin, is a jaded, frivolous misanthrope, a *poseur* full of spleen and ennui, in whom desire takes the form of a wariness of desire, and who kills his friend Lensky in a senseless duel. Moreover, he survives to live a spiritually vacuous life, which conservative critics do not generally expect of their tragic heroes. Yet there seems no reason not to call Onegin, who almost ruins Tatyana's life and destroys the point of his own, a tragic figure, however the sprightly, self-ironizing levity of the poem's tone may run counter to the sobriety of its content. The work is at once tragic and satirical. Pechorin, of Lermontov's *A Hero of Our Time*, is a similarly disreputable figure, languid, heartless and predatory, a man who deliberately sets out to attract a woman and then callously spurns her. Marlowe's Faust, Barabas and Edward the Second, Chapman's Bussy D'Ambois, Shakespeare's Timon and Coriolanus and Ibsen's Hedda Gabler or John Gabriel Borkman are all similarly unattractive figures; yet critics who might well hesitate to allot tragic status to the Bazarovs of this world are generally keen to concede it to the likes of them.

To suggest that characters such as Onegin and Pechorin might be seen as tragic would appear to violate the classical precept that tragic figures should evoke pity. But for one thing, it is not impossible to pity the morally repugnant, and for another thing what inspires pity should surely be less some isolable personality than the action as a whole. Pechorin is a tragic figure less because he is to be personally pitied than because he is part of a deeply sorrowful narrative which involves spiritual breakdown and ruin. Ben Jonson's monstrous Catiline and bloodstained Sejanus, who is finally torn apart by the Roman mob, are no more congenial than Shakespeare's Richard III, but they are monumental tragic figures even so. In fact Jonson is specifically anti-Aristotelian on this score, having Terentius comment in Act 5 of *Sejanus* that it is unwise to pity the great when they take a tumble. Tragedy depends less on compassion for specific individuals than we might think, though it is no doubt possible to muster some for the blood-weary Macbeth in his last desperate hours.

To suggest that we can feel pity for the morally repulsive is a dangerous proposition. There is a moment in Dante's *Inferno* when the poet is rebuked by his guide for pitying the damned, since this would imply that God's punishment was less than just. But though Dante does not seem to consider the lost souls of the *Inferno* tragic, since they brought their chastisement on themselves, there is no need to agree with him. What would it mean to pity Adolf Hitler? In what sense might he be seen as a tragic character? One answer might be that for all we know, Hitler might well have turned out in different circumstances to be a valuable human being. What is pitiable is not the man himself, but the waste and monstrous warping of humanity which his wickedness represents. It is true that we cannot be sure that pity is an appropriate response here. We do not know enough about how human beings are formed to be certain that Hitler could ever have turned out differently. What one might call the social-worker theory of morality seems scarcely adequate to explain his malevolence. Yet we probably know enough about human formation to be aware that even the slightest injury or deprivation at a vulnerable stage can be enough to turn us into ogres; and we cannot yet rule out the possibility that Hitler and other evil men and women might in some subjunctive world have emerged as worthwhile people. But even if they had, the pity concerns this possibility; it is not a matter of compassion for the man himself. There is nothing about him to evoke it.

Most tragedies end unhappily, but a fair number do not. Aristotle himself is notably casual, not to say self-contradictory, on the matter. A sad ending was not essential for Greek tragedy, though it was dominant. At one point in the *Poetics* he prefers a happy ending to an unhappy one, perhaps because it can achieve *catharsis* without being too brutal, but at another point he seems to change his mind. If there is any truth in the theory that tragedy has some obscure roots in sacrifice and fertility cults, which there may not be, then destruction in these rites results in renewal rather than catastrophe. They are examples of 'tragedies' which end well. Plato extends the word 'tragedy' to the *Odyssey*, which does not end badly at all, and remarks that Homer is chief of tragic poets. More than a third of Euripides's tragedies end well. Of Aristotle's two favourite tragedies, one (Euripides's *Iphigenia in Tauris*) ends well, while the other (*King Oedipus*) does not. *Paradise Lost* ends with the Archangel Michael's prediction of a felicitous future for humanity, but this does not annul the tragedy of the Fall. David Hume remarks in his *Treatise of Human Nature* that many tragedies end happily.[13] Hegel thought it was one-sidedness, not death, which constituted the tragic action, and does not regard the death of the hero as essential for the reconciliation. You can always say: 'He got his daughter back in the end, but it was tragic that he had to endure so many years of hardship and despair searching for her.'

A tragic protagonist does not have to die, even though there are times when it would be more merciful if he did. James Tyrone in Eugene O'Neill's *A Moon for the Misbegotten* lingers on even though he is spiritually dead, in contrast with, say, Faulkner's Joe Christmas in *Light in August*, who is castrated and murdered. A hero may live and prosper, like Aeschylus's Orestes, Calderon's Segismundo or Kleist's Prince Friedrich. Tragedies which end with condign punishment might be said to end both well and badly. It is good that the villains are made to howl, but bad that their viciousness makes it necessary in the first place. John Marston's satirico-tragic *The Malcontent* is full of disasters yet ends happily, as Malvole unmasks himself as the deposed Duke Altofont and spares Mendoza's life. The same dramatist's *Antonio and Mellida* is similarly laced with tragic villainy yet has an implausible, tongue-in-cheek happy ending. Lavretsky in Turgenev's *A Nest of Gentlefolk*, whose first wife cheats on him while his second lover spurns him for a convent, leads a tragic enough existence but finally attains a degree of tranquillity, in contrast with the same author's Rudin, who fails the woman he loves and ends up sacrificing himself on the barricades of 1848. Happiness in Turgenev is usually fragile and fleeting, not least for the guilt-ridden, solitary Sanin of *Spring Torrents*. Dostoevsky's *The Brothers Karamazov* ends on an affirmative note, with Alyosha and his boys pledging their love for each other. Aeschylus's *The Suppliants*, in which the daughters of Danaus flee the rapacious sons of Aegyptus, is the first play of a trilogy which probably ended happily, like the *Oresteia* and the Prometheus trilogy. There are mixed endings such as Aeschylus's *Seven Against Thebes*, where the city is saved but only at the price of the mutual slaughter of Eteocles and Polynices, which will in turn set in motion the tragedy of Antigone.

Euripides's *Alcestis* draws to a happy conclusion, as Alcestis is returned from the shades by Heracles to the husband for whom she has sacrificed her life. The murderous Medea, in Euripides's version if not in Franz Grillparzer's, is whisked divinely aloft to escape justice for her crimes. Grillparzer's finest play, *Sappho*, ends miserably, as the eponymous heroine, stung with jealousy over Melitta's love for Phaon, casts herself into the sea. In Franz Wedekind's *Lulu*, the prostitute protagonist is brutally murdered; but Shakespeare's *Macbeth* concludes with the villain receiving his just deserts. Despite a killing, Corneille's *Le Cid* reaches a benign conclusion, with Chimena reconciled to Rodrigo, and the same is true of Corneille's *Cinna*, as the emperor Augustus magnanimously pardons Cinna's conspiracy against him. The play is a tragedy in the medieval sense of a drama of high seriousness about the fortunes of the great, but nobody is actually killed. Corneille's Polyeucte, on the other hand, meets his death as a Christian martyr, but the result is a spiritual triumph, as his lover Pauline and her father Felix are converted by his saintly example to the Christian faith.

Tragic practice, then, is a considerably more mixed affair than most tragic theory. A felicific calculus of Greek tragedy would suggest that most of the plays fail to end in complete debacle, which is not to suggest that their conclusions are euphoric. Schiller's *Don Carlos* ends badly, with the murder of the Enlightenment liberal Posa by the absolutist Philip and the arrest of the revolutionary Don Carlos himself. But there is little doubt that the days of the *ancien régime* are numbered and that the political future lies with Posa. Bourgeois optimism thus coexists with formal tragedy. The same author's *Maria Stuart*, a powerful, fast-paced drama which displays a fine economy of structure, is also formally tragic in its conclusion, as Maria is sent to her death by Queen Elizabeth; but she dies with monumental dignity, outfacing her own guilt as a murderer, forgiving her enemies and thus outflanking in magnificence of soul the great (and feminist-minded) Elizabeth herself. The play thus demonstrates Schiller's belief, argued in his essay on tragedy, that there is an inner freedom which resists all mere earthly defeat, and which, like the Kantian sublime, knows that its infinite sovereignty is more than a match for whatever might threaten it.

Egmont has an ending which reflects Goethe's ambiguous attitude to tragedy. Its hero confronts death at the hands of Spanish autocracy as a martyr for the colonized people of the Netherlands; but a concluding tableau side-steps this tragic finality by showing the protagonist enshrined with Freedom, who bids him be of good cheer, informs him that his death will secure liberty for the province, and sends him marching triumphantly off to die for freedom. Goethe's *Iphigenia in Tauris* ends happily with Orestes and Electra forgiven and set free by Thoas the king of Tauris, while the protagonist of *Torquato Tasso*, a near-paranoid, potentially tragic figure, clings finally to Duke Antonio as his saviour. As for Jean Racine, dramas like *Andromache*, *Britannicus* and *Phèdre* involve violence and destruction, but there are no deaths in *Bérénice*, which ends in reconciliation, while in *Athalie* the murderous Atalie is herself killed so that freedom and justice may triumph.

Perhaps happy and unhappy endings are beside the point because what matters is mutability, rather than any specific kind of conclusion. The sheer fact of an ending, in the sense that this is all of the action that we spectators will witness, highlights the transience of both happiness and unhappiness, and brings to mind the condition to which both will eventually lead, namely death. But whether death itself is happy or unhappy may depend in part on whether we have learned in life the lessons of mutability. Those who live in a way which denies the fragile, provisional nature of things, but cling instead to absolute ends, are unlikely to make an easy death.

Whether tragedies end well or badly, however, traditionalists insist that their primary agents must be of noble stature. There cannot be a common-life tragedy, any more than there can be a farce of emperors. For William Hazlitt, Coriolanus can be tragic, but not the mob which hounds him: 'There is nothing heroical in a multitude of miserable rogues not wishing to be starved', he comments of the Roman populace in the play, demonstrating that even radical Whigs have their patrician prejudices.[14] Tragic protagonists, in Aristotle's eyes at least, must also be reasonably though not outstandingly virtuous, a fact which is not always easy to square with their genteel provenance. Indeed, the English word 'gentleman' records in compact form the tangled history of relations between moral and social stature. As David Farrell Krell sardonically remarks, the characters of tragedy are better than the average run of humans, 'and they prove it by killing their fathers and sleeping with their mothers, or by serving up their brother's children to him, or by sacrificing their children in order to assure the success of a military adventure'.[15] Eminent individuals generally have more opportunities for wrongdoing than obscure ones, so that finding a morally principled member of the ruling class is usually no simple matter. A character in Jane Austen's *Mansfield Park* remarks that being honest and rich has become impossible.

It might also be thought that *too* high-born a hero would violate the Aristotelian precept that we, the audience, must be able to identify with him; but Pierre Corneille claims that this is too crassly literal a reading of Aristotle's requirement, and reminds us that even kings are men.[16] Even so, one modern critic finds Corneille's own Le Cid too heroic to engage our sympathies.[17] One might say the same of the tedious chivalric virtues of the hero of John Dryden's *Aureng-Zebe*, a play full of ersatz exoticism and excessively automated rhyming couplets. The neo-Aristotelian critic Elder Olson can find no taste of tragedy in Eugene O'Neill's *Mourning Becomes Electra* because the characters are too ordinary to be valued highly ('all that anyone knows is that the Mannons are having a rather bad time')[18] and don't represent anything likely to happen to us. It is hard to see how Euripides's *Ion* or Middleton's *Women Beware Women* do this any more effectively, unless Olson led a more exciting life than one might have suspected. Whereas he is of the elitist opinion that 'you cannot display the full range of character, thought, and passion in a language founded upon what the ordinary man thinks, feels, and says in an ordinary situation',[19] the Whiggish Richard Steele holds that we are much more likely to feel sympathy for someone not socially elevated above us. Steele sees men and women as naturally narcissistic, so that they 'believe nothing can relate to them that does not happen to such as live and look like themselves'.[20] Jean-Jacques Rousseau, who detested the theatre, considered it fortunate that tragedy presents us with such improbably gigantic beings that their vices are scarcely more likely to corrupt us than their virtues are likely to improve us.[21]

There are several reasons for this traditional preference for patricians. For one thing, the fortunes of the great are thought to be of more public or historic moment than the affairs of the lowly. The high/low distinction is thus a public/private one too: the illustrious are symbolic representatives of a more general condition, and can thus catalyze a more world-historical tragedy than their more parochial, less well-connected inferiors. Falls from a towering height make more of a splash. Indeed, even falling might prove something of a luxury: the protagonist of V. S. Naipaul's *The Mimic Men* remarks that 'the tragedy of power like mine is that there is no way down. There can only be extinction' (ch. 1). The anti-tragic teaching of a poet like Horace is to keep your head down and trust that a low profile will save you from disaster. Thomas Hardy believed much the same. As far as the public dimension of tragedy goes, Raymond Williams is right to see that the eighteenth-century shift to bourgeois or domestic tragedy represents in this respect both loss and gain: the sufferings of the untitled can now be taken seriously, but the general, public character of tragedy is by the same token steadily abandoned.[22] There is, supposedly, less historically at stake in the ruin of an artisan than of an arch-duke, though the case is harder to sustain when it comes to a Corsican corporal or a first-century Palestinian vagrant. There is also usually a politely veiled implication that genteel upper-class souls feel their undoing more keenly than cowherds. But you can regard the afflictions of cowherds as tragic in the ordinary-language sense while denying that they are tragic in the more technical sense of the term. In modern times, to assume that common consciousness is invariably false consciousness may give rise to a spiritually if not socially aristocratic hero, one who can soar above this web of necessary illusions to perceive a truth denied to the populace.

For another thing, cowherds supposedly haven't that much to lose, unlike corporation executives or arch-dukes. The bigger they come, the harder they fall. Schopenhauer, despite seeing tragedy as commonplace and everyday, thinks even so that the powerful make the best protagonists – not because they are necessarily noble-spirited, but because their more extravagant plunges from grace render the tragedy more grippingly terrible for the spectators. The misfortunes of a middle-class family, he considers, can be resolved by human help, whereas kings must either look to themselves or be ruined. This overlooks what might be called the widow's mite syndrome: the near-destitute may cling more tenaciously to what meagre possessions they have, and feel their loss more sharply, than one who has more than enough to squander. But tragedy should also centre on the exalted because, as Sir Philip Sidney claims with disarming candour in his *Apology for Poetry*, seeing them come unstuck provides some much-needed *Schadenfreude* for their downtrodden underlings. If you are disgruntled with your plebeian place in life, the sight of a prince being toppled from his throne may remind you that your own lot, precisely because it is harsher, is also more secure. 'High place is desirable', comments Agamemnon in Euripides's *Iphigenia in Aulis*, 'but, when attained, a disease.' Or as Aethra pithily observes in the same author's *The Suppliant Women*, 'the gods stretch greatness in the dust'. The mighty are both blessed and cursed, and thus, as we shall see later, have something of the ambivalence of the tragic scapegoat. But such tumbles on the part of the pre-eminent also remind you that if this can happen to them then it can all the more easily happen to you, thus curbing your *ressentiment* in this way too.

Among those who adhere to this tragic aristocratism is the early Georg Lukács. For him, tragic heroes must be genteel for philosophical reasons: since tragedy is a matter of spiritual essences rather than empirical contingencies, only the portrayal of such privileged figures will allow it 'to sweep all the petty causalities of life from the ontological path of destiny'.[23] Princes, in other words, are not distracted from their edifying projects by the need to bath the baby or fix a sandwich. But they are also in Lukács's eyes the only figures whose conflicts grow directly out of their own situation rather than result from accident or external forces, which satisfies the Aristotelian requirement that the tragedy should not be sprung *ex machina*. In Hegelian terms, the more prestigious the protagonist, the more immanent the tragedy. In any case, since Lukács holds rather strangely that the essence of tragedy is solitude, such august figures, marooned on their lonely pinnacles, are more likely to fulfil this demand. 'In vain did our democratic age', he comments in *Soul and Form*, 'wish to establish the right of all to participate in the tragic; vain was every attempt to open this heavenly kingdom to the poor in spirit.'[24]

Lukács's tone is not exactly one of regret, and neither is George Steiner's, when he proclaims that 'there is nothing democratic in the vision of tragedy'.[25] The form, he tells us, presupposes the high life of courts, dynastic quarrels and vaulting ambitions because it deals essentially with the public sphere.[26] This curiously overlooks the fact that the middle classes had their public sphere too; indeed, the very concept is drawn from that social history. What of Büchner's Danton, or stout burghers like Ibsen's Stockmann, or the tragic figures of Thomas Mann's *Buddenbrooks*? In what sense is *Middlemarch* more private than *Macbeth*? Hegel is adamant that tragic pity is 'not excited by ragamuffins and vagabonds',[27] but Oedipus is not far from this condition at Colonus. Theodor Adorno's tone about tragedy is rather more ambiguous: the form has died, so we are informed, because 'nobility' has fallen victim to cultural 'vulgarity'. Yet Adorno, in typically dialectical style, also insists that though nobility in art must be preserved, its collusion with social privilege and political conservatism must be exposed.[28]

Horace is already warning in 'On the Art of Poetry' against too abrupt a descent in theatrical performance from tragedy to the satyr play which traditionally accompanied it. No actor who was presented just a moment ago as a hero or king, he advises, should be suddenly 'translated into a dingy hovel and allowed to drop into the speech of the backstreets'.[29] Aristotle remarks in the *Poetics* that the 'grandeur' of the form is of fairly recent vintage, emerging as it did from comic diction and satyr plots. According to Werner Jaeger, the democratic rot set in remarkably early: Euripides and others 'finally vulgarized tragedy into a drama of everyday life'.[30] In the hilarious slanging match between Euripides and Aeschylus in Act 2 of Aristophanes's *The Frogs*, the populist-minded Euripides accuses Aeschylus of writing bombast, 'great galumphing phrases, fearsome things with crests and shaggy eyebrows. Magnificent! Nobody knew what they meant, of course.' The older poet goes in for 'high-flown Olympian language, instead of talking like a human being.' Tragedy, Euripides complains, was in a dreadful state when he inherited it from his senior colleague, swollen with high-falutin' diction. It was he, he boasts, who got her weight down, putting her on a diet of finely chopped logic and a special decoction of dialectics. Everyone in his plays – women and slaves, masters, maids, aged crones – is always hard at work talking, which he proudly describes as 'democracy in action'. In a gesture worthy of Brecht, he adds that the public have learnt from him how to think and question, to ask 'Why is this so? What do we mean by that?' Dionysus, who is in on the quarrel, sardonically confirms that no Athenian can come home nowadays without asking 'What do you mean by biting the head off that sprat?' or 'Where is yesterday's garlic?'

Aeschylus, in his turn, sees this as no more than spreading a general spirit of subversion: 'now even the sailors argue with their officers – why, in my day the only words they knew were "slops" and "yo-heave-ho"!' The younger poet has stuffed his dramas with pimps and profligates, women giving birth in temples and sleeping with their brothers; as a result, the city is full of lawyers' clerks and scrounging mountebanks, with not a decent athlete left in the place. In the spirit of a Noel Coward confronted with an upstart John Osborne, he loftily defends his patrician characters: 'My heroes weren't like those market-place loafers, swindlers and rogues they write about nowadays: they were real heroes, breathing spears and lances . . . I didn't clutter my stage with harlots like Phaedra or Stheneboea. No one can say I have ever put an erotic female into any play of mine.' 'How could you?' Euripides flashes back, 'You've never met one.'

In his preface to *Samson Agonistes*, Milton inveighs against introducing 'trivial and vulgar persons' into tragic art. The spiritual snobbism of this tradition has not gone unresisted. Raymond Williams opens his *Modern Tragedy* by remarking that he has witnessed tragedy of several kinds in his own 'ordinary life', though 'it has not been the death of princes'.[31] He then goes on to speak of a dead father, a divided city and a world war.

George Steiner, however, remains unpersuaded. Crises in Ibsen, he remarks, can be resolved by saner economic relations or better plumbing, but (he adds with splendid *hauteur*) 'if there are bathrooms in the houses of tragedy, it is for Agamemnon to be murdered in'.[32] In tragedy, he informs us, 'there are no temporal remedies . . . The destiny of Lear cannot be resolved by the establishment of adequate homes for the aged'.[33] Nor, one is tempted to retort, can the destiny of the aged. But the case is disastrously flawed. Agamemnon may not be caught visiting the bathroom, but he is part of a drama which indeed achieves its temporal resolution in the *Eumenides*. Plato, who took a dim view of the kind of democracy which is celebrated in that play, also had a notoriously low opinion of tragedy, and the two aversions may not be unconnected. Plenty of tragic protagonists could have led peaceable lives if only they had not slept with their mothers, contracted syphilis, been betrayed by their lovers or murdered a monarch. Most tragedy is in that sense remediable, including that of classical antiquity. The catastrophe, to be sure, is sometimes predestined by a prima-donna-like god or the star-crossed history of a house; but for the most part it would not have come about if some previous, avoidable event had not happened as well. It is not true, as Nietzsche suggests, that 'tragedy deals with incurable, comedy with curable suffering'.[34]

In his 'Study of Thomas Hardy', D. H. Lawrence argues that tragedy is the preserve of the spiritual aristocrat, and complains: 'Why must the aristocrat always be condemned to death?'[35] Lawrence sees tragedy as the monopoly of those mighty souls who defy petty social convention and insist instead on being true to themselves. They are the heroic elite who are faithful to the larger morality of Life, rather than to some despicable suburban code. Lawrence's naive Romantic libertarianism pitches 'Life' (unambiguously fruitful) and 'society' (unequivocally oppressive) in simplistic opposition. The tragedy of modern times is that such life-figures, full of passional splendour and animal vitality, are cravenly sacrificed by their petty-bourgeois creators on the altar of social decorum. In the old days, it was different: Oedipus, Macbeth and Lear are necessarily overthrown, since their quarrel was with Life itself, which for Lawrence will brook no defiance. But Tolstoy's Anna Karenina, along with Thomas Hardy's Tess Durbeyfield, Eustacia Vye, Sue Bridehead and Jude Fawley are all ritually immolated, allowed to go under by authors who, alarmed by the spontaneous forces they have unwittingly let loose, step in to cut these magnificent creations vindictively down to their own puny size. Tess Durbeyfield, who is up against nothing more imposingly ontological than rape and poverty, predatory patriarchs and economic exploiters, should, one assumes, have exultantly carried all before her. Unusually among the high modernists, Lawrence is a resolutely anti-tragic thinker, for all the most discreditable of reasons.

Lawrence's view of Hardy is actually a view of Lawrence; but Hardy's tragic narratives are nevertheless relevant to the question of high-life heroes. In the honourable humanist tradition of George Eliot, Hardy recognizes that tragedy can be found on small tenant farms on far-flung provincial moors, in seedy coastal resorts and down the backstreets of university cities. Like Eliot's, his fiction insists that the destinies hidden away in these inconsiderable corners are as absolute for their bearers as they are for the denizens of courts and cathedrals. Yet like Eliot too, he is not quite tonally at ease with his own heterodoxy, and as in the case of Eustacia Vye will occasionally wheel on stage some rather lumbering tragic machinery in order to force his point home. The imagery in which he frames the action is sometimes incongruously askew to its substance. By the time of *Jude the Obscure*, the civilization which produced classical tragedy is now explicitly the class enemy, a sphere of fetishists and spook-worshippers which thwarts your own stumbling progress towards civility. But before Hardy presses against this outer limit of literary and social decorum, after which he was to fall silent as a novelist, he gestures rather portentously to classical motifs in order to dignify the inconspicuous fate of some rural artisan or female farm labourer, rather as he tries too hard at times to write in the grand style of the London literary coteries in order to signal that the World Spirit is alive and kicking even in deepest Dorset. But the self-consciousness with which this is done may only seem to disprove the case. It is hard at this historical point to find a literary language which is both common and resourceful, lucid and sharable yet the bearer of momentous meanings. As far as that goes, the nineteenth-century division of labour between poetry and prose, the discourse of spiritual insight and the idiom of social description, has done its damage.

Herman Melville's Ishmael insists in *Moby-Dick* that he is dealing 'not [with] the dignity of kings and robes' but with the 'democratic dignity' of the arm 'that wields a pick or drives a spike' (ch. 26). But since the source of democracy for Melville is God himself, no loss of tragic sublimity is involved. Even so, the novel has to apologize with facetious unease for presenting such low-life figures as whalers, rather as *Adam Bede* has to suspend its narrative for a moment to defend in tones of genial patronage its dealings with the petty-bourgeois Poysers. 'If, then, to meanest mariners, and renegades and castaways', Melville writes, 'I shall hereafter ascribe high qualities, though dark; weave round them tragic graces . . . if I shall touch a workman's arm with some ethereal light; if I shall spread a rainbow over his disastrous set of sun; then against all mortal critics bear me out in it, thou just spirit of Equality, which hast spread one royal mantle of humanity over all my kind!' (ch. 26). Melville has no doubt that a tragedy populated by carpenters and harpooners is a thoroughly political act, just as Alessandro Manzoni is aware of the portentous political impact of making the leading actors of *The Betrothed* a silk-weaver and a peasant woman. They represent what the novel calls the 'gente di nessuno' ('nobody's people'), that 'immense multitude', as Manzoni puts it elsewhere, 'passing on the face of the earth, passing on its own native piece of earth, without leaving a trace in history'.[36] With *The Betrothed*, the masses make one of their earliest entries into literary history. A later nobody's person is Myrtle Wilson of F. Scott Fitzgerald's *The Great Gatsby*, whose squalid death in a motor accident is described by the novel as her 'tragic achievement' (ch. 8). Perhaps this is meant to be ironic, since getting yourself killed by a car is scarcely an achievement. But perhaps it is not, since what Myrtle has achieved in doing so is tragic status.

Hardy and Eliot, like Wordsworth in the popular tragedy of 'Michael', are both drawn to obscure forms of blight and desolation, to those trapped in the sheer stifling monotony of spiked dreams and baulked hopes, as well as dealing in more dramatic forms of tragedy. This did not especially endear them to those Victorian critics for whom common-life tragedy was 'too near the truth' to be agreeable.[37] Both authors, with Darwin at their elbow, see evolution itself as dismantling the barriers between high and low. An evolutionary world is an ironic one, since you can never be sure which humble, trivial-looking life-form will evolve in the fullness of time into something quite momentous, in the arduous trek from the mollusc to monopoly capitalism. The text of the world is thus at any particular moment unreadable, since you would have to be able to view it retrospectively, in the light of what it might lead to, to interpret it aright. Anyway, in the proto-modernist text of evolution, classical hierarchies are alarmingly undercut, as we can never be quite certain how important anything is, and as the inglorious secretes a potentially subversive power. Just as Jacques Derrida perversely unlocks the grand thematics of a text by seizing upon some stray little signifier buried shyly away in a footnote, so Hardy recognizes that drama of world-historical proportions can hinge on a mislaid letter or belated gesture – that the trope of an evolutionary universe is not only irony, but bathos. In such a world, the ordinary may be pregnant with a world-shaking meaning of which it betrays no trace. As Anton Chekhov remarks: 'people are having a meal at the table, just having a meal, but at the same time their happiness is being created, or their lives are being smashed up'.[38] In the social or evolutionary web, the real significance of one's existence is always elsewhere, as a subtext weaving itself invisibly in and out of your actions, a social unconscious which sets the scene for your individual fortunes but never stages an appearance there. The commonplace and the cata-strophic, as in Auden's poem 'Musée des Beaux Arts', are the recto and verso of a single process.

Tragedy and democracy meet in the novel, then; but it is not the only place where they effect an encounter. Arthur Schopenhauer is one of the few philosophers to recognize tragic ordinariness in drama. In tragedy, he writes, we see 'the greatest misfortune, not as an exception, not as something occasioned by rare circumstances or monstrous characters, but as arising easily and of itself out of the actions and characters of men, indeed almost as essential to them, and this brings it terribly near to us'. There is no need for colossal errors or unheard-of accidents, simply that 'characters as they usually are . . . in circumstances that frequently occur, are so situated with regard to each other that their situation forces them, knowingly and with their eyes open, to do one another the greatest injury, without any one of them being entirely in the wrong'.[39] Tragedy for Schopenhauer is at once the product of an imposing metaphysical force – the Will – and as intimate and unremarkable as breathing. It is a yoking of the everyday and elevated evident in his own name. We are moving here towards a sense of the quotidian nature of tragedy that August Strindberg would recognize, and away from the view of a modern critic, N. Georgopoulos, that the circumstances which the tragic hero encounters 'are extraordinary – beyond human comprehension, on the other side of the human nature the protagonist brings to them . . . non-human'.[40] It is hard to see that the circumstances which help to bring low Mark Antony (having sex with an enemy of Rome) or Strindberg's Miss Julie (having sex with a sadistic servant) are sublimely unfath-omable. Georgopoulos does, however, make a number of references to Moby-Dick, who is admittedly more inscrutable than Tennessee Williams's Big Daddy or Wedekind's Lulu. It is another example of allow-ing a mere one or two texts to determine one's sense of the form as a whole.

Lessing is another who speaks up for that apparent oxymoron, demo-cratic tragedy. For him, the rank of the protagonist is unimportant; the Jewish hero of his play *Nathan the Wise* is a prosperous, generous-hearted bourgeois, not an aristocrat. With Marlowe's Barabas and Ben Jonson's Volpone, the business of material acquisition can be graced, in however tongue-in-cheek a fashion, with cosmic imagery, evidence enough that the mercantile classes are still in their heroic heyday. Indeed, middle-class tragedy of some sort goes back as far as the Renaissance, with dramatic pieces in England like *Arden of Feversham*. Balzac remarks in *Lost Illusions* that 'the anguish caused by poverty is no less worthy of attention than the crises which turn life upside-down for the mighty and privileged persons on this earth' (Part 2, ch. 1). *Eugénie Grandet*, he comments in the course of that novel, is 'a bourgeois tragedy undignified by poison, dagger, or blood-shed, but to the protagonists more cruel than any of the tragedies endured by members of the noble house of Atreus'. *The Human Comedy* is full of tragedies of little men like César Birotteau, a mediocre petty-bourgeois perfumier caught up in the snares of a predatory capitalism. Flaubert's Madame Bovary is a commonplace enough tragic figure, though the emotionally anaestheticized style in which she is presented is also a satirical comment on her lower-middle-class pretensions. The novel thus has its tragedy and disowns it at the same time.

It is true that, with the onset of modernity, politics ceases by and large to provide fit meat for tragedy. It is no longer the valorous, spectacular stuff of the feudal or absolutist order but bloodless and bureaucratized, a matter of committees rather than chivalry, chemical warfare rather than the Crusades. In a drama like *Egmont*, Goethe is still drawing on the more charismatic politics of an earlier period. But social and economic life in the modern age provide plenty of opportunities to compensate for this declension. Indeed, a trace of this now-defunct heroism survives in the very totalizing ambitiousness of Balzac's enterprise, the title of which evidently recalls Dante, and which according to one critic represents 'the last chance for an artist to make sense of a whole society in all of its inter-related details'.[41] Balzac's heroic endeavour is to bestow universal status on the egregiously unheroic middle classes, raising them to the dignity of the tragic while retaining an expansive, essentially comic vision of their actual fortunes.

'The tragedians are wrong, grief has no grandeur', writes John Banville in his novel *Eclipse*. Grandeur is indeed the wrong word; but the implication that tragedy is one thing and ordinary life another is unwarranted. Indeed, one of the ironies of Enlightenment is that at the very moment when tragedy is being denied, it is also being extended. Enlightened Man turns his face from all that high-pitched talk of rank, evil, mystery, honour and cosmic fatality to address the more sublunary matters of political reconstruction, social well-being, historical progress. But because this project involves universal equality and the unique value of each individual, absolutely anybody can now be a tragic figure. And since politics is increasingly supposed to involve the common people, each one of them has a destiny as potentially world-historical as Cinna's or Le Cid's.

Moreover, as capitalism overrides the barriers between hitherto cloistered communities, levelling difference and privilege to uniformity, it creates a common world in which everyone's destiny is perpetually at stake. As the film director Michelangelo Antonioni once put the point: 'Who can be a hero in a nuclear age? Or for that matter, who can't be?' Tragic heroes and heroines are now to be found loitering on every street corner, as each individual's fate becomes in principle as precious as every other's and your world-historical crisis threatens to shatter my existence too. For modernism, to be sure, something more than this may be required. To alchemize the base metals of daily life into the pure gold of tragedy, one may have to take these men and women and push them to the very limit of their endurance. But tragedy, that privileged preserve of gods and spiritual giants, has now been decisively democratized – which is to say, for the devotees of gods and giants, abolished. Hence the death-of-tragedy thesis. Tragedy, however, did not vanish because there were no more great men. It did not expire with the last absolutist monarch. On the contrary, since under democracy each one of us is to be incommensurably cherished, it has been multiplied far beyond antique imagining.

This carries further implications. For most traditionalist theorists, as we have seen, only the sort of destruction which discloses a sense of ultimate value can be judged tragic. And this value generally emerges through the act of resistance, performed by a specific kind of agent. With democracy, however, things are different. For now it is taken for granted that men and women are uniquely valuable *as such*, which would hardly have occurred to Augustus Caesar. They do not need to be duchesses, guerrilla fighters, strenuous combatants in the battle of life, hapless victims of an invidious fate, moral innocents or acutely conscious of their plight to earn our sympathies. Schopenhauer talks of leaving the conclusion to the spectator, meaning perhaps that it is we who assume the value which makes the action tragic, rather than leaving it to vigorous self-affirmations on stage. This is why, under democracy, tragic protagonists do not have to be heroes to be tragic. The only qualification for being a tragic protagonist is that you are a member of the species. What category of member, as far as rank, profession, provenance, gender, ethnicity and the like go, is a supremely indifferent affair. As with censuses, there are certain questions which one need not ask.

It is this revolutionary, properly abstract equality which postmodernism, like the rulers of pre-modern regimes, finds so distasteful. Most of what we need to know, for tragedy to occur, is that a man or woman is being destroyed – for who says 'humanity' now says 'ultimate value'. A modern tragic protagonist does not have to demonstrate this humanity in eye-catching form, since it is we who presuppose it in any case. The tragedy rests as much upon our assumptions as on what the play or novel argues. Thus the ending of Ernest Hemingway's *A Farewell to Arms*, as the protagonist leaves the corpse of his partner behind him in hospital, is calculatedly affectless and anaestheticized, with the flat, deliberately downbeat tone typical of some modernist writing. It does not invite us to regard the death as tragic. Yet we do so in any case, because being modern readers we need no such rhetorical exhortation. All we need to know is that someone is dead, and something perhaps of the circumstances. How much of the circumstances is a debatable point. Perhaps we need to know that whoever is dead did not just expire peacefully in bed at a grand old age; or that they were not in such intolerable pain that death was what they desired; or that they were not hanged for crimes against humanity. Yet while this might make the death non-tragic for some, it would not necessarily do so for others. You can always argue that death is tragic in itself, or that it is tragic that someone should want to die anyway, or that we are not wholly responsible even for acts of genocide.

Tragic democracy thus cuts through the jealously patrolled frontiers between tragic resisters and non-tragic victims, those debacles which allow us a glimpse of supreme value and those which do not, those cut down by accident and those by some updated version of destiny, those who are engineers of their own undoing and those afflicted with ruinous misfortune from the outside. Far from there being 'nothing democratic in the vision of tragedy', as George Steiner asserts, absolutely nobody is safe from tragedy in such a world. The Enlightenment, commonly thought to be the enemy of tragedy, is in fact a breeder of it. It is worth recalling that tragic art began in a society which called itself a democracy, indeed in its Aeschylean form is much preoccupied with the provenance of that political order.

One might well complain that if tragedy demands no more of human beings than to be human, then it demands too little of them, and we purchase our tragic stature on the cheap. Is tragedy really just some sentimental humanism, as eighteenth-century domestic tragedians like John Lillo seem to have believed? Are we all equal in the eyes of Zeus? To claim that anyone can be a tragic subject, however, is not to suggest that every tragedy is as poignant or momentous as every other. The loss of a child may be more catastrophic than the loss of a fortune, or even than the loss of one's mind. The point is just that there are now no distinctions in principle between potential candidates for such cataclysms. Tragedy returns as everyday experience at exactly the point when a democratic age has grown wary of it as ritual, mystery, heroism, fatalism and absolute truth. And after the Enlightenment's insistence on our common humanity will come Schopenhauer, for whom the malignant Will stirs in our most casual gestures; Marx, for whom death-dealing conflicts are masked by the Apollonian consensus of bourgeois democracy; Nietzsche, who detects a repressed history of blood and horror in the fashioning of civilization itself; and Freud, who likewise sees culture as the fruit of barbarism and for whom we are all potential monsters, as the criminal features of Oedipus can be traced in the blissfully innocent countenance of the infant.

There is another problem with the democratization of tragedy. The more everyday it is, the harder it is to abolish it altogether. In challenging the elitism of some traditional tragic theory, one would seem to confirm its sense of the imperishability of the tragic. It is easier to get rid of princes than to eradicate lethal accidents, flawed relationships, routine human breakdown and betrayal. Or at least, some of these conditions could be eliminated only along with our freedom, so that when it comes to tragedy we have to take the kicks with the ha'pence. This is a dilemma to which Raymond Williams in *Modern Tragedy* is insufficiently alert. Williams really wants to argue two cases about tragedy, both of them deeply rooted in his socialist humanism. The first, aimed at the elitists, is that it is a profoundly ordinary affair; the second, aimed at the conservative pessimists, is that it has assumed in our time the shape of an epic struggle which can in principle be resolved. It is not clear that these two cases are wholly compatible with each other.

If tragedy, as John Jones argues, centres more on an action than a character, a condition rather than a personal quality, then much of the debate about high and low protagonists is in fact irrelevant. What began as a technical point about how best to represent the action – choose an eminent personage because his fall has more of a moral and dramatic impact – later becomes an ideological affair of noble souls and patrician sentiments, part of tragedy's campaign against a despicably ignoble modernity. Since then, there has been a gradual scaling down from seigneurs to salesmen. As John Orr perceptively comments, this shift has also been one from Old to New Worlds, as the passing of the tragic baton or buskin from Ibsen, Chekhov and Strindberg to Eugene O'Neill, Tennessee Williams and Arthur Miller also represents a shift from bourgeois to proletarian.[42] One might also see it as a shift from hero to victim, though there are plenty of the latter in Euripides.

This advance in democracy has not been unqualified: in Robert Bolt's *A Man for All Seasons*, the Common Man turns up at the end in the guise of Thomas More's Executioner. While the Nazis were settling into power in Germany, W. B. Yeats was still, astonishingly, producing heroic dramas like *The King of the Great Clock Tower* and *The Herne's Egg*. He greeted the outbreak of the Second World War with *The Death of Cuchulain*. In the age of radio, pogroms and mass unemployment, Yeats still populates his stage with a motley crew of tinkers, beggars, Fools, witches and peddlers, most of whom would probably have been locked away for life in reformatories in the Ireland of his day. *The Herne's Egg*, which comes complete with a cast of Congal king of Connacht, Aedh king of Tara, the priestess Attracta and the regulation Fool, was written in the year the Nazis seized Austria. Yet if Ireland had its Aedh and Attracta, it also had Paddy Maguire, the broken, sexually frustrated small farmer of Patrick Kavanagh's great tragic poem 'The Great Hunger'. One thinks also of a tragic working-class figure such as Gervaise Macquart of Emile Zola's *L'Assomoir*, a laundress who struggles to acquire a position and then, through no fault of her own, loses business, reputation, daughter and dipsomaniac husband and meets with a squalid death from poverty and alcoholism.

Georg Büchner's extraordinary Woyzeck, half-visionary, half-schizoid, is perhaps the first proletarian hero in tragic drama, a down-at-heel soldier who stabs his unfaithful partner Marie, and as the play's language moves near to surrealism grasps through his madness a kind of truth. Büchner anticipates Bertolt Brecht in his belief that morality is mostly for the well-heeled, and his revolutionary pamphlet *The Hessian Messenger* is a splendidly swingeing piece of populist rhetoric for which he narrowly escaped arrest. If *Woyzeck* places a working-class figure centre-stage, Gerhart Hauptmann's *The Weavers* presents working people, most unusually in the history of drama, not just as individual victims but as a social class.

One of the finest tragedies of working-class life is Zola's *Germinal*, which presents a misery and exploitation which are anything but universal. They belong to a highly specific historical condition, a ferociously particularized struggle between labour and capital, and are all the more powerful on that account. To universalize them – to regard Etienne Lantier as some allegorical representative of Man – would be to trivialize and dilute them. It is curious that the champions of universality never seem to consider this possibility, just as it is strange that they are usually also such doughty advocates of the uniquely particular. The two are by no means always compatible. *Germinal* remains an incomparably compelling tragedy even though it ends with a courageous vision of political hope – of the germination of a new social order, as a 'black avenging host ... thrusting upwards for the harvests of future ages' will finally crack the earth asunder (Part 7, ch. 6). The only authentic image of the future, as Zola understands, is the failure of the present. In a classical tragic insight, Lantier remarks of the impoverished miners that their starved bodies, if they go under, will do more for the people's cause than any prudent politics. But it is not that he wants to go under: he is a martyr rather than a suicide, who becomes a scapegoat for the massacred miners and is stoned. It is better not to live as a tragic martyr or scapegoat; it would be infinitely preferable if there were no greedy mine-owners in the first place. Tragedy is not a matter of masochism, of grovelling self-abasement, of the glorification of suffering. But if such suffering is forced upon you, there may be ways of turning it into the preconditions of a changed existence.

Büchner's and Brecht's plebeian protagonists are for the most part social rebels, whereas just the opposite is true of the prototype of popular tragedy of our time, Arthur Miller's Willy Loman. Loman, whose very name indicates his modest status, meets with his death not because he challenges a false social order but because he is too self-destructively eager to conform to it. *Death of a Salesman* seems deliberately designed to scandalize the Dorothea Krooks of this world: apart from the fact that Loman's tragedy does spring from his own situation, and that he could be seen as a representative figure, the play manages to violate almost every tenet of tragic theory. Willy is far from noble, though he is morally speaking on a par with his audience; he is more victim than agent, and puts up little resistance to the forces destroying him; he does not accept his suffering as necessary, and if he goes willingly to his death it is for pragmatic reasons only; he understands precious little of what is happening to him, and so flouts the doctrine of *anagnorisis*; the issues at stake are historically specific ones, quite the reverse of timeless; there is nothing expiatory about his suffering, though there is something selfless about his dying; his fortunes are in no sense preordained, and his death rights no sort of moral balance and confirms no kind of cosmic justice. All this, one might argue, nonetheless relies on traditional notions of high-born suffering, if only to generate dramatic impact by bowling such stereotypes audaciously over. One might even claim the same of Othello, who is ruined by a handkerchief rather than dying in battle. Loman discloses a kind of value in his sheer self-deceived tenacity of commitment, his courageous refusal to back down from the problem of his identity; as Miller himself observes in the Introduction to his *Collected Plays*, Willy cannot settle for half, but must pursue the dream of himself to the end. It is not, however, the kind of value which fortifies our faith in the justness of the human condition, least of all in that bit of it known as American capitalism.

Miller sees the social laws which govern Willy's actions as being as inexorable as classical fate, 'no less powerful in their effects upon individuals than any tribal law administered by gods with names'.[43] Loman is not, in his author's eyes, entirely bereft of self-awareness: he is haunted by the hollowness of the objects in which he has invested his selfhood, like Hegel's *comic* character in the *Aesthetics* who identifies with an inherently false aim and makes it the one real thing in his life. To say that Willy cannot verbalize his situation, Miller claims, is not to suggest that he is ignorant of it. Even so, Miller rightly insists, complete consciousness is not possible for human subjects, and there is 'a severe limitation of awareness in any character'.[44] After Freud, *anagnorisis* is bound to look more ambiguous. In fact it can always be argued, as we have seen already, that such self-blindness deepens rather than dilutes the tragedy. To go to one's death like Willy Loman without ever having known who one was is arguably more poignant than to enter it in the full panoply of tragic self-consciousness, which in such situations is anyway a limited sort of value.

In Miller's eyes, Loman is brought to his death by refusing to give up on his desire, keeping faith with a law – the law of success rather than love – which is in fact baseless. Yet it is only such laws which make life supportable for many under their punitive sway. Without the law which declares that a social failure has no right to live, life would be painfully befuddling for many men and women. Like Conrad and Ibsen, then, Miller is not wholly censorious of such enabling fictions. It is true that what matters for him is not law but truth; but this is not quite the same as a contrast between falsehood and reality. For the truth in question is the quasi-existentialist one of integrity rather than of validity; it is the truth of one's unfaltering fidelity to an ideal, even if the ideal is false and one's fidelity to it finally lethal. What matters for Miller when it comes to tragedy, here as in *A View from the Bridge*, is what he calls an 'intensity of commitment', which may well be commitment to a spurious goal. The real tragedy of Willy Loman is that he has no choice but to invest his admirably uncompromising energies in a worthless end.

In the throes of one particular crisis in *Death of a Salesman*, Biff Loman urges his father to back off, reminding him that people like themselves are a dime a dozen. Loman, in a movingly dignified response, rounds on his son and declares: 'I am not a dime a dozen! I am Willy Loman, and you are Biff Loman!' (Act 2). And the truth is that they are both right. Biff urges the cold-eyed reality of the capitalist market-place, where individuals are indifferently exchangeable, whereas Willy appeals to the humanist ideology – all individuals are unique (or, as the present-day American banality goes, 'everybody's special') – which cloaks and ratifies that indifference. If Biff is both right and insulting to insist on the bleak reality, Willy is both correct and deluded to deny it. There is, as Ibsen knew, a tragedy of demystification, denunciation, violent unmasking; but there is also the more tortuous tragic experience of clinging to one's delusions because in a false situation this is the only way to preserve, in however mystified a guise, a few shrivelled seeds of truth. Human individuals are indeed uniquely valuable, however much the proposition is also a pernicious piece of ideology. Ordinary experience may be laced with a large dose of delusion, but it can also speak the truth. It is this which is overlooked by the elitists of tragedy, for whom only those perched loftily above the masses can pierce the veil of false consciousness and peer boldly into the abyss.

Chapter 5

Freedom, Fate and Justice

'Tragedy is the image of Fate, as comedy is of Fortune', writes Susanne K. Langer.[1] The statement is more elegant than accurate. There is, for example, no discussion of fate or the determining sway of the gods in Aristotle's *Poetics*. Aristotle thinks that the development of a tragedy should be natural and necessary, less diffuse and digressive than the epic, but this is more of a formal than metaphysical requirement. He excludes accident, but seems to mean by 'necessity' something more like a probable or coherent chain of causality than some metaphysical fatality. The early Hegel, however, saw the decline of the idea of destiny as closely bound up with the fall of the ancient *polis*, both events to be lamented from the standpoint of an errant modernity. Jean Anouilh's *Antigone* is a modern *locus classicus* of this assumption that tragedy and fate walk hand in hand. As the Chorus of the play remarks, 'The machine is in perfect order, it has been oiled ever since time began, and it runs without friction . . . Tragedy is clean, it is restful, it is flawless . . . Death, in a melodrama, is really horrible because it is never inevitable. In a tragedy, nothing is in doubt and everyone's destiny is known. That makes for tranquillity . . . Tragedy is restful; and the reason is that hope, that foul deceitful thing, has no part in it. There isn't any hope. You're trapped.'

Tragedy here has the shapely necessity of art itself, and part of our delight in it is thus sheerly aesthetic. The skeletal diagram of destiny is embodied in the spare economy of the art work, which exudes the stillness of death. Neither art nor destiny betrays the slightest stain of contingency. Unlike the more diffuse, capacious epic or novel, tragic art displays a certain inevitability in its very formal rigour, and like destiny it combines this stringency with a certain mysteriousness. Nothing could not have happened as it did, just as the narrative of the *Odyssey* or *Orlando* is now fixed and frozen for all time, thus saving us the fatiguing psychical labour of imagining alternative twists and turns, or wondering as with some more avant-gardist text which pieces go with which. Once tragedy is cast into artistic form, then as W. B. Yeats remarks in 'Lapis Lazuli', 'It cannot grow by an inch or an ounce'. Form itself thus becomes a kind of transcendence of the tragic materials. Friedrich Hölderlin writes to a friend that tragedy is the strictest of all poetic forms, starkly unornamented and proudly denying all accident.[2] It is interesting to observe the direct relation here between fate and formal integrity.

Tragedy, on this view, is the abolition of the subjunctive mood. The form thus caters wonderfully to our endemic indolence, our desire that all the work should have been done for us before we even arrive on the scene. The serene composure of tragedy, its bland, mummified features, is akin to both art and death, which is to say a matter of both its form and its content, and the law of the artefact is the inscription within it of a higher providence. In Schopenhauerian fashion, you can now look upon your own star-crossed life with something of the estranging, serenely contemplative gaze with which you might impassively survey the downfall of another. Tragedy is the present lived as though it were the past, tempering the excitement of a 'What comes next?' with the consoling certitudes of an ending we read back at each point into the evolving action. It involves what the Irish philosopher William Desmond calls 'the posthumous mind', as we watch these living events in the backward shadow cast by the deaths in which they issue.[3] Paul Ricoeur sees the spectators of a tragedy as 'wait[ing] for the certainty of the past absolute to supervene upon chance events and the uncertainty of the future as if it were something new'.[4] We move backwards and forwards simultaneously, mixing freedom and fatality, rather as for Freud we are pitched between the unfurling dynamic of *Eros* and the backward drag of *Thanatos*. However savage or sanguinary the tragic conclusion, it is at least a predictable one, and this assurance may console us a little for the discomforts of pity and fear. Such, at least, is the doctrine of tragic destiny.

There are at least two ironies in Anouilh's pronouncement. For one thing, it is curious to see such an old-fashioned piece of tragic dogma in such a boldly revisionist work, which treats Antigone as some kind of existentialist heroine or maverick guerrilla fighter engaged less in an act of sororal piety than in a self-assertive *acte gratuit*. For another thing, there is little sense of destiny in Sophocles's own play. The act of leaving Polynices unburied was never carved in stone, and Antigone would probably have been saved from death if the newly remorseful Creon had gone straight to her prison rather than attending first to her brother's corpse. It is not true that all tragic actions are predetermined. Of Shakespeare's tragedies, only *Macbeth* would seem to merit the description. The tragic outcome of Lope de Vega's *The Knight from Olmedo* would have seemed predestined to the play's original Spanish audiences, who would have been aware of the legend in which the Knight, Alonso, meets his death at the hands of his rival in love Rodrigo; but there is no such *déjà lu* about same author's *Punishment without Revenge*. And if not all tragedy is determined, not all determinism is tragic. Spinoza is an out-and-out determinist for whom nothing could have happened other than it did, but his philosophy, as we shall see later, is the reverse of tragic. Thomas Hobbes is also a devout determinist, and a tragic thinker to boot, but he is not tragic because he is a determinist.

If tragedies *are* predetermined, then their protagonists are either puppets or waging war on the inevitable. Whether the inevitable has foreseen and factored in their resistance, as God, being omniscient, must have factored in one's prayer, is one question which then arises. But puppet-like status disqualifies characters from tragedy for most conservative commentators, which is to say for most commentators. Oscar Mandel, despite censuring as non-tragic any action not governed by fate, thinks that 'Hardy's philosophy (if we can flatter him with this term) makes tragedy all but impossible'[5] because it reduces his characters to mere pathetic victims. Victims, Mandel believes in now-familiar style, can move us but can't be tragic. For this, one requires a little more spirit and initiative on their part. It might follow from this that Tess Durbeyfield's seduction by Alec D'Urberville was more tragic if it was not a rape than if it was. Mandel also ignores the fact that there are a number of resourceful, adaptable non-fatalists in Hardy's fiction. But if tragic protagonists are at least free to resist their inevitable ruin, doesn't the fact that they do so comment rather unfavourably on their intelligence? It is true that they may not know whether they are predestined to destruction or not, as the Calvinist cannot be sure that she is one of the elect. Anyway, the inevitable is usually unpleasant, and unless you oppose it you may never find out how inevitable it was in the first place. But to battle it with eyes wide open, like Macbeth in his final hours, is to tread a thin line between reckless courage and bovine obduracy. If all the lifeboats have been launched, why not just have a drink in the bar?

Even so, fruitless rebellion is a way of squaring up to death which the modern age has much admired. There is a gloomy existential allure about the idea of going down fighting, which is the final refutation of utilitarianism. Utilitarianism calculates the consequences, whereas this kind of snarling, last-ditch self-affirmation damns them, preferring the aesthetic beauty of an act performed entirely for its own sake, a mutinous expression of value which will get you precisely nowhere. Indeed, the act performed at the point of death will quite literally have no consequences for oneself, and so is peculiarly privileged. Thus the chicken-hearted Hirsch spits defiantly in the face of his executioner in Joseph Conrad's *Nostromo*, affirming his identity for the first and last time. There are similar moments of truth in Dostoevsky. Walter Benjamin sees tragedy as breaching what he calls 'demonic fate', for in it humanity becomes aware that it is superior to its gods. 'There is', he writes, 'no question of the "moral world order" being restored – instead, the moral hero . . . wishes to raise himself by shaking that tormented world'.[6] Tragedy is a strike against destiny, not a submission to it. For Schelling, there is no greater dignity than to know that one is up against a death-dealing power but to wage war on it even so. Thom Gunn speaks in his poem 'Lerici' in *My Sad Captains* of those who when drowning 'Dignify death with fruitless violence, / Squandering all their little left to spend'. If you have to go out, you might as well do so with a grandiloquently rebellious gesture, demonstrating your patrician contempt for the forces which have brought you to nothing, and thus wresting value from the very jaws of ruin. The very way you square up to death reveals an energy which negates it.

This is not the same as desiring death. It is not Antony's 'But I will be / A Bridegroom in my death, and run into't / As to a lover's bed' (*Antony and Cleopatra*, Act 4, sc. 14). Antony will disarm death as one might disarm a tiger or a burglar by moving resolutely towards it, hailing it like a lover and so non-plussing it, divesting it of its daunting majesty. By performing one's death in this style, treating it as an event in one's life rather than just as its biological conclusion, one both embraces and transcends it, freeing oneself of its intimidatory power precisely by snuggling into its erotically alluring bosom. Contrary to Lear's logic, something will come of nothing. By negating the negation, a positivity may emerge. Antony is thus the opposite of the ethically inert Barnadine of *Measure for Measure*, a Musil-like psychopath so spiritually torpid that he objects to being executed only because it interferes with his sleep. Sunk in moral sluggishness, Barnadine is so heedless of death that he must be persuaded actively to perform it ('Persuade this rude wretch willingly to die' (Act 4, sc. 3)) so that his punishment will have some meaning. In the face of the most terrible manifestation of the real, we are required to become accomplished actors. Otherwise death will not constitute an event in Barnadine's life, lapsing from the sphere of value to the realm of blunt biological fact, and the law will stand in danger of being discredited. Death has no power over those who already move among the living dead. Without the complicity of its subject, authority is bereft of legitimacy. Those who live their lives meaninglessly, with all the ataraxy of death, are unnerving parodies of those who strive to appropriate their own deaths in order to live more fully.

Despite being a prisoner, Barnadine is an enviable image of absolute liberty. But he is free only because he cannot invest anything at all with meaning, least of all himself. If he is unperturbed by the thought of death, it is in a sense because he is dead already. His opposite number in the play in this respect is the condemned Claudio, who is terrified of death but who, like Antony, promises himself that 'If I must die, / I will encounter darkness as a bride. / And hug it in mine arms' (Act 3, sc. 1). Only in this way can fate be converted into freedom. Gunn's strenuous swimmers, by contrast, don't accept death at all, but find a way of yoking it violently to the service of life, using it to spit in the face of destiny. Their prodigal self-squandering is the closest they can come to immortality. They are not martyrs, and neither is the death-charmed Antony. The martyr does not want to die, but by accepting his or her death manages to socialize it, puts it on public show and converts it to a sign, places it at the emancipatory service of others and thus salvages some value from it.

The opposite attitude is typical of the later W. B. Yeats. Yeats's 'tragic joy', a doctrine he inherits from Nietzsche, is all about a conceited contempt for death, laughing nonchalantly in its face to show how little heed a gentleman pays to such squalid necessities. Yeats sees himself in grotesque spirit as a wild old wicked man dancing ecstatically on his own grave, or as the haughty, hard-living Anglo-Irish landlord snapping his fingers in the face of the Celtic *canaille* dragging him down into the mire. This insane ecstasy expresses itself not in the chortlings of comedy but in what Simon Critchley calls in another context 'a *manic* laughter: solitary, hysterical, verging on sobbing'.[7] Death is an intolerable discourtesy, and like other such petty-bourgeois vulgarities is best treated by pretending that it isn't there. Yeats will accordingly rise regally above his own extinction, write his own epitaph in order to pre-empt the event, gather it into the artifice of eternity as the gyres which will shuttle him into a superior form of existence are already beginning to whir. All this is less a confrontation with death than a disavowal of it, turning it into a paper tiger so that one can buy one's transcendence of it on the cheap. It is not the response of the Yeats who knew that whatever seeks to be whole has first to be rent, who starts at the cry of a stricken rabbit, or who movingly feints being unable to continue with a poem because of his grief over a dead friend.

There are examples of this militant self-affirmation in the art of classical antiquity. Prometheus is one name which springs to mind. On the whole, however, the idea of the autonomous individual pitting her free will against an external fate is a relatively modern one. There is no exact ancient Greek equivalent for the notion of free will. Prometheus in

Aeschylus's drama, if the play is indeed his, will be free in the future, but, as it were, by necessity; and Zeus in the play is predestined to fall, but not if Prometheus intervenes to save him. The interplay between freedom and providence, in other words, is more subtle than a simple antithesis. The ancient Greeks knew themselves to be morally responsible agents, but not quite in the modern sense morally *autonomous* agents. The boundaries of the self seem for them more fluid and porous than for us. They perceived an irreducible ambiguity in human existence which made it hard to categorize actions simply as 'willed' or 'fated', 'free' or 'necessary'.

Indeed, we late moderns, coming after the heyday of the self-determining subject, are conscious of much the same ambiguity. There could not be a freedom which was not somehow constrained. Constraint is constitutive of liberty, not just a curb on it. Pure freedom, Albert Camus reminds us in *The Rebel*, is the freedom to kill. I am not free to play golf if I have not mastered the rules of the sport, or able to execute my project of self-realization if social conventions and the laws of Nature never stay still for more than a moment. A wholly unpredictable world would be the ruin of our liberty, not the ground of it. Indeed, this would not be a bad description of some Euripidean tragedy, portraying as it does a world so arbitrary and undecidable that the very notion of responsible agency is grievously undermined. It is a lack of determination, not an excess of it, which is stymying here, just as for Bertolt Brecht, with his well-known 'This man's sufferings appal me because they are unnecessary', it is the fact that a tragic action is *not* inevitable which sharpens our sense of outrage.

Whatever champions of contingency we might be, we cannot help expecting with part of our mind that the world will make sense, and feeling vaguely cheated if it does not. Perhaps this accounts for why injustice, which is a kind of senselessness, makes us so furious. Kant's third *Critique* is one instance of this pathos, this hunger for significant pattern in a universe which coldly repudiates it. Since we cannot get by in social life without some notion of debts, deserts, equitable exchanges, it is hard to resist the temptation to read them into the cosmos itself and demand a similar punctilious rationality from its operations. We do not really expect that virtue will be rewarded in our sort of world – not even, these days, in fiction; but it is testimony to what one might call a weak utopian impulse that we still cannot help feeling mildly scandalized when it is not.

Tragedy is not supposed to be a matter of luck; but is it not more tragic to be struck down by an illness which afflicts only one in a million than to die of old age? The medieval notion of the wheel of fortune suggests that tragedy may just randomly afflict you, as opposed to the supposedly more dignified notion that it must arise organically from your own conduct. But it is easy to think of situations in which the former is more tragic, in the common-or-garden sense of more profoundly sorrowful, than the latter. It is not invariably true, as Northrop Frye suggests, that tragedy is 'an epiphany of law, of that which is and must be'.[8] This is just as vapid as most universal statements about the subject. It does not apply, for example, to *'Tis Pity She's a Whore* or *The Cherry Orchard*. The early Walter Benjamin believed just as unquestioningly that all tragedy moved under the sign of fate. The alcoholic Consul of Malcolm Lowry's *Under the Volcano* reflects to himself that 'even the suffering you endure is largely unnecessary . . . It lacks the very basis you require of it for its tragic nature' (ch. 7). Yet Lowry's disintegrating protagonist, whether his torments are necessary or not, has a claim to being one of the great tragic figures of modern fiction.

Geoffrey Brereton makes the astute point that tragic situations need not be irreparable ones, since it makes sense to say 'Surely something can be done to *relieve* the tragic plight of the refugees'.[9] Less promisingly, however, he holds that it is not tragic for a powerful force to defeat a weaker one, since this is a predictable and so non-shocking conclusion. For the United States to wipe North Korea from the planet would thus, one assumes, be regrettable but not tragic or shocking. Pure accident is not tragic in Brereton's eyes, but neither is the unavoidable, such as natural calamities which could not have been foreseen or forestalled. For the phenomenologist Max Schleler, by contrast, it is the avertible which is non-tragic.[10] But Brereton believes that to speak of tragedy, we must be able to say that something went wrong which might have gone right. And this is to say that the idea of tragedy includes a sense of failure lacking in the idea of fate.

Brereton's argument confuses two different cases. It is true that if nobody had ever done anything but crawl in the gutter, and had no conception of any other way of life, it is hard to see how this could be called tragic. Failure and tragedy are comparative terms. But they are also comparative terms in this sense, that if something goes right for me which does not go right for you, you can still be called a tragic failure even if there was never any chance of your being otherwise. Equally, it is not true that the unpreventable is never a matter of failure, and thus of tragedy. You may fail because of forces beyond your control.

It may be that tragedy itself first emerges when a civilization is caught between fate and freedom. 'The tragic sense of responsibility', write J.-P. Vernant and P. Vidal-Naquet, 'emerges when human action becomes the object of reflection and debate while still not being regarded as sufficiently autonomous to be fully self-sufficient.'[11] It emerges, in other words, in some twilight zone between politics and myth, civic and religious allegiance, ethical autonomy and a still cogent sense of the numinous. To be able to pose the question 'To what extent is humanity the source of its own actions?', or 'Am I doing this or not?', suggests both an anxiety in the face of determining forces, and the kind of moral self-reflection which, for the question to be posable at all, can put those forces into question. Democracy brings in its wake a quickened sense of individual self-determination; yet the ancient Greeks are aware that actions acquire their meaning not subjectively but from their location within the symbolic order, an order governed by inscrutable forces (the gods) which are beyond one's dominion, and which like the Lacanian Other have a habit of returning your words and actions to you in scrambled, alien or inverted form. Even so, as with Oedipus, it is through this garbling that their truth is disclosed to you.

For Hegel, it is this disjunction between the self-understanding of human subjects and their actual social and historical positions, between the intentions embodied in human practices and the processes set in motion by them, which is the very dynamic of historical development.[12] That our purposes are outstripped by their effects, that we may not measure up to our own actions, that we always to some degree act in the dark, that understanding is always after the event – these are insights common alike to Hegel and Sophocles. Indeed, it is just this dislocation between impact and intention which the Greeks know as *peripeteia*, suggesting not simply a reversal but a kind of irony, double-effect or boomeranging, aiming for one thing but accomplishing another. Some tragic actions do this on a grand scale, bending themselves spectacularly out of shape; but in doing so, they write large an indeterminacy which belongs to the structure of everyday conduct. It was such *peripeteia*, for example, which led to the British conquering India, at least in the view of the Victorian John Robert Seeley. 'Nothing great that was ever done by Englishmen', Seeley writes, 'was done so unintentionally, so accidentally, as the conquest of India . . . in India we meant one thing, and did another.'[13] Having arrived simply to carry on a spot of harmless trade, the British, such are life's little ironies, unaccountably found themselves owning the place.

Quite who is acting is then as much a question for Greek tragedy as it is for the psychoanalytic theory which casts a backward glance to it. Tragic protagonists receive their actions back from a place which they cannot fathom, a realm of Delphic opaqueness and sibylline slipperiness which is nonetheless implacable in its demands. Just as the Lacanian subject can never be sure whether it has deciphered the demand of the

Other aright, since that demand has to pass through the duplicitous signifier, so the Greek protagonist moves fearfully in a realm of half-legible signs and portents, groping timorously in darkness among baleful powers, perpetually at risk of stumbling up against some forbidden frontier, overreaching himself and bringing himself to nothing. And this state of emergency is routine.

In this perilous condition, there can be no sure distinction between agent and victim, my action and yours, human and divine, subjective intention and objective effect. For tragedy to be possible, the realms of the human and the divine must be both distinguishable and inseparable,[14] caught up in some intricate logic of collusion and opposition. Oedipus, horrified by the oracle's prediction, flees from Corinth straight into the arms of his destiny; in his case, 'I was fated' and 'I doomed myself' come to much the same thing.[15] It does not occur to him in the play to excuse himself because his actions were unintentional, since his guilt is not subjective. Fate and freedom are not so separable: Oedipus's *moira* or allotted portion in life is woven into his conduct in a way best captured by the Freudian concept of overdetermination – so that while it is undeniably he who acts, there is also an otherness which acts in him. Indeed, it may be that Oedipus's tragedy is predicted rather than predetermined – that his actions are freely undertaken even though they are foreseen. For Christian faith, likewise, God sees what I will freely do in the future because he is omniscient, not because he forces me to do it. Nor can God foretell what is inevitably going to happen, since in an open-ended universe there is no such thing as what is inevitably going to happen, and thus nothing to be foretold. Even the Almighty cannot see what doesn't exist. God for Thomas Aquinas is not an external fatality like an earthquake but the very ground of human freedom, so that it is only by a radical dependency on him that we are able to be ourselves. He is the otherness installed at the core of the self which enables us to be the source of our own actions, over which we can thus never assert some proprietorial right. God is the necessity of human freedom.

The characters of Greek tragedy, so Oliver Taplin argues, are represented most of the time not as puppets but as reasonably free agents working out their own destinies. Sometimes, however, they are seen in more fatalistic terms, and at other times in both ways together.[16] Human freedom is expressly denied in the Prologue to Euripides's *Hippolytus*, but there seems nothing foredoomed about, say, the sufferings of Philoctetes. Greek tragedies quite often suggest that their narratives are not in the least predestined, and not one of Aeschylus's characters conforms to the standard model of destiny. Joseph Addison tells us in an essay in *The*

Spectator that tragedy subdues the mind to the dispensations of providence, but there is not always any obvious providence to subdue ourselves to. Eteocles in *Seven Against Thebes* sees himself as doomed to fight his brother, but the Chorus warns him against such corrosive fatalism. The ancient Greeks, a people not unknown for their philosophical proficiency, were perceptive enough to recognize that determination and free agency are subtly interwoven. In the dense intermeshing of human affairs, not least in as exiguous a space as the ancient city state, it is no simple matter to decide whether an action is mine or not, or to unravel the unfathomably complex effects bred by a single act of one's own in the lives of others. It is this condition which we might call the social unconscious.

No action is ever purely one's own, so that it makes sense to ask 'Is this action mine, am I doing something here or not?' as it does not make sense to ask 'Whose pain is this?' (For psychoanalytical thought, it also makes sense to ask: 'Who is desiring here?') There is no unswerving trajectory between intention and effect, which is to say that our actions are 'textual'. The question 'Am I responsible for my actions?' thus cannot be answered in the terms in which it is commonly proposed, since it betrays too thin a conception of what it is to act. Which is not to say that we are thereby absolved from moral responsibility as the mere playthings of the gods, functions of genetic codes or products of social institutions. We are not, for example, to blame for the drastic effects and reorderings which our sheer presence in the social order inevitably brings in its wake; but since some of these consequences are bound to be destructive, it is also a question of what the ancient Greeks saw as objective guilt, Christians call original sin, and the Romantics knew as the nameless crime of existing. Our free actions are inherently alienable, lodging obstructively in the lives of others and ourselves, merging with the stray shards and fragments of others' estranged actions to redound on our own heads in alien form. Indeed, they would not be free actions at all without this perpetual possibility of going astray.

This is a condition as common in Sophocles as it is in Ibsen or Hardy. In the hands of Marx, it is transformed into the theory of commodity fetishism. For George Simmel, it represents the fundamental tragedy of modern culture. Hegel saw fate not as alien, but as a consciousness of one's self as somehow hostile. What the self confronts is not some exterior law, but the law which it has itself established in the course of its conduct, which now looms over it like a curse. Actions sow their consequences interminably in the most unforeseeable spots, rippling out like radio waves in the galaxy; but they can never be recalled to source, so that the moment of free decision, like the jump in Conrad's fiction, is also a kind of irreversible fate. You can decide to jump, but not to undo the decision once it is taken. Such moments of crisis in Conrad – Jim's fatal jump in *Lord Jim*, Winnie Verloc's stabbing of her husband in *The Secret Agent*, whatever it is that Kurtz gets up to in the jungles of *Heart of Darkness* – go significantly unrepresented by the novels themselves, reported at second hand, squinted at sideways or examined only in retrospect. In a deterministic universe, free actions are bound to seem bafflingly opaque, so that while one can portray the moment just before and just after some mighty upheaval of the human subject, the event itself slips through the net of the sayable.

So it is that freedom comes to invert itself into fatality, as projects which seemed at the time transparent and intentional slip from our grasp to form a field of anonymous forces in which we are no longer able to recognize our own confiscated subjectivity. It is this ambiguous condition, one in which we are neither fully responsible nor absolved from guilt, to which Christian theology gives the name of original sin – 'original' not in the sense of dating back to an ominous encounter with a reptile in a garden but in the sense of *a priori*, given from the outset, transcendental rather than transcendent, inescapably entwined with the roots of our sociality. One might call it objective guilt, if that did not have too Stalinist a ring, though the phrase has a Sophoclean ring too. But it is a *felix culpa* or happy Fall, one up into history and liberty rather than down to biology and the beasts, since such built-in destructiveness is a necessary correlative of our freedom, and could be eradicated only along with it.

Perhaps things are tragic not because they are ruled by a pitiless Law but precisely because they are not. After Darwin, we still have development, but development without a *telos*. It is the death of a certain vision of purposive totality. Thomas Hardy's universe is a perspectival one, not a totality, which is to say that his fiction grasps an object in a way which implies a subject. Indeed, this is one source of his celebrated irony, since irony is a clash of perspectives in which the same object appears in different aspects. Perspective is, so to speak, the phenomenological form of irony, irony fleshed out as situation or event. Perhaps the darkling thrush perched high on its branch can see something which you on the ground can't, in which case you should beware of absolutizing your own *fin-de-siècle* moroseness. Absolutizing their own viewpoint is quite often how Hardy's characters come to grief. Such perspectival perception has a characteristic Hardyesque wryness, realism and humility about it, a chastening recognition that there are probably things going on in the middle distance which might turn out to render your own vantage-point invalid. As a character in Büchner's *Danton's Death* observes: 'There is an ear for which the riotous cacophony that deafens us is but a stream of har-monies' (Act 4, sc. 5). Pespectivism may block from us the absolute truth, but it also holds open the possibility of a way of seeing less dispirited than our own, and so tempers the tragic vision. We may not see life steadily and see it whole, but we can always speculate that there *is* such a whole, since our own experience is so palpably partial. The fragmentations of modernity can thus be turned optimistically against themselves.

If Hardy is an atheist, it is because he sees that there is no vanishing-point at which all these perspectives converge. God would be the name for the Omega point at which these conflicting ways of living and seeing might bundle up into a totalized vision; but such a metalanguage is ruled out for Hardy by the nature of an evolutionary universe. Not because evolution testifies to the less than recent or less than edifying origin of the human species, but because it means a world of clashing, angled, decentred life-forms. It is reality itself, not just the art which portrays it, which is provisional, selective, unfinished, so that the only truly realist art would be a detotalized one, a 'series of seemings' as Hardy himself put it. In a body-blow to classical liberalism, truth and partisanship are no longer at daggers drawn. Bias is somehow built into the world. The-ology is thus a subject without an object. It is in this sense that Darwin puts paid to divinity, not just in the matter of monkeys.

Totality, then, is now a scientific as well as a philosophical non-starter. Even if God existed he would be irrelevant, since the structure of the world is such that we could not live our lives at such a transcendent point. There could simply be no human life there, any more than there could be on Pluto. Hardy would have had no problem with Derrida's appar-ently outlandish assertion that 'there is no outside-text'. There is nothing, that is to say, which is not intricately woven through with other morsels of the world, no identity which stands proud of its historical context. God, like little Father Time in *Jude the Obscure*, or indeed like a naturalistic nov-elist, might have the unnerving ability to view our lives in the round; but this, as with Father Time, is allied with his impotence. And if God is a logical impossibility or absentee landlord in this piecemeal, partisan world, it follows that an Immanent Will or President of the Immortals must be just the same, which at least rules out those kinds of tragic fatal-ism along with deistic optimism. That there is no totality is for Hardy a fact rather than a value. A non-totalized world is no more necessarily bleak or malevolent than one made of green cheese – unless by bleak and malevolent you mean, as Hardy's characters sometimes mean, that the world doesn't underwrite any particular human perspective.

This may be thought tragic, but it could just as easily be seen as liber-ating. If reality does not automatically speak the language of revolt, neither is it fluent in the idiom of reaction. It does, however, speak the language of freedom, if only in the negative sense that, having no particular opinions of its own, it throws you back upon your own decisions. The universe no longer speaks a specific language, which then leaves you free to invent your own. But the price one pays for this is to surrender the comforts of naturalism. Nature no longer grounds human value, so that humanity's freedom is also its tragic solitude. The schism which opens between Nature and culture is at once the source of our dignity and the truth of our alienation. We are still in a sense grounded in Nature – but only in the ironic sense that the contingent nature of consciousness is now a material fact, its superfluity confirmed as structural. Our divorce from Nature is natural, not just a queasy feeling or state of mind. For T. H. Huxley rather than the naturalistic Herbert Spencer, we must construct our cultures against the grain of Nature, a proposal which is as courageous as it is depressing. If teleologies have broken down, then the world has no direction; but this also means the collapse of malignant teleologies like Schopenhauer's, freeing us from being the pliable instruments of providence into a dangerous but delightful autonomy.

Evolution, then, is an antidote to tragic absolutism, materialism a riposte to the metaphysical. There is always another way of seeing where that one came from, to ironize one's own standpoint; and this is a pluralism rooted in material struggle, in the clash of life-forms rather than in some blithe Arnoldian equipoise. Yet if this perspectivism is in one sense at odds with tragedy, it is in another sense the inner structure of it. Hardy's novels are constantly showing us how what appears vital from one viewpoint figures as marginal from another, so that tragic collision is built into a clash of interpretations. A hermeneutical world is likely to be a violent one. Besides, if life-forms are intricately but not *organically* bound up with each another, you can never calculate exact outcomes, any more than you can in the market-place. Actions taken at one spot in this great web will resonate throughout the whole tangled skein, breeding noxious effects where one least expects them.

So tragedy and irony are bound up together. For Hardy, tragedy springs from the way things are randomly interwoven, not from their predestined nature. That everything is subtly bound up with everything else is by no means an invariably comic way of seeing, whatever Hegel or Joyce may have considered. It is, for example, a property of paranoia, which Freud thought the closest thing to philosophy. The ending of *Middlemarch*, to be sure, will try with a certain pathos to lend this textuality a comic twist: if nothing exists in isolation, then the obscure acts of goodness that a much-chastened Dorothea Brooke will perform in the future will diffuse their benign effects through the web of society as a whole. To act anywhere is to act everywhere. It is one of the more subtle rationales for reformism.

There are other senses in which freedom and fatality are twinned. 'Self-determination' is the modern jargon for freedom; in Spinoza's view a free animal is not undetermined but self-determining. A free being is autonomous rather then unconstrained, meaning that the law according to which it lives is its own. Liberty is not the antithesis of law, but the self-bestowal of it. And since the law of one's being is absolute, freedom is rooted in a kind of necessity. But the term 'self-determination' also suggests setting limits to one's liberty in the act of exercising it, diminishing the self in the process of realizing it. The self-determining animal is also a self-thwarting one, which simply to fulfil its boundless freedom must become a slave to finitude. To practise one's freedom is thus to betray it. The subject is lord over itself, but therefore its own obedient vassal. In opening up horizons, we ineluctably impose frontiers; in choosing one course of conduct, we leave others eternally unrealized, allowing such absences to shape the future. The future is composed quite as much of what we did not do, as of what we did. To act in one way is to leave ourselves with only a meagre set of further options, so that we can quickly paint ourselves into a corner. Many a tragic character ends up by doing this. The Good Angel of Marlowe's *Doctor Faustus* makes it clear to Faustus that his damnation is not inevitable, that he can still repent, but Faustus has so hardened his heart, or perhaps had it hardened for him by a Calvinist God, that this possibility has been thrust out of reach. Or think of Schiller's Wallenstein, who acts too late and finds himself manipulated by forces beyond his control. In this sense, we do not need the gods to deprive us of choices, coerce us into tragic dilemmas or compel us down cul-de-sacs, since we are perfectly capable of doing all this for ourselves.

This twinning of freedom and fatality can also take a political form. Rather as Descartes provisionally surrenders what he knows in order to repossess it on a surer footing, so the bourgeois individual must freely surrender to the state his private identity in order to receive it back, incomparably enriched, in the form of public citizenship. What you receive back in this mighty exchange of identities is not just your transfigured self, now in its authentically communal form, but all other such corporate identities along with it, which are similarly enriched by your own self-giving. Since the self-subjection must be general, the upshot is liberty all round. A mutual submission cancels all the way through. As a democrat or republican, I submit myself to the very law which I simultaneously impose upon you, finding my autonomy in this necessity just as you find yours. Freedom is obedience to self-imposed sovereignty.

This, roughly speaking, is Jean-Jacques Rousseau's doctrine in *The Social Contract*. But if the private individual *must* make such a move for republican society to survive, is not her decision for freedom itself coerced? It seems that we are forced freely to submit to the coercion of a law which will make us free. Resolving this conundrum is no doubt one aim of Rousseau's notion of the General Will, that built-in predisposition to reach a consensus of true interests which all individuals share, and which is the universal, quasi-transcendental condition of any specific social compact. The General Will cannot be wrong, since it cannot be wrong to will the good and desire a peaceable social existence; but people can certainly be mistaken about what counts as these things in practice, not least the chauvinistic, illiberal, oligarchically minded Rousseau himself. The notion of the General Will thus places an end-stop on the regress of freedom and coercion, since it is itself really neither. It does not make sense to speak of willing the General Will, since we do not will the rational conditions which make for sociability; but neither are they forced upon us.

To be free, then, means to will the necessary conditions of freedom. And if it is liberty we desire, we have no choice about this. So liberty and necessity go hand in hand. But it is also possible to combine the two through a kind of *amor fati*, hugging one's chains and making one's destiny one's choice. This is to treat freedom as the knowledge of necessity, embracing the inevitable in the form of a free decision. For the German philosophical heritage, as we shall see in a moment, this is one way in which the idea of tragedy can solve the problems of post-Kantian modernity, uniting freedom and determinism, the noumenal and the phenomenal, in a single act. To be 'absolute for death', in the words of the Duke of *Measure for Measure*, is to embrace one's own finitude; and it is in this active anticipation of an ending, which for Heidegger is possible only for *Dasein* or that mode of being distinctive of the human, that an authentic existence lies. It is in this moment of truth, for Heidegger, that *Dasein* is free.[17]

Yet for *Being and Time* our being-towards-death is a fact as well as a value, since it is *Dasein*'s lack of totality, the fact that it is always pitched out ahead of itself, which generates the movement by which it anticipates at every moment that elusive self-completion which only death can signify. And since this is the movement which we know as temporality, it is death which brings *Dasein* into existence as a temporal being, as well as a finite one aware of its lack.[18] Death is foreshadowed in the unfinishedness of every one of *Dasein*'s instants, which is no doubt one of the several meanings of St Paul's 'we die every moment'. And though this Heideggerian doctrine was to find some sinister resonances in the death cult of fascism, its fidelity to lack and finitude, along with its sense of death as a detotalizing force, could also foster an altogether more radical politics.

The permutations of freedom and necessity vary from thinker to thinker. For Thomas Hobbes, to be free means to be unhampered by external forces; but this is quite compatible with determinism, since the opposite of determinism for Hobbes is not freedom but contingency. Or there is the case of Machiavelli, who comments that 'prudent men always and in all their actions make a favour of doing things even though they would of necessity be constrained to do them anyway'.[19] He himself views Fortune as something less than dire necessity: a man of exceptional *virtu* or civic spirit can always master it, as in the notorious chapter 25 of *The Prince*, where he speaks of Fortune as a woman who needs to be taken by force. The same may happen in tragic art: Calderon's Segismundo in *Life is a Dream* finally masters his fate, whereas Don Lope of the same author's *Three Judgements In One* does not. Or there is Frederick Engels, for whom freedom is famously the knowledge of necessity, in the sense that only by grasping the laws of Nature and society can we mould them into the medium of our self-realizing.

Again, there are the existentialists, who stand Engels's formula on its head, as in W. H. Auden's Sartrian claim that 'We live in freedom by necessity'. Freedom is now a condition to which we are condemned, a force which will have its own sweet way with all the intractability of doom. Fate is not just what frustrates our freedom, but what binds us to it. You can believe with the Sartre of *The Flies* that men and women are free but do not know it, and flee from this frightful responsibility to the deceitful solace of the Law; or you can hold with Rousseau that if human beings cravenly refuse their freedom then they should have it forced upon them. For the Sartre of *Being and Nothingness*, the past is unchangeable, but it does not determine the present. On the contrary, it is the present which determines the past, both in the sense that I assume responsibility for all that I have ever done, and in the sense that I can always define my past in a way which contributes to my freedom in the present. If you want to have a particular sort of past, you have to act in a particular way.

For the Walter Benjamin of *The Origin of German Tragic Drama*, freedom and fatality are alike in that both turn their back on the mechanistic realm of causality. For Friedrich Nietzsche, the two realms converge in art, where the contest between freedom and compulsion becomes undecid-

116

able. You can say that a poet or painter creates freely, but this freedom seems to spring into being with all the irresistible force of a tidal wave. Much the same could be said of the 'authentic' action of the existentialists. What defines your freedom, in the end, is what you find you cannot walk away from. And as far as this goes, you do not have all that much choice. Ironically, it is what we cannot help doing which is the key to our liberty. This kind of compulsion, a modern-day equivalent of the ancient Greek *daimon*, can be found in Kant's notion of freedom as fidelity to a law which bears in on us with ineluctable authority. For Kant, our belief in freedom is itself necessary; indeed, it is as much a necessity of reason as our belief in the law of contradiction. The Kantian moral law is a version of ancient Greek destiny for the modern age, and just as sublimely unintelligible. There are moral as well as material necessities. Among these would seem the impulses to freedom and justice, which will not let us rest until they have had their way. It is for this reason that we have grounds for political hope, not because of some postmodern fantasy of the death of necessity and the endless pliability of the world, a vision which no doubt derives as much from cosmetic surgery and short-term employment contracts as it does from Jean-François Lyotard.

There is another sense in which freedom and determination are linked. If we can act upon the world, then it must be determinate, already shaped in a way which enables our agency. But if that agency is to be real, the world must also be open-ended, less than fully formed or ontologically complete. One can express this duality in temporal terms, as Kant does: the past is a matter of causal determinism, while the future is a question of ends and thus of freedom.[20] What is fact from one perspective is value from another. There is a void in reality which our free agency needs to fill. For Sartre and Lacan, our subjectivity is itself a kind of void or *néant*, the sheer process of negation through which one situation transcends itself into another so as to constitute what we call history. The root of being is lack of being. And though this history feels open and unpredictable as we are fashioning it, it may present itself in retrospect with all the necessity of a natural law. As Fredric Jameson puts it, historiography shows us 'why what happened (at first received as "empirical" fact) had to happen the way it did'.[21] Freedom, once narrativized, reads like necessity. An example of this is Goethe's *Wilhelm Meister*, in which, as Jameson points out, what seems fortuitous at the time can be retrospectively read as the plottings of the novel's secret brotherhood, and thus as providential.[22] And this despite the fact that Goethe himself distinguished between chance and fate, assigning the former to the novel and allotting the latter to tragedy. The historical narrative, too, may appear one of either freedom or necessity, depending on whether you are living it forward or reading it backward.

Aristotle seems to contrast not freedom and necessity, but inner and outer necessities. There is a dash of psychological determinism about his thought. Indeed, if the *hamartia* or moral flaw which supposedly causes tragedy is built into our temperament, and is less sin than innocent error, how can we be held responsible for it? Necessity is not always outside us: there is one's *daimon* or bent of character, which for both Goethe and Lessing had all the force of destiny. An 'authentic' action is one which springs from the core of the self; but you might therefore quite as well call it irresistible as call it free. For Goethe, there can be a tragic collision between one's purely empirical freedom and the inexorable dynamic of one's inner character. Such fate is a central theme of *Elective Affinities*. Garcia Lorca's tragedies share much the same view: 'You have to follow the path of your blood', as the Woodcutter of *Blood Wedding* counsels the restive young bride who runs off with an old flame on her wedding day. For D. H. Lawrence, nothing is more coercive than what he calls spontaneous-creative life.

In his *Philosophy of Art*, Schelling assumes that tragedy must deal in destiny, and asks whether there can be a modern version of it. He replies that Shakespeare replaces fate with character, which now stands forth as an insuperable necessity. For the ancient Greeks, he argues, the gods often inflicted error on humanity, and their brand of fate is thus flawed; but this cannot be the case with the perfect God of Christianity. So fate as a cause of tragic downfall must shift instead to character, which can no longer be regarded as free. It is the destiny of our selves which proves hardest to elude. It is a doctrine which leaves some Romanticism with a problem: if character is destiny in the sense that one cannot be false to oneself, what value is there in being true?

It is simple-minded, then, to pitch freedom against fate as an inside against an outside. Or, indeed, as an autonomous subject against a recalcitrant object. In this respect, one might contrast Shelley's *Prometheus Unbound*, with its polarizing of an oppressive God and a glorified rebel, with Aeschylus's rather more nuanced drama on the subject. In the modern epoch, the pact which Greek tragedy strikes between fate and freedom begins to break up, as a self-determining subject squares up to an external compulsion. As freedom becomes less a description of a situation than an inner faculty, the idea of free will is born, and along with it a number of Cartesian conundrums. Is a free action always the result of an act of will? When I act freely, am I conscious of an act of volition? Or does it just mean that nobody is holding a gun to my head? If there is something called an act of will, does it occur a split second before the action itself, or does it accompany it throughout, fading gradually away like a painful twinge or a delectable taste? On this view, we are free inside, but everywhere empirically in chains; and how we can inhabit both of these spheres simultaneously is a question which Kant finds notoriously difficult to answer.

It can be claimed that it is tragedy, rather than Kant, which supplies the solution. It is a solution which Hegel finds physically incarnate in Greek theatre, as the free activity of Spirit is distanced by masks, ritual, dance and Chorus into the anonymous image of destiny. Fate is just the outer garb of freedom, the expressionless features it turns to the world. If tragedy reconciles freedom and necessity, then it bridges the gap between pure and practical reason which the critical philosophy itself could never span.[23] Simon Critchley argues that this, in effect, is the reason for the 'massive privileging of the tragic' in the post-Kantian era, a theme 'which has an almost uncanny persistence in the German intellectual tradition'.[24] The role of the aesthetic in general is now to bridge the chasm between Nature and freedom, fact and value, epistemology and ethics; but for Hegel, Schelling, Schlegel, Hölderlin, Hebbel, Schopenhauer, Heidegger and their progeny, tragedy goes one step further and actually thematizes the contest between freedom and fate. This is why, for most of these thinkers, it is the most precious aesthetic form of all. Tragedy is an imaginary solution to a real contradiction plaguing modernity, and is thus the very prototype of ideology. Oscar Mandel writes that 'the tragic idea survived the loss of the gods and it survived the loss of the tragic hero';[25] but if it did so, it is largely because it went on to play a key role in the internal conflicts of bourgeois culture.

If this is so, one can appreciate why the philosophy of tragedy is for the most part so airily indifferent to human suffering. What is at stake here is less an experience than a theoretical problem. Such theorizing fails to heed Adorno's warning that 'if thought is not measured by the extremity which eludes the concept, it is from the outset in the nature of the musical accompaniment with which the SS liked to drown out the screams of its victims'.[26] And since the theoretical problems at issue are no longer of any great moment, at least in the ways they were classically framed, tragedy is no longer the supremely cherished form that it once was. It has not died, just ceased to be so ideologically crucial. For the post-Kantians, however, tragedy is of well-nigh divine importance. It is, in effect, a secular version of God, since nobody unites the two realms in question more dexterously than a being whose freedom is a necessity of his nature – the only being, moreover, whose existence is actually necessary, unlike otters, chief executives and lumps of limestone. Schelling's philosophy culminates in what he names Indifference, a state in which freedom and necessity blend undecidably into one; and this – another profane version of the Almighty – is the essence of tragedy, too. Tragedy achieves this blending in a number of ways. It may end by incorporating the hero's free action into its own majestic teleology; or it may demonstrate how that freedom was always already reckoned into the equation, and so is itself a kind of necessity; or it may show, conversely, how necessity itself is not blind but, rather like the Kantian sublime, has the enigmatic purposiveness of a subject. Or, as we have seen already, it may show the hero freely submitting to his fate, choosing the inevitable and so reclaiming it for human liberty.

In tragedy, as in Schelling's account of human nature, the conditions are ripe for 'necessity to be victorious without freedom succumbing, and in a reverse fashion for freedom to triumph without the course of necessity being interrupted'.[27] The tragic hero, Schelling argues, can rise above necessity through his disposition towards it, and so be vanquished and triumphant at the same time. In his *Letters on Dogmatism and Criticism*, he argues with a faintly perverse flavour that the supreme testimony to human freedom, so Greek tragedy demonstrates, is voluntarily to accept one's punishment for an unavoidable crime. In allowing the hero to struggle against fate, and so to behave as though he were free, Greek tragedy pays tribute to his liberty. Providence shapes our ends, but in so doing contrives in us the consoling illusion that we do so ourselves. Ishmael reflects in Melville's *Moby-Dick* that though he cannot tell why the Fates set him down for a whaling voyage, one which will end in tragic disaster, he can see a little 'into the springs and motives which being cunningly presented to me under various disguises . . . cajol[ed] me into the delusion that it was a choice resulting from my own unbiased freewill and discriminating judgement' (ch. 7).

Like the Sartrian existentialist, the Greek protagonist in Schelling's eyes chooses to be responsible for all that he has done, wittingly or not; but since he can do so only by embracing death, he loses this freedom in the act of gaining it. A textbook example would be Heinrich von Kleist's *Prince Friedrich von Homberg*, in which Homberg is sentenced to death by the Prussian state and subsequently pardoned, but determines to be executed anyway so as to glorify the law, exercise his supreme freedom, and accept responsibility for his actions. In a final irony, the gallantry of this resolution saves him in any case. The hero of Kleist's story *Michael Kohlhaas* also submits to his execution as his just deserts. By sacrificing his own finitude, the hero identifies with fate and in doing so achieves a transcendence of it. The power to abandon one's creaturely existence must be a power which springs from beyond it; so that in sacrificing

120

oneself to destiny one makes oneself its equal. Tragedy thus represents both victory and defeat for freedom, but also for necessity; each is simultaneously conqueror and conquered. In English writing, one thinks of the ending of George Eliot's *The Mill on the Floss*, or of Milton's *Samson Agonistes*, in which Samson can triumph over his Philistine enemies only by bringing himself to ruin. In psychoanalytical terms, the oedipally insubordinate hero worsts the Name of the Father, but expiates his guilt for this transgression by being crushed in his turn.

Death itself dismantles the opposition between fate and freedom, since it is in one sense preordained and in another sense accidental. We cannot avoid dying in some kind of way, but what kind of way is a contingent rather than pre-scripted affair. The coroner's category of accidental death applies in a sense to every expiry there is, if by accident we mean less chance or misfortune than non-necessity. One might always not have died of bowel cancer or toppling drunkenly into Vesuvius, whereas it would not be possible not to die at all. Death is thus in one sense always accidental and in another sense always predetermined. It also undoes the opposition between the immanent and the externally caused, since even if we are run down by a truck our death remains an internal affair, a closing down of our biological systems, just as much as if we expire of old age. In this sense, all death is natural, even death on the gallows or in the trenches. Death is a link between the alien and the intimate, between mighty determining forces and the secret recesses of subjectivity. Like the desire with which it is so closely affiliated, it is at once inalienably mine and utterly impersonal, existential value and everyday fact, that which springs from the depths of my being yet is intent on annihilating it.

In an Hegelian age of political hope, tragedy is a negative demonstration of the supremacy of Reason and freedom. In staging a passing disruption of providence, it serves to show just how triumphantly invincible it is. Driven underground by the enlightened humanitarianism of the earlier eighteenth century, tragedy reappears at the heart of Europe in the century's closing decades as a negative image of utopia, the lineaments of a fathomless liberty beyond all law, and so – once again – as a secularized theology. The tragic protagonist fails in the face of an indomitable destiny, just as the imagination shrinks and quails when confronted with the fearful majesty of the sublime. But both failures yield us a glimpse of a higher order of freedom and justice, which can be lit up only by the flames which consume the protagonist. In both tragedy and the sublime, the infinite is made negatively present by throwing the limits of finitude into exposure. By the inevitable collapse of whatever strikes against its authority, an ultimately unfigurable Reason is brought dimly into focus.

In this sense, tragedy overturns rebellion and reinstates the Law. Yet in doing so it reveals that the love of freedom which drives the hero to his death is also its own. Destiny is simply the mask worn by liberty, compulsion the way Reason makes itself felt in the phenomenal world. There can thus be no final antagonism between authority and revolt. Freedom, did the insurgent hero but recognize it, is the stuff of the very sovereignty against which he pits his forces. And tragedy is the name we give to the moment of truth in which this recognition breaks upon him. In the act of being beaten down, the tragic hero is forced to contrast his own puny strength with the power of providence, and in doing so discovers that same infinity of power within himself. Just as the sublime throws the limits of our understanding into stark relief, while yielding us in the process an oblique sense of infinity, so tragedy humiliatingly exposes the limits of our powers, but in thus objectifying our finitude makes us aware of an unfathomable freedom within ourselves. By being newly aware of the boundaries of our being, we sense an eternity of power beyond them. The stupendous secret to which tragedy makes us privy is that this fifth-columnist Law was on the inside of us all the time, covertly at work in our very drive to overthrow it. Law and desire, had we but known it, were in cahoots behind our back from the outset.

So defeat is also victory, since the power which crushes us is shown to be our own free spirit in objectified form. And necessity is worsted as well as triumphant, unmasked as liberty in misrecognized guise. The hero submits to death, which may seem a victory for fate. But since he does so freely, knowing that death is his own gateway to infinity, he transcends fate in that very act. The freedom by which he embraces his finitude implicitly disproves it. The conservative moral of tragedy is that there is no need to revolt, since the Law is the law of freedom. The radical message is that you need to revolt to find this out – that only the sacrifice of the finite can manifest the truth that infinite freedom is the secret of the world. Politically speaking, then, this version of tragedy is an appropriate form for those who still affirm liberty but are distinctly allergic to actual revolution. In the aftermath of the French Revolution, such ideologues were scarcely in short supply.

For Schlegel as much as for Schelling, tragedy deals with a sublime battle between freedom and necessity.[28] Friedrich Hebbel speaks of the strife between the individual and the Idea within which his claim takes shape. The claim is no purely individual affair, to be set against the public sphere; it is itself a matter of necessity, driven on by the world-historical process. Yet it proves fatal to the protagonist who makes it. D. D. Raphael, along with a whole raft of twentieth-century critics, finds in tragic art a collision between the forces of necessity and a self-conscious resistance to their sway.[29] For Paul Ricoeur, the tragic narrative is also one of destiny – but it is a doom put into suspense by the free resistance of the hero, which then causes fate to hesitate and appear like contingency. It is as though the freedom of the hero introduces a vital germ of uncertainty into the heart of destiny, and it is from this seed that the tragic action flowers.[30]

There are problems, however, with this antithetical vision. Tragedy for this vein of thought is supposed to be immanent, arising from the protagonist's own actions. And this immanence is closely allied to the idea of fate. By banishing extraneous causes, tragedy becomes a closed world with all the taut coherence of destiny. It works by its own internal logic, just like its self-determining hero, who by staying austerely faithful to his own being comes to resemble a work of art. Like the artefact, the hero steadfastly unfolds the implications of his situation without straying into the superfluous or accidental. Yet there is a moral price to be paid for this aesthetic purity. If the protagonist is really so self-contained, he risks becoming responsible for his own undoing and hence dispelling our pity. To evoke sympathy, his actions must breed effects or spring from causes for which he is not entirely to blame. As Paul Ricoeur points out, the Greeks in Aeschylus's *The Persians* can feel compassion for their Persian enemies partly because they can see that it is the gods who have crushed them.[31] Mount Olympus thus lets humanity off the moral hook. But if this in turn is overstressed, what becomes of the hero's self-moving powers, the very essence of his freedom? How can his actions be allowed to escape his control if his autonomy is to be complete?

In practice, of course, tragic actions are never so self-contained. Their agents are brought low not just by their own contrivance but by external forces – say, sheer accident, or the malevolence of fate. But fate is rather too metaphysical a concept for modernity, even if it has its own ersatz versions of it; and accident is too demeaning a cause of tragic catastrophe. 'It is no longer possible', declares Yeats, 'to write *The Persians, Agincourt, Chevy Chase*: Some blunderer has driven his car on to the wrong side of the road – that is all.'[32] A hero cannot come to grief by getting his cloak entangled in his chariot wheels, since such random events are essentially meaningless, and there must be nothing in tragedy which fails to signify. Tragedy is in this sense the paradigm of art in general. As Georg Lukács remarks of the form: 'All the relationships of life have been suppressed so that the relationship with destiny may be created'.[33] To be fated is to have one's end in one's origin, devaluing the empty time in between; and since suffering is a question of temporality, this may well be downgraded along with it. Trifling occurrences are too vulgar for tragic status, as Mandel reminds us: *The Duchess of Malfi* fails in his view to qualify as tragic because the Duchess, as women will, 'babbles a little, and thereby fatally reveals to the evil Bosola that Antonio is her husband', while Agamemnon meets his death 'simply by returning home', a lamentably unglamorous way of departing from this world.[34]

Chance, like the unique particular, is not intelligible to classical scientific inquiry; it is illegible, non-typical, and nothing more can be learned from it than from a gust of wind or scattering of raindrops. What is in fact being rejected here is less the accidental than the empirical, which poses a perpetual threat to tragic essentialism. Indeed, the division within tragedy between the essential and the empirical is reflected in the discrepancy between tragic theory and tragic practice. The former is really a kind of Platonic version of the latter, shorn of its embarrassing inconsistencies, so that tragedy can be extracted as an ideology or theoretical position in its own right from a host of deeply divergent texts. What tragic essentialism finds distasteful is randomness, contingency, the unravelling text of the empirical and everyday – in a word, comedy. Comedy is the domain of the non-intransigent, of those crafty, compliant, unkillable forms of life which get their way by yielding. Its adaptive, accommodatory spirit is thus the very opposite of tragic deadlock and clenched resolution.

But accident is also a threat to tragedy because the agent ceases to be the source of her own action, lapsing instead into ignoble passivity. The refusal of accident, the necessary immanence of tragedy, and the self-affirmation of the agent, are closely allied conceptions. The great modern-day philosopher of tragic contingency is the Heidegger of *Being and Time*, for whom authenticity lies in seizing upon one's 'thrownness', the fact that one has been pitched headlong into existence without ever having been invited, and living it out with all the resoluteness of a preordained project. But there is another motive for the refusal of accident in tragic theory. If tragedy springs not from chance but from the protagonist's own conduct, then this may risk alienating our sympathies, but it might also serve to temper the injustice of the tragic suffering itself. To the modern mind, this is hardly the case if the tragedy is sprung simply by a blunder. But if you think of *hamartia*, somewhat implausibly, as a moral transgression, or consider like the Greeks that subjective guilt is not the point at issue, then the hero remains partly to blame, and the pain inflicted on him seems less gratuitous. You can even interpret the tragic flaw less as a defect which causes the tragedy than as a blemish which makes the hero's sufferings more palatable. Even so, the problem is not easily settled. Either tragedy results from accident, which is undignified; or from destiny, which is unjust; or from the hero's own actions, which makes him unpalatable. The best solution is a careful balance of the last two, but this is not easy in an age which has little belief in destiny in the first place.

The irony of *peripeteia* is that what you do is and is not your own. No doubt this is what Northrop Frye has in mind when he claims in *Anatomy of Criticism* that tragedy involves both incongruity and inevitability. Cleanth Brooks dismisses the idea that suffering is ever just imposed on tragic protagonists; they must incur it by their own free decisions. It is hard to see how this is true of Iphigenia, Desdemona or Hedvig Ekdal of Ibsen's *The Wild Duck*. It also comes embarrassingly close to implying that such protagonists are responsible for their own undoing, and so get what they deserve. A humanist insistence on free agency threatens ironically to issue in a lack of humanity. No doubt spotting this danger, Brooks hastens to add that the hero 'at the least . . . finally wills to accept [his suffering] as pertaining to the nature of things'.[35] It is not clear why you should accept your suffering if it is not your fault, or quite what distinguishes a hero here from a masochist. Brooks thinks that one should accept one's tragic anguish because it brings 'knowledge of the full meaning of one's ultimate commitments',[36] which seems a rather drastic way of discovering them. Perhaps academic types set rather more store on self-knowledge than those less eager to wade through mayhem and misery to attain it.

Many so-called accidents are not in fact meaningless because they are not in fact accidents. Just as purposive action always has its residue of the non-intended, as the notion of *peripeteia* would suggest, so non-intentional actions are also the by-product of purposes. And most so-called natural disasters are disastrous but not natural. Besides, to call the world arbitrary and chaotic is to make sense of it in a particular way. Virginia Woolf made a distinguished career out of doing so. It also carries with it a number of sensible implications: that we are vulnerable to chance and should be on our guard against the unpredictable, that it is dangerous to assume that we ever are in total command, that we can only provisionally plan for the future, and so on. The random and arbitrary are not in this sense beyond meaning. How the Woolfs of this world *know* that the human condition is chaotic is another question. One would seem to need a powerfully totalizing perspective to assert any such thing.

But the downgrading of accident has deeper roots. For Raymond Williams, it springs from 'the separation of ethical control and, more critically, human agency, from our understanding of social and political life'.[37] What kind of a society is it, he inquires, which can find no ethical content or agency in events such as war, famine, work, traffic and politics, but which treats them instead as sheer contingencies? In any case, you can trivialize events by calling them destined just as much as by calling them accidental. 'Does not the term "tragedy", Slavoj Žižek asks, 'at least in its classical sense, still imply the logic of Fate, which is rendered ridiculous apropos of the Holocaust? To say that the annihilation of the Jews obeyed a hidden necessity of Fate is already to gentrify it.'[38] Žižek is mistaken to assume that tragedy, even classical tragedy, invariably involves fate; but he is right to see that the notion can actually sanitize suffering, and Euripides is unlikely to have demurred.

For scholastic thought, it would be self-contradictory to see accident as essential. For Hegel, the accidental cannot be the typical, and it is on the latter that tragedy turns. Yet dramas like Sean O'Casey's *Juno and the Paycock* are crammed with contingencies while being none the less tragic for that. There is nothing predestined in the downfall of the Boyle family, unless bad company, chronic fantasizing, alcoholic bravado, sexual seduction, financial fecklessness, political betrayal and an aversion to work are all disabilities inflicted by the gods. Yet it is just this pattern of historical accidents which can then be seen as typical of a more general condition. And while there is nothing preordained about poverty and sexual exploitation, there is nothing accidental about them either. Like most of social existence, they fall somewhere between the two. When Raymond Williams speaks of revolution as 'the inevitable working through of a deep and tragic disorder',[39] he does not mean that it is inscribed in the stars, but neither does he mean that it is fortuitous. Many tragedies are tragedies of fortune rather than fate; their point is not that wicked deeds backfire by some inexorable logic, but that life is a precarious business for the wicked and innocent alike. It is too arbitrary to have a shape about it, whether malign or beneficent.

In Voltaire's sentimental tragedies, chance tends to replace destiny. The plays stress the avoidability of catastrophe, and tend to conclude with compromise and reconciliation. If this is an expression of bourgeois optimism, it has its socialist equivalent. For Bertolt Brecht, a rejection of metaphysical fate must be actually built in to the dramatic form itself. What he rather misguidedly calls 'Aristotelian theatre' – misguided because Aristotle, as we have seen, believes in unified plots but says nothing about fate – presents a seamless narrative which denies the audience the freedom of the subjunctive mood, thus reinforcing its political fatalism. A dramatic structure thus precipitates a whole ideology. His own 'epic' or episodic theatre, by contrast, 'would at all costs avoid bundling together the events portrayed and presenting them as an inexorable fate . . . nor does it wish to make the spectator the victim, so to speak, of an hypnotic experience in the theatre'.[40]

A unity of dramatic form reflects itself in the doped consciousness of the spectator, which needs to be stirred into self-division by the joltings of montage, disconnected episode, contradictory character, multiple possibility. Brecht seems oddly to believe that mutability is inherently good, rather as Samuel Johnson maintained that it was inherently evil. If there is a fate, then for Brecht it is 'no longer a single coherent power; rather there are fields of force which can be seen radiating in opposite directions'.[41] Like many a radical, he obediently subscribes to a reactionary definition of tragedy, which he then predictably proceeds to spurn. Tragedy is about inevitability, and thus a politically noxious form. Yet the anti-determinist *Mother Courage* is a supremely accomplished piece of tragic theatre, even though its protagonist is a low-life, hard-bitten opportunist who learns nothing from her sufferings. If Brecht is anti-tragic because he believes that tragedy can be avoided, so are a great many tragedies.

Like Williams, however, he is too reticent about the fact that there are tragedies which, as it happens, cannot be avoided. 'As it happens' is an essential qualification: most tragic episodes which prove inevitable do so for contingent reasons. Given that the hospital was out of drugs, the child was bound to die. On the other hand, 'most' is an essential qualification: even with well-equipped hospitals, there are always likely to be those dead before their time. Tragedy of some sort is in this sense unavoidable; but this is not because it is the gods' generous-hearted way of giving us a chance to demonstrate how resplendently robust we are. Fatalism of a sort, despite Brecht's choleric protests against it, is sometimes a reasonable response. There are indeed situations about which there is nothing to be done. By the end of the novel, there is probably no way of saving Jude Fawley or Tess Durbeyfield. There are also dilemmas, as Racine, Ibsen and Hardy knew, in which you cannot move either way without creating intolerable damage. What matters is neither optimism nor pessimism but realism, which depending on the situation will sometimes assume the one form and sometimes the other. Albert Camus reminds us in *The Rebel* that the knowledge that suffering and injustice will never be entirely eliminated is part of the experience of tragedy. But this does not mean that there is nothing to be done in any situation.

There is another sense in which contingency can be tragic. Late modernity, as we shall see later, is plagued by a sense of gratuitousness, lacking any solid foundation to its forms of life. The scandal and glory of any particular event is that it might just as well never have been; and this is true also of the work of art, which must now incorporate into its forms an ironic awareness of its own arbitrary, ungrounded nature, as the closest it can approach to what used to be called truth. If the work of art, like the sphere of ethics, must now become its own law, legislate for itself, it is largely because there is nothing but quicksand beneath its feet. The

127

price these spheres must pay for their proud, new-found autonomy is thus distressingly high. Everything is now at once a marvellous gift of being and alarmingly unmotivated. The problem for modernity is not one of an all-powerful destiny, but the fact that there seems to be no destiny at all. William James argues in *Pragmatism* that a world with a God may well still burn up or freeze, but 'where he is, tragedy is only partial and provisional, and shipwreck and dissolution not the absolutely final things'.[42]

The narrative of Creation, in other words, would seem to give some point to the world. This is ironic, since the theological meaning of 'creation' is exactly that there is no point to the world. It was brought to birth not as the last step in some inexorable causal process, but purely out of God's gratuitousness. Creation is that which might just as well never have been, and is thus the final refutation of an instrumental rationality. This, indeed, is part of the meaning of God's transcendence. He transcends his creation in the sense that it is not necessary to him, and he did not have to bring it about. The world is gift, not fate. It has its source in freedom, not compulsion. Like the artist and his product, God fashioned the world just for the hell of it, as a quick look around it will no doubt confirm.

Even so, modernity has need of its own grand narratives of fate, just as it fashions its own myths despite its hostility to earlier ones. One such substitute for the gods is Nature, whether in providential Wordsworthian form, or in such rapacious guise as the unappeasable ocean of J. M. Synge's *Riders to the Sea*. In its later phases, the modern epoch will come to accept that randomness rules, that the world is no longer story-shaped, that fate is what we fashion rather than endure. Fate and linear time stand or fall together; and the latter is now thrown into question as progressivist hopes begin to falter, and as modern experience becomes so fractured and convoluted that syntax or narrative can only steamroller their way over what is best grasped as an intricate synchrony of the senses. The senses know no straightforward temporality, as perceptions interlace and sensations merge; and since modernism is among other things an epochal shift from reality to experience, from how the object is to how it strikes an observer, phenomenological time comes to oust chronology. The story, as in Benjamin's essay 'The Storyteller', now has a charmingly pre-modern, artisanal aura about it, as the trace of a world before the death of the genetic and consequentialist fallacies for which to know a thing is to know where it came from and where it is going.

If fables of destiny are undermined from one direction by the sensory overload of modern life, they are undercut from another by the unconscious, which as Freud reminds us is a stranger to narrative, and which loops time round itself to create bizarre new constellations between the very old and the very new. The very old is the best image we have of the very new, since it has not happened for such a long time. Even in late modern and postmodern culture, however, destiny of some sort is still much in vogue. It is just that it now has names like power and desire, forces every bit as lethal, capricious and implacable as the effects of a squabble on Mount Olympus. Freud speaks of destiny as having migrated in modern times to the family. Every domestic hearth is now a potential house of Atreus, all the way from Garcia Lorca's *The House of Bernada Alba*, with its clutch of squabbling, sexually frustrated women terrorized by a domineering matriarch, to the lighter version of this imbroglio, Brian Friel's *Dancing at Lughnasa*.

In its more buoyant phase from Hegel to Comte, however, modernity comes up with Progress or Reason as profane substitutes for providence. Hegel writes of the 'rationality of destiny',[43] as though the blind forces of fate have now taken on the more intelligible form of *Geist*. Schopenhauer's doctrine of the voracious Will insists that nothing could be further from the truth; but in general tragedy, one of the last preserves of the arcane and archaic, must now be rendered transparent by middle-class Enlightenment. Reason is as unbending as fate, but ultimately beneficial. Whereas fate has force but not necessarily significance, Reason has both. Indeed, the idea of fate is interestingly ambiguous in this respect. It hovers somewhere between sheer brute force and the idea of a narrative which adds up. Like Darwinian evolution, which has a logic but not a purpose, it suggests a kind of pattern, but not necessarily one which makes moral sense. The Greek gods, taken as a whole, scarcely do that. Hence the belief that fate is blind, which suggests that it has the unity of an agent but not the shaping intelligence. Conservative critics of tragedy quite often assume that pattern or symmetry must be valuable in themselves, but some tragedy exposes this as a false equation.

Even if the story adds up, then, this is not necessarily to say that it is rational in the sense of reasonable. It may reveal a meaning, but that does not mean that it is just. You can have necessity without benevolence, law without virtue. And this then allows some critics of tragedy to shift attention from the injustice of things by stressing their intelligibility instead. On the other hand, you can try to excuse the tangible injustices of tragedy by stressing their lack of intelligibility. In his tersely entitled *Tragedy*, W. MacNeile Dixon, a critic distinctly averse to rational lucidity, sees the very inequities of tragedy as a sign of the mysterious inexplicability of the cosmos, and thus squeezes some perverse value from it. If the choice is between sublimity and intelligibility, mystery and rationality, he will plump in each case for the former.

129

Franz Kafka's description of the law in *The Trial* has just the ambiguity of a necessity without justice. Like the Greek concept of *dikē*, the law is logical but not equitable. On the contrary, it is vengeful and vindictive, and the point is to placate its wrath by striving to preserve it in a state of equilibrium. As with the nineteenth-century conception of Nature, or indeed the Foucaultian notion of power, the law is a vast, self-regulating organism which will compensate for being disrupted at one point by spontaneously producing a counter-force at another, thus remaining sublimely unaltered as a whole. It is as impenetrable as a jellyfish. As the priest tells Josef K in the 'In The Cathedral' episode: 'One does not have to believe everything is true, one only has to believe that it is necessary'. One admires the internal symmetries of this secretive, spiteful law rather as one might admire the form of a work of art whose content one found thoroughly repugnant.

At least fate has a certain consistency, which is more than one can say for chance or fortune. To see the world as governed by chance is to see it as not governed at all. John Milton writes in *Paradise Regained* that he treats 'Of fate and chance, and change in human life', but it is not clear that these are the near-synonyms the line might suggest they are. Mutability, for example, may be either tragic or comic, depending on what it is that mutates. Whatever the *carpe diem* school of thought, ephemerality is not tragic in itself, not least if what passes away is injustice or atrocious pain. It is a recognition of transience, and of the consequent pettiness of pomp and power, which finally persuades Segismundo in Calderon's *Life is a Dream* to put aside his tyrannical conduct. Nor is permanence inherently positive if it means, say, the extraordinary historical persistence of women's oppression. But neither is it always drearily monolithic. It would be pleasant if justice were a permanent human condition, whatever the champions of plasticity might believe.

For Oscar Wilde in *The Critic as Artist*, the scientific principle of heredity is simply the fearful symmetry of nemesis returning in new guise. The process is dramatized in Zola's *Nana*, where Nana is really Nature's vengeance on a corrupt, libidinous society. It crops up too in Eugene O'Neill's *Mourning Becomes Electra*, in which Lavinia and Orin turn inexorably into the images of the parents they have murdered. The past returns in that neurotic compulsion known as revenge. The dead never lie down and will always prove stronger than the living, since so many generations of them have gone into the making of those currently alive. The dead, so to speak, have the statistical advantage. George Eliot writes in *Felix Holt* of Nature as a great tragic dramatist, meaning perhaps that it deals in fateful symmetries. But society itself can be seen as a second

Nature. You can substitute the laws of humanity for the laws of God, as Benjamin Constant suggests in *Adolphe*: 'the laws of society are stronger than the will of men; the most compelling emotions dash themselves to pieces against the fatality of circumstances' (ch. 6).

Naturalism is just such an attempt to find in human history something of the inexorability of natural or metaphysical law. The imperishable laws of Nature can stand in for a more traditional sense of immortality, while their unfathomable depths can compensate for the loss of religious mystery. One can thus reap the consolations of teleology without the handicap of supernaturalism. Comtean positivism is an anti-tragic creed, rejecting Hegelian negativity and its disruptive political overtones for the solid self-identity of the present, and the progressive laws which will carry it into an even more sanguine future. At the close of Zola's novel *The Earth*, Jean the peasant speculates that Nature makes use even of our petty, degraded natures for its own inscrutable ends – that even our vice and crime may somehow be essential to it. It is a recycling of seventeenth-century rationalism in nineteenth-century evolutionary guise. If evolution needed its blunders and cul-de-sacs in order to produce its finest organisms, then a species of theodicy is back on the intellectual agenda, and tragedy is consequently hard to come by.

There is a dash of Nietzsche here too: the crime, horror and bloodshed of human genealogy will be retrospectively justified by the *Übermenschen* to whom it will give birth. To regard humanity in this light also involves an anti-tragic distancing, shrinking the species back to its humble place within the cosmic whole. 'And how important is human misery', Jean muses, 'when weighed against the mighty mechanism of the stars and the sun?' (Part 5, ch. 6). If evolution decentres Man, it dislodges tragedy along with him. Even so, the narrative of *The Earth* is tragic enough, as the grasping old peasant Fouan, a low-life French King Lear, is betrayed and destroyed by his murderously quarrelsome children.

The pseudo-scientific aura of naturalistic art represents a disavowal of tragedy, as the anaesthesia of the style transcends the squalid sensationalism of the contents. This is as true of Joyce and the early George Moore as it is of Gustave Flaubert. Tragedy, as in Schopenhauer's aestheticizing of the form, is shorn of its affects. But since few things are more sensationalist than the clinical, as pornographers are aware, this has the paradoxical effect of intensifying the bleakness. For conservative theorists of tragedy, however, such naturalism is the reverse of tragic. It centres on suffering rather than agency, biology rather than history, victimage rather than affirmation. It is too seedy, low-life and disenchanted for tragic status, but also too deterministic, which means that its characters are too quiescent to muster much heroic resistance. Its subjection of men and

131

women to enslaving forces is memorably imaged in the figure of the paralysed Madame Raquin in Zola's *Thérèse Raquin*, who, rather like the unmoved naturalistic author himself, can record events but is unable to respond to them.

Conservative theories of tragedy rank science, determinism and naturalism as among the main modern enemies of the form – strangely, since classical tragedy can at times be determinist enough. Among their other defects, such doctrines leave no space for the autonomous subject – though this, as we have seen, did not exactly flourish in classical antiquity either. Walter Kerr believes that Freud, a determinist in his eyes, has helped to scupper the possibility of modern tragedy, while Patrick Roberts doubts that psychoanalysis is such a full-blooded determinism but concedes that it limits our freedom.[44] Other critics, conversely, claim that modern-day determinism has actually renewed the tragic spirit. Henri Peyre maintains that in a world of wars, technology, revolutions and the like, modern humanity can no longer be sure that it is master of its own fate, so that tragedy stages a reappearance. What has buried the form for some has resurrected it for others.[45]

There is, in fact, an intriguing inconsistency in this case. Traditionalist critics of tragedy defend the free individual against a soulless modern determinism; but since they believe in a providence to which we must submit, they also rebuke an errant individualism. W. MacNeile Dixon, for example, questions whether the tragic hero is responsible for his own fate, since this for him smacks too much of bourgeois self-determination. But he also recognizes that self-responsibility is the only way in which the catastrophe can be morally justified – and even then only in part, since tragedy has a habit of meting out disproportionate penalties. At the same time, though the idea of destiny is a more exalted affair than a contemptible mechanistic determinism, it is not easy to overlook their embarrassing affinities. There is, to be sure, a difference between seeing men and women as guided by a mysterious providence, and seeing them as determined by their genes, infantile years or economic mode of production. But both ways of seeing cut the individual brusquely down to size, so that old-fashioned advocates of tragic fate are in danger of reproducing in more spiritual guise the very collectivism of which they complain. Yet if they opt instead for a defence of individual responsibility, they are equally at risk of endorsing some of the less savoury aspects of the middle-class modernity they abhor. Tragedy is both the showcase of liberal humanism and its subversion.

What are we to make of the constant emphasis on tragedy as predestined, mysterious and life-affirming? Why does this critical clamour so often drown out the cries of misery and howls of anguish emanating from the works themselves? One answer is that tragedy, as we have suggested already, is a kind of secular theodicy. The ancient Greeks had less need for such a science, since their gods were a fairly scurvy bunch in any case; but Christianity posits a perfect God, who is then notoriously hard to square with his less than perfect creation. The existence of evil is one of the most convincing arguments against religious faith, and no religious apologist has ever dealt with it convincingly. Like theology, tragedy is disturbed by the presence of evil in the world, and seeks in some rather gestural way to account for it. In general, the tragedians have had as little success in this enterprise as the theologians. But if tragedy is predetermined, then this at least shifts the responsibility for such evil from our own shoulders; if it has an aura of sacred mystery, then we can only profane it with such obtusely rationalist questions as 'Why?'; and if it is life-affirming, then at least some good springs from its negative features, which is some sort of justification for them. If butchery and betrayal are predestined, then we can make a necessity out of a vice. Or we can see them as only partly determined, in which case we can also shift some of the blame on to the protagonist. If you are partly the architect of your own overthrow, as in Aristotle's theory, this raises fewer uncomfortable questions about the injustice of the world in general. It is a choice between excusing the hero and exculpating the gods.

Even so, the embarrassing fact remains that tragedy, in traditionalist eyes, is supposed to disclose the presence of a cosmic order, but ends up all too often showing just how appallingly unjust the world is. It is this disconcerting truth which must somehow be negotiated. Frank Kermode proposes a suggestive parallel between the delusions of paranoia, which lead men and women to feel that they are being unjustly persecuted, and tragic plots;[46] but the fact is, as the old joke has it, that a good many of these tragic paranoiacs really are being persecuted. The notion of necessity is convenient here, however, since if the tragedy is predetermined there is a sense in which arguing the toss over how just or unjust it is is beside the point. The doctrine of fate is among other things a caveat against raising tactless questions. What happens, happens; and the fact that it had to happen means that it is pointless to inquire any further. 'The hero must fall', observes Northrop Frye, '. . . it is too bad that he falls.'[47] And that, in the end, is all there is to say. The supposed mysteriousness of the tragic, its resistance to mere secular reasoning, can be exploited to cover over its cruelty. And the pleasure we take in the tragic action, a pleasure which itself raises some unease among commentators, can be seen as a sense of exaltation released in us by destruction, thus transforming this morally rather shady enjoyment into a justification of suffering.

Yet none of this can be accomplished without a good deal of disingenuousness. A. C. Bradley tells us in *Shakespearian Tragedy* that tragedy is about waste, but that we feel the worth of what is wasted, so that the action is not in vain. The experience therefore does not leave us 'crushed, rebellious or desperate',[48] qualities which middle-class men of his time were in the habit of associating with the mutinous lower orders. If tragedy is too palpably unjust, then it might stir up socially disruptive protest. The law which destroys the hero, Bradley assures us, is neither just nor benevolent, but nor is it indifferent and malicious. Since this pretty well exhausts the options, it is difficult to know quite what it is. We observe injustice; yet there is no fatalism at stake, and certainly no question of a *spiteful* fate. Tragedy discloses a moral order.

In any case, so Bradley argues in an abrupt switch of gear, the agent of tragedy is largely responsible for his own ruin, which would seem to strike the question of whether there is a malevolent or benevolent order somewhat redundant; though Bradley remarks elsewhere that we are made to feel that the protagonist is 'in some degree, *however slight*, the cause of his own undoing',[49] which is a somewhat different emphasis. But it is a necessary one as well, since if the hero is largely the cause of his own collapse, then as we have seen already, the question of whether he can evoke our commiseration becomes a troubling one. And though Bradley claims in justification of the tragic catastrophe that the hero is seriously flawed, the flaws he actually mentions – pride, credulousness, irresoluteness, excessive susceptibility to sexual emotions – are hardly hanging matters.

Yet Bradley, bewilderingly, describes these rather minor blemishes as 'evil', as though it were depraved of Hamlet to procrastinate. Having just listed some tangible instances of tragic injustice (Cordelia, Lear, Othello and the like), he comments rather unexpectedly that tragedy is an 'example of justice'. 'The rigour of the justice', he concedes, 'is terrible, no doubt . . . but . . . we acquiesce, because our sense of justice is satisfied.'[50] This seems to suggest that we acquiesce in excessively rigorous punishment, usually known as injustice, because it is just. Do we really accept the death of Cordelia as no more than her deserts? For what crime is Racine's Hippolytus destroyed? What sin has Hieronimo in Kyd's *Spanish Tragedy* committed for his son Horatio to be murdered?

Like a good many other critics, Bradley seeks to absolve tragedy of undue brutality by the negative strategy of scoffing at the doctrine of poetic justice. To expect a play to reward the virtuous and punish the vicious, as Thomas Rymer demands, would be painfully unsophisticated. Tragedy, after all, must be an imitation of life, in all its moral chequeredness. But this is not the issue. The question is why a form which

134

shows the innocent being torn limb from limb should be acclaimed as the highest expression of human value. Having deployed this tactic to exculpate tragedy, however, Bradley instantly resorts to another. Reaching rather nervously for his Hegelian hat, he remarks that tragedy is not in fact a matter of justice or injustice at all, even though he has informed us earlier that it is an example of justice. Karl Jaspers makes a similar claim, dismissing the justice or otherwise of destiny as 'irrelevant', 'mere petty moralism' which confuses tragedy with such sublunary matters as sickness, despair, evil and death.[51]

As with Hegel, so Bradley argues, we do not judge the competing claims at stake, even though he himself has just been liberally scattering evaluative epithets about Shakespearian characters. But Hegel does not hold that we should refrain from judgement; he believes rather that both poles of the tragic conflict are justified. The problem is that there are too many judgements, not too few. And the fact is that we do of course judge between Othello and Iago, Pastor Manders and Oswald Alving. But though justice and injustice are not the issue, Bradley adds that the moral order which tragedy discloses is ultimately beneficent, 'akin to good and alien from evil'. It is hard to see what kind of cosmic order can be akin to good but indifferent to justice.

The moral order, Bradley reassures us, is not capricious, but operates 'from the necessity of its nature'.[52] This makes it sound ominously like fate, which is not quite the same as a benign providence. But at least it is not capricious fate – so we can draw some comfort from the fact that being roasted slowly on a spit was actually planned by the heavens, not just the result of some careless oversight on their part. There is, however, a tension here between Bradley's moralism and his Hegelianism. The moral order may be positive; but if tragedy is to be immanent rather than accidental, it must generate this evil out of its own substance, and thus begins to sound rather sinisterly like the Gnostic God. How can the order be moral yet contain its own destructiveness? Bradley cushions the bad news that tragic destruction is built into the world by telling us that *Geist* is 'driven to mutilate its own substance',[53] which sounds a less disagreeable way of describing, say, the slave trade than some other accounts of it. The moral order is sound in the sense that it finally drives out evil, though only by a tragic waste of good. There would seem, however, no more point in protesting against this automatic, remorselessly self-regulating system than in attributing moral purposes to the central heating.

Like many a critic of tragedy of his day, Bradley draws implicitly on Victorian notions of inexorable physical laws, which if breached will exact their deadly retribution. To transfer this notion in Comtean style to human affairs then has the benefit of suggesting that these, too, are inexorable processes beyond moral judgement. Thomas Carlyle's universe, for instance, is a Calvinist mechanism of strict, self-regulating tit-for-tat: you reap as you sow, so that, for example, the cosmos will wreak its automatic revenge on idleness. But since this is a just order, and its penalties are eye-for-an-eye rather than excessive, it is not by and large a tragic one. Disaster is always the result of sin, if not necessarily your own, and thus in some cosmic sense your own fault. It is a familiar right-wing doctrine: those who are diseased or starving, not to speak of those who are impoverished or out of work, are in some obscure or not-so-obscure way responsible for the fact.

In the end, Bradley throws in the towel. Tragedy may not be entirely moral, but Shakespeare was not trying to justify the ways of God to men or write *The Divine Comedy*. Tragedy is simply tragedy, and there is nothing more to be said. Tragedy would not be tragedy 'if it were not a painful mystery'.[54] After all his conceptual twistings, Bradley can finally muster nothing more than a resounding tautology. A lengthy process of analysis is finally thrown to the winds with a saving allusion to mystery. It is the last refuge of a sophist.

Not all critics are so tortuously inconsistent. S. H. Butcher has no reservations in believing that 'through (the hero's) ruin the disturbed order of the universe is restored and moral forces reassert their sway'.[55] Leo Aylen informs us that 'though [the Greek dramatists] could never express their belief that the ultimate order was moral, they certainly felt it was, or at least that it ought to be'.[56] This is rather like arguing that there is no adultery in Hollywood, or at least there ought not to be. Schiller goes one further, with his florid claim that 'the experience of the victorious power of the moral law is so high, so real and good, that we are even tempted to be reconciled to evil, which we have to thank for it'.[57] It is almost worth violating the moral law by butchering an entire village, just to have the satisfaction of knowing the law's ultimate victory. 'To have been great of soul', H. D. F. Kitto piously intones, 'is everything.'[58] What is murder compared with magnanimity? The pattern of destiny, Kitto thinks, may cut harshly across the life of the individual; but 'at least we know that it exists, and we may feel assured that piety and purity are a large part of it'.[59] Hecabe does not seem quite so assured in Euripides's *The Women of Troy*, when she remarks that 'I see how the high gods dispose this world; I see / The mean exalted to the sky, the great brought low'. Adrastus adds in *The Suppliant Women* that 'gods are cruel, and men pitiable'. The closing lines of Sophocles's *The Women of Trachis* contain a scorching denunciation of divine injustice. Heracles in Euripides's play is tormented but totally blameless; Medea is guilty but gets off scot-free.

Andromache in *The Women of Troy* is innocent yet doomed to a dreadful fate.

But this is Euripides, with whom tragic submission is already declining into churlish rebellion. Yet Sophocles's Oedipus, another innocent, tells the Chorus at Colonus that he has 'endured foulest injustice'. A. J. A. Waldock's rather too briskly iconoclastic *Sophocles the Dramatist* thinks that the gods emerge from Sophoclean drama with no credit at all – an over-emphatic case, but a refreshingly unorthodox one.[60] The Chorus of Aeschylus's *Prometheus* rebukes the hero for his wrath, pride and obstinacy, but seems to believe even so that Zeus's chastisement of him is immoderate. Schopenhauer claims that Greek tragedy is inferior to its modern counterpart exactly because its protagonists *don't* embrace their destinies, unlike the brand of Christian resignation which turns gladly from the world as so much dross.

By no means all Greek protagonists concede that their suffering is justified, accept their guilt or confess that the calamity follows from their own behaviour. And they are mostly quite right not to do so. It is the theorists of tragedy, not the victims of it, who imagine that they do, or at least that they should. Richard B. Sewell claims that no ancient Greek hero gladly embraces his or her destiny, even if the result of doing so is that 'suffering has been given a structure'.[61] We have met before with this aesthetic concern with the form of suffering, rather than its content. George Steiner believes that tragedy needs the intolerable presence of the gods, but the truth is that its characters would often be a lot better off if they were absent. If tragedy does require the gods, it is not always, as Steiner seems to suppose, because they lend it a suitably numinous depth, but because without the petty machinations of Mount Olympus the tragedy might never have come about in the first place.

Kitto seems to think in his cerebral way that the sheer existence of a cosmic pattern is reassuring, as though a random but non-ruinous world would not be preferable to a plotted but malignant one. Like other enemies of contingency, of which the prototype is arguably paternity, he overlooks the fact that accidental suffering may not be cosmically meaningful but may still be significant. Value does not necessarily depend on metaphysical significance. The Mona Lisa or regular dental treatment are valuable, but not metaphysically so. Conversely, pattern does not necessarily imply meaning, as with a snowflake. Although life has been cruel to Oedipus, Kitto generously concedes, 'nevertheless it is not a chaos ... We are given the feeling that the Universe is coherent, even though we may not understand it completely'.[62]

It seems cold comfort. If Oedipus is cut down by fate, then it might have been better for his health had there indeed been chaos rather than cosmos. Much tragedy would seem testimony to neither, but to the more disturbing fact that an order exists but that it is not just. This is then the metaphysical equivalent of a radical political case. As far as Kitto's coherent universe goes, there is not much evidence of it in *The White Devil* or *The Revenger's Tragedy*, not to speak of Edward Bond's *Saved*. 'Complete malignity', declares T. R. Henn, 'makes tragedy without meaning.'[63] There must, in other words, be a positive order if it is to be intelligibly violated, just as you must receive an invitation in order to turn it down. But there are plenty of tragic works which suspect that there is no such order at all, or that it is actively malevolent.

E. R. Dodds writes breezily of the 'puerile idea' of poetic justice, which he brusquely dismisses as 'nonsense'.[64] Rather less brusquely, Joseph Addison points out in *The Spectator* that if the virtuous are always shown as successful, there is no room for tragic pity. Demanding that tragedy should reward the virtuous and penalize the vicious is indeed a piece of simple-minded moralism. In the eighteenth century where it originates, it is also (though Kitto curiously fails to mention this) a flagrant piece of ideology, as didactic critics stand guard against setting a bad moral example to the lower classes. Wickedness must not be seen to prosper on stage, if your life and property off-stage are to be secure. Even so, it is remarkable how rarely this suave, tough-minded dismissal of poetic justice reckons the cost of its rejection. In rescuing tragedy from moral naivety, it does so only by acknowledging that a good deal of it brutally flouts the very moral order which the critics of poetic justice value so highly. It is the mentality of a certain type of old-style Oxbridge don, who would rather be thought wicked than naive.

Lessing, who is on the whole progressive when it comes to tragedy, holding that the rank of an unfortunate man is neither here nor there, nevertheless warns tragic poets against playing too much on our sense of universal injustice and making us shudder at the incomprehensible ways of providence, since these are futile emotions. In any case, he insists, we do not need these tactics to teach us submission, since cool reason can do it for us less distressfully. The case is explicitly ideological: if we are to retain confidence and joyful courage, so Lessing instructs the tragedians, it is essential that we should be reminded of such terrors as little as possible.[65] Gloom, once again, is socially subversive. Even Lessing is not so brazenly ideological as Plato, however, who insists in *The Republic* that if the political state is to be secure, playwrights should not portray the gods as unjust, and should show how those who are punished reap benefit from it.

'Where there is compensation', declares George Steiner, 'there is justice, not tragedy.'[66] This, once again, is inaccurate. Many tragedies end with the dispensation of justice; what is tragic about them is that so much bloodshed should have proved necessary to attain it, or that there should be crimes which call for such stringent penalties in the first place. The Book of Job is Steiner's example of a narrative of justice rather than tragedy; but even if Job is finally comforted, was it not tragic for him to suffer so much affliction in the first place? Why should it be true that all's well that ends well? *The Bacchae* remains a tragedy even if you think that the dismembering of Penthus is his just reward for arrogant impiety towards a god. I. A. Richards shares Steiner's grim view of tragic endings, insisting that 'the least touch of any theology which has a compensating Heaven to offer the tragic hero is fatal'.[67] Yet Richards finds joy at the heart of tragedy even so – though it is 'not an indication that "all's right with the world" or that "somewhere, somehow, there is Justice"; it is an indication that all is right here and now in the nervous system'.[68] What Richards effusively describes as the greatest and rarest thing in literature comes down to a matter of mental hygiene.

Some commentators seem actually to relish tragic injustice, drawing it ostentatiously to our attention. Georg Lukács comments in *Soul and Form* that in tragedy 'sentence is passed ruthlessly upon the smallest fault',[69] as though nothing could gratify us more deeply. As judged by the theorists, most of them conservatives, it is a virulently illiberal form. In the same spirit, Jean Racine remarks proudly in his preface to *Phèdre* that 'the smallest faults are severely punished' in the play, as though this were a recommendation. Justice for the Jansenist Racine is dispensed by a hidden God whose ways we should not even expect to be intelligible to us; it is enough for us to know that, God being God, they are divine. If the Almighty transcends our discourse, then his actions are not just, but neither are they unjust. Despite this, Roland Barthes argues in *Sur Racine* that Racine's universe is manifestly unjust, and that in order to rationalize this men and women must fabricate some guilt for themselves. Tragic characters are thus born innocent, but become guilty in order to save God's face.

Northrop Frye maintains that 'tragedy is intelligible because its catastrophe is plausibly related to its situation'.[70] But it is not the intelligibility which is in question; it is the fact that a supposedly auspicious providence seems to dole out injury to the innocent with such profligate abandon. The catastrophe is plausible in the sense that it springs from the situation, but not in the sense that it is proportionate to it. Milton's Samson in *Samson Agonistes* complains that God seems to inflict punishments 'too grievous for the trespass or omission'. By the end of *King Lear* it is as though the play finally unleashes its grotesque violence on the audience themselves, rounding on them sadistically and rubbing their noses in its revolting injustices until they are tempted to whimper that they can take no more. Samuel Johnson certainly couldn't. As Sadhan Kumar Ghosh points out, 'it is the disproportion and not the punishment that constitutes the true terror of tragedy'[71] – so much so, indeed, that he believes justice and tragedy to be quite incompatible.

Indeed, on one theory of tragedy, the penalty *must* be disproportionate. As we have seen, the tragic hero must be reasonably virtuous in order to win our compassion, and thus cannot wholly deserve his or her punishment. There is a kind of French neo-classical tragedy, so-called *tragédie heureuse*, which presses this doctrine to an extreme: poetic justice has to be executed, since the hero is perfectly incorruptible and so cannot be destroyed. As John Dryden argues in his *Essay on Dramatic Poesy*, only the good-living but misfortunate will evoke our compassion – so that if tragedy is to elicit a suitable response from us, it would seem forced to acknowledge that the universe is less than equitable. The strength of the form, its nurturing of human sympathies, is thus directly related to its moral embarrassments. If we are to be struck with admiring awe at the sight of a largely innocent victim heroically resisting his fate, we cannot avoid being equally struck with indignation at the fact that he should have to suffer at all.

The mirror-image of disproportionate punishment is forgiveness, which returns less than expected rather than more. Forgiveness breaks the circuit of tit-for-tat, disrupting the economy of come-uppances. It sets aside the strict exchange-values of justice with a cavalier gesture, rising above the dull, petty-bourgeois logic of debits and deserts. In fact, the equivalence of an eye for an eye was itself for the Old Testament a matter of mercy: it meant that you should exact in punishment no more than you had been deprived of. It is a corrective to the wrong sort of excess. Infinite Justice, the code-name briefly bestowed on the US campaign against terrorism, is in one sense the kind of oxymoron one would expect of official military rhetoric. The right sort of excess, by contrast, is forgiveness. Forgiveness is both lavish, since a form of generosity, but also a kind of negation, refusing to return like for like, plucking something from nothing. As such, it is a utopian gesture which stands for a moment outside the rules of the game. A refusal to retaliate goes along with what seems its opposite, the extravagance of giving more than is actually demanded, offering your cloak as well as your coat or walking two miles rather than one. This is a kind of carnivalesque mockery of the neurotically exact equivalences of justice, with an eye to a future world where they will not be so important. Until that time, however, a measure-for-measure ethics remains essential, not least since the weak would be ill-advised to rely on the whimsical generosity of the powerful. Justice, with its book-keeping logic, binds us to the world as it is, but without it the powerful would have a field day. And exorbitant gestures like for-giveness are quite often the prerogative of the mighty, as well as being sometimes self-indulgent. But this is not to say that such gestures cannot put justice creatively into question, as injustice puts it into question in all the wrong ways.

How mercy is to flourish without making a mockery of justice is a problem with which Milton grapples in *Paradise Lost*. In a similar way, Shakespeare's *Measure for Measure* contrasts the kind of letting-off which is really just airy indifference with one which has to reckon the cost. And there are always some, like the psychopathic Barnadine, who cannot be forgiven because they do not speak the language of moral value any more than they speak Bulgarian. Barnadine is like the innocent of William Golding's novel *Free Fall*, who cannot forgive because they do not under-stand that they have been offended against. The dead cannot forgive either. They cannot relieve us of our guilt and anger that they are no longer here.

There is an influential vein of thought for which the purpose of tragedy is didactic. But if tragedy is predestined, how can it warn you against what you can do nothing about? And if it is lacking in justice, how can it foster integrity? The very excess which deters us from immorality also fails to persuade us of the form's moral soundness. In any case, it is sometimes our virtues, not our vices, which bring us to grief. Tragic art, to be sure, can teach you 'upon how weak foundations gilden roofs are builded',[72] as Philip Sidney insists, and thus act as a bulwark against hubris. It can also reconcile you to your humble place in life, as the Earl of Shaftesbury sug-gests: tragedy 'consists in the living representation of the disorders and misery of the great; to the end that the people and those of a lower con-dition may be taught the better to content themselves with privacy, enjoy their safer state, and prize the equality and justice of their guardian laws'.[73] This tags an eighteenth-century moral on to a medieval definition.

Yet tragic art would seem on much marshier terrain when it comes to morality. This does not matter much in our own day, for which art is the very opposite of didacticism, even though one admired literary mode continues to be the sermon. 'Tragedy does not yield moral lessons', insists R. P. Draper.[74] But it presents problems for a more moralistic age. What is ideologically desirable is some version of poetic justice, yet this is exactly what will fail to convince. David Hume maintains that seeing the virtuous suffer is disagreeable, but Joseph Addison rejects the doctrine of poetic justice as contrary to nature and reason.[75] Henry Fielding's novels end with poetic justice, but they do so with an ironic air, signalling that it is now only in fiction that the wicked will get their come-uppance and the good their marriage partners. In real life, so Fielding intimates in the mischievous gap between artistic form and empirical content, the villains would probably end up as archbishops. The more fiction celebrates poetic justice, the more subversively it draws attention to the lack of it outside the text. When the sorrowing Renzio of Manzoni's *The Betrothed* muses that 'There's justice in this world in the long run', his more disenchanted narrator adds, out of his earshot so to speak: 'How true it is that a man overwhelmed by grief no longer knows what he is saying!' (ch. 3).

Even so, the idea that the good will prosper is not wholly unfounded. As Rosalind Hursthouse puts it: 'We think that (for the most part, by and large) if we act well, things go well for us'.[76] To be just, prudent, compassionate and merciful is more likely to protect us from harm than to be reckless, unjust, hard-hearted and vindictive. But not necessarily so. We still cannot avoid blunders, bad luck, psychopathic room-mates, crooked colleagues, falling prey to malevolent forces. Manzoni's Don Abbondio in *The Betrothed* is naive to suppose that 'unpleasant accidents do not happen to the honest man who keeps to himself and minds his own business' (ch. 1). Virtue is at once the best recipe for happiness, and as Fielding recognizes a way of making ourselves vulnerable in an unprincipled world. This is why it is admirable and ludicrous at the same time, like the word 'virtue' itself.

Tragic theory is accordingly caught between an ideologically unnerving pessimism and an implausible poetic justice. It seems that tragedy can encourage compassion only by confessing injustice. This dilemma would be eased if the theory could shed its prejudice that only the morally admirable are fit meat for pity. The English are said to have taken a long time to see Napoleon as a tragic figure. Yet though Voltaire's characters Zamore and Orosmane are both murderers, they are to be pitied rather than condemned in the eyes of their soft-hearted author. Pushkin's Boris Godunov has killed the crown prince to seize the tsardom, but his death is treated sympathetically by the play and he emerges finally as a positive figure. Albert Camus argues in *The Rebel* that we regard injustice even to one of our enemies as repugnant. Schopenhauer holds in his usual nonconformist style that we can pity tragic protagonists even when their sufferings are merited and when they show no self-recognition. He also comments in his saturnine way that we, the spectators, are probably well capable of much of the wickedness we see on stage. And indeed, thoroughly non-pitiable characters are sometimes allowed to escape justice. A flagrant case in point is the pathologically jealous Gutierre Alfonso Solís of Caldron's *The Surgeon of Honour*, who has his wife bled to death for infidelity but is punished for the crime only by being forced to marry another woman.

Schopenhauer scoffs that 'only the dull optimistic Protestant-Rationalist or peculiarly Jewish view of life will make the demand for poetical justice and find satisfaction in it'.[77] The tragic hero in Schopenhauer's view knows that he atones not for his own sins, but for the crime of existence itself. Tragedy, in other words, contains both the justice and injustice of sacrifice: the act of sacrifice is a necessary expiation for some communal crime, yet its victim must be innocent. Yet if tragedy disowns poetic justice, how can it be morally edifying? This is not a problem for Schopenhauer himself, who will have no truck with such idealist absurdities as moral edification; but it is certainly one for more moralistically minded critics like John Dennis, who maintains that every tragedy should be a high-minded homily, chastising the bad and protecting the good.[78] Rousseau was not convinced: since, he suggests, one detests the crimes of a Phèdre or Medea just as much at the beginning of the play as at the end, where is tragedy's moral lesson?[79]

The lesson is usually that one should beware of breaching the moral order. Usually, though not always – not, in fact, for Walter Benjamin, who sees tragedy as a shaking of the moral cosmos by one who has recognized himself to be superior to its gods. But though almost all the critics we have examined agree that tragedy presupposes such an order, the case is far from proven. Indeed, the truth might well be the contrary. It can be claimed that tragedy springs not from violating a stable order, but from that order being itself caught up in a complex transitional crisis. And this then modifies the simplistic 'free hero versus determining cosmos' ideology of the form. 'Transition is the zone of tragedy', declares Karl Jaspers,[80] while Benjamin sees tragic theatre as an historically necessary passage from myth to philosophy.

The classicists J.-P. Vernant and P. Vidal-Naquet see Greek tragedy as emerging from a tension between old religio-mythical ways of thought and new politico-legal ones which still remain cloudy and contested. 'Tragedy', they announce, 'is born when myth starts to be considered from the viewpoint of the citizen.'[81] Greek theatre is a combination of the primitive and the progressive, of Dionysus and Apollo, of elemental forces and the collective pondering of moral questions to arrive at a rational conclusion. If it is a theatre of cruelty, it is also a forum for civic debate. Moses Finley thinks that the dramatists, and especially Euripides, probed 'with astonishing latitude and freedom into the traditional myths and beliefs', and links this to the democratic ambience of fifth-century Athens.[82] Martha Nussbaum writes in Love's Knowledge that to attend ancient tragic drama was 'to engage in a communal process of inquiry, reflection, and feeling with respect to important civic and personal ends'.[83] The tragic poets were becoming the chief ethical teachers, in ways which clearly rattled the likes of Plato.

To see Greek tragedy as poised between the heroic–mythical and the rational–legal is to say that, like Freud, it is struck by the paradox that the very forces which go into the making of civilization are unruly, uncivil, potentially disruptive ones. This is most obvious in sexuality, at once anarchic passion and anchor of domestic life. But much the same is true of material production – the raw, earthy energies on which civilization is reared, and which bulk large in the myth of Prometheus. What holds in these cases applies equally to the ethico-legal sphere, in which justice is both thwarted and promoted by the archaic drive for vengeance. Political power, however enlightened, is still caught up in perils and taboos. If the Dionysian is both dreaded and revered, this deep-grained ambivalence extends to the making of civilization as a whole, an ambivalence which the Faust myth also encodes. Vernant and Vidal-Naquet thus reject the teleological reading of the *Oresteia* as a laborious trek from chthonic powers to civic legality; the drama is about both at once, about the law and the Eumenides together.

For Northrop Frye, in an unwonted flash of Marxist insight, the tragic drama of both fifth-century Athens and early modern England 'belong to a period of social history in which an aristocracy is fast losing its effective power but still retains a good deal of ideological prestige'.[84] There is a case that major bodies of tragedy spring up at times of crucial socio-political formation, as with the birth-pangs of the ancient *polis* or the Renaissance nation-state. 'The ages of comparatively stable belief', writes Raymond Williams, '. . . do not seem to produce tragedy of any intensity.' Rather, the form's most common setting seems to be 'the period preceding the substantial breakdown and transformation of an important culture'.[85] A traditional order is still active, but increasingly at odds with emergent values, relationships, structures of feeling. This may also be the case with modernism, which, so Perry Anderson has argued, tends to flourish in still tradition-bound societies which are nonetheless experiencing for the first time the ambiguously alarming and exhilarating impact of modernization.[86] Indeed, modernism produces a distinguished body of tragic art, though not necessarily one centred on the stage.

In a powerfully suggestive essay, Franco Moretti sees Renaissance tragedy as staging the culture of absolutism in its process of dissolution.[87] It represents the steady degeneration of such absolute sovereignty, but in conditions in which those caught up in this decline can no longer comprehend it. As a governing class in historical decay can no longer grasp its situation, the initiative is passed to the theatre spectators themselves, who must now, without an absolute authority to guide them, think and judge for themselves. As such, they represent the first glimmerings of the rational public sphere of later middle-class society, which likewise repudiates traditional authority for critical debate. Tragedy, on this view, is a vital mechanism in the evolution from late-feudal to bourgeois culture.

It is, then, an essentially transitional form, the fruit neither of cosmos nor chaos. It is the product neither of faith nor doubt, but of what one might call sceptical faith. It may spring, for example, from the clash between a remembered sense of value and what seems a predatory, degenerate present. Tragic disenchantment is possible because idealism still is. Or it may dramatize the deadlock between the asphyxiating burden of the past and a wistful striving for the future, between which the present is squeezed to death. This is so in both Ibsen and Chekhov. For Hegel, tragedy often reflects a strife between past and present, with the tragic hero torn apart in the contest between them. The protagonist may be like Hamlet out of joint, askew to his time, either a too-early avatar of a new world or a washed-up survivor of an old. Goethe's Götz von Berlichingen is a type of the latter; but there is also, as Marx argued, the revolutionary whose hour has not yet struck, of whom Thomas Münzer is exemplary. Marx thought Lassalle's choice of Franz von Sickingen for the eponymous hero of his tragedy a false move in this respect: von Sickingen, intended as a harbinger of the future, is in fact an aristocratic hang-over from the *ancien régime*.[88]

Shakespearian tragedy can also be seen in such transitional terms. Shakespeare is attracted by the traditional idea of inherent values and stable identities, but he is also an advocate of difference in so far as he recognizes that things, including human subjects, must be mutually constitutive just in order to be themselves. Intrinsic values are a kind of resounding tautology; as Wittgenstein puts it in *Philosophical Investigations*, there is no more useless proposition than that of the identity of a thing with itself. Yet the alternative would seem in Shakespeare to be a perilous brand of relativism in which all identities become contextually defined and so are no longer consistent identities at all. Difference or mutuality, positive in itself, has a kind of 'bad' infinity lurking within it, so that one value or identity can become confounded with another in a process which threatens to level them all to nothing. Money, language and desire are the plays' three prime examples of this promiscuity, which risks undermining all unity and stability. Yet since this is also true of the extravagantly metaphorical language in which the drama makes its point, it is hard to eradicate this perpetual mingling and exchanging of identities, which is a source of both tragedy and comedy, without eliminating creative powers along with it. Equally, it is hard to oppose the hard-faced new ideologists like Edmund, Iago or Lady Macbeth, with their hubristic belief in endless self-fashioning, without acknowledging that such transgression is a condition of human history and agency as such.[89]

The opposition between order and transgression can anyway be dismantled. For one thing, the Law has a vested interest in our iniquity, since if we did not kick over the traces it would be out of business. For another thing, it is 'orderly' of us to transgress, in the sense that a perpetual crossing of boundaries is part of our nature, not some lamentable deviation from it. One word for such constant transgression is history. Not to have any very stable location is built into the order of the labouring, linguistic animal. A distinctively human regime is one with an immanent power to surpass itself. Language is exactly such a formation. It is this capacity for transgression which makes a cultural system work, rather than simply disrupting its regular operations. Tragedy sometimes detects a kind of skewedness or brute dissonance at the heart of things, as some intimation of the Real – say, incest, or being served up the flesh of your butchered infants – irrupts into an ethical order which usually survives by keeping such horrors at bay. Without this excluded Real, however, no ethical order would be able to function.

Not all tragedy is of this kind; some of it is not especially horrific or outrageous but simply sorrowful. Yet such glimpses of the Real are both fascinating and obscenely enjoyable – so that even as the mind is shaken to its roots, stunned and violated by the terrors it has witnessed, clamouring that such things cannot conceivably be possible while knowing full well that they are taking place, it also grasps that this askewness beyond signification is somehow necessarily part of the way things work. Without this blindspot at the centre of our vision, this screaming silence at the core of our speech, we would be unable to see or speak at all. There is something out of place or, in Lacanian phrase, *ex-time* at the very heart of order, whether it is a repressed desire or a suppressed group or class, which helps to keep it going. It is this necessity, this otherness or out-of-place element which we need in order to be in place at all, which lurks within the ideas of fate and Will, and of which the Christian God is a more benign instance. It may also inform the Christian doctrine of original sin, the belief that transgression is part of the way we naturally function, an essential structure of our species-being, and that this is a felicitous state or *felix culpa* because it is the source of our achievement as well as of our self-undoing.

The word 'order' suggests a coherent system. But this is rarely the actual context of tragedy, in the sense that scholars once used solemnly to imagine a shapely entity known as the Elizabethan World Picture. As

Raymond Williams points out, ancient Greece was 'a culture marked by an extraordinary network of beliefs connected to institutions, practices and feelings, but not by the systematic and abstract doctrines we would now call a theology or tragic philosophy'.[90] But if order is not quite as stable as it may appear, neither is transgressive desire anything but routine. For Spinoza, our desires are themselves determined, while for Freud desire has the anonymity of an impersonal order. Desire for Freud is not defined by its object, which is quite gratuitous; instead, it goes all the way through it and comes out somewhere on the other side, to rejoin itself. Desire in the tragedies of Racine has just this merciless, inhuman quality, as a sort of natural catastrophe which suddenly rears its head and knocks you sideways. It is a sickness or affliction to be lamented as deeply as death, and from which death is often the only exit. Racinian theatre is one in which desire continually misses its target, so that its strict economy is often enough a balance of non-reciprocities, a failure of symmetry all round, as one character loves another who loves another. Andromache loves her dead husband Hector, Pyrrhus loves Andromache, Hermione loves Pyrrhus and Orestes loves Hermione. In *Britannicus*, Nero is in love with Junia, beloved of Britannicus; Titus of *Bérénice* loves Bérénice but casts her off, while Antiochus loves her unrequitedly. Phèdre loves Hippolytus, who detests her, Aricia loves him too, and Hippolytus loves her in return.

All this then gives rise in Racine's drama to the series of mismatchings, mystifications, backfirings, double effects, mutual misperceptions, counter-productive strategies, self-undoings and self-divisions by which desire may finally cancel itself out into death. This stringent neo-classical form is less a matter of equipoise than of a tight web of mutual thwartings, which seems harmonious only because all the characters are potentially engulfed in such conflict. The homogeneous language hints at this claustrophobic enclosure even as its elegance rises above the appalling savagery it portrays. These mannered patricians are also libidinal monsters. There is constant disruption within the most rigorous order, so that disruption becomes itself a kind of sinister symmetry, the pitiless repetitions of desire. The choice for a Phèdre is between being ravaged by this unforgiving law, or destroyed by the equally unrelenting edicts of society.

It is true that, viewed from another angle, desire is a wayward, anarchic force which plays havoc with duty and violates the bonds of friendship, kinship, legality, civic allegiance. Desire, as the eighteenth- and nineteenth-century novel is aware, is no respecter of social distinctions, which is one reason why it is so baneful. To see desire as anarchic is no doubt particularly tempting for a rationalist age, one for which emotion can only be defined as the rival of reason; there can be nothing here of classical morality's idea of *reasonable* desire, any more than there can be for postmodern thought. But passion is a register as well as a delirium, a remorseless fate as well as a random infection. Love is at once inevitable and fortuitous: this irreplaceable person is the only conceivable object of it, even though of course it could always have been someone else.

Though characters like Phèdre act and scheme as free agents, they are determined at every point by this ruthlessly impersonal yearning, which divides them so radically from themselves that they can only look on helplessly as their passion carries them to their ruin. Desire brings with it suffering and self-repression, so that as in Goethe's *Werther* one fears it as one might dread a hideous crime or virulent contagion. Its opposite would seem less hatred than health. Love is a lethal addiction which makes you a stranger to yourself, forces you into dissembling, disavowal, self-torture, and can veer in the blinking of an eye into its opposite. The one you love is also your deadly enemy, as indeed is the part of the self that loves. The typical condition is thus one of ambivalence, as creative and destructive impulses become tragically intertwined. Much the same is true of Euripides's *Medea*, Lorca's *Yerma* and Edward Albee's *Who's Afraid of Virginia Woolf?*, which like *Medea* has a *Kindermort*, though this time a purely imaginary one.

Even if there is some sort of order in the world, it may be fitful and ambiguous, its ordinances both coercive and inscrutable. Kafka's fiction is the *locus classicus* of this double bind, but it can be found more generally in Protestantism and the idea of the *Deus absconditus*, in the vision of men and women groping among the semi-legible tokens of a darkened world for an assurance of salvation which is forever denied them. For this way of seeing, things are not rational in themselves; they are rational only because God has arbitrarily decreed them to be so. A similar arbitrariness belongs to the Law in general, which cannot be rationally motivated since it would then be subordinate to reason and so lose its absolute authority. The Law can retain that authority only by being a resounding tautology ('The Law is the Law!'), an empty signifier whose imperative 'Obey!' is as intransitive as the orders of one who simply wishes to be in command, not to get something accomplished. Kafka's Josef K. has to write a statement of defence against a crime which has not been specified. 'What do they want of me?', 'What am I supposed to do?', is the anxious query of the subject who stands before the Law, wondering whether it can fathom this unreadable text and whether the Law has interpreted its own demand aright.

If there is no justification before the Law, it is for one thing because the Law says nothing which you could argue or agree with; it has no

content beyond the sheer performative act of asserting its own dominion. It therefore has the formalism of all pure violence, and is as impervious to argument as a psychotic. Raskolnikov reflects in Dostoevsky's
Crime and Punishment that all the great lawgivers of humanity have been
bloodthirsty because they have all been bold innovators; the bearer of
the new, of that which as yet lacks legitimacy, is in this sense akin to the
criminal. The avant-gardist and the malefactor are twins. Hegel saw
history as the product of creative tyrants drenched in blood and imagination, murderous prodigies who were forced to transgress moral frontiers and trample others underfoot simply because they were in the van
of progress. It is a tragic view of human civilization: Hegel did not believe
there was much happiness for men and women beyond the private
sphere, and saw history as largely devoid of such fulfilments.

'What do they want of me?' is also the question of the protagonist of
Kafka's *The Castle*, who can never be sure whether the Castle authorities
are 'hailing' him personally or quite unaware of his existence. 'My
position here', he protests, 'is very uncertain.' Was he summoned for a
purpose, or by some administrative oversight? At one point the bureau-
crat Klamm calls out Frieda's name, but K. speculates that he may not
have been thinking of her at all. It is hard to know what to demand of
the Law apart from a sheer recognition of one's existence; but this is
either so formal or so total a demand, either everything or next to
nothing, that it is not easy to say what would count as meeting it. How
would K. recognize recognition? The Castle's pronouncements, he is told,
are not to be taken literally ('You misconstrue everything'), and perhaps
there is no metalanguage or single source of utterance in the Castle in
any case. K. is told after a while that there are 'control authorities' but
no Control Authority. He naturally wants to get on terms with these
authorities, since he may then find out what he is supposed to do, make
some sort of difference; but if an authority is a power which precedes
and pre-empts you, then perhaps it has all been decided in advance and
K. is wasting his time. It is impossible to tell whether things are random
or rigorously determined. To be forgiven, you must first of all prove that
you are guilty, which the Castle denies; there can be no salvation for the
innocent. It may also be that the Castle, like the Mosaic Law in the eyes
of St Paul, can only condemn rather than pardon. The Law has its uses,
but as Paul recognizes it will only show you where you have gone wrong,
not instruct you in how to go right.

K. is told that his happiness will end on the day when he discovers
that the hopes he has placed in Klamm are vain, which sounds like the
opposite of a successful Lacanian analysis. For the subject to realize
that it has no foundation in the Other, that nothing can unambiguously

guarantee it, is the glimmerings of Lacanian wisdom, not the end of felicity. It is the moment at the end of J. M. Synge's *The Playboy of the Western World* when Christy Mahon, having advanced from depending on his father to relying on the admiring fantasies of the community, comes to realize that there is no sure ground of identity in either of them and abandons them both for a narrative of perpetual self-invention. Kafka's K. does not give up on his desire for recognition, and the intended conclusion of this unfinished fable represents a compromise: he is issued with no official guarantee or legitimation of his position in Castle society, but on his death bed, worn out by his struggle, the news comes through that though his legal claim to stay in the village is invalid, he is allowed because of certain auxiliary circumstances to live and work there.[91]

The Law is not the opposite of desire, but the taboo which generates it in the first place. In this sense, as we shall see later, it is a little like tragedy, which is supposed to provoke the very emotions which it then proceeds to purge. Paradoxically, it is only through the Law that we can have access to the desire which it prohibits, since the prohibition is the first we learn of it. 'If it had not been for the law', writes St Paul to the Romans, 'I should not have known sin. I should not have known what it is to covet if the law had not said, "You shall not covet."' (Romans 7: 7). In this sense, it is the Law which tells us what to desire. Franco Moretti points out that in the fiction of Balzac and Flaubert, the hero only really desires what others wish him to desire.[92] In the form of the Freudian superego, the Law is insanely vindictive and brutally sadistic, plunging men and women into madness and despair. This vengeful, paranoid Law is out of control, sick with desire, spreading havoc in the name of stability, raging against the fragile ego with death-dealing ferocity.

As if this were not enough, the Law is also obtuse, deaf to the truth that the subject is unable to obey its childishly unreasonable demands, and blind to the fact that its violence is excessive even for its own ends. It has all the arrogance of power with none of its craftiness. Those who cling most submissively to this august power may be the most guilty, since it is always possible that, like the ice-cold Angelo of *Measure for Measure*, their eagerness to conform is an unconscious defence against their urge to rebel.[93] Like the sublime, the Law is both fearful and alluring; indeed for Kant, the moral law is the ultimate form of sublimity. The holy terror of the sublime is the way in which Nature points beyond itself to the moral law in its very raging destructiveness. Once sublimated in this way, those destructive forces seem to be redeemed: they now take the form of moral authority itself, in all its daunting majesty. Yet because this authority is unrepresentable in itself, it can be imaged only by Nature, and so is bound to have an aura of Nature's chaos and callousness still clinging to it. There is a parallel here with tragedy. Tragic destruction points beyond itself to a law which seems to justify it; yet that law has itself more than a touch of frenzy, disorder and injustice about it. Whether it is a solution to strife, or a higher expression of it, is then not easy to judge.

It may be in any case that order and the powerful individual, at least in the modern era, are not commonly found together. Hegel, like Max Weber after him, thought that the bureaucratic state had more or less put paid to heroes, so that the more stability one has the fewer colourful mutineers one is likely to breed. A. C. Bradley bemoaned the effect of a world of 'trousers, machinery, and policemen' on 'striking events or individual actions on the grand scale'.[94] Quite why an heroic world should be a trouserless one is not clear. Besides, order and transgression cannot be polar opposites, since the law is its own transgression. Its origin, as Edmund Burke knew, is bound to be lawless, since there is no law before the Law, and the establishment of the Law must therefore have been arbitrary and coercive. Conversely, the coercion of the Law requires a general consent to the institutions of authority. Civilized society for Burke is simply the process by which, over time, this violent origin or aboriginal crime becomes mercifully erased from human memory, so that illegitimacy modulates gradually into normality. Civility is just violence naturalized. At the source of any human history lies some primordial trespass or taboo-breaking, which has now been thrust judiciously into the political unconscious and cannot be dredged to daylight without risk of severe trauma. Those radicals who hark back to this illicit source would reopen the primal scene, uncover the father's shame, snatch the veils of decency from the unavoidably tainted sources of social life and expose the unlovely phallus of the Law.[95]

This collusion between Law and desire is obvious enough in revenge tragedy. Revengers like Chapman's Bussy D'Ambois or Vindice of *The Revenger's Tragedy* turn by some fateful logic into the image of those they hunt down, growing less and less distinguishable from them. If Vindice punishes the wicked, he also gloats over doing so. The revenger is both criminal and law-enforcer, custodian of order and violator of it. Ferdinand, the symbol of authority in Webster's *The Duchess of Malfi*, is a monster of evil. To clamour for justice as an avenger is to be sucked into the very order which denies it, accepting its warped reciprocities, its exchange-values, its barren tit-for-tat logic. Only by some gesture of absolute refusal, some gratuitous act of foregoing and forgiveness, might one cut the knot of this situation, breaking the deathly circuit; yet this is to allow injustice to flourish, so that it is not easy to distinguish such transcendence from criminal indifference. Perhaps one needs to step back from this self-fuelling violence to some meta-position which foreshadows death, where all odds are struck even, reading that death back into the present in the gesture which we know as mercy. It is in this spirit that Walter Benjamin writes of death as the form of the tragic protagonist's life, rather than just its end.[96] Yet this creative levelling of values is ominously close to a kind of cynicism.

All of these cat-and-mouse collusions between law and rebellion cast doubt on some simple antithesis between cosmic pattern and individual trespass. One of our most abiding desires, if Freud is to be credited, is a desire for the Law itself, a passion for self-laceration. And this, as we shall see, plays its part in tragic pleasure. Moreover, if transgression is to be real, so must be the Law it flouts, which means that transgression cannot help confirming the very power it infringes. Crime must imply value if it is to be authentic, so that the anarchist is almost as much a zealot for law and order as the archbishop. The Marquis de Sade cannot logically be a nihilist.

Dorothea Krook claims that the torments of tragedy are necessary, and are accepted by protagonists as such, even if they are innocent. Their pain is redemptive and expiatory, makes the mystery of suffering intelligible, reaffirms the moral law and achieves reconciliation. There are no doubt a few tragic works of which this is true, but it is false of the great majority, from *Antigone* and *Othello* to *John Gabriel Borkman* and *The Seagull*. It is the critics' desire for moral harmony, not the tragedians', which is at stake here. To see human anguish as bound up with the rending and reinforcing of a cosmic order is an attempt to justify the indefensible. It is like claiming that the loss of life in a shipwreck at least testifies to the magnificent power of Nature. Indeed, this is more or less the opinion of Hölderlin, for whom tragedy is a necessary sacrifice of the human which allows Nature to appear as such. But this, like other such apologias, is cast in the high-toned language of German idealism, and its more objectionable implications are thus easily passed over. Such philosophers of Nature, sublimity and the intolerable presence of the gods need to recall that tragedy is traditionally about pity as well as fear, a topic to which we may now turn.

Chapter 6

Pity, Fear and Pleasure

Tragedy, that most virile of art forms, began as a fairly effeminate business. One of the several reasons why Plato banishes it from his ideal republic as the key example of irrational art is because it allows us to indulge dangerously unmanly emotions such as pity and fear. We should not give rein in art to passions which we would restrain in reality, even though Plato grudgingly admits how enjoyable they can be. The pity we feel for others is in danger of infecting ourselves; it is hard to be compassionate without feeling sorry for ourselves as well.[1] Leo Tolstoy harbours a rather similar theory of emotional infection in *What is Art?* As for fear, a surplus of it obviously threatens the masculinist virtues of toughness and self-discipline on which the polity rests. Plato has some more creditable reasons for his wariness of tragedy, not least his belief that a true understanding of law, wisdom and justice would eliminate it from life. Philosophy is the antidote to the tragic. But the topic brings out the worst in him as well as the best.

Aristotle's ingenious riposte to this censure is the doctrine of *catharsis*, which accepts Plato's premises while denying his conclusions.[2] Tragedy can perform the pleasurable, politically valuable service of draining off an excess of enfeebling emotions such as pity and fear, thus providing a kind of public therapy for those of the citizenry in danger of emotional flabbiness. We feel fear, but are not inspired to run away. We are, so to speak, shaken but not stirred. In this sense, tragic drama plays a central role in the military and political protection of the state, organizing the appropriate feeling-complex for these ends rather as Bolshevik *Proletkult* saw art as an organizing principle of new kinds of feeling appropriate to Soviet Man. The French neo-classical critic Rapin argues that tragedy hardens us against fear, as we grow accustomed to seeing those more eminent than ourselves coming to grief, as well as disciplining us to spare our pity for those who most deserve it.

Tragedy is thus an instrument for regulating social feelings, and its purpose, as Milton writes in the preface to *Samson Agonistes*, is 'to temper and reduce [the passions] to just measure with a kind of delight'.[3] Philippe Lacoue-Labarthe sees Greek tragedy as a politics of emotion, insisting that pity and fear are political rather than psychological notions. Pity refers to the social bond, whereas fear refers to the danger of its dissolution.[4] They thus correspond roughly to the roles which Edmund Burke in his aesthetic treatise respectively assigns to the beautiful and the sublime – the former as the graceful affinities and acts of mimesis which bind social life together, the latter as the disruptive dynamic or restless enterprise which dissolves it only to recreate it anew.[5] Tragedy, one might argue, is a blending of beauty and sublimity: it trades in the ordinary social relations of love and politics, but sees these as opening on to an otherness which they cannot entirely master.

For Aristotle, then, tragic theatre is a refuse dump for socially un-desirable emotions, or at least a retraining programme. Whereas Brecht believed that the audience should check in their excessively tender feelings with their hats and coats, Aristotle holds that we should leave them behind us as we exit. As Walter Kaufmann paraphrases him: 'confused and emotional people will feel better after a good cry'.[6] But perhaps not, so the implication runs, self-disciplined types like you and I. F. L. Lucas, displaying a well-nigh postmodern sensitivity to cultural difference, thinks that Aristotle's theory 'may have been truer for an excitable Mediterranean race'.[7] The conflict between Plato and Aristotle is thus one familiar today between mimetic and therapeutic theories of pornography or media violence. Either the stuff drives us to real-life brutality, or it has exactly the opposite effect. Nietzsche espoused the mimetic theory and rejected the doctrine of *catharsis*: for him, instincts were strengthened the more they were expressed.[8]

Aristotle claims in the *Poetics* that pity and fear are intertwined. We pity others for what we fear may happen to ourselves, and those inca-pable of the one feeling are thus impervious to the other as well. Pity is thus self-regarding, as it is for some modern philosophers, though else-where in his work Aristotle distinguishes between this self-centred emotion and compassion or philanthropy. Pity turns into fear, Aristotle remarks in the *Rhetoric*, when its object is so intimate that the suffering seems to be our own. Pressed to a limit, then, the distinction between the two feelings becomes well-nigh undecidable. Both are rooted in the imagination – in the case of pity, in the reconstruction of another's feel-ings, in the case of fear in a vision of what might happen to ourselves. Aristotle does not consider that you can pity those who brought their misfortune on themselves, an opinion shared by Martha Nussbaum but not, as we have seen, by the present study.[9] It seems rather flinty not to feel a twinge of compassion for someone who wrenches his car steering-wheel in a momentary flare of irritation and ends up without any limbs. Nussbaum usefully stresses, however, that you can't feel pity without feeling potentially vulnerable or insecure yourself, not least if pity is as self-regarding as Aristotle seems to think.

Not every critic is as hard-nosed as Aristotle on this score. The soft-hearted Lessing, whose ideas of sympathy were influenced by Adam Smith, thinks that we can sympathize even with evil persons.[10] David Hume asserts that 'we pity even strangers, and such as are perfectly indifferent to us'.[11] But there is a submerged dilemma here, as we have noted in the previous chapter. If protagonists are too faultless then they risk being too passive, their suffering becomes repugnant, and it is not easy to claim with the apologists for cosmic order that tragedy has much to do with justice. But if they have a hand in their own downfall, it is hard for some critics to see how we can sympathize with them, and so feel their undoing as tragic rather than deserved. But we can, in fact, feel for those whom we find disagreeable. Oscar Mandel asks whether we like Emma Bovary well enough to make the novel tragic, but Emma is tragic whether we like her or not.[12] All we need to know to assess whether her career is tragic is whether she is human, not whether she is appealing, self-destructive, saintly or high-born.

There is thus a kind of flaw or potential weakness at the root of pity, which makes it sound rather less of an unpleasantly *de haut en bas* affair. If we were fully self-contained we could not have compassion for others; indeed we would have a touch of the psychopath about us. John Dryden may be mistaken to rank pity as 'the noblest and most god-like of virtues', as he does in his preface to *Troilus and Cressida*; but it is not necessarily just odious patronage either, even though we speak more easily of the object of pity than the subject of it. Hetty Sorel in George Eliot's *Adam Bede* is denied her appropriate tragic status in just this way. In fact, for some critics tragedy and pity make uneasy bedfellows: you don't look down on those you see as tragic, while pity might involve just such condescension. Hegel manages to be patronizing to pity itself, which in tragedy must be superior stuff to the common-or-garden species. 'Mere' pity and fear, he declares, are inferior to the higher ends of the art. For Hegel, the long tragedy of the Jewish people can rouse neither pity nor terror, only horror. It has nothing of the beauty and grandeur of the Greek heritage, incapable because of its utterly transcendent God of incarnating the divine in the human sphere. In one of the tortuous absurdities which litter the theory of tragedy, Jewish tragedy for Hegel, in the words of one of his interpreters, is 'bereft of any tragic dimension'.[13]

Aristotle's doctrine is homeopathic: tragedy arouses feelings of pity and fear only to purge them, cleansing us of too much terror and tender-heartedness by feeding us controlled doses of these very passions. We are allowed to indulge these feelings, but only in the process of slimming them down to size. There is thus an oddly circular quality to tragedy, which stimulates in order to syphon off. It is more like primal scream therapy than music hall. And just as our response to tragedy strangely mingles pain and pleasure, so this process of purgation is similarly ambivalent: the feelings being released are painful in themselves, but the act of easing them is pleasurable. We may pass over in decorous silence the obvious analogy to this act of enjoyably voiding an achingly burdensome load. But this dialectic of pain and pleasure is a doubled one, since both sensations are at work in pity and fear in the first place. The eighteenth century was well aware of the smug glow of sentimentalism which pity could involve, and an age fascinated by the sublime was no stranger to the suggestion that terror could be enthralling.

How self-interested is pity? Thomas Hobbes sees it in characteristically egoistic style as the 'imagination or fiction of future calamity to ourselves, proceeding from the sense of another man's calamity'.[14] Pity can be a species of *Schadenfreude*, agreeably reminding us of our own freedom from harm in contrast with another's misery. Joseph Addison presses this case to a sadistic limit: the greater the hero's misery, the deeper our delight. Amartya Sen writes that 'it can be argued that behaviour based on sympathy is in an important sense egoistic, for one is oneself pleased at others' pleasures and pained at others' pain, and the pursuit of one's own utility may thus be helped by sympathetic action'.[15] For Sen as for Kant, an empiricist or Humean notion of sympathy, whereby we copy or reflect others' emotions directly in ourselves, can be no sound basis for morality, since it is always bound to betray a self-regarding subtext. Sympathy and empathy, however, are not always clearly distinguished in the theory of tragedy. There is no moral value in the mere act of empathy. Becoming Henry Kissinger by an act of imaginative identification does not mean having compassion for him, not least because I have just suspended the self which might exercise it. Sympathy implies the existence of distinct identities. If Keats does manage to become the nightingale he can logically reap no fulfilment from the fact, since there will be no Keats around to reap it.

It may be, as the philosophical egoists argue, that I feel for your trouble only because I can imagine having the same affliction myself; but there is a difference between feeling *for* and feeling. I do not have to feel your pain, in the sense of mimetically recreating it within myself, to feel for you. There is a difference between feeling sorry for you and feeling your sorrow. It is a Romantic error to suppose that feeling for must involve feeling. It is the emotional equivalent of the belief that in order to understand someone else's meaning you must grope your way into her mind. Empiricism breeds Romanticism: if we are all trapped in our solitary experiential worlds, then only some extraordinary faculty like imagination, intuition or the moral sense could conceivably leap the gulf between us. But you can sympathize with someone racked by birth contractions without being anatomically capable of being racked by them yourself, just as you can judge a flautist to be execrable without ever having played the flute. A bankrupt who testily rebuffs your sympathy because you have never been bankrupt yourself is not just someone who is hard to console, he is someone who has failed to grasp the concept of sympathy. It is even possible to feel for someone's trouble more keenly than they do themselves. It may be that I want to relieve you of your despair just so as to feel less sympathetically suicidal myself. But you can also want to help someone out without feeling much beyond the desire to help them out, just as you can empathize with another's misery without feeling the slightest impulse to alleviate it. You may think it serves them right, or relish the aesthetic spectacle of their distress, or be masochistically reluctant to stop enjoying the sensation yourself.

The philosopher Henri Bergson maintains that if pity were just a question of sympathizing with someone's pain, we would shun it as too unpleasant; it must also express a desire to help. But Bergson also believes that pity expresses a desire to suffer: 'the essence of pity is thus a need for self-abasement, an aspiration downwards'.[16] True pity for Bergson consists not in commiserating with suffering but in desiring it. We sympathize with someone in distress out of a grovelling need to feel as low as they do. It is, he thinks, as though Nature is committing some great injustice which causes the sorrow, and it is necessary to rid ourselves of complicity with such injustice by this 'unnatural' yearning. Masochism, after all, is not so easily discounted. Even if sympathy is not empathy, we can still feel intensely when faced with another's sorrow, and this may well prove both harrowing and delectable. Dostoevsky writes in *Crime and Punishment* of 'that strange inward glow of satisfaction which is always found, even among his nearest and dearest, when disaster suddenly strikes our neighbour, and from which not one of us is immune, however sincere our pity and sympathy' (Part 2, ch. 7).

If Hobbes is an egoist about pity, David Hume is a semi-egoist. In his *Treatise of Human Nature* Hume discusses pity with tragedy directly in mind, arguing that fear involves sympathy just as Aristotle claims the opposite. But 'sympathy' is an ambiguous term here, meaning less compassion than the sheer ability to imagine another's emotional state; and it therefore follows logically that we can only fear if we can imagine what it is we fear. Hume thinks that we are all spontaneous impressionists or naturally mimetic animals, vividly receptive to others' feelings and able to reproduce them in ourselves; but it is not clear how self-regarding or altruistic this faculty is. Hume is a genial, sociable soul, but also a fly, worldly one with a wry sense of humanity's self-interestedness; and these two aspects of him blend a little uncertainly in his treatment of the subject. Thus he writes that 'the direct survey of another's pleasure naturally gives us pleasure, and therefore produces pain when compar'd with our own. His pain, consider'd in itself, is painful to us, but augments the idea of our own happiness, and gives us pleasure.'[17]

This seems to blend altruism and self-interest, sympathy and *Schadenfreude*; though the case is at once more and less admirable than this suggests. On the one hand, if sympathy for others really is natural, then it can be scarcely more meritorious than bleeding or breathing. On the other hand, Hume does not argue that we take malicious delight in another's misery, just that our own happiness is enhanced by the contrast. He calls this a 'pity revers't'. Nor does he claim that we resent the pleasure of others, just that it makes our own lack of it more painfully evident. Anyway, why exactly pity mingles pain and pleasure is clear for Hume: the pleasure is self-regarding, while the pain is other-regarding. And this would seem to draw on a further distinction between feeling and feeling *about*: we feel another's pain or pleasure spontaneously, mimetically, but we have feelings about it as well, which involve concepts, judgements, comparisons and the like. It is not, however, quite so sharp a difference as all that – for pleasure in another's pleasure seems to involve interests, not just natural reflexes. We delight in someone else's delight, but we are also delighted to do so for self-interested reasons.

That natural sympathies are also non-moral ones is equally a problem with the eighteenth-century Irish philosopher Francis Hutcheson.[18] A zealous anti-Hobbesian in the Gaelic-dominated school of benevolence, Hutcheson believes that we have an innate, spontaneous sense of compassion for others prior to all reasoning and self-interest.[19] Disinterestedness for him means not some bogus impartiality but that decentring of the self into others which is the practice of sympathy. Desiring the good of another regardless of our own interests is known to postmodernism as a spurious neutrality, and to more traditional ethical thought as love. Virtue, for Hutcheson as for Shaftesbury, is an end in itself, a matter of pleasure rather than duty rooted deep in our species-being, and the moral sense is a source of intense, quasi-aesthetic enjoyment. Hume inherits something of this doctrine from Hutcheson, holding that we are governed by sentiment rather than reason and that we pity others antecedent to all rational calculation. But this Hutcheson-like spontaneity is for him never entirely distinct from self-interest, since 'our concern for our own interest gives us a pleasure in the pleasure, and a pain in the pain of a partner'.[20] By the same token, however, injuring another is bound to cause their hatred of us to reflect itself in us as self-hatred. 'Custom and relation', Hume remarks, 'make us enter deeply into the sentiments of others; and whatever fortune we suppose to attend them, is render'd present to us by the imagination, and operates as if originally our own.'[21] It is not easy to say whether this is more selfless than it is self-regarding.

There are thus several ways of accounting for tragedy's peculiar blending of pleasure and pain. You can argue with Hume that pain and pleasure coexist when we witness another's affliction; or that painful feelings may be pleasantly purged; or that tragedy presents distressing contents in an artistically enjoyable way; or that it is on intimate terms with the sublime, which daunts and dispirits even as it stimulates. You can even go the whole hog and see tragic pleasure as a sheer unadulterated joy in others' misery. But few beyond Nietzsche are bold enough to do that.

Jean-Jacques Rousseau is another who believes in a natural force of pity prior to all reflection, 'which the utmost depravity of morals is hardly able to destroy – for we see daily in our theatres men being moved, even weeping at the sufferings of a wretch who, were they in the tyrant's place would only increase the torments of his enemy'.[22] If we needed to rely on anything as flimsy as reason to move us to compassion, the human race in Rousseau's view would probably by now be extinct. Pity for him is the fount of all social virtue; it is what plays the role of law and morality in the state of nature, and what saves us from being monsters. Rousseau toys with the hypothesis that pity is just empathy, a feeling which puts us in the sufferer's place, but thinks rather oddly that this gives his case for altruism more force rather than less.

St Augustine seems aware in his *Confessions* that there is a streak of cruelty in the kind of pity which finds itself helpless before a hopeless situation. The frustration involved in this can fester into sadism, as a kind of psychical defence against one's impotence. There is a *post-factum* fatalism about pity which is at odds with its implicit utopian impulse. Schopenhauer has profound compassion for the world precisely because it cannot be changed. Samuel Beckett wryly observes that the sufferer in tragedy is at least spared the despair of the spectator, though this may be truer of his own plays than of some other drama.[23] Pity may simply be a sign that the catastrophe has already happened, and that all that is left to us is to lament it. It is embarrassingly parasitic on unhappiness. In this sense, it is appropriate that one of our earliest historical discussions of

159

the emotion occurs in the context of theatre, where the spectators, physically divorced from the stage and unable to intervene in the action both by social convention and because it is fictional, can do little but look on aghast as a pre-scripted disaster runs its ordained course in lofty indifference to their own desires. A theatre which affirms human value and agency also provides in its very structure a graphic image of fate, passivity and alienation. Pity is a spectator sport.

Brecht will accordingly transform the theatrical apparatus itself, seeking to turn the estrangement it creates into a politically constructive force, as well as to dispel on stage the illusion of predestination. Empathy may be an epistemological intimacy, but it also demands a distance across which one can fantasize; so that the space which allows an audience to dream can be turned into one which exhorts them to question. The refusal of empathy and the critique of pity are thus related to one another as form to content. For Brecht as for Blake, pity is the lachrymose face which exploitation turns to the world. Indeed, in *The Threepenny Opera* it has become a flourishing industry all of its own.

For the eighteenth century, what Raymond Williams calls 'the contrast of pity with pomp'[24] belongs with an ideological assault on the traditional ruling order by its middle-class humanitarian opponents. There is a shift in sensibility from admiration (heroic and patrician) to pity and tenderness (domestic and bourgeois). Pity is the feel-good factor of the eighteenth century.[25] Pathos, tearfulness, *tendresse*, the meek, melting emotions, domestic pieties, chevaliers of the drawing-room, sentimental optimism, the cults of sensation and benevolence, a sanguine trust in Christian providence rather than an old-style pagan fatalism: if all this swooning and snivelling is a potent critique of upper-class barbarism and *hauteur*, it also proves largely incompatible with the creation of tragedy. Indeed, in the hands of its leading apologist Lessing, it involves a full-blooded historical revisionism which sidelines neo-classical drama, stomping-ground of the frigid nobility, and re-draws the lines of tradition from the Greeks and Shakespeare straight to the middle-class present. One result of this bold new cartography is a false alliance of Sophocles and Shakespeare from which the theory of tragedy has still not entirely recovered.

Lessing's own drama *Nathan the Wise* ends with a positive orgy of embracing and reconciling, while Voltaire's tragedies of sensibility appeal similarly to sentiment rather than reason. 'What's a tragedy that doesn't make you cry?' he inquired, and a piece like *Oreste* resounds with the noise of incessant wailing. *Merope*, a domestic drama about maternal love, reveals a robust underlying optimism: human nature is essentially beneficent, tyrants are mostly unhappy, men and women are the guileless victims of misfortune. It is the kind of emotional buoyancy which also informs Rousseau's *La Nouvelle Héloise*, in which an illicit love affair on course for tragedy is averted by Julie's renunciation of Saint-Preux and her spiritual rehabilitation.

Few commentators on tragedy question the validity of Aristotle's categories of pity and fear. James Joyce even adds an extra scholastic twist to them in *A Portrait of the Artist as a Young Man* by distributing them between a response to the sufferer and a response to the cause of the suffering. Yet Oscar Mandel, scarcely the most dissident of critics, sounds a surprisingly negative note, wisely doubting whether the complexity of our response to tragedy can be mechanistically divided into two determinate and necessary emotions.[26] Walter Kaufmann is doubtful that any ordinary spectator fears meeting the fate of an Oedipus or Prometheus, while Raymond Williams speaks scornfully of an eighteenth-century culture which 'comes to see the spectator as a detached and generalized consumer of feelings'.[27]

Pity-and-fear is certainly an inadequate formula for tragic experience. Yet it gets at the idea that there can be something chastening about tragedy, in the full complexity of that term: humbling, subduing, shocking, rebuffing, restraining, purifying, disciplining, tempering. And the formula, however reductive, suggests something of the dialectic of otherness and intimacy which tragedy can involve. Pity, roughly speaking, is a matter of intimacy, while fear is a reaction to otherness. St Augustine speaks in his *Confessions* of a light which shines through him and fills him with terror and burning love: 'With terror inasmuch as I am utterly other than it, with burning love in that I am akin to it'.[28] It is in fact possible to see these emotions as actual opposites: the opposite of love is probably more fear than hatred. Thomas Hobbes sees all human actions as springing from either pride (the desire for power, in effect) or fear, the former impelling us to appropriate an object and the latter to repel it.[29] We are pushed towards things and away from them, rather like tragic pity and fear; and this mechanistic psychology of appetencies and aversions survives as late as I. A. Richards. Richards sees tragedy as bringing pity, which is the impulse to approach, and fear, which is the reflex to retreat, into perfect equipoise.[30] Malcolm Lowry, who was a Cambridge student and may have heard Richards lecture, quotes this formula in *Under the Volcano*, though he wryly adds a third possibility: 'the conviction it is better to stay where you are' (ch. 8). In the rather different world of *Dialectic of Enlightenment*, Max Horkheimer and Theodor Adorno examine the tension between identification and dread – between the mimetic desire to merge with the world, and the terror of being taken over by alien forces which this brings with it.

161

Confronted with another's suffering, we can imagine ourselves vacil-
lating between 'This could be me!' to 'This, I'm glad to say, isn't me', 'This
mustn't be me!' (the didactic message of tragedy), and 'This can't be me!'
(however much I identify, there remains some residue of otherness here,
some gap I can't cross). 'This is and is not me' might then crystallize part
of what the pity-and-fear precept is groping for. Perhaps this is among
the reasons why incest has been such a recurrent theme in tragic art.
Incest is a kind of irony, whereby a thing is monstrously compounded
(sister/daughter, father/brother), both itself and something else; and this
compression is reflected in the lean economy of the tragic form, as though
incest presses this taut structure of contradictions to the point of self-
parody. One can even compound the compoundedness with a double
incest, as in Thomas Mann's *The Holy Sinner*, in which a child of incest
then marries his own mother. Incest is a matter of keeping things in the
family, thus disclosing what a fearful deformity this community of affections can breed. Aristotle perhaps meant more than he knew when he
remarked in the *Poetics* that tragedy is mostly a family matter. But incest
is also an enigma of affinity and otherness, identity and difference,
marking the point where the one glides into the other. Excessive
intimacy results, ironically, in alienness – both because it brings down
the cutting edge of the differentiating law between those involved, and
because to be too close to the sources of one's own identity is to come
up against a traumatic otherness which lies in wait for you there. To
merge with the parent is to come too near to the tabooed sources of one's
own identity, and like Oedipus to be blinded by this excess of light. Only
by establishing a distance from yourself, as in any act of knowledge, can
you know yourself for what you are; but this risks a different kind of
estrangement.

Incest, like Sophocles's *King Oedipus*, is all about arithmetic – about
non-resolvable equations or mathematical impossibilities ('two makes
four', 'two into one won't go'). Among other things, it concerns the
paradox that alterity is the ground of intimacy. Otherwise we could never
escape the narcissism of relating only to ourselves – though even this is
not conceivable without another who, like the Delphic oracle, can tell
me who I am. There is something self-thwarting or unthinkable about
human relationship, of which incest is simply an outlandish example.
Having daughters for sisters and sons for brothers reflects a conundrum
built into relationships as such. There is an alienness at the core of the
self which is pitilessly indifferent to it, yet without which there could be
no speech or subjecthood at all. It is the blindspot which allows us to see,
as Oedipus will see truly only when his eyes are put out. Oedipus is both
stranger and kinsman to others, so that pity and fear, in the sense of the

akin and the alien, are at work in the drama itself. The audience response to the play thus mirrors its content. We, too, are both strangers and kins-folk to Oedipus. Tragedy is the art in which the ambiguities on stage are also the ambiguities between stage and spectators.

Oedipus, master of riddles, works out his equations and equivalences only to discover that he has cancelled himself to zero in the process, left himself out of the reckoning, subtracting himself from the imposing figure of kingship to become the cypher of a beggarly exile. The man who forces Nature in the shape of the sphinx to yield up its secrets also vio-lates Nature in his outlawed love. The incestuous one is out-of-joint, the joker in the pack who disrupts the symbolic order of kinship but signifies its latent contradictions, and so incarnates the forbidden truth of the very kingdom from which he is cast out. Like all such liminal figures, as we shall see later, he or she is thus both sacred and soiled, holy and cursed; and this will be the condition of Oedipus when he arrives at Colonus to die. The incestuous one is an abomination who confounds essential dis-tinctions; but since desire is in any case no respecter of such boundaries, this vilified figure is also representative of the way of the world, of the social unconscious, of some nameless crime or obscene commingling inherent in existence itself.

The motif of incest, central to Shakespeare's *Hamlet*, crops up in Lope de Vega's *Punishment without Revenge*, in which Federico has an affair with his stepmother Casandra instead of marrying his cousin Aurora, he and Aurora having been brought up like brother and sister. It also haunts the tragic drama of Racine, not least *Phèdre* and *Britannicus*. 'Incest, rivalry among brothers, murder of the father, overthrow of the sons – these are the fundamental actions of Racinian theatre', writes Roland Barthes, who detects Freud's myth of the primal, parricidal horde lurking somewhere at their root.[31] There is a hint of incest in the brutal Ithocles's treatment of his twin sister in John Ford's *The Broken Heart*, and the theme breaks dramatically into the open in the doomed, world-defying passion of Giovanni and Anabella in *'Tis Pity She's a Whore*. The play ends with a *Liebestod* which finds an echo over the centuries in the ending of Ibsen's *Rosmersholm*.

Incest in Ford is a closure or perfect mutuality; his protagonists can transcend a vicious society, forging their own absolute, autonomous uni-verse in its place. Something of the same is true of Catherine and Heath-cliff in *Wuthering Heights*, who may be half-siblings. Hippolito of Thomas Middleton's *Women Beware Women* is gripped by an illicit passion for his niece Isabella, and persuades her that he is not her uncle to further his desires. There may be an incestuous component in Ferdinand's furious antagonism to his sister's marriage in John Webster's *The Duchess of Malfi*,

while Spurio and the Duchess of *The Revenger's Tragedy* are locked in incestuous liaison. D'Amville in Tourneur's *The Atheist's Tragedy* makes a das-
tardly incestuous proposal to Castabella, and incest bulks large in *Mirra*,
a tragic drama from the pen of the eighteenth-century Italian dramatist
Alfieri.

In Thomas Otway's *The Orphans*, Charmont is suspiciously opposed to
the marriage of his sister Monimia, who secretly weds Castalio but sleeps
with his brother Polydore by mistake. Both partners feel the pollution of
incest and cast themselves out; Castalio then kills Polydore. Count Cenci
commits an incestuous outrage on his daughter Beatrice in Shelley's *The
Cenci*, though the illicit relationship between Cain and his sister Adah in
Byron's *Cain*, which results in the child Enoch, is rather more excusable,
given the scarcity of alternative sexual partners at the time. The spectre
of incest looms up only to be dispelled in Lessing's *Nathan the Wise*, while
in Schiller's *Don Carlos*, Carlos is in love with the queen his stepmother,
a passion which is betrayed to his despotic father. Almost all of the
main relationships in Eugene O'Neill's *Mourning Becomes Electra* (Ezra
and Lavinia, Lavinia and Orin, Orin and Christine) are implicitly incestuous, and incest also informs Arthur Miller's *A View from the Bridge*. In
what Raymond Williams calls 'liberal' tragedy, aspiration always bears
with it a burden of guilt, so that in the very act of striking for freedom
you confront yourself as a stranger. Incest, with its mingling of identity
and otherness, can then become a metaphor of this self-division, as it
does in Ibsen's *Ghosts*.

'Incest', argues Franco Moretti, 'is that form of desire which makes
impossible the matrimonial exchange that . . . reinforces and perpetuates
the network of wealth.'[32] It is thus a kind of radical politics in itself, a
shaking of the symbolic order to its roots. In an incestuous relationship,
what the two partners share is an out-of-jointness, and this meeting in
no-man's-land is true also of pity and fear. In the deepest sense, to
exclaim 'This isn't me!' of the tragic victim is not to disown the agony
but to acknowledge it. It can mean that confronted with this unbearable
pain, all identity, including one's own, has now dwindled away, leaving nobody even to make an act of identification. What we share, in
Lacanian parlance, is no longer a question of the imaginary – rivalry,
mimesis, antagonism, sympathetic identification – or of the symbolic –
difference, identity, alterity – but of the Real. Which is to say that we
encounter each other on the ground of trauma, impasse, an ultimate dissolution of meaning, and seek to begin laboriously again from here.

To weave all three Lacanian categories together: tragedy portrays
conflicts in the symbolic order – political strife, sexual betrayal and
the like – with which we are invited, not least through pity, to make an

imaginary identification; but this imaginary relation is disrupted by fear, which is to say by the intrusion of the Real. Only relationships based on a mutual recognition of the Real – of the terrifyingly inhuman installed at the core of the other and oneself, for which one name is the death drive – will be able to prosper. What has to be shared, to by-pass a mere mirroring of egos, is what is foreign to us both. And this is what is expelled from the world of consciousness and civility. It is only on the basis of the askew, the *ex-time*, the ejected, that a community of compassion can be constructed. The cornerstone of a new order has to be, like Oedipus at Colonus, the reviled and unclean.

This requires one particular conjugation of pity and fear which the philosophers of tragedy have for the most part passed over in silence. It involves coming to pity what we fear, finding our own selves reflected in the abhorrent and abominable, and thus reinscribing the imaginary in the Real. For the conservative, monsters are other people; for the liberal, there are no monsters, only the mistreated and misunderstood; for the radical, the real monsters are ourselves. If the philosophical egoists are right that pity always betrays its adulterating admixture of self-interest, then it must be transferred from the domain of the imaginary, where self-in-other holds sway, to the register of the Real. It is here that we can effect a more enduring encounter by meeting on the ground of what excludes both self and other, of what disrupts our imaginary identities from within while being at the same time the very matrix of them. It is this inhospitable terrain, this kingdom whose citizens share only the fact that they are lost to themselves, which we hold most deeply in common, not a mutual exchange of egos; and a certain type of tragedy – *King Oedipus* and *King Lear* most memorably – is able to achieve this transference and disclose this truth. But it is by no means the only specimen of the art there is, or an account of the form as a whole. It is of no particular relevance to *Titus Andronicus, The Spanish Tragedy, The Jew of Malta* or *The Cherry Orchard*.

If pity is not to remain in the imaginary sphere of the ego, as it does with Hobbes, Hume and Rousseau, it has to open out into some less personal, more anonymous, 'non-human' dimension, and it is this which 'fear' can be made to signify in Aristotelian theory. If we are to escape the sealed circuit of the self, or the equally windless enclosure of self and other, we have to have sympathy for the other precisely as monstrous, to feel for the blinded Oedipus or crazed Lear in their very rebarbative inhumanity. And this demands an answerably 'inhuman' compassion, which is far from agreeable. For the Judaeo-Christian tradition, this inhuman form of compassion is known as the law of love. To see the Old Testament as concerned with ritual observance, and the New Testament as ousting this legalism with love and interiority, is a sophisticated piece of Christian anti-semitism. The law upheld by the Jews of the Old Testament is itself the law of love, which Jesus as a devout Jew declares he has come to fulfil rather than abolish. Jesus has not come to put sentiment in the place of obligation. Nobody gets crucified for doing that.

There is nothing objectionable in itself about obeying a list of edicts, as long as one recognizes that this is for the tenderfoot who is still in need of guidance. This is why St Paul thinks of the Law as an infantile affair, mostly for children. As long as we still look upon the ethical as a higher authority which rebukes and rewards us, we have not yet grown up. Indeed, we have not made much of an advance on dogs, let alone toddlers. What is inscribed on tablets of stone must be written on hearts of flesh, so that, as Paul observes in his epistle to the Romans, we can 'die' to this death-dealing Law and be discharged from its burdensome sway. Like the rules of art, the Law fulfils itself when we learn to do without it and acquire the spontaneous habit of virtue instead. Like the rules of art, too, part of what the Law intimates to us is when to throw it away. Once we have grown into virtue we can dispense with having to turn up the books all the time, as a fluent speaker of Arabic can dispense with a dictionary. At the same time, ritual fades into the background, as for the New Testament we stumble towards the profoundly unwelcome recognition that salvation is ethical (feeding the hungry, visiting the sick and imprisoned and so on) rather than cultic. But the logical fulfilment of the Law is also death, since those who love well enough are likely to be disposed of by the state.

But how can love be a matter of law? How can one be commanded to love? Is not 'Love one another!' as absurd as 'Find this joke funny!', or 'Feel jealous in four seconds' time!'? This would doubtless be the case if compassion was largely a question of feeling, as Romantics mistakenly assume. For one kind of moralist, what matters most in ethics is imagination. Only by this mimetic faculty can we know what it feels like to be someone else, and thus treat them like ourselves. The ethical begins to blur here into the aesthetic, to the consternation of Immanuel Kant. But sympathy, as we have seen, is not a matter of empathy, and if it were it would scarcely be such a rare commodity. It is here that the apologists for the imaginary must yield ground to the champions of the Real. Nobody expects us to feel a warm glow for whoever disembowelled our pet wombat, simply to treat him justly and humanely, not to respond in kind, and so on. And since this disemboweller could be anyone, love is also a matter of law in the sense that it is as indifferent as unconscious desire to any particular individual, which is to say that it is unconditional.

It is not a question of being sensitively attuned to cultural and ethnic peculiarities in the suavest postmodern style, but of acknowledging that anyone whatsoever has a claim on you, regardless of their culture. In this sense, compassion is ruthlessly impersonal. It is not dependent on one's emotional whims.

Love is thus no respecter of persons, and above all no respecter of families. There is nothing in the least lovely about it. The New Testament has significantly little to say of the family or sexuality, those fetishes, respectively, of Christian conservatives and radical postmodernists, but what it does have to say of the family is distinctly hostile. We are not supposed to grant our nearest and dearest any special priority when it comes to compassion. In any case, love within the family is just as much an obligation as it is outside it. David Hume thought that natural affections of this kind were a duty; it was not up to us whether we cared for our children. It helps to like them, of course, but it is not indispensable. As Nagg replies to Hamm in Samuel Beckett's *Endgame*, when irritably asked why he engendered him: I didn't know that it'd be you.

That love is not primarily a question of feeling is why the paradigmatic case of it is how you treat strangers or enemies rather than friends. If we have to love others in all their traumatic, repugnant selfhood, then it is in a sense always as enemies, potentially devastating threats to our own identity, that we encounter them. Anyway, what could be less praiseworthy than loving a friend? It would be like being awarded a certificate for enjoying sex or chocolate. To love one's neighbour as oneself is delightfully undemanding, if by this is meant loving an alter ego. It is in this imaginary register that it is usually understood. But in another sense it is not easy at all, since it is not easy to love oneself, as opposed to pampering oneself, thinking highly of oneself, being brutally self-interested and the like. One would not be at all eager to be treated by some people in the way they treat themselves. Blaise Pascal thinks that our concupiscence makes us hateful to ourselves, so that to love ourselves can only mean that 'we must love a being who is within us but not our own self'.[33] And this *ex-time*, for psychoanalytical thought, is the Real. One has to love oneself as one is, in all one's moral squalor, which is how one has to love others too. To feel for others as oneself is thus to feel for them as they are, rather than as imaginary replicas of oneself. It is to know them in the Real rather than the imaginary. It is to love even that 'inhuman' thing in them which also lies at the core of ourselves. And far from being delightfully undemanding, this is well-nigh impossible. It is what it would take for us to be free, but it may well be beyond our power.

Even so, it is this impersonality, which seeks to engage others as they actually are, in all their existential unloveliness, which ironically prevents compassion from being abstract in a more damaging sense, which is to say not really compassion for *this* person at all but a promiscuous openness airily indifferent to its object. You have to love me not just in my general human shabbiness, but in that unique form of hideousness which is all my own. Moreover, as if all this were not fatiguing enough, unconditionality also means non-reciprocity. The commandment is simply 'Love!', not 'Love and you'll get something in return!', or 'Love only those who display the most disgustingly obsequious devotion to you!' Compassion is inhuman in this sense too, in this reckless refusal to calculate interpersonal consequences, breaking violently with the natural order of credit and debit, the regulated symmetries of the symbolic order.

If love is a law, then the distinction between private sentiment and public obligation is dismantled, and compassion is thrust beyond the private arena into the political domain. In bourgeois society, these spheres are both separate and secretly related. If hard-headed politicians are much given to sobbing in public, not least in the United States, it is because sentimentalism is the pragmatist's corrupt version of feeling, the most authentic brand of it he can muster, rather as the bohemian is the scandalized burgher's image of the artist. The catch in the throat, and catching them by the throat, are not so different. On this view, feelings are private and arbitrary, whereas public responsibilities are graven in stone. In fact, feelings can be quite as rational as chess, and public obligations as arbitrary as hair-styles. Some important ethical consequences flow from this dismantling of the opposition between private and public, some of them relevant to socialism. Generosity, for example, becomes a public obligation. Having one's needs cared for beyond the call of duty is no more than one's due. We have a right to expect mercy, to calculate on the incalculable. Non-reciprocity becomes a matter of routine.

There is one final sense in which one can speak of the law of love. W. H. Auden's rather too grandiloquent line 'We must love one another or die', which he was later to reject, nevertheless captures the political truth that unless we cooperate we are unlikely to survive. Philosophers have sometimes puzzled over whether one can progress from a fact to a value; but here, perhaps, is an unexpected example of just such a shift. Our material situation is such that only valuing one another is likely to keep it going.[34] Without such value, we may well end up with no facts at all. We have long been aware that human beings are so constructed as to require affection if they are to flourish; but it looks, politically speaking, as though they may now need it just to survive.

'Why does tragedy give pleasure?' is among the hoariest of philosophical questions, akin to 'Why is there anything at all?' or 'Why is there evil in the world?' There has been no shortage of answers. Tragedy gives pleasure because the purging of excessive emotion is enjoyable in itself; because we take pleasure in mimesis as such, even representations of disasters; because tragic art shapes suffering into a significant pattern, containing it while rendering it agreeably intelligible; or because it puts our own petty troubles in chastening perspective. We revel in the steadfastness of the human spirit in the face of mind-wrenching calamity, or find an epistemophiliac satisfaction, however morose, in learning the truth and knowing the worst. We relish tragedy because observing the wretchedness of others is a source of malicious delight to us, or because we enjoy pitying its victims, which is always at some level a pleasurable self-pity as well. We reap moral and intellectual fulfilment from seeing the balance of cosmic justice harmoniously restored, though we also enjoy identifying with the rogues and rebels who disrupt it. Moreover, there is pleasure to be had from symbolically rehearsing and so disarming our own deaths, which fictional representations of death allow us to do.

Further answers to the question are not lacking. It is imaginatively gratifying to identify with someone else, however unenviable his or her plight, and in tragedy this carries with it an agreeable sado-masochistic bonus. Tragedy is satisfying because it allows us to indulge our destructive fantasies while knowing that we ourselves cannot be harmed, thus unleashing in us the delights of the death drive in culturally reputable guise. This libidinal joy in wreaking havoc may mix with our moral sense that there is indeed some value in suffering. We find fulfilment in the moral education which tragedy puts us through, and find it enjoyable simply to be so intensely stimulated, whatever the horrific nature of the stimulus. 'When it is well structured and well performed', writes Amélie Oksenberg Rorty, 'tragedy conjoins sensory, therapeutic and intellectual pleasures. Pleasure upon pleasure, pleasure within pleasure, producing pleasure.'[35] Compared with the *jouissance* of *Gorboduc* or *Saint Joan*, sexual orgies would seem for many an ardent critic to pale into insignificance.

Some of our pleasure in tragedy no doubt springs from simple curiosity. We don't witness brutal murders every day, and are thus intrigued to come across them even in fictional form. Indeed, the fact that they are fictional is the basis of one theory of tragic pleasure: for David Hume, in his essay on tragedy, we enjoy in art what we wouldn't in life. J. M. Synge's play *Deirdre of the Sorrows* ends by contrasting the harrowing deaths of its protagonists with the joy which recounting their legend down the ages will bring. Form plucks a kind of victory from defeat, thus reversing the tragic action itself. Tragedy is an imitation, and imitation for Hume is always agreeable; in any case, the eloquence of tragic art mitigates the discomfort of it. But this still does not account for why we find *disasters* in art enjoyable. That we enjoy imitation as such casts no light on the specific thrill which catastrophe, real or imagined, brings in its wake. And though eloquence may mitigate the tragedy, it may also intensify it, as Hume himself suggests when he imagines giving a father too graphic an account of the death of his favourite child.

It is true that we know people are not really being butchered on stage, which allows us to enjoy the spectacle with an easy conscience; but why *do* we enjoy it? The argument from fiction simply pushes the question back a stage. Philip Sidney tells us in *An Apology for Poetry* of an abominable tyrant who had pitilessly murdered a great many people, 'yet could not resist the sweet violence of a Tragedie'.[36] But Sidney is speaking here of being moved to pity by tragedy, not of relishing the torment of it, so that the case is no different from someone shedding tears over images of the down-and-out while creating mass unemployment in his company. There is nothing particularly puzzling about this: if the unemployed began to break his windows, he would stop weeping soon enough. In his *Spectator* essays on the art, Joseph Addison thinks that tragic pleasure, which leaves a 'pleasing anguish' in the mind, arises from comparing our own secure situation to the havoc on stage. His view is shared by Lucretius, who writes in *De Rerum Natura* of how sweet it is to behold a shipwreck from the safety of land – not, he adds, that we are glad that others should be afflicted, but because it is always pleasant to witness an evil from which you yourself are exempt. As with Hume, there is a difference between being glad about others' suffering absolutely, and being glad about it relatively. The Marquis de Sade, who reputedly paid someone to walk up and down outside his window in the pouring rain, was probably reaping both kinds of benefit.

Edmund Burke, however, in his essay on the sublime and the beautiful, can catch himself feeling no such satisfaction, even though he sees sublimity as a delight in pain. He also makes the hard-headed point that we do not, in fact, always prefer fictional to real-life suffering. A crowd, he argues, will desert a theatrical spectacle in droves to witness a real-life execution. Those critics who see tragedy as mollifying by its art what we would find unbearable in life have obviously overlooked the traffic jams of ghoulish voyeurs around aircraft accidents. The idea, anyway, is that real-life grief becomes sweetly agreeable when mitigated, and the same is true of artistic sorrow, where the tempering is achieved by form and fiction. But it is surely not true that we always enjoy pain when it is virtual rather than actual. I do not find having my teeth pulled out without anaesthetic in the least seductive even as a hypothesis, so that our relish for harm cannot be just a matter of its fictional packaging.

Burke believes that 'terror is a passion which always produces delight, when it does not press too close, and pity is a passion which is accompanied with pleasure, because it arises from love and social affection'.[37] Art is no doubt one way in which the terror can be kept at arm's length, but it is not the only one. If the crowd who surge from theatre to gallows were to be threatened with hanging themselves, their enjoyment of the scene might conceivably be diminished. Maybe any kind of spectatorial stance towards suffering, not just that of art, can make it sometimes pleasurable. Contrary to Hume and Addison, however, he maintains that some tragedy is the more pleasurable the less fictional it is: 'The prosperity of no empire, nor the grandeur of no king, can so agreeably affect us in the reading, as the ruin of the state of Macedon, and the distress of its unhappy king'.[38] Reading of the ruin of the state of Britain might prove a less delectable matter, for one of its most loyal servants; but having gleefully underlined the joy we take in others' miseries, Burke then provides an unexpectedly edifying explanation of it. It is true that 'there is no spectacle we so eagerly pursue, as that of some uncommon and grievous calamity',[39] but this apparent sadism is in fact altruism: unless we were attracted by suffering, we would shun real-life scenes of it and so fail to come to the aid of the victims. Our enjoyment of others' woes is thus a cunning device whereby Nature strengthens rather than loosens our social bonds. Sadism is really solidarity. The theory is as ingenious as it is implausible. Why should we put an end to our pleasure by rushing to the aid of the injured, unless the impulse to help is always for some reason stronger than the pleasure itself? Why not just let them lie back while we enjoy it?

The critic Maud Bodkin believes that tragedy is enjoyable because it gives us a 'tribal' feeling of the renewal of group life through sacrifice. It is doubtful that this is what theatregoers are feeling on the way out of *Blasted* or *The Quare Fellow*. Franco Moretti offers a more original (though less grandly universal) proposal in *The Way of the World*: the modern world valorizes unhappiness and takes pleasure in disconsolate endings because this eases bourgeois society's bad faith about not living up to its own principles. If only some external force had not intervened, perhaps it might have done. Destiny thus relieves it of responsibility, which is always an agreeable sensation.[40] Perhaps this is one reason why the word 'happiness' is so pallid a term in our lexicon, almost as embarrassingly unusable as 'love'. It also suggests a placid, rather bovine inertia, at odds with the frenetic dynamism of capitalist society. Unhappiness sounds somehow more real – both because, historically speaking, it is, but also, as Moretti suggests, because we can eagerly embrace it as retribution for our failings.

171

Perhaps we enjoy tragedy simply because we like to be stimulated, as Descartes considered. William Hazlitt thought something of the same, believing that the object of our stimulation was less important than the fact of it.[41] This, which one might call the anti-boredom theory of tragic pleasure, was fairly popular in the neo-classical period: Dennis and Rapin both advanced versions of it. Perhaps Samuel Beckett, whose work makes even tedium a pleasure, serves to refute the case. The Abbé Dubos observed that we go to tragedy because it is more pleasant to be grieved than to be bored. Better to be jolted alive by emotion than fester in ennui. This, however, might be true of other art forms as well; it does not yield a theory of specifically tragic pleasure. People, after all, have been known to die of laughing at comedy, which sounds stimulation enough.

Or it may be, as some eighteenth-century commentators maintained, that providence has considerately mollified all strong emotion with an accompanying balm. A kind of *catharsis* is divinely built in. Other critics of the period held that the pleasure of tragedy lay in moral satisfaction – either in the fulfilment of poetic justice, or in an enhanced sense of our own benevolence when we grieve over downfall and injustice. One might perhaps more accurately call this moral self-satisfaction. The Earl of Shaftesbury makes tragic pleasure sound an upliftingly moral affair when he writes of how 'the moving of our pleasures in this mournful way, the engaging them in behalf of merit and worth, and the exerting whatever we have of social affections and human sympathy, is of the highest delight'.[42]

For Schopenhauer, the jubilation of tragedy arises from our disengagement from the world and renunciation of the will to live. There is a glum sort of pleasure to be gained from recognizing that the world and the will can afford us no final satisfaction, and so are not worth our attachment to them. This is the joy of an ultimate freedom, which knows itself to be invulnerable because like the depressive or melancholic it has withdrawn all investment from reality. The subject is simply no longer at stake enough to be injured, and the sense of immortality which this breeds is an additional source of solace. What is really immolated in tragedy is thus less the hero than the ego of the spectator. The pleasures of tragedy are nirvanic. Indeed, this is true for Schopenhauer of the aesthetic in general, which estranges the torture-chamber of this world to a kind of theatrical charade, its shrieking and howling stilled to so much idle stage chatter for the audience's enraptured, indifferent contemplation.

The sublime is therefore the most typical of all aesthetic states, allowing us as it does to gaze upon daunting immensities with utter equanimity, serene in the knowledge that they can no longer harm us. As

Danton remarks in Büchner's *Danton's Death*: 'I'm flirting with death; it's very agreeable, making eyes at him through a spyglass like this, from a nice safe distance' (Act 2, sc. 4). In the sublime, the ego fantasizes a state of exultant invulnerability, thereby wreaking Olympian vengeance on the forces which would hound it to death. We can indulge the masochistic pleasures of the death drive safe in the knowledge that we are unkillable. Tragedy, or the aesthetic, is thus for Schopenhauer a momentary victory over both *Eros* and *Thanatos* – over the will to live, but also, as a phantasm of indestructibility, over death. Instead, like the tragic scapegoat itself, we find ourselves in some limbo or liminal state between the two. The aesthetic triumphs over death by coolly pre-empting it, acting it out already in the detached indifference of the artefact, drawing its sting by committing a sort of spiritual suicide before the grave can lay claim to it. It thus transcends life at the same time.

There is also something self-defeating about this condition, however, since as long as the ego still delights in its dissolution, it cannot have attained it. In tragedy, we feel for others because we know that their own inner stuff, the cruel Will, is ours too; but at the same time we spurn the Will's blind futility, freeing ourselves from its treacherously life-enhancing illusions. This is Schopenhauer's own version of the dialectic of pity and fear, intimacy and alienness, as we are drawn to a suffering which we acknowledge as our own, while through the framing, tranquillizing power of the aesthetic, we distance ourselves derisively from the whole grotesquely pointless spectacle.

A. D. Nuttall writes in his *Why Does Tragedy Give Pleasure?* of 'that strange sweetness of fear and grief' which characterizes our response to the art,[43] while Plato speaks in the *Philebus* of the spectators of a tragedy rejoicing in their grieving. He also writes in the *Phaedo* of Socrates's death as evoking both pain and pleasure in Phaedo himself ('a quite weird sensation, a sort of curious blend of pleasure and pain combined').[44] It is not just that we feel glad and grieved at the same time, but that we feel glad about our grief. Pentheus in *The Bacchae* savours the distress which he feels while peeping voyeuristically at the female revellers, as though he is the spectator of a tragedy within a tragedy. Our response, in other words, is not just ambivalent but masochistic. And since this grievous delight springs from identifying with the victims on stage, it is also sadistic, since the only way to perpetuate it in ourselves is to wish them to suffer more. Seeing them in torment makes us feel their misery ourselves, makes us enjoy feeling it, and so makes us want to put them through further pain. As Freud puts it, speaking of life rather than tragic art: 'The sadism of the superego and the masochism of the ego supplement each other and unite to produce the same effects'.[45]

No author is more aware of this than Dostoevsky, whose fiction is laced with sado-masochism from one end to the other, and whose characters wallow in the intricate delights of being mortally affronted. In this world of abruptly illogical emotion, in which everyone seems to be in a permanent state of pathologically morbid irritability, few experiences are more familiar than squirming humiliation. A fellow Russian, Vladimir Nabokov, is another virtuoso of this condition. Having manoeuvred themselves into a mortifying situation, Dostoevsky's ruined gentlefolk, buffoonish landowners and socially paranoid clerks cannot resist the impulse to persist in their grotesquely grovelling behaviour until they have magnified their degradation, both as a reckless assault on others and as a violence wreaked on themselves. Marmeladov of *Crime and Punishment* drinks to deepen his misery and exults in being beaten by his wife, while Raskolnikov courts his own downfall in his cat-and-mouse game with the investigator Porify. 'The moth flying into the candle of itself' is how the novel describes his self-immolating urge. There is a different aura of perversity about the fascinatingly complex, depraved wife-poisoner Svidrigaylov. The neurotically sensitive narrator of *Notes from Underground* is another case of self-abasement, while Father Zosima counsels Alyosha Karamazov to 'seek happiness in grief'.

Most critics, however, are made distinctly uneasy by the sado-masochistic theory of tragic pleasure. Northrop Frye writes a shade too briskly that 'the pleasure we get from [the blinding of Gloucester] has nothing to do with sadism',[46] while A. D. Nuttall, though generally more open to Freudian insight, is similarly sceptical of the case. Oscar Mandel informs us, in what could no doubt be read as a classic gesture of denial, that 'the argument that our pleasure derives from malice (*schadenfreude*) has often been refuted and demands no further attention'.[47] Far from being often refuted, it has rarely been addressed, except by the tragedians themselves. A character in August Strindberg's *A Dream Play*, for example, comments that 'people have an instinctive horror of other people's good fortune'. On the whole, critics have preferred rather more high-minded explanations of tragic pleasure, as in D. D. Raphael's bland assertion that 'our pleasure arises from the feeling that one like us reaches the greatest heights'.[48] But the question is rather why we smack our lips at seeing him topple from them. Nietzsche has no doubt that sadism is the solution: 'To see others suffer does one good', he writes gleefully, 'but to cause others to suffer even more so.'[49] Even the high-toned Matthew Arnold remarks that 'the more tragic the situation, the deeper becomes the enjoyment', which smacks of a most un-Arnoldian sadism.[50] Herman Melville observes in *Moby-Dick* that 'all men tragically great are made so through a certain morbidness' (ch. 16).

There is no reason why one should be forced to choose between humanist and psychoanalytical explanations.[51] Tragic pleasure works on a number of levels. Freud himself seemed to think that both cases captured something of the truth, remarking as he did that the average individual is both more and less moral than he imagines. When it comes to the question of moral value, his writing outdoes the humanists as well as undermines them. Slavoj Žižek notes that in staging suffering as an aesthetic spectacle, there is something abusive at tragedy's very core.[52] The psychoanalytically minded critic can accept this while still finding value in the form, but the humanist usually has trouble with this dual response. If tragedy is the highest achievement of the human spirit, it might seem grossly demeaning to speak of it in terms of sado-masochism, as though one were to discuss *The Divine Comedy* in terms of rubber fetishism. But why should sado-masochism be demeaning? If Freud is to be believed, it is an indispensable structure of the psyche, without which we would not work as human subjects. If it is perverse to find pain gratifying, then since we are all subject to what Žižek calls the 'obscene enjoyment' of the death drive,[53] which commands us to take delight in our own dissolution, it is hard to know who exactly is supposed to represent the norm.

One can imagine a three-step process here. First, the humanist resists the suggestion that our pleasure in tragedy is anything but morally pure. Then, perhaps, she may be reluctantly persuaded to acknowledge an element of *Schadenfreude* in the tragic crisis, even coming to see her former insistence on its moral sublimity as something of a psychical defence. But what if the recognition of *Schadenfreude* is a defence too? What if we would rather confess our enjoyment of another's agony than acknowledge the shaming truth that the destruction we most revel in is our own? Could our wryly conceded sadism be yet another mask for the death drive?

St Augustine is a good deal less coy than many a modern critic, speaking in his *Confessions* of tragedy as a joy in another's pain. He understands what it is to be seized by a 'pernicious pleasure' or 'miserable felicity'. As one who has himself perversely sought out shame and suffering, sinning simply so as to relish his own festering corruption, he ponders the question of why a man should yearn to be made sorrowful 'by beholding sad and tragical events, which he would not willingly suffer in his own person'. Grief is a pleasure to us, and he who grieves 'remaineth enraptured and weeps for joy'.[54] Perhaps, Augustine speculates, it is pity we like to savour rather than sorrow, though sorrow may be its inevitable accompaniment. We should be content, he considers, to love grief from time to time, but we must beware of uncleanness – so that his argument

175

here borders on Aristotle's doctrine of *catharsis*. This, one should recall, is the post-conversion Augustine looking back on his reprobate, sado-masochistic self, and drawing a suspiciously rigorous line between compassion and self-pleasure. It is impossible, he declares, to pity another truly while wishing that he might persist in his misery so that one might persist in one's enjoyment of it. But the fact that the idea even crosses his mind is itself perhaps revealing. True pity is rather too sharply distinguished from the bogus variety, compassion severed from self-interest.

But if some tragic drama is so compelling, it is partly because it is able to have its humanist cake and eat it. Tragedy of this kind is sublime in both humanist and psychoanalytical senses – pleasurable, majestic, awe-inspiring, suggestive of infinite capacity and immeasurable value, yet also punitive, intimidating, cutting us savagely down to size. We see men and women chastised by the Law for their illicit desire, a censure which with admirable economy satisfies our sense of justice, our respect for author-ity and our impulse to sadism. But since we also identify with these malcontents, we feel the bitterness of their longing, a sympathy which morally speaking is pity, and psychoanalytically speaking is masochism. We share their seditious passion, while reaping pleasure from castigating ourselves for such delinquent delight. Pity brings us libidinally close to them, while fear pushes them away in the name of the Law. But we also fear our own pity, alarmed by our own dalliance with destruction. Not all tragedy pitches insurrection against authority; but when it does, it satisfies the sombre demands of the superego while letting the death drive ecstatically loose. And this does nothing to alter the fact that the issues at stake remain ethical and political ones, questions of justice, violence, self-fulfilment and the like. Few artistic forms display such impressive erotic economy, and perhaps none caters so cunningly to our sadism, masochism and moral conscience all at the same time. Few, also, reveal such a close mirroring between the transactions on stage and the trans-actions between stage and spectators.

If tragedy has something of the melancholic joy of the sublime, it also displays for some critics a similar structure. The pain of the Kantian sublime springs from a recognition of finitude: we strive to measure up to some unfathomable Law or Reason, but inevitably fail. The sublime thus has an oedipal structure. But if our finitude is thus thrown into harsh relief, so by contrast is the august infinity which we crave; and in the very act of striving and failing to attain it, we act out a freedom in which we can hear a dim echo of the sublime power itself. In falling short of the Law or the Absolute, we acknowledge our affinity with it, recog-nizing that our only true dwelling place is within its own eternal homelessness. In a similar way, the hero for classical tragic thought reveals an unfathomable value in the very act of plummeting from the heights to which he climbs, so that the experience is spiced with both pain and pleasure. In psychoanalytical terms, it is a dead heat between the Law and desire. The sadism of the superego, and the masochism of baffled desire, are both satisfied; but desire also steals a maliciously enjoyable march on the Law, feeling both gratified and guilty for doing so. At the same time, it makes the momentous discovery that Law and desire are secretly at one – that the infinity which it encounters *is* desire in a different guise, and that the deepest design of the Law is not to forbid our desire but, on the contrary, to demand that we indulge it. But since the desire in question is the death drive, it is the Law of desire which has the last laugh.

Chapter 7

Tragedy and the Novel

We speak of the comic novel, but rarely of the tragic one. Drama seems to have laid exclusive claim to tragedy. 'In God's name, why call a thing a tragedy, unless it is meant to be a play?' asked an exasperated nineteenth-century reviewer of a minor work of Byron.[1] Is this because there is something inherently untragic about the novel? At first glance, it is tempting to believe so. 'The history of the decline of serious drama is, in part, that of the rise of the novel', observes George Steiner,[2] and one could no doubt forge some sort of narrative out of this sequence. A tragic theatre bound up with the despotic absolutism, courtly intrigue, traditional feuds, rigid laws of kinship, codes of honour, cosmic world-views and faith in destiny of the *ancien régime* gives way in the novel to the more rational, hopeful, realist, pragmatic ideologies of the middle class.

What rules now is less fate than human agency, less codes of honour than social conventions. Work and home, not court, church and state, become the primary settings, and high politics yields to the intrigues of everyday life. It is a shift from the martial to the marital – the former being part of a problem, the latter of a solution. The public realm of tragedy, with its high-pitched rhetoric and fateful economy, is abandoned for the privately consumed, more expansive, ironic, everyday language of prose fiction. And this, for some, is certainly a loss: some critics, as Henri Peyre suggests, blame the death of tragedy on the novel, which 'captured the essentials of tragic emotion, while diluting and often cheapening it'.[3] Thomas Mann thought rather disdainfully that democracy was 'the state for novels', which were not to be confused with Culture.[4]

No doubt there is something in this historical case. It is hard, for example, to think of many tragic novelists in England before Hardy, James and Conrad. There are a few major pieces of tragic fiction (*Clarissa*, *Wuthering Heights*), and a number of arguable near-misses (*The Mill on the Floss*, some later Dickens novels), but no sizeable, distinguished body of tragic fiction. The temper of eighteenth- and nineteenth-century English fiction, the heyday of the making of the English middle class, is anti-tragic. It is not until that class moves into its epochal decline in the later nineteenth century that the tragic novel emerges as a major form. Tragedy, having been overtaken by the novel, catches up with it again. The mutedly affirmative ending of *Middlemarch*, along with *Daniel Deronda*'s mixture of personal tragedy and political salvation, marks a transitional point. Utopia has now to be either scaled down or exported. It is the nearest to the tragic note that, before James and Hardy, seems ideologically permissible in the English novel.

Nor is it simply a matter of England. Alessandro Manzoni's *The Betrothed*, a novel which constituted something of a founding event of Italian modernity, begins by claiming to draw upon a seventeenth-century narrative whose high tragical style it simultaneously rejects as unsuitable for the modern reader. This tattered manuscript, which speaks of 'grievous Tragedies of Horror and scenes of fearful Wickedness', is scorned by the self-consciously up-to-date narrator as full of 'bombasti-cal declamation', crammed with the kind of vulgar extravaganzas of which sophisticated modern readers have had a surfeit. Yet this sharp distinction between *passé* tragic rhetoric and matter-of-fact novelistic modernity undermines itself as it goes along. For one thing, the seventeenth-century author himself obsequiously apologizes for treating 'persons of small import and low degree', so that the declension from high tragedy to low democracy is already contained within the former. For another thing, Manzoni's present-day narrator concedes that much of the *ur*-narrative runs quite smoothly and naturally, whatever its occa-sional baroque flourish; and he does, after all, decide to make use of the story himself, recasting the language and sequence of events in modern-izing terms. In a final irony, the content of Manzoni's novel, with its vil-lainous abduction, warfare, plague and famine, is high-tragical enough for even the most archaic of tastes.

What we have here, in short, is a minor allegory of the novel form's troubled relations with its generic precursors, as the former, proudly pro-claiming its revolutionary break with the latter, finds itself inescapably parasitic on them. As with the Marxist conception of the relations between liberalism and socialism, it is a case of revolutionary continuity. Even so, Manzoni has already proleptically absorbed the lesson which Marx will preach in his *Eighteenth Brumaire of Louis Bonaparte*, drawing his narrative, but not his poetry, from the past. And this class struggle at the level of literary form is reflected in the substance of *The Betrothed*, as a licentious aristocratic assault on that most characteristic of bourgeois institutions, marriage, is finally repulsed. The pious, pacific middle-class virtues triumph over a predatory, anarchic nobility – which is to say that the novel form wins out over tragedy.

Yet polite Europe had been shaken to its core in the late eighteenth century by a tragic novel, *The Sorrows of Young Werther*, from an author notoriously averse to the tragic mood; and although the modern reader may well feel that Goethe's lavishly self-pitying hero's only tragic flaw was not to kill himself a good deal sooner, there is no denying that few tragic narratives since Richardson's *Clarissa* have traumatized their readerships on such a remarkable scale. The nineteenth-century French novel, in addition, is hardly starved of tragic plots. Stendhal, Balzac, Flaubert: in the wake of a bourgeois revolution rapidly turning sour, all of these authors come up with major works of tragedy. And while Dickens, whatever his overall darkening of mood, is still just about managing to pull off satisfactory settlements in *Bleak House*, *Little Dorrit* and *Our Mutual Friend*, Herman Melville in the United States is producing a magnificent piece of tragic fiction which ends in utter disaster. *Moby-Dick* needs to be in prose, since it deals with a catastrophe of the common people; but to grant these whalers the tragic dignity which is their due it must also break the bounds of realism with its burnished Shakespearian rhetoric, setting a Satanic hero cheek-by-jowl with detailed information on blubber hooks and the bone-structure of the sperm whale. We should not, then, generalize too quickly from the example of Britain, in some ways the least typical of European cultures, which had had time to put the tragic upheavals of its seventeenth-century political history behind it and, as the world's first capitalist nation, embark on an expansive programme of industrialization at home and imperial conquest abroad.

In *Theory of the Novel* Georg Lukács sees epic and the novel as 'extensive totalities', in contrast with the 'intensive totality' of drama. But Goethe's *Faust* is hardly as intensive as some might wish, and Woolf's *The Waves* is scarcely extensive. Nor is it quite true that the novel deals with interiority and the drama with action: what of Cervantes or Fielding on the one hand and Racine or Chekhov on the other? Even so, the suspicion that there is something inherently untragic about the novel-form is hard to shake off. Franco Moretti sees one type of novel, the *Bildungsroman*, as precisely this, with its harmonious integration of individual and society, freedom and happiness, self-determination and socialization. This inherently progressive, optimistic form exhibits a 'triumph of meaning over time',[5] and like most kinds of novel 'makes normality interesting and meaningful *as* normality'.[6] Classical literary genres often showed scant interest in the everyday, and postmodernism has an ingrained suspicion of normality, which it dogmatically rejects as always and everywhere oppressive; but in between the two comes this fascination with the mundane, foreign alike to the pastoral on the one side and the peripheral on the other.

No doubt it is almost impossible for us now to recapture the imaginative excitement felt by those reared on a diet of tragedy, elegy and homily at the emergence of a form which seemed to find the commonplace and quotidian extraordinarily engrossing, assuming in its Protestant manner that spiritual dramas were hidden behind every shop front and under every frock coat. Moretti thinks this fictional world quite incompatible with revolutionary crisis, and Flaubert's *Sentimental Education* might be adduced to support his claim, as the callow young Frédéric Moreau shambles on with his aimless, supremely trivial existence while the French revolution of 1848 is in full flood just around the corner. Moretti comments that what the *Bildungsroman* is really about is 'how the double revolution of the eighteenth century could have been avoided'.[7] *Madame Bovary* is about the tragic destruction of a deluded young woman; but as though to make the point that the rhetoric of tragedy cannot coexist with the fiction of the commonplace, the novel scrupulously refuses in its style the emotions which its action would seem set to provoke.

Whereas tragic drama, so the argument goes, distils some pure moment of crisis from the ruck of life around it, the novel is a species of imaginative sociology which returns such intense, isolated moments to the flow and counter-flow of history, patiently unravelling the rather less exotic, workaday forces which went into their making, and in doing so relativizing judgements which in their dramatic form can seem a good deal more stark and intractable. In the topography of the novel there are fewer precipices and hairpin bends, fewer walls to be forced up against. The novel on this view is a matter of *chronos*, of the gradual passage of historical time, whereas tragedy is a question of *kairos*, of time charged, crisis-racked, pregnant with some momentous truth. Aldous Huxley argues in his essay 'Tragedy and the Whole Truth' in *Music at Night* that the novel tries to tell the whole truth in all its irrelevant contingency, and so dilutes the chemical purity of tragedy. To shirk nothing, not to exclude, is not to be tragic. And in the great ocean of irrelevancies which is contemporary life, tragedy has accordingly retreated. The tragic bent of Stendhal and Pushkin, as Moretti points out, means that they show less delight in a thickness of social texture, less digressive fascination with sheer contingency, more readiness to come straight to the dramatic point.[8] Indeed, one might see Stendhal's ambitious, world-renouncing heroes as having strayed from some high tragedy into a novelistic world which is altogether too prosaic for them, and from which they finally beat a disdainful retreat.

This discrepancy in Stendhal between idealism and worldliness, or tragedy and the novel, dramatizes the bourgeoisie's transition from their heroic to their pragmatic phase. By the time of Flaubert, the clash between the two has become purely farcical, as idle dreaming and a degraded world push each other deeper into self-parody. It is as though Stendhal's protagonists refuse to survive into this dismal epoch, choosing instead to die with their dreams intact because unrealized. For them, the conflict between pragmatism and idealism is still a tragic one, even if love can provide an heroic alternative to the politics of disenchantment. Indeed, it is conducted in Stendhal with all the scripted precision of a military campaign.

The heroes of these fictions, trapped between the poetry of the revolutionary past and the prose of the post-Napoleonic present, internalize this contradiction as schizoid beings, at once absolutist and opportunist, authentic and charlatan, noble and mediocre, principled and unscrupulous, altruistic and self-interested, passionate and calculating, admirable and ridiculous. Split between worldly ambition and *contemptus mundi*, their canny outer conformity is matched by an obdurate inner refusal, in an epoch when power and idealism are no longer reconcilable. The very impulse which drives them to scale the social hierarchy is also the sense of spiritual superiority which leads them finally to spurn it. In proto-modernist fashion, the self is no longer destiny but performance, a matter of protean masks and brilliant improvisation. Adept at playing the political game, Julien Sorel of *The Red and the Black* and Fabrizio del Dongo of *The Charterhouse of Parma* nevertheless refuse to give up on their revolutionary desire and are borne to destruction by it. Both illustrate Pushkin's lines in *Eugene Onegin*: 'To see life as a ritual play / And with the decorous throng to follow / Although one in no manner shares / Its views, its passions, or its cares!' (ch. 8, 11).

Julien, one of Nature's aristocrats, is in the end too high-minded even to bother to carry on living; and since his life has anyway been a kind of calculated self-monitoring and self-experimenting, it has a dissociated quality about it which prefigures his death. Like the classical Spanish picaro, he ends up finding the world void of truth, full of nothing but fraud, graft and odious class privilege, and his death by execution is really a cool-headed form of suicide. He is well aware that the law which sends him to his death is class law, that his real crime has been social climbing. If he has no wish to defy this law, it is out of contempt for it, not respect. Ideals are still absolute, but they can no longer be realized; and this, for Stendhal as for Lucien Goldmann in *The Hidden God*, is a tragic condition. Passion and energy still flourish, but in an exploitative society they need to look sharp for themselves, and thus breed a calculating self-interest which threatens to undermine them. Fabrizio keeps up the outward shows as a fashionable young preacher, but remains fixated on the idealistic Clelia and withdraws from the world when she dies.

As Franco Moretti points out, freedom and happiness cannot be harmonized for Stendhal as they can be in the classical *Bildungsroman*. In the end, there can be no compromise between tragic extremism ('I can see nothing but a sentence of death that distinguishes a man', Mathilde airily remarks in *The Red and the Black*) and the shabby trade-offs of everyday life. Tragedy is intransigent, the novel built out of compromise, and Stendhal's heroes disappear down the gap between the two. Yet even though the political world of these fictions is violent and corrupt, it retains an aura of glamour and adventure, of spies, scheming Jesuits and court imbroglios, as though these were almost the last novels in which high politics could still be the stuff of drama. Politics, Stendhal remarked, could still be heroic in Italy but not in England, where battles and executions had yielded ground to numbers and taxes.[9] With Flaubert and Zola, we will have vacated this swashbuckling political sphere for the more mundane world of social existence.

Whether or not tragedy and the novel are incompatible, it is certainly hard in the modern period for heroism and the common life to intersect, and in writers like Sean O'Casey they do so only to engage in mutual travesty. One way out of this problem is to set your tragic action on some pre-modern margin where, as with Synge's *Riders to the Sea*, Yeats's *Deirdre*, Lorca's *The House of Bernarda Alba*, Tennessee Williams's *Suddenly Last Summer* or some of William Faulkner's tragic fiction, ordinary life itself seems more ritualized and intense, emotions more raw and exposed. The sea is another conveniently histrionic backdrop for a tragic art baulked by modernity, from Herman Melville to Joseph Conrad. In his valuable essay in an historical reading of tragedy, John Orr notes that late nineteenth-century European tragic theatre springs largely from the peripheries, from Scandinavia, Ireland, Spain or Russia: 'Tragic drama could not have sprung from the major epicentres of European capitalism at the time, nor chosen its tragic protagonists from the urban bourgeoisie of the major nations'.[10] One might add that these are for the most part societies in which the conflict between tradition and modernity was peculiarly acute at the time. If modern life is too humdrum for tragedy, then, you can pitch the conflict in some more elemental setting in which honour or blood-guilt or ritual mourning still thrive. Faulkner's warwearied, ghost-thronged, dynastic, patriarchal South of racial strife and decaying gentility is one such likely location. *Absolom, Absolom!*, which dramatizes the destruction of a protagonist as representative of a dynasty, remarks of Quentin that 'his very body was a hall echoing with sonorous defeated names: he was not a being, an entity, he was a commonwealth. He was a barracks filled with stubborn back-looking ghosts still recovering, even forty-three years afterward, from the fever which had cured the disease' (ch. 1). Meanwhile, Faulkner's garrulous, overblown style signals that all this, despite its provincial landscape, is undoubtedly Literature.

Tragedy, on the view we are investigating, is more at home in the short story than the novel proper, a less well upholstered form in which, as with Chekhov and Kipling, the narrative can be more easily pared down to a single moment of disruption or disclosure. In George Eliot's hands, the novel can avoid tragedy because its task is to trace the complex chains of causality which weave themselves into the present, thus letting explanation take the place of condemnation. *Tout comprendre est tout pardonner.* The realist novelist and the political liberal make natural bedfellows. Moreover, this kind of intricately hermeneutical fiction can also take us beyond the external facts into a phenomenology of them, of how their lights and shades fall differently in different centres of consciousness, and so forestall absolute judgements in this way too. There are no villains in Eliot, just egoists, which is to say those who are incapable of becoming novelists. For imagination and human sympathy, in the English empiricist tradition, amount to much the same thing; and the subtle flow and recoil of sympathies of the novel, always of course within a containing form, becomes a political paradigm, perhaps now the sole surviving place where sympathy and authority, local affections and an allegiance to the whole, can be at one. There is an anti-tragic ethic at work here: wickedness springs simply from a lack of imagination. De Sade's monstrous manipulators, who can imagine all too well what their victims are suffering and thus relish it all the more jubilantly, take a somewhat less sanguine view.

Honoré de Balzac is no doubt the greatest imaginative sociologist of all, yet his fiction is strewn with tragedies: the vengeful malevolence of cousin Bette, the persecution of the unworldly Pons, the hubristic downfall of the callow young Lucien de Rubempré, the Lear-like humiliation of Goriot, the suicide of Esther in *A Harlot High and Low*, the cruel devastation of Eugénie Grandet, the madness of Gobseck. Yet these warped, blighted lives help to compose a Human Comedy, not a tragedy, since the emergent bourgeois society to which they belong is still robust, extravagant, even heroic – 'comic' in the sense of swarming with God's plenty, and offering readers this pullulating diversity of life-forms for their delectation. Balzac writes in *Cousin Pons* of 'this terrible comedy'. There is a monstrous energy at work for which even evil is magnificently theatrical, more Satanic than suburban. And this is partly because while Stendhal deals with the superstructure, Balzac's sphere of interest is the base. If everyday life can be heroic in the latter case but not the former, it is because Stendhal's bailiwick is the institutions of court, church and state, of political machinations in high places, all of which in post-revolutionary society are now incorrigibly squalid and self-interested; whereas Balzac writes not just of bourgeois society but of *capitalist* society, of the thrills and spills of high finance, wolfish competitors and rapscal-lion adventurers, as narratives of fearful instability and melodramatic fluctuations of fortune collide and diverge as in some great stock exchange of the literary imagination. Something of the same voracious, quasi-pathological energy can be found in Dickens, whose irrepressible imaginative vitality can carry him through the most sombre of scenarios. In the very act of unmasking the barbarities of Dotheboys Hall in *Nicholas Nickleby* he is tempted for a moment to see the funny side of things, and the quickening rhythms of the railway passage in *Dombey and Son* reveal an excitement at this vision of progress quite at odds with the fact that these black monsters are officially a symbol of death. His imagination is too copious and histrionic to be tragic, as the sheer energy of the act of writing surmounts whatever gruesome scenes it represents.

To see the novel as an antidote to tragedy is to view it as an intrinsi-cally liberal form, decentred, dialogical and open-ended, a champion of growth, change and provisionality as anti-tragic modes. Indeed, one might expect Mikhail Bakhtin, the most eminent exponent of this case, to contrast the rough-and-ready democracy of the form with the more aloof, auratic presence of tragedy, which, rather surprisingly, he fails to do. On the contrary, he links tragedy and laughter in opposition to a browbeating rhetoric. Both tragedy and laughter, he comments, strive to expel fear from change and catastrophe; but the former does this by a kind of 'serious courage, remaining in the zone of closed-up individual-ity', whereas laughter responds to change with 'joy and abuse'. Tragedy, then, is no more than a poor cousin of carnival; but they link hands in their hostility to 'moralizing and optimism, to any kind of premature and "abbreviated" harmony in what exists (when the very thing that would accomplish the harmonizing is not present), to abstract idealization and sublimation. Tragedy and laughter equally fearlessly look being in the eye, they do not construct any sort of illusions, they are sober and exact-ing.'[11] Tragedy and laughter would both seem to Bakhtin to be forms of moral and epistemological realism, and his caveat against premature har-monizing strikes a rare note in commentary on the tragic. Idealization, sublimation, false euphoria and hastily constructed symmetries litter the theory of tragedy from end to end, so it is bracing to have this gesture of dissent from one of the finest philosophers of culture of the modern age.

Yet tragedy in Bakhtin's eyes remains an inferior mode to carnivalesque laughter. Indeed, it is precisely from the tragedy of the self-
enclosed individual life, rigorously bounded by life and death, that the
carnivalesque redeems us. This great celebrant of knockabout libidinal
laughter and communal *jouissance* has in fact a chillingly sombre view of
the vulnerability of the individual life, which tragic art supposedly takes
as its subject-matter. The tragic plot is set in motion by a transgression
which for Bakhtin expresses nothing less than the 'profound crime (the
potential criminality) of all self-asserting individuality'.[12] Tragedy can
raise such individualism, in itself a somewhat feeble affair, to the status
of major art; and it is thus quite a different matter from the nit-picking
literary realism for which individualism means everyday security and stability, a way of life which 'avoids death and real struggle, which takes
place in the most comfortable and secure locations of banks, exchanges,
offices, rooms, and so on'.[13] What this renowned theorist of the novel
contrasts unfavourably with the spendthrift, extravagant gestures of carnival and tragedy is precisely the stuff of the novel. Or at least its more
buttoned-down, naturalistic variety. Tragedy and carnival are all about
change, abrupt reversals, the larger than life, in contrast to the seedy continuities of everyday life; and the question for Bakhtin is whether the
history of the novel cannot itself be re-read in these carnivalesque, anti-
naturalistic terms.

Carnival brings together dramatic disruption and street-wise wisdom,
reconciling the exceptional and the everyday. The wisdom of the folk
is resolutely anti-tragic, as against the world-view of their more large-
gestured, fate-ridden superiors. The Nephew of Diderot's *Rameau's
Nephew* is such an anti-tragic populist – sponger, wit, clown, chancer,
debunker, hedonist and cynical operator rolled into one, a spontaneous
materialist whose mimicry is a canny form of adaptation, and who is thus
unlikely to come to grief. The philosophers have sought to interpret the
world, whereas the people know that the point is to survive it. The determinism of Diderot's Jacques the Fatalist, in a novel which reads like a
curious *mélange* of Sterne, Fielding, carnivalesque and *conte philosophique*,
also reflects a traditional strain of popular stoicism. What was once a
matter of cosmic destiny is for Jacques a matter of routine causality. Life
blindly, obdurately persists, which may be cold comfort but which at least
deflates high-toned tragic rhetoric. The common people, fit subjects for
the 'low' tragedy of affliction and fruitless toil, are not yet fit subjects for
'high' tragedy since they have yet to make their dramatic entry as an
agent on the political scene. The folk have yet to become the working
class.

All the same, there is a long-lasting bond between low life and the metaphysical, if not exactly the political, in that most venerable of novelistic forms, the picaresque, in which the travelling rogue finally sees through the ontologically hollow forms of social existence. If the novel is the genre of social mobility *par excellence,* who better to exemplify this errancy than the solitary picaro? And how many artistic forms of such venerable lineage place an unscrupulous con-man at their centre?[14] If the novel is the most gregarious of literary forms, then ironically the richest range of social experience can be portrayed through the unfettered wanderings of one stripped of home, occupation and social relations. And if he is enough of a hard-bitten chancer to see others as they are, rather than to perceive them in some solemnly mystified literary mode, then all the better for social realism.

The novel, with its Cervantes-like ironizing of idealism, can at least encourage you not to expect too much, and so not to lapse into postures of disenchanted gloom. The very qualities which for Samuel Johnson or Laurence Sterne make ordinary life a constant process of thwartings, vexations, irritabilities and petty disappointments are also what deprive it of the grandeur and finality which might lend themselves to tragedy. Moreover, the sheer temporality of the novel brings with it some bleak hope: nothing lasts, including unhappiness. There is always the eager expectancy of exchanging one variety of it for another. Temporality, to be sure, can also be a tragic medium: once executed, actions are eternally irrevocable, and will bear their blighted fruit in the future. But as long as there is time there is the promise of redemption, and the novel form seizes advantage of this fact.

The realist novel preserves a delicate equipoise between conflicting viewpoints, shifting its focus with impeccable equity and good manners so that now one centre of consciousness and now another is lit up. All of these various components must be totalized, gathered into a whole, but with no detriment to their unique specificity. It is this which Hegel means by 'typicality'. There is still need for a metalanguage, as there is for a political state; but like the liberal state this metalanguage is hospitable to a diversity of life-forms, and can govern them only by listening to them attentively. There are deadlocks and contradictions, some of them tragically irresolvable; but these are overcome in principle by the literary form itself, whose complex unity thus becomes a discreet utopian gesture. The novel presents conflicts, but in the form of their potential resolution; and one way it does this is by personalizing them, shifting social questions metonymically on to individual ones, so that a marriage, a benevolent employer or a long-lost cousin can provide the solution to one's woes. When the realist novel in nineteenth-century England arrives at some ideological impasse, it tends to reach back to older, pre-realist fictional modes like Gothic and folk tale, rummaging among their repertoire of rather shopworn devices until it can pluck out some convenient stratagem – an unexpected legacy, a ghostly voice in your ear – which might move the story forward. In an Austenite world of a few distinguished families, this strategy may be plausible enough; but there are social and political forces which resist such figuration, and by the time of Henry James and E. M. Forster the novel will be uneasily aware that it survives partly by repressing them.

The Irish poet Patrick Kavanagh once remarked that tragedy was underdeveloped comedy, meaning perhaps that to put a tragic crisis back in context, to discursify it, is to defuse it.[15] Moretti thinks that the *Bildungsroman*, or perhaps the realist novel more generally, cannot survive too much fracture and disruption. In its more expansive, capacious way, it is sceptical of the tragic or existential moment of truth, the throw of the ontological dice on which all is supposed to turn. 'It is a constant elusion of historical turning-points and breaks', Moretti comments, 'an elusion of tragedy and hence . . . of the very idea that societies and individuals acquire their full meaning in a "moment of truth".'[16] Goethe's Wilhelm Meister finally abandons the search for the one definitive act in which his destiny will shine forth; Sammy Mountjoy of William Golding's *Free Fall* is unable to nail down the key moment when he lost his innocence however far back he pushes his narrative. There is no isolable origin, as the textuality of the novel and of Mountjoy's career proliferate beyond any natural source or closure.

Rüdiger Bittner argues boldly that tragedy is falsifying for just this reason, that it pursues a moment of totality which is untrue to what we are, as dispersed, time-ridden creatures: 'the totality of the tragic hero is not something we lack. It is an illusion. There is no such thing as one's all that could be put at stake. The decision in tragedy is void: we do not stand nor do we fall because, unlike the towering hero, we are in many places. Tragedy errs.'[17] Henri Lefebvre has similar reservations about existentialism, a creed which he upbraids for having 'drawn closer to everyday life . . . only to discredit it', devaluing it in favour of 'pure or tragic moments – criticism of life through anguish or death, artificial criteria of authenticity, etc.'[18] Tragedy, in short, is in this view an extremist form, a crystalline structure of forces and counter-forces, in contrast with what Franco Moretti sees as the middle-of-the-road normality of the *Bildungsroman*. And the novel is anyway more democratic than the theatre because it allows us to control our own participation. On this view, tragic art is about symmetry, nemesis, swift retribution, actions deflected suddenly into their opposites, a whole cruelly inexorable logic which demands a stringent unity of action, and which can only be diluted by the discursive. The novel, moreover, is much better suited than the drama to charting formation and development, themes which bulk large in the bourgeoisie's cultural repertoire.

This is not, however, quite the whole truth. Moretti and Bittner are right to be wary of what one might call the Room 101 or Lord Jim's Jump syndrome – the dubious modernist belief that there is some privileged word, gesture or action which will incarnate the whole of one's selfhood as surely as the Romantic symbol fleshes out the infinite. The difference between modernism and Romanticism is that this moment is now remarkably hard to pin down. But why should one assume that what you scream out when someone straps a cage of starved rats to your face is the truth? Most of us would say anything whatsoever. One might also dub this the Lord of the Flies syndrome – the quintessentially modernist dogma that beneath the smooth, paper-thin surface of civilization brood chthonic forces which betray its unspeakable truth, and which will burst forth in some dreadful epiphany once you dump a bunch of schoolboys without cricket bats and a prefect on a desert island. The plentiful modernist literature of anti-epiphany – Joyce's scrupulously anti-climactic *Dubliners*, the unblemished emptiness of Forster's Marabar caves, the windy Chapel Perilous of *The Waste Land*, the inconclusive relationship of Birkin and Ursula in *Women in Love*, the bungled encounters between Stephen and Bloom in *Ulysses* – is then merely the obverse of this credo.

Yet the Room 101, Jim's Jump and Lord of the Flies syndromes all derive from novels, not tragic drama; and though *Free Fall* never really pinpoints the moment of its hero's lapse from grace, it does yield him a transfigurative epiphany of grace when he is released from the broom cupboard. Perhaps even realism is now extremism, since extremism is the way of the world. If there is a sense in which the modern world is perpetually in crisis, then tragic drama has no monopoly of the moment of truth. Indeed, it is this conviction which informs one of the most imperishable of all literary studies, Erich Auerbach's *Mimesis*, for which the triumph of a gradually evolving realism, all the way from the Old Testament to the fiction of Emile Zola, is to take the common life, and those lowly social characters who embody it, with an unprecedented seriousness. 'Seriousness' is as much a keyword for Auerbach as it is for tragic theory; and for *Mimesis* one supreme test of whether everyday life is being accorded its due status is whether it is regarded as a fit medium for tragedy. The elevated figures of Racine and Corneille are secluded from everything 'base and creatural', as is the art of baroque absolutism in general, while Goethe and Schiller shy away from mixing a forceful realism with a tragic conception of their age.

It is in the great post-revolutionary realist novel above all, in the writing of Stendhal and Balzac, that the apparent oxymoron of *tragic realism* is fully achieved, which for Auerbach will reach its apotheosis in Zola. Art must spring from 'the depths of the workaday world and its men and women',[19] disclosing a 'serious treatment of everyday reality, the rise of more extensive and socially inferior human groups to the position of subject-matter for problematic-existential representation'.[20] This comic or tragic literary populism is at daggers drawn with more portentous, hierarchical art forms such as classical tragedy, which exalt the tragic personage and its 'princely passions' above the surrounding social universe, and which find a sinister echo in the elitist postures of grandeur which drove the Jewish Auerbach from Nazi Germany into exile in Turkey. In this moment of world-historical danger, a lineage of plebeian, humanistic realism, which like the Judaeo-Christian scriptures mixes the sublime with the sublunary, must be summoned to bear witness against the bogus sublimity and mythological anti-humanism of fascist culture.

In any case, it is surely a mistake to see tragedy as invariably hinging on a stark moment of truth. Goethe remarks in *Wilhelm Meister's Apprenticeship* that things in drama hurry on apace and the active hero carries all before him, whereas the typical hero of a novel is more passive. John Synder argues that in tragedy 'no Homeric wandering or delay is permitted, just the appallingly straight and narrow way towards victory, loss, or draw'.[21] This surely underestimates the number of tragic zigzags one comes across (*Hamlet* arguably takes them as its theme), just as Moretti perhaps makes a little too much of the hybrid, wryly unheroic, hospitable nature of the novel.

If there is Scott, Austen, Edgeworth and Eliot, there is also the more absolutist, uncompromising fiction of Stendhal, Hawthorne, Melville, Conrad and Dostoevsky. Thomas Mann's *Buddenbrooks* is all about process, degeneration, genealogical continuities, but *The Magic Mountain* would not be the same without Hans Castorp's epiphanic insight in the snow. If *War and Peace* ends before the disruption of social order by the Decembrist insurrection, devoting its last word instead to marriage, *Anna Karenina* is a full-dress tragedy. Tolstoy portrays a definitive crisis of conversion in *The Death of Ivan Ilyich*, where the emotionally autistic Ilyich experiences a joyful revelation of love on his deathbed, as well as in *Resurrection*, where there is a renewal of life for the penitent sinner Nekhlyudov. And Virginia Woolf's fiction is all about privileged moments plucked from the flow of profane time.

To refine the distinction, however, is not to reject it. The stage does indeed generally demand more swashbuckling moments of truth than the study. And if the novel of high realism is a compromising, commodious form, there is a strain of tragic drama which is all about a refusal of compromise. Henry James writes that 'the old dramatists ... had a simpler civilization to represent – societies in which the life of man was in action, in passion, in immediate and violent experience. These things could be put upon the playhouse boards with comparatively little sacrifice of their completeness and their truth. Today we're so infinitely more reflective and complicated and diffuse that it makes all the difference ... '[22] Modern manners are too nuanced, oblique and undemonstrative for an heroic art, and because of this we need a narrative voice-over, which the novel can give us with less strain than the modern drama, which will help us to unravel these subtleties, not least where inarticulate characters are concerned. The less eloquent and sophisticated thus fare rather better in the novel than on stage, having, so to speak, an interpreter at their side, which is perhaps another reason why the novel is a more popular, democratic form than tragic drama.

Indeed, the relations between the two genres can be seen as an allegory of the relations between the middle class and aristocracy – the middle class needing to hijack for its own political ends something of the grandiloquence and ceremonial forms of its superiors, while feeling these forms to be too shackling and simplistic for its own psychologically intricate life-world. Wilhelm Meister begins by elevating the Muse of Tragedy over the figure of Commerce, but by the end of the novel, having met with no particular success on stage, he will acknowledge commerce as the true form of nobility, one which moreover can be trusted as a bulwark against political revolution. Commerce is nervous of disruptions and upheavals, just like the novel. Like the novel, too, it is all a matter of plot, of establishing connections between far-flung elements and drawing them into an elaborate yet orderly whole. Wilhelm's companion Werner even goes so far as to praise double entry book keeping as 'one of the most beautiful inventions of the human mind' (Book 1, ch. 10), not the most universal of opinions. But the problem, as Matthew Arnold will recognize later, is how to lend this heroic but essentially private early-bourgeois culture an imposing public presence; and Wilhelm's own improbable solution is the theatre, in which middle-class figures can exchange their private identities for public personae and appear on stage as gentlemen of culture able to beat the nobility at their own game. The new bourgeois public sphere will be the theatre, casting the run-of-the-mill narratives of middle-class privacy into a more sociable symbolic form.

Realist fiction usually works from the inside of a culture, as a dramatization of everyday life in what Schiller calls somewhere 'its intimate and sweet well-being'. It is no particular part of its task to submit that life to a comprehensive critique. Such fiction is thus redolent of a sense of being relaxedly at home in secular experience, whatever the world's grievous problems; it contrasts with those art forms for which what seems problematic is now nothing less than everyday experience itself. Tragedy, on the other hand, can easily exude a sense of homelessness. One would not say of a typical Balzacian or Tolstoyan hero, as Lucien Goldmann comments in *The Hidden God* of the tragic protagonists of Racine, that they are present and absent in the world at one and the same time. And if the novel prizes psychological realism, dissecting the sometimes murky roots of character and conduct, then its very form tends to sabotage the kind of heroism which depends on a tactful repression of all that. As with spouses and servants, the novel has too much inside knowledge to be dazzled by the sumptuous gesture or the outward show. It is hard to heroize characters whom we have known at such close quarters for the duration of four or five hundred pages, as opposed to figures we see strutting for a couple of hours on stage. And though dramatic performance is a more 'real-life' affair than reading, there is a sense in which, exactly because of this, it is also more artificial, and so more prone to idealization. At least novelistic characters are not real people pretending to be barons or beggars.

Franco Moretti makes the point that the economic domain is not represented in the *Bildungsroman* – in Goethe, for example, or Austen – indeed, that it scarcely figures 'in the great narratives of the last two centuries'.[23] Given one's sense that the middle classes seem to have passed that time doing precious little but making money, this is certainly a striking lacuna. But the reason is surely clear: there is no stable narrative of growth and maturity to be derived from the random fluctuations and chance connections of the market-place, so that bourgeois ideology is in this sense at odds with its own material infrastructure. One might see a contrast here between the *Bildungsroman* and the picaresque forms of Fielding, Defoe and Smollett, whose characters are not especially supposed to evolve and who move episodically through a set of chance encounters which have force but not necessarily meaning. Narrative, by contrast, is the shaping of event into meaning, and there is notably little of this in a Defoe novel, in which adventures accumulate with all the arbitrary, potentially infinite self-generation of capital itself, and which have eventually to be abruptly truncated for fear that they might go on forever. 'What comes next?' is really the only question to ask in the midst of this breathless narrational syntax, which exchanges one exotic item for another within the levelling medium of its bloodless prose-style.

Fielding's fiction, on the other hand, is a curious blend of the two modes, and the meaning of his novels lies somewhere in the ironic gap between them. We are supposed to believe that there is some organic sense or providential pattern to this arbitrary assemblage of rogues and grotesque mishaps, even though we catch the author signalling archly behind his hand that such providence exists only because we happen to be in a novel. Jane Austen's novels give us a record of experience, but along with it the norms by which that experience should be judged and corrected; and literary form is one vital bearer of these norms. But form in other hands can easily become ironic, since like the Law in St Paul it only serves to show us how far the shabby content of our lives falls short of it. Anyway, if the realist novel's task is to reflect an empirical world which lacks an immanent design, then its form, as Laurence Sterne was not slow to realize, can only be gratuitous, an enormous con-trick or *trompe l'oeil*. Literary form means editing, excluding, manipulating, all of which Sterne sees with *faux* benevolism as a kind of cheating on the reader, a literary equivalent of aristocratic *hauteur* and dominion. Representation is not compatible with reticence, and Sterne will therefore throw form warm-heartedly to the winds, thus befuddling his readers in cordially sadistic style.

No sharper contrast between tragedy and the novel could be found than in Georg Lukács's *Theory of the Novel*, for which tragedy deals in spiritual essences and the novel in a degraded empirical existence. The distinction is zealously endorsed in much of Yeats's writing on the subject. Lukács's theory of genres here is essentially Kantian: whereas epic reveals meaning to be still immanent in common life, tragedy stages a conflict between what is (the common life) and what should be (*Sollen*), finding an embodiment of the latter in the tragic hero. After epic and tragedy in ancient Greece comes philosophy, in which essences will cut adrift from existence altogether, so that philosophy is itself a tragic phenomenon, a form of spiritual homelessness. In the later, Marxist Lukács, these two domains of fact and value will be reintegrated by realism. In the meantime, however, tragedy survives into the modern era, since being 'alien' to life it is unaffected by historical change; but epic declines into the novel, as immanent meaning gives way to a world abandoned by God.

In a strict sense, the novel for the early Lukács is a post-tragic genre, since it follows on the historical heels of the classical trio of epic, tragedy and philosophy. Yet in another sense it is indeed tragic, as a form in which essence and existence can never coincide, in which meaning and value

193

are always elsewhere, and in which form must be subjectively, and thus arbitrarily, bestowed. Form is in this sense the death of fate. Lukács thus manages to make all novels sound like modernist ones, as a subject plunged into crisis confronts a contingent world, incident and interiority are forced apart, a slippage occurs between deed and meaning, and the only possible totality is an abstract, artificial one. As totality grows more inorganic in a world which has ceased to be story-shaped, the gap between it and the sensuous minutiae of life is thrown into ironic exposure – which is to say that the Lukács who was later to reinvent Marx's lost Paris manuscripts also more or less predicts Joyce's *Ulysses* eight years before its appearance.

One might risk the paradox that the novel is a tragic form for the early Lukács, whereas tragedy is not. Since it spurns the empirical, a realm of which Lukács was never particularly enamoured, tragedy is an elevated, affirmative affair, far less to be mourned than to be celebrated. The highest human value resides in an artistic form which turns its back on human existence. There is a kind of tragic art for Lukács which feels the power of that existence, shun it though it may; but there is another variety in which the world of spiritual essences consumes life entirely away, freeing tragic passion of 'human dross' and reducing to ashes everything that is merely human. This Platonic world, which unlike the postlapsarian novel knows no time, sets its face against life as such: if the essence takes on sensuous existence in the figure of the hero, it is only so that he can die and transcendence can thus be rendered visible. In a Kantian distinction, the 'intensive totality' of the drama is a matter of the 'intelligible', whereas the epic and the novel revolve on the empirical. There is, however, a problem for tragedy here, since the more its spiritual essences recede from the empirical world, the longer stretches the road which the hero must travel to discover them, which then threatens to undermine tragedy's 'intensive totality' or slenderness of construction. As the essence withdraws, it necessarily complicates the empirical domain, and so highlights the distance between them even more.[24]

Whatever spiritual homesickness Lukács might discern in the very structure of the novel, the fact remains that some of its most eminent modern practitioners have turned their face from the tragic. Given the generally sombre, angst-ridden mood of modernism, this comes as something of a surprise. Marcel Proust, perhaps the finest of modern novelists, uses his art to salvage the complex organic unity of his narrator's life, which can then be presented whole and entire, without rupture or discontinuity. The famous Proustian epiphany may suspend time, but it is pressed here into the service of connecting, disinterring, excavating, redeeming, of resisting the erosions and dispersals of temporality. As the novel draws to its close, the peal of the bell on his parents' garden gate is still fresh in the narrator's ears, linked in an unbroken series from childhood to the present. Here, with a vengeance, is the novel form's resistance to revolutionary crisis. The final note of *Remembrance of Things Past* is an affirmative one, as the narrator, his life focused to a pure point by his consciousness of impending death, takes up the task of writing his great work. If that work is enabled by death, it is also a way of vanquishing it.

Robert Musil's *The Man Without Qualities* treats the prelude to a tragic cataclysm, the First World War, with wit, satire and surreal humour, while Lawrence's fiction, as we have seen, is doctrinally hostile to tragedy. There are Lawrentian characters who are unfulfilled or unfulfilling, but these are merely the walking wounded of a war in which Life will always have the upper hand. The true hero of Lawrence's novels, that unfathomable force which he calls spontaneous-creative life, will simply discard such empty husks, casting them off as so much waste produce and rolling serenely on its path, seeking for some more vibrant instrument through which it can achieve expression. There is nothing tragic about those who are tossed on to the dustheap of Life, since they are mere ontological cyphers, men and women who have denied the god in themselves and so have consigned themselves to perdition. A profound anti-humanism thus lies at the root of Lawrence's metaphysic: the distinction which matters is not between humans on the one hand and snakes or gentians on the other, but between those organisms which are able to become the sensitive transmitters of Life itself, and those which are not. A sunflower, or a cell glimpsed down a microscope, may incarnate this force more wondrously than a man or woman.

There is a full-blooded determinism at work here, for all Lawrence's Romantic libertarianism. Life itself cannot be worsted, and will thrust its way ruthlessly towards self-realization. At the quick of the self lies that which is implacably alien to it. It is only by uttering what is not ourselves, laying ourselves obediently open to its inscrutable stirrings within us, that we can flower into autonomous selfhood. Men and women are strangers to their own being, and must simply look on wonderingly as it goes its own sweet way, superbly indifferent to their own petty egos. Human agency for Lawrence is no more than a bourgeois-humanist myth. For him, the unforgivable blasphemy is to try to dredge this mystery of spontaneous life into daylight, force it under the dominion of the interfering intellect, wrench open the buds of today to predict the bloom of tomorrow. But Life will exact its vengeance from all such unholy humanism; and this is a triumphalism which cannot coexist with tragedy.

Lawrence's art makes up in part for the crudity of his metaphysic, which is more than can be said for George Bernard Shaw. Shaw, whose metaphysic might be described as vulgar Lamarckianism laced with a bluffer's-guide version of Nietzsche, believes similarly in the triumph of Life, though in his case it is known as Creative Evolution. The Shavian superman is he in whom this force has finally attained self-consciousness, and so can pursue its enigmatic ends all the more effectively. Among those purposes might well be the final conquest of death. There can be no irrevocable breakdown or failure in this brutally progressivist world. In this evolutionary brand of cosmic rationalism, sin, crime and loss will all finally be briskly recycled as success, a belief to which Shaw's fellow Dubliner Yeats was also no stranger.

Shaw's bumptious, self-satisfied prose style is a fitting medium for this doctrine. He couldn't for the life of him see what was poignant about Wilde's *De Profundis*, a work which with characteristic perversity he regarded as exhilaratingly comic. 'It annoys me', he writes, 'to have people degrading the whole [Wilde] affair to the level of sentimental tragedy.'[25] 'Sentimental', to be sure, is a smack at the British, and as an Irish interloper himself, with nothing but his wits and words to hawk, Shaw understood Wilde far better than most observers in the metropolitan nation. He also shrewdly recognized that the spiritually chastened Wilde of the prison writings was among other things just another assiduously cultivated persona. Having sported a number of masks in his time, Oscar was now trying on Jesus Christ for size. Even so, Wilde's career was straight out of a textbook of tragic theory, as the supremely gifted, virtuous (but not too virtuous) protagonist scales the heights of achievement, hubristically overreaches himself, comes undone in a way inherent in his character but for which he is only partly to blame, and in doing so falls victim to nemesis, inspiring pity among many and fear among his homosexual confrères in particular.

Shaw felt for his colleague, but he was as deficient in the tragic sense of life as a hamster. With his baroque fantasies of transcending matter entirely, he regarded the fragile, creaturely nature of the human species largely as an obstacle to the life of unbridled thought. Saint Joan, in Shaw's supposedly most mature tragic drama, represents these cerebral fantasies in the thin disguise of a cross-dressing French peasant. She is another of Shaw's *Übermenschen*, an allegorical cut-out, an embodiment of the pure force of Progress which yearns to cut through the tiresome complexities of the human and historical. Shaw gives the vitalist game away, shamelessly exposing something of the ideological crassness which underlies the far more intricate art of a Lawrence. His work is almost enough to make one appreciate the value of agony.

As for that other lower-middle-class Dubliner James Joyce, one might well see the Stephen Dedalus of *A Portrait of the Artist as a Young Man* as a stereotypical figure of modernist tragedy, solitary, Satanic, self-exiled and disaffected. This particular *Bildungsroman* ends on an inconclusive note, with neither harmony nor narrative closure. Yet Stephen is not Joyce, and *Ulysses* will insert this potentially tragic tale into the everyday social context of Bloom and Molly's Dublin, thus blending the genres which we have been contrasting. In the meeting of Stephen and Bloom, a tragic modernism encounters a comic naturalism. The doom-laden narrative of Stephen is continued from the *Portrait*, but also suspended and ironized by other standpoints. If he achieves no particular integration himself, the novelization of his identity crisis, weaving it in and out of the exaggeratedly commonplace story of Molly and Leopold Bloom, achieves a kind of reconciliation on his behalf.

Stephen's high-toned tale is needed among other things to prevent *Ulysses* from lapsing into a mere elephantine parody of naturalism; but by dialogizing it, pitching Stephen's rather priggish rhetoric against some less fastidiously self-conscious voices, Joyce pulls off the rare trick of making tragedy seem brittle and emotionally regressive in contrast to comedy. For us moderns especially, the idea that tragedy is somehow *deeper* than comedy is almost irresistible, despite Bakhtin's claim that laughter 'has the deep meaning of a world-outlook, it is one of the most essential forms of truth about the world in its entirety, about history and man'.[26] If one wanted to nominate an English comic thinker in this deep sense of the term, Shaftesbury might spring to mind. Isn't it in the end more courageous to affirm in the teeth of the nightmare of history? Or is this not a vital moment of tragedy as well?

Comedy of this kind borders on the quasi-mystical faith that, whatever the appalling evidence to the contrary, all is somehow ultimately well. It is not always easy to distinguish this compassionate detachment, one much in evidence in Joyce, from the dissociated vision which turns tragedy into comedy by amusedly aestheticizing the cosmos, which is also much in evidence in Joyce. The comic tradition which stands behind him is that of Catholic medieval Europe, of Dante rather than Dickens, and in Joyce's writing the *sanitas*, equipoise and serenity of that outlook merge with, of all things, a species of materialism. Indeed, when he described himself as having the mind of a grocer, not quite the kind of claim one could imagine on the lips of a Yeats or an Eliot, he might have been referring both to his scholastic impulse to categorize and the unflagging mundaneness of his imagination. But he is a high-class, de luxe grocer, preoccupied with the endless possible permutations of matter, of the way the same few lowly elements can be combined according to certain great abiding laws to produce texts, subjects, histories, languages and the like. *Finnegans Wake* is the ultimate *combinatoire*, the code of all codes. But since nothing can ever finally perish in these mighty cycles of birth, copulation and death, for Joyce as much as for Yeats, this represents another rejection of absolute breaches and losses, a celebration of the commonplace and continuous, and thus another form of resistance to tragedy. The very indifferent levelling of things which threatens a certain classical notion of value is converted to a value in its own right, as Molly Bloom's sleepy indifference to difference might also articulate a deeper kind of acceptance.

Yet not all forms of levelling are comic, as E. M. Forster's *A Passage to India* is aware. There is also the cynical undermining of value and meaning which is the echo in the Marabar caves – that sense that everything exists but nothing has value which finally infiltrates Mrs Moore, as a kind of fearful inner chaos which saps her identity and claims her life. If the British imperialists rank all too rigidly, their more liberal kinsfolk revolt against such brutal hierarchies by keeling spectacularly over into nihilism. The liberal belief in the sympathetic self, pressed too far, becomes an 'Oriental' scepticism of the very concept of selfhood. Levelling of this kind, as we shall see later, is akin to what Milan Kundera calls the demonic. Besides, when it comes to Joyce, there is a strain of denial or disavowal in this comic vision, which he nurtured as Europe was exploding into flames around him. Just as Yeats's whirring gyres and cycles serve among other things to compensate for a history which is now in the process of dispossessing him and his social kind, so Joyce defies absolute loss and breakdown by thrusting it back into the Viconian cycles of dissolution and renewal. This makes death a part of life in the manner of the Irish wake, stripping it of its intimidatory aura and satirically belittling it. But it is non-plussed by those losses which are indeed absolute, at least for those involved; and this, once one has discarded the consolations of the cyclical, includes an alarming number of deprivations, including all human deaths. Yeats and Joyce share a suspicion of linear time which some see as rooted in Irish culture; but Yeats in his radical-extremist, apocalyptic way looks on the shift from one historical cycle to another as violent, tumultuous and so potentially tragic (one thinks of 'Prayer for My Daughter'), whereas Joyce in his more mundane, social-democratic style rejects any such histrionic vision for continuity-amidst-change.

If death is an elusive topic to grasp, it is not only because it is, so to speak, the last thing we experience, but because it occurs at the juncture of meaning and non-meaning, value and fact. My death is at once what distinguishes me from the ruck of my fellow creatures, since nothing could more graphically illustrate the fact that there is only one of me, while at the same time locking me into the species as one of the most banally predictable of biological events. That this unique individual should perish is an utterly commonplace affair. Death is a democratic business, since unlike most tragic theory it reveals that what is ultimately precious about us is not this or that quality of character but just the bald fact of our irreplaceability. And as far as that goes, we are all on a level. The simple fact of our passing matters more than how we shape up to it. What death makes of us is more fundamental than what we make of it. But for the comic outlook of a Joyce, nothing is irreplaceable, least of all Stephen Dedalus's father, who crops up in less dishevelled guise in the person of Leopold Bloom. And though life passes into death and out of it again, there is little sense of the price which this may involve. What you lose on the semiotic swings you make up on the Viconian roundabouts. In this respect, Joyce's art is sometimes not far from the more callow or cavalier aspects of Yeats. Since one can hardly speak of the cosmos having to reckon the cost of the loss of a rabbit, this vision, once projected on to history as a whole, issues in an idea of sacrifice which is largely confined to the self-abnegation of art. The true ascetic is now the aesthete.

Bakhtin writes of the tragedy of the self-enclosed individual life, a tragedy which, one might add, springs not least from the fact that such a life would be hellishly unintelligible to itself. What a certain bourgeois fantasy half-guiltily conceives – the idea of that which would be utterly, inalienably mine – would actually be a condition of frightful chaos, since what is in principle intelligible to me alone would actually be as meaningless to me as to anyone else. The poststructuralist critique of the 'proper' is out to show that what appears tragic for bourgeois humanism – alienation, appropriation, reification and the like – is actually comic, always-already at work, part of the very conditions of our sociality. Franco Moretti has pointed to this mutation in the case of modernism: 'Benjamin and Adorno associated "fragmentary" texts with melancholy, pain, defencelessness, loss of hope; today, they would evoke the far more exhilarating concepts of semantic freedom, de-totalization and productive hetereogeneity'.[27]

In a similar way, Bakhtin points out that the reification of the word, its free-standingness of a specific act of intention, is a necessary condition of its multiplicity of meaning, just as one might argue that objectification of some sort is an essential condition of all relationships. Whatever else human beings may be, they are most certainly natural objects. Otherness, unfinishedness, hybridity, indeterminacy and the like thus shift over from being lethal assaults on identity to being the very grounds of it. Which is to say, shift over from tragedy to comedy. All selfhood must be refracted through the Other – though if this for Lacan is the only way we can come into our own, it is also a potentially tragic form of alienation. Whereas Jacques Derrida and his acolytes tend merely to invert the *status quo ante*, so that what used to be seen as an unbearable loss of the proper, authentic or originary is now grasped as enabling and productive, Lacan, a far more tragic philosopher, is alive to both the gains and the losses of this vein of thought. The subject risks losing itself in the very medium which allows it to emerge into being.

The signifier of the inconceivable state which would be intelligible to me alone is death, which we have to do entirely for ourselves, and which we can know nothing of from the inside because, not being an experience, it has no inside. The idea that everything will carry on as usual after my death is at once, so to speak, a dead certainty and a paradigm of the purely speculative, since there is of course no way I could verify it. It is also in a curious way the ultimate validation of materialism, of the existence of an objective, independent world which will not only not notice when my own particular consciousness fizzles out, but will also be casually looking the other way when everybody else's does as well. No suggestion could be more offensive to those brands of linguistic idealism for which, since the world and discourse stand or fall together, we can transcend our mortal flesh in fantasy. As with all idealism, self and world are locked here in imaginary collusion; and if this lends a rather fragile quality to the world, dependent as it is on nothing more well-founded than our discourse, it also lends a reassuringly ontological feel to our subjecthood.

There are other such profane intimations of immortality. Nationalism, for example, for which what is imperishable is the people, and which is thus, despite its tragic history, an anti-tragic creed. One thinks also of Raymond Williams's socialist-humanist declaration 'I die, but we do not die',[28] which would be rather more persuasive in a pre-nuclear age. For Bakhtin, our mode of immortality is known as the body – not, as for postmodern theory, the 'constructed' body, since this belongs to culture and so in principle to tragedy, but a grosser version of this rather suave postmodern fiction, one which concerns digestion as well as discipline, shitting as well as sexuality. The Foucaultian body is the site of potential tragedy, of an insidious inscribing and oppressing. It is not, to be sure, tragic in actuality, since the body is itself a stand-in for the kind of interiority which would be needed to experience the tragic as such, an interiority to which Foucault is almost pathologically allergic. The Bakhtinian body, by contrast, is comic, utopian, a principle of solidarity rather than an index of exploitation, a force for stubbornly surviving continuities rather than a delicate locus of difference.

There is something to commend the case that the novel and tragedy are uneasily allied. The classical Spanish picaresque novel, as we have seen, unmasks the vanity of the world, perceiving its metaphysical emptiness but striking a pragmatic bargain or working compromise with it. Novelists like Scott, Manzoni and Sholokov all write against a backdrop of historical tragedy, yet labour through to some final affirmation. Scott retains his progressivist, middle-of-the-road vision; Manzoni ends *The Betrothed* with some wan hope for a kinder world; while the Sholokov of *And Quiet Flows the Don* sustains his faith in the Bolshevik experiment despite the local tragedies it entails. For the young Georg Lukács, form and content, value and fact or culture and life are tragically at odds; for the later theorist of the novel, they are harmonized by a utopian form known, ironically, as realism.

Yet realism, after all, is only one style of fiction. The belief that the novel form is *ipso facto* untragic springs largely from generalizing this privileged strain of it to the genre as a whole, as well as from an exaggerated respect for the classical doctrine that tragedy is always a question of crisis. The classical realist novel certainly aims for settlement and *détente*, repair and restitution, marriage and meaningful identity, whatever the destruction and disenchantment it must wade through to arrive there; but what of the novel which comes after it? *The Counterfeiters, The Outsider, A Farewell to Arms, Light in August, Under the Volcano, The Grapes of Wrath, The Power and the Glory, The Death of the Heart, The Third Policeman, The Ante-Room, The Last Tycoon, Lolita, Pincher Martin, Bend Sinister, Guerillas, American Pastoral, Beloved, The Life and Times of Michael K*: the list is arbitrary enough, but the common tragic milieu is unmistakable. From roughly the end of the nineteenth century, a genre which had struggled to avoid tragedy in the name of the morally inspiring succumbs to it on a dramatic scale, as the middle-class order which bred it passes its historical zenith and enters into the long ice-age of the twentieth century.

As for tragedy being a question of crisis, it can surely be quite as much a condition as an event, which lends it to novelization remarkably well. Indeed, one of the greatest of all tragic novels turns on a momentous non-event, a tragic violation which is not represented at all, which indeed has no need to be represented, and which according to one or two rather fancifully minded critics may never actually have happened. In the very bosom of modernity, with English civilization apparently at its most blithely self-assured, Samuel Richardson writes the astonishing *Clarissa*, in which tragedy and the commonplace are inseparable. The novel was to be a model for one of the greatest French fictions of the age, Laclos's *Les Liaisons dangereuses*. In the very home of progress and liberty, a repressed, mutilated humanity breaks abruptly through, as the tragic condition of women challenges the comic vision of men.

Clarissa, a novel whose heroine has a tragic precursor in the anorexic Penthea of John Ford's *The Broken Heart*, is a work of refusal and renunciation, coldly turning its back on an everyday world whose every detail it finds irresistibly fascinating. In spurning a world it desires, it becomes a novel about sacrifice, and its heroine is one of the great sacrificial scapegoats of world literature, intelligently in command of her dying and unswerving in her resolve to withdraw herself through death from the social currency of violence and dominion. As her body wastes gradually away to become a stark signifier of a more general state of victimage, her unconscionably prolonged dying turns her death into a public theatre in which the evils of an exploitative society can be put scandalously on show.

Like a Jamesian heroine, Clarissa wins with empty hands, turning her passivity into a form of practice, so meekly pacific that her death unleashes, Samson-like, a sadistic violence on her persecutors, so piously pledged to virtue that she shakes the foundations of a society which pays no more than lip-service to it. Richardson, usually a reader-friendly author remarkably adept at public relations, was deaf to the pleas of those outraged readers who wanted his heroine to live. He saw that poetic justice would suggest that her kind of virtue wins its reward in this world, thus freeing the social order which hounded her of its responsibility.[29] The death of Clarissa is both tragic negation and utopian transcendence, and John Kerrigan is surely right to suggest that the novel 'offers a counter-example to the familiar, half-persuasive thesis that Christianity is inimical to tragedy'.[30] Clarissa is one of the great tragic figures of English writing, though as one critic points out, Aristotle would not have found her so. She is too innocent, and the injustice of her death thus too repellent.[31] It is another case of the strange discrepancy between tragic theory and tragic practice.

Chapter 8

Tragedy and Modernity

Few thinkers could be more foreign to the spirit of tragedy than Benedictus de Spinoza. The son of a Portuguese Sephardic Jew who emigrated to the Netherlands, Spinoza was expelled from the Amsterdam Jewish community for heresy, had close links with Anabaptist Mennonites, came under the influence of Descartes and in turn powerfully inspired Goethe and Coleridge. As a member of a reviled minority, he was an apostle of tolerance and liberal enlightenment, a doughty demythologizer of the Bible and a scholar renowned for his charity and humility. In our own time, several of his doctrines have cropped up in heavy Marxist-Leninist disguise in the writings of Louis Althusser.

God for Spinoza is a self-causing cause: he acts solely by the laws of his nature and is therefore free, though he is not free not to act in this way. God is necessarily the way he is. That which is free exists by the necessity of its own nature, rather than being determined by some external force. The human mind is part of God's intellect, and Nature is part of his infinite substance; so the laws of Nature follow from God's nature, and they, too, could not be other than they are. All things have their essence in the mind of God, and to know God, which means to understand how things are and must necessarily be so, is the highest human attainment, the blissful state of intellectual love.

The virtuous for Spinoza are those who live according to such reason, and therefore lead lives which are serene, resigned and profoundly untragic. If you grasp why the person who has offended you could not have done otherwise, you are bound to feel less outraged by the injustice. Determinism is conducive to tolerance, not despair. Whatever seems to the virtuous individual 'impious, horrible, unjust, or disgraceful, arises from the fact that he conceives these things in a disturbed, mutilated, and confused manner: and on this account he endeavours above all to conceive things as they are in themselves'.[1] Reason, objectivity and disinterestedness are on the side of love and mercy, not of oppression. Nothing in the world happens by chance – 'In the universe there exists nothing contingent'[2] – and this lack of fortuitousness is what makes the world non-tragic. If nothing could have happened other than it does, there is no point either in lamenting or vigorously resisting it. The populace, however, live by imagination (Althusser's 'ideology') rather than reason ('theory'), and are therefore ignorant of the causes of things, believing themselves to be free. Freedom is the ignorance of necessity.

The reasonable individual returns love for hate, and has no fear of death. Virtue is no more teleological than the universe itself: just as the world, being part of God's substance, has its end in itself, so only the unschooled masses imagine in spontaneously utilitarian spirit that things are good or bad in so far as they cater for human happiness, failing to grasp that virtue is autotelic. True virtue is to desire what will preserve you in being, so that self-interest lies at its root; but this is a reasonable form of self-regard which obeys the general laws of Nature and is perfectly compatible with friendship, peace and love. To seek what is useful for yourself is to seek what is most useful for others. There is no tragic conflict between individual and society, and no sadistic delight in others' sorrows: 'every one led by reason desires for his fellows the good he desires for himself'.[3]

It is not the most seductive of world-views for the twenty-first century. Indeed, it represents everything that is commonly thought wrong with the thought of modernity:[4] rationalist, scientistic, totalizing, metaphysical, universalist and blandly upbeat. A touch of tragedy would do it no harm at all. For Spinoza, as for Leibniz and Vico, evil is simply good grasped out of context; for him as for Descartes, the essence of humanity lies in the intellect, an opinion which would seem to confuse persons with dons. But one should not forget that these rebarbative doctrines go hand in hand in Spinoza with a revolutionary humanism which preaches a brand of liberal pluralism, puts humankind in the place of God and affirms the democracy of the populace as the most fertile form of politics.[5] In any case, one should not reduce a whole complex epoch to one set of doctrines. For there is a tragic modernity just as much as a progressivist one; and if dialectical thought is in demand in the modern era, it is because the two are intimately allied.

This is why there is irony in the proposal that the idea of tragedy is a full-blooded critique of modernity. Indeed, the ironies are multiple. For one thing, tragedy is on hand in the modern age to deflate a vainglorious bourgeois humanism, one which buys its affirmations on the cheap. And there is plenty of that in the discourses of the modern epoch, from Bacon to Bakunin. Romanticism has its tragic conflicts, but on the whole it would prefer to blame ruin and affliction on the powers which oppress

204

the human subject, rather than contemplate any central flaw in that subject's constitution. Byron's Manfred, for example, finally defies the evil spirits which come to claim him and rebelliously asserts the utter self-dependence of the human mind. By the time of Sartre, this faith in the sacredness of self-determination has become so ardent that almost any appeal to conditioning forces becomes a case of *mauvaise foi*. Tragedy can submit all this jejeune talk of Man and his infinite capacities to a sobering reminder of death and fragility, of humankind's extreme strangeness to itself, its fugitive career, volatility of selfhood and transcendental homelessness. Yet the idea of tragedy, as we have seen, is hardly well equipped for this chastening task, given its own inclination to a self-vaunting humanism which passes cavalierly over the fact of human frailty. The idea of tragedy is in this sense another version of bourgeois humanism, not an antidote to it. Or perhaps it would be more accurate to say that it counters the more dewy-eyed, callowly utopian brands of humanism with a more conservative variety of the same creed.

So it is that tragedy, in the hands of the theorists rather than the practitioners, moves into a democratic era with a fond backward glance at honour, hierarchy and heroism, and opposes ancient fate to modern freedom. It elevates the value of suffering above the drive to eradicate it, repudiating reason for myth, history for eternity, accident for essence. Tragedy pits a patrician rhetoric against the demotic idiom of the modern, clinging to unbending commitments which will brook no workaday compromise. What makes life meaningful in its eyes is not love or friendship, but death. It scorns the notion of secular progress, and is sceptical of the self-determining subject. Happiness is for shopkeepers, not tragic heroes, who have something more precious to pursue. 'Tragic drama', writes George Steiner, 'tells us that the spheres of reason, order, and justice are terribly limited and that no progress in our science or technical resources will enlarge their relevance'.[6] Tragedy, which plays the role of wisdom to the knowledge of science, *Vernunft* to *Verstand*, is thus the very paradigm of what we know today as the Humanities, or of what has been traditionally known as *Kulturkritik*.[7] At the same time, in its suspicion of reason, order and progress, this brand of genteel reaction has more than a little in common with a supposedly radical postmodernism.

This view of tragedy, astonishingly, arises in an era which has witnessed more real-life tragedy than any other in history. While the scholars have been speaking of tragedy with caught breath as estimable and ennobling, or issuing elegiac laments for its decline, history has been awash with warfare, butchery, disease, starvation, political murder. It is true that as suffering has escalated apace, so by and large has our sensitivity to it. The most bloody of epochs has also been the most humanitarian. This is not just cosmetic, though it is doubtless that as well; it is also because a humanism and individualism which are sources of that destructiveness can also have a genuine respect for human life. But it is in this blood-soaked period that tragedy is declared, bemusingly, to be either dead or of absolute value.

In a further ironic twist, the former claim usually entails the latter, since the death of tragedy is generally mourned as the passing of something ultimately precious. But both assertions are responses to the havoc and butchery, not just disavowals of it. If tragedy is dead, then as we have seen already it is because it posits a sense of value which a history of terror has supposedly extinguished. And if it is of absolute value, whether alive or dead, it is because it represents a reaction to modern barbarism. It is just that what it complains of in that era is usually science, democracy, liberalism and social hope rather than injustice, exploitation and military aggression. In this sense, it remains bound to the very social forms which it disowns.

What happens to tragedy in the twentieth century is not that it dies, but that it mutates into modernism. For a major strain of modernism also belabours a middle-class society with which it nevertheless remains complicit, castigating its spiritually derelict condition from the right rather than the left. Modernism, too, can be rancorously anti-democratic, stridently elitist, homesick for the primitive and archaic, in thrall to spiritual absolutes which spell the death of liberal enlightenment. And if modernism lends the tragic impulse a new lease of life, it is not least because of the return of mythology. In the late modern era, mythical destiny shows its face again in the guise of vast, anonymous forces – language, Will, power, history, production, desire – which live us far more than we live them. The human subject, lately so proud of its free agency, once more seems the plaything of mysterious powers, and eternal recurrence itself recurs, this time in the shape of the commodity form. As human life becomes as collective as in pre-modern times, the atavistic and the avant-garde form curious new affinities. For Joyce and Beckett as much as for pre-modern mythology, change is just a variation on the same imperishable old items. History loses its sense of direction, giving way to the cyclical, the synchronic, the epiphany of eternity, the deep grammar of all cultures, the eternal now of the unconscious, the primitive energies at the root of all life-forms, the moment in and out of time, the still point of the turning world, the collapse of novelistic narrative.

Yet modernity never really needed reminding of tragedy. To assume so is to reduce a complex formation to a single, crassly triumphalist doctrine, a grand narrative of progress which rides roughshod over individual lives. Arthur Schopenhauer recounted one such grand narrative, that of the Will, but there was nothing teleological about it, and certainly nothing triumphant. On the contrary, it was one of the most remorselessly tragic fables which modern history has witnessed. It is a mistake to suppose that all grand narratives are forever striving onwards and upwards. Though modernity recounts several such tales, they do not exhaust its narrative repertoire. There are also stories to be told of deadlock, contradiction, self-undoing, which represent the dark underside of the fables of progress.

The philosopher Georg Simmel portrays one such contradiction, which he bluntly names tragic. In his essay 'On the Concept and Tragedy of Culture', he argues in Hegelian style that spirit can be realized only in forms which alienate it, and which then come to assume an ominous objective logic of their own. Indeed, Simmel's essay is an early anticipation of the Death of the Author doctrine, an anti-intentionalist case which stresses the immanent logic of cultural forms and their lack of a single producer. Since it belongs to spirit to estrange itself – since its self-separation is ironically inherent to it – the result is a classically tragic condition. Alienation is a kind of *peripeteia*, in which self-realizing swerves into self-loss. Indeed, possession must logically imply loss: I can only speak of an object as authentically mine if it is potentially alienable, which is why I cannot describe my body or a backache as a possession. 'Even in its first moments of existence', Simmel writes, 'culture carries something within itself which, as if by an intrinsic fate, is determined to block, to burden, to obscure and divide its innermost purpose.'[8] Culture is self-deconstructing, as the burden of objectified spirit comes to overwhelm the subjective life. As the protagonist of André Gide's *The Immoralist* remarks, 'Culture, which is born of life, ends up killing it'. Culture is what makes life worth living, but it is also what emasculates life's vital energies in a tragically self-consuming process.

For Nietzsche, Freud and Simmel, civilization is life turned destructively against itself, however indispensable this ironic doubling may be. Material production gives birth to a culture which its own philistinism undermines. As the advocates of *Lebensphilosophie* warn the neo-Kantian formalists, cultural forms are bound to betray the diversity of life in the very act of expressing it. Mikhail Bakhtin thus turns to the novel, with its mongrelized, open-ended, perpetually unfinished forms, as one solution to this dilemma.[9] For the Freud of *Civilization and its Discontents*, culture is locked in tragic conflict with the very destructive forces it is supposed to transcend. To create civilization involves sublimating part of our primary aggressiveness, diverting it from the ego and fusing it with *Eros*, builder of cities, to subdue Nature and rear our institutions. The death drive, which lurks within our aggressivity, is thus tricked out of its hostile intentions and harnessed to the business of constructing a social order.

To do this, however, involves renouncing instinctual gratification; and to enforce this painful sacrifice, some of our aggressive energies must be hijacked to form the superego. But every renunciation of instinctual fulfilment strengthens the authority of this brutal autocrat, intensifying its sadistic power and thus deepening our guilt. The more admirably idealist we grow, the more we stoke up within us a lethal culture of self-hatred. And the more we sublimate *Eros* into the building of banks and opera halls, the more we deplete its internal resources, leaving it a prey to its old antagonist *Thanatos* or the death drive. The more civilized we become, then, the more we tear ourselves apart with guilt and self-aggression. Culture and death are not rivals after all. There is a tragic self-mutilation at the very root of civilization. It is just that civilization needs this savage parody of itself in order to function. Psychoanalysis is the science of desire; and the lesson it has to teach is that desire is the tragedy of everyday life, at once luridly melodramatic and as banal as breathing.

The contradictions of idealism is a familiar motif of modernity. Bourgeois society is awash with admirable ideals, but structurally incapable of realizing them – so that what Simmel sees as the self-marring nature of all culture is here at its most acute. Since this stalled dialectic between an impotent idealism and a degraded actuality is inherent to the bourgeois social order, and incapable of being resolved by it, it might well be termed tragic. It is there in comic mode in the altercation between the lofty-spirited Philosopher and the streetwise Nephew in Diderot's *Rameau's Nephew*. Proclaiming values which it can never realize, modernity is caught up in the chronic bad faith of a performative contradiction. Lucien Goldmann in *The Hidden God* sees 'tragic man' as caught between an ideal which is compelling but increasingly absent, and an empirical world which is present but morally worthless. Since absolute value has ebbed from everyday life, the tragic protagonist is driven to refuse the world; but if absolute value has vanished, then he has nowhere to launch his refusal but from within the very world he spurns. He must thus recognize and rebuff that world at the same time, in a simultaneous yes-and-no which for Goldmann contains the seeds of a dialectical rationality. All that is left of transcendence now is the yearning for it.

Like the hidden God, the tragic hero is present and absent in the world at the same time, unable either to stay or leave, bereft of an alternative for exactly the reasons which make him restive with what he has. As Georg Lukács remarks in *Soul and Form*, a tragedy is that form in which 'God must leave the stage, but must yet remain a spectator'.[10] If God is fully present in his creation then he robs it of autonomous value, as well as depriving his creatures of freedom; but his absence equally plunders the world of meaning, and the tragic protagonist is caught in this metaphysical cross-fire. His freedom is assured, but for the same reason he can now practise it only in a paltry world. Moreover, God's ominous silence, the loss of heaven, makes that world more precious at the very moment that it highlights its perishability.

Kant, on this view, is a tragic philosopher. For Goldmann, he is stuck with *Verstand* but beguiled by *Vernunft*, still hungering for ideal values – freedom, totality, the universal ethical community of ends – which are now opaque and unknowable, thrust into the realm of the noumenal and so cut off from the phenomenal sphere in which they are supposed to be active.[11] This at least seals them from harm, but only at the cost of entombing them, like someone so anxious to preserve his strength that he never gets out of bed. The ideals are secured – but only by being sealed off from the empirical world, so that they dwindle to dim abstractions and hence, in effect, fail to be secured at all. Like the God of Jansenism, or indeed the noble ends of bourgeois society, such values are present and absent simultaneously. It is as though the domain of tragedy and the novelistic landscape of everyday life are both in good working order, but divided from each other by an ontological gulf.

Ultimate values undoubtedly exist, but how they come to do so in this profane world must remain a mystery. If there is value at all, then it can only be in relation to ourselves, a relativity which then threatens to undermine it. Spinoza, an early specimen of a long line of anti-realist moral philosophers, thought that value-terms like 'good' and 'bad' named nothing in the world itself. So did Thomas Hobbes. By the time of Wittgenstein's *Tractatus Logico-Philosophicus*, value has been banished from the world altogether, along with the subject. We cannot span the abyss between the world-for-us and the world-in-itself, though we can abolish the latter altogether by arguing like Berkeley that objects are just complexes of perceptions, with no fatal slippage between how they are and how they appear to us. Ontology thus becomes phenomenology. We are rescued from tragedy at the cost of never escaping from our own skins.

The hiddenness of God is also a concern of the greatest tragedian of late seventeenth-century England, John Milton. Like many eminent works of art, Milton's great tragic poems are not timeless but askew to their time. Unlike, say, the writings of John Dryden or the Earl of Rochester, they are not quite at one with their historical conjuncture. They belong not so much to their chronological moment as to the revolutionary period which precedes it, as the mythologizer-in-chief of the

English bourgeois revolution, he and the revolution having now both fallen on hard times, turns to address the question of how that republican paradise came to be lost. An historical tragedy has occurred, which Milton's poetry must decipher in its own mythopoeic fashion, placing a political debacle within a longer eschatological narrative of sin and salvation. The course of history no longer seems to manifest the deity: God is a *Deus absconditus* – indeed, for the Milton who clings to the Arian heresy, inherently so. The Father is not fully incarnate in the Son but remains aloof and unfathomable. For orthodox Christian theology, the Incarnation means that God is no longer the austere patriarch or Name of the Father but suffering flesh and blood, friend and fellow victim; but Milton must keep these two persons of the Trinity rigorously separate, for fear no doubt that the mercifulness of Christ might be tainted by the despotic high-handedness of the Father. In a classically Protestant scenario, Christ's love is needed to shield us from the Father's wrathful justice, as a sympathetic defence attorney might save you from a grilling at the hands of a particularly irascible judge.

It is this which Blake has in mind when he calls the Satanic God of Milton and others 'Nobodaddy'. In the Old Testament, the word 'Satan' means 'accuser', and represents the image of God of those who need for their own purposes to see him as an avenging judge. It is the image of God cultivated by the respectable and self-righteous, who believe that if only they can placate this fearful patriarch by cultic ritual and impeccable conduct then they can bargain their way to heaven. It is the reverse of the image of God as a broken body, as an executed political criminal. In Milton's austere Arian theology, the Name of the Father is not dethroned but appeased. Despite his commitment to sense, discourse and reason, there is thus an unspannable gulf between God and humanity, which the English people's failure to realize the kingdom of heaven on earth has done nothing to narrow. Nor has it been eased by the growing rationalism of the age. For the Protestant puritan, moving fearfully in darkness amidst fragments of revelation, God is just but utterly inscrutable. As Frank Kermode comments, Milton's God 'often seems indifferent to human beings; he seems not to understand them. His plots cause them excruciating pain and are unrelated to the human sense of justice. He is contemptuous of equity, even of sanity.'[12] It is much the way Euripides thought about his own particular clutch of deities.

The God of *Samson Agonistes* seems especially erratic in this respect. The poem contains one of the most powerful denunciations in literature of God's so-called justice. God is justice and reason, but in a sense impenetrably different from ours, as one might speculate that a tarantula had some notion of elegance but one light years removed from our own. His ways must by definition be just because he is God, as a Cambodian's day-dreams must by definition be those of a Cambodian; but it does not follow that God's sense of justice meets our own criteria of equity. It is not clear, for example, why disobeying him over so trifling a matter as an apple should be enough to plunge human history into nightmare for the next few millennia. But this is to resort to reasons, and part of the problem is that reason is really just what God arbitrarily decides on. He is not ruled by rationality himself since he created it, rather as an absolute monarch is the ultimate anarchist since he is not bound by his own edicts. On a Catholic view, God wills what is good; on a certain Protestant view, things are good because God wills them. Had the fancy taken him, he could always have willed that genocide was praiseworthy. If some things just are good or bad, independently of whether God wills them or not, then this would seem to curb his freedom, and the cosmos ceases to be clay in his hands. But unconstrained freedom, freedom to declare that torture is commendable, is both vacuous and tyrannical, like the God of *Paradise Lost* in the eyes of, say, William Empson in *Milton's God*. We will see the same problem later in the case of existentialism.

For some modern thought, it would seem true that we are free and yet not free at all. This is the case with both Kant and class society. In Kant's view, what can be known must be determinate, and this is the world as it is known to pure reason. The empirical self falls within this realm, being causally determined and so unfree. But our acting in the world belongs to the sphere of freedom or practical reason; and if the world is determinate, then our action is unable to alter it. So the world upon which we act must be indeterminate, capable of being given a struc-ture which it does not have already, if our freedom is to have meaning. But if this is so, then the world on which we act must be unknowable, since the knowable is the determinate. The (phenomenal) world we know thus cannot be the same as the (noumenal) world on which we act, so that theory and practice, pure and practical reason, are necessar-ily at odds. Knowledge and freedom are at odds in this sense too, that to act effectively we would need to know the effects of our actions in advance, which would then negate our freedom. We act necessarily in the dark, but as the world grows more complex, this becomes all the more dangerous. The ideal situation in the market-place would be for me to know the future but for you not to.

Neither can we know that we are free agents, since our freedom is noumenal, too. We can only have faith that we are. Fideism, here as else-where in modern thought, is the logical outcome of positivism, empiri-cism or phenomenalism. If knowledge can have no truck with value, faith can have no affinity with fact. This inevitable discord between theory and practice crops up, sometimes with tragic overtones, in so improbable an assortment of thinkers as Nietzsche, Freud, Sorel, Conrad, Althusser and Paul de Man. If we are to act constructively, we must at all costs repress the knowledge which informs us that the agent has no real unity, that he or she is wholly exchangeable with another, that what appear to the agent to be rational motivations are actually emotional prejudices, that there are no inherently valuable ends, and that the world on which we act is unfathomable, indeterminate or coolly indifferent to our projects. A certain amnesia or self-blindness is a condition of selfhood, not a deficiency of it.

Much the same is true for David Hume, who having reduced identity to a fiction, reason to imagination, morality to sentiment, causality to custom and belief to feeling, feels the need to decamp from the philosophical havoc he has wreaked by carefully cultivating an Apollonian false consciousness. Having calmly knocked the foundations out from beneath social life in his study, Hume strolls out to play backgammon and make merry with his friends, assured that theory is one thing and practice another. 'Very refined reflections', he writes with a palpable air of relief, 'have little or no influence upon us.'[13] The clubbish is a refuge from the conceptual. Theory, far from securing social practice, actually disables it. If intuition assures you that there is truth, truth informs you that there is just intuition. In an ironic reversal which Wittgenstein would later re-echo, it is common sense which is metaphysical, assuming that there is some unimpeachable ground to social custom, and philosophy which arrives hot-foot with the monstrous news that custom rests on nothing more unsinkable than itself. The symbolic order is 'supported' by a Real which is nothing at all, and Hume has had a forbidden glimpse of this ghastly truth. He has been forced by his own irresistible chain of reasoning into a waste land beyond all reason.

In a rare moment of panic, the normally suave Hume confesses that he feels himself to be 'some strange uncouth monster', banished from all human commerce by his sceptical reflections and 'left utterly abandon'd and disconsolate'.[14] It is not even as though this Edinburgh Oedipus can console himself with the thought that he is speaking the truth, since truth is precisely part of what he has called into question. Must not his belief that belief is just a vivid sort of feeling apply to itself? In a curious irony, the philosopher becomes an anti-social outcast, a hairy prophet howling in the wilderness, not because he proclaims some apocalyptic truth or spearheads some sensational revolution, but because he delivers the altogether more disturbing message that social practice and the habits of human nature are all we ever have. If this is so, then it is doubtless all

212

the more alarming to feel yourself forced out of them. For where then is there to go?

The quest for the absolute can never be justified, as Kantian critique sketches the frontiers between what can be intelligibly spoken of and what cannot. But the hope for it is never entirely eradicated, and will make its presence felt among other places in the *Critique of Judgement*'s reflections on the sublime. Just as the sinner can never be justified but goes on hankering wistfully for evidence of salvation, so it is hard to relinquish totality, even if the only evidence for it we have is the wan faith that the rubble of atomistic facts we see around us can surely not be the whole story. Pascal, for Goldmann, is another such tragic thinker, since he accepts this mechanistic vision of the world at one level while refusing it at another. The bourgeoisie cannot give up on its ideals, but it cannot realize them either; and the less it can do so, the more unpalatably abstract those ideals become. The more rationalized and regimented its world grows, the more it must appeal to spiritual values to legitimate it, only to find that it has rationalized them away just when they are most needed.

It is possible, however, to see Kant's programme as much as an antidote to tragedy as an example of it. The point is to forego metaphysical extravaganzas, moderate your passions, avoid hubris, know yourself and your limits, cultivate reason and restraint. A world purged of heady speculation and apocalyptic zest is one poor but honest. Reason may be a sublime idea beyond comprehension, fact and value eternally disjunct, the world ultimately unknowable, its purposiveness a hypothesis, freedom an unthinkable enigma and the Absolute strictly off-bounds; but all this leaves you with a manageable sort of place to live in, however bleak and monochrome. There is a kind of tragic renunciation at work here, as Kant austerely declares anathema all fervid Romantic conjecture and turns his face heroically from the forbidden fruit. It is an ancient remedy for tragedy: don't overdo it and you won't come a cropper. Such an anti-tragic spirit is alive in the sceptical, self-ironizing prose style of Montaigne, a writer with what Claude Rawson has called 'a temperamental shrinking from catastrophic perspectives',[15] just as it can be detected in the wily, accommodating pragmatism of that bugbear of stage tragedy, Machiavelli.

Even so, it is alarming that the sources of freedom should be so obscure, since bourgeois society can then lend no sure foundation to its most treasured value. If the essence of Man is his freedom, then he is bound to slip instantly from his own grip, find himself reduced to a sort of cypher at the very height of his affirmation. As soon as you try to pin down this protean, quicksilver thing called freedom or subjectivity, it slides through the net of signification and leaves you grasping at thin air. A human subject who could be known would be a determinate object, and so not a subject at all. The free subject, the founding principle of the whole enterprise, cannot itself be represented in the field which it generates, any more than the eye can capture itself in the field of vision. The subject is rather the incalculable element or out-of-place factor which allows that field to emerge into existence in the first place. What our knowledge tells us is that we are beyond its reach.

Subjectivity is thus both everything and nothing, the productive source of the world yet a mute epiphany or pregnant silence. You can glimpse it out of the corner of your eye, but it evaporates as soon as you stare at it straight. It cannot be reckoned up with the objects among which it moves, since it is the power which brings them to presence in the first place, and so must lie on some altogether different plane. The self is not an object in the world but a transcendental viewpoint upon it, a prodigiously structuring force which is at the same time sheer vacuity. The subject is a residue or leftover, rather as the theory of evolution brings with it the sobering insight that human consciousness is an accident, an excrescence, the result of sheer absent-mindedness on the part of a Nature intent on other matters.

Like the sacrificial scapegoat of tragedy, this subject is at once the cornerstone of the social order and yet surplus, excessive, marking the limits of the knowable by the very fact that it lies beyond them. Like the sublime, all we can comprehend about it is its incomprehensibility. This poses a problem for Romanticism, which needs to know which of the self's various impulses are authentic, springing from its inward necessity. These are the desires which must at all costs be acted upon; but if the self is a searchless chasm they are not easy to identify, or to distinguish from desires which are false or trifling. This deep subjectivity is at once an infinity to be revered and an abyss in which one is sunk without trace. Absent and present in the world at one and the same time, the bourgeois subject is itself the great tragic hero of the modern epoch. For Jewish antiquity, there could be no graven image of God because the only image of God was humanity. Now that humanity has usurped his place, it too has become unrepresentable, so that all true philosophy must be iconoclasm. In a classical tragic rhythm, the rise of Man is also his disappearance. Like celebrities promoted out of the public eye, the human species rises without trace. The human has replaced the divine as the locus of absolute value; yet if God is dead, then as Nietzsche saw there is no vantage-point outside the human from which a judgement of its value could logically be made. The death of God, whatever Feuerbach may have thought, thus threatens to drag humanism down in its wake.

So it is that Blaise Pascal sees humanity as a site of contradictions, acclaiming Man and deriding him at the same time. He is a creature full of error whose precious reason is the sport of every wind, whose primary principles are intuitive rather than rational, and whose most cherished values are culturally relative. 'There is nothing just or unjust but changes colour as it changes climate. Three degrees of latitude upset the whole of jurisprudence and one meridian determines what is true.'[16] Custom, for Pascal as for Hume and Burke, is the sole foundation of justice, and force and concupiscence the ignoble motivations of all our actions. The only reason for clinging to custom is that it is customary to do so. Habit is a kind of second nature, but nature is no more than habit or convention in the first place. Our lives, governed by a perpetual drifting of desire, are a compound of boredom and fretfulness, and our knowledge is quite without foundation. In science and mathematics, principles 'which are supposed to be ultimate do not stand by themselves, but depend on others, which depend on others again, and thus never allow of any finality'.[17] False consciousness is our natural condition: at the core of human existence lies the monstrous trauma of death and the threat of eternal perdition, yet nobody loses as much sleep over this as they do over some imaginary affront to their honour. What we call reality is just the set of shabby illusions which shield us from death, a kind of Soho of the psyche.

Yet we should pause before dramatically unveiling a postmodern Pascal. For this is also the man who hymns the magnificence of humanity, a magnificence quite inseparable from its absurdity. 'Man's greatness', he writes, 'comes from knowing he is wretched; a tree does not know it is wretched.'[18] Two negatives make a positive: by doubling our dismal state, raising it to the second power of self-consciousness, we can hope to surmount it. Indeed, the greatness of humanity can be deduced from its misery, since only a creature which knows itself capable of greater things could feel so thoroughly disconsolate. If there is no sense of value, there is no tragedy; if we were less precious, we would be less morose. The truth of the human condition can thus be captured only in the language of antithesis and oxymoron. Man is vile and great, bold and timid, credulous and sceptical, and Pascal's own task, rather like that of the psychotherapist, is to exalt him when he humbles himself and humble him when he exalts himself – not, to be sure, in order to adapt him to some utterly illusory mean, but to bring him to understand that he is 'a monster that passes all understanding'.[19] Monstrosity is our natural condition, not a deviation from it. It is not that the human subject is sometimes fine and sometimes vile but that it is both together, and so represents an aporia which baffles thought. 'Man', Pascal writes, 'transcends man.'[20] He is the activity of ceaselessly eluding himself, the process of his own self-opaqueness.

Like the tragic scapegoat – like Oedipus at Colonus – the human subject is both 'glory and refuse of the universe', 'feeble earthworm' and 'repository of truth'.[21] The subject is superfluous ('refuse'), excremental, inherently out of place, yet this weakness is also a sort of exaltation. The paradox of humanity is that it seems built for redemption but cannot attain it; and for Pascal it is in this contradiction that one may glimpse the profile of God. The point is not to renounce reason (Pascal is no fideist), but to turn it against itself and practise it otherwise; and this can be achieved only by forsaking reason as we know it. Only through the surrender of reason could we truly know ourselves, since reason, for Pascal as for Freud, is more a barrier against such self-knowledge than a highway to it. Just as the rules governing a procedure sometimes intimate when to improvise on them or throw them away altogether, so reason needs to exceed or transform itself – but only when it judges that it is reasonable to do so: 'It is right, then, that reason should submit when it judges that it ought to submit'.[22] There must come a point where reasons simply run out or point beyond themselves. Explanations, as Wittgenstein remarks in the *Philosophical Investigations*, must come to an end somewhere; it is just that they themselves have an important hand in deciding where. It is reasonable that reason should not go all the way down.

To hold that there are some beliefs which do not need justifying by other beliefs is to be a foundationalist. But you can also hold that something does not need a foundation because it is self-founding. It is its own ground, end, cause and reason, rather than resting on some ontological bedrock beneath it. This is the case with modernity's conception of freedom. As Albrecht Wellmer points out, the Enlightenment insists that norms can now find their justification only in the will of humanity, rather than in God or Nature or tradition; but this insight must have been a vertiginous one, an experience of freedom which was 'either chilling or exhilarating'.[23] Exhilaratingly, it means that humanity is free to refashion itself; chillingly, it means that there is nothing beyond this freedom to lend it an ontological seal of approval. If there were, then our freedom would be constrained. To give oneself the law is both the supreme form of dignity and a hollow tautology.

The modern subject requires some Other to assure it that its powers are genuine and its freedom authentic. Otherwise it behaves like the man in Wittgenstein's *Philosophical Investigations* who cries 'But I know how tall I am!' and places his hand on top of his own head. Yet such otherness is also intolerable to the subject, reminding it of a world which it

216

has failed to saturate with its own subjectivity. There can be no subject without objectification, yet this is exactly the way in which the subject comes to lose track of itself. It needs others in order to be itself, but continually finds that this dependence infringes its autonomy. As the poet Bernard O'Donoghue puts it, 'Our faultline: that we're designed / To live neither together nor alone'.[24]

On the other hand, if the world the subject addresses is no more than a thinly disguised version of itself, all its relationships become narcissistic. It is like another of Wittgenstein's foolish figures, who passes money from one of his hands to the other and believes that he has made a financial transaction. Perhaps the subject can know itself as an object simply through self-reflection, which might be a way of keeping its objectivity within the charmed circle of its own consciousness. But to do this means splitting itself in two, carving up its own unity in the act of trying to grasp hold of it. The subject is sovereign, but like a monarch in exile it has no real kingdom to rule over. As Kierkegaard puts it in *The Sickness Unto Death*, the one who chooses his own identity is a 'king without a country', and his subjects live in a condition where rebellion is legitimate at every moment.

So it is that the dream of freedom can quickly sour to nightmare, as the defiant boast of the modern ('I take value from myself alone!') dwindles to a cry of anguish ('I am so lonely in this universe!'). The humanist subject is a manic-depressive creature, discovering to its consternation that in appropriating Nature it has appropriated its own objectivity along with it. Besides, quite how it manages to act upon Nature at all is a mystery, since for this, subjectivity requires a body; and as it cannot tolerate a particle of matter in its make-up, it is hard to see how it can bind itself to anything so gross. In this sense, too, the human subject is a conundrum or contradiction, as the monstrous unity of two universes, one composed of matter and the other of anti-matter, which for Descartes meet somewhere around the pineal gland.

The paradox of freedom is that it severs you from the world in which you practise it. Once again, self-realization involves self-estrangement. The price of liberty is eternal homelessness. Freedom can find no fitting objective correlative of itself in any one of its works, a fact which threatens to strike all of them trite and arbitrary. A desire which is acted upon thus comes to seem just as fruitless as one which is not. The more the subject feels its freedom to be necessary, the more dismayingly contingent its existence becomes. For Machiavelli, our appetites are insatiable and our fulfilments confined, so that 'the human mind is perpetually discontented, and of its possessions is apt to grow weary'.[25] Shakespeare's Troilus puts it rather more memorably to Cressida: 'This is the monstrosity in love, lady, that the will is infinite, and the execution confin'd; that the desire is boundless, and the act a slave to limit' (Act 3, sc. 2). Desire is the great tragic protagonist of modernity, striving and forever falling short, entangling itself in its own too-much.

So much is clear from the philosophy of Sade, for whom Nature is a meaningless chaos and the highest desire the orgiastic experience of nothingness. *Pace* the petty hedonists and utilitarians, one must desire everything regardless of the consequences, taking one's cue from Nature and living for death and destruction. Sade's is the *ne plus ultra* of the philosophy of freedom; but so, too, are the melancholic writings of Giacomo Leopardi, who believes that 'everything is evil, existence is evil and ordered to evil',[26] and for whom we are creatures built for a happiness which nature simply does not accommodate. Ennui – the pure hankering for infinite fulfilment – is the way the mind feels the emptiness of existence, the only experience which keeps it from non-being. For having discovered that there is no satisfaction, desire finally comes to take itself as an object, and it is this craving for its own emptiness, a version of the death drive, which keeps us listlessly in motion. What for postmodernity is the thrilling subversiveness of desire is for modernity a prolonged disenchantment. The furious freedom of the modern age is at odds with feeling at home in the world; and to make us feel that we and the world are partners, mirror-images, locked in an imaginary collusion, is one vital end of ideology. In this sense, the bourgeoisie is a threat to its own ideology. Freedom and happiness are now to be reconciled only in exceptional places, such as the realist novel. Or, for that matter, in the exceptional mind of Hegel, for whom the subject may unite with the world without threat to its spiritual freedom, since the world itself is simply spiritual freedom in material disguise.

If freedom is at odds with happiness, it would seem equally at war with reason. Not, to be sure, for Kant and Hegel, but for the kind of libertarianism for which any rational foundation to liberty must inevitably limit it. If you can give reasons for freedom, then you have already dislodged its priority and blemished its purity. On this eccentric modern theory, to drink because you are thirsty is a kind of coercion. One thus buys one's freedom at the cost of its foundedness, which means that it is as precarious as it is precious. One outcome of this libertarianism is the *acte gratuit*, the act performed purely to prove one's freedom, like Lafcadio Wluiki throwing a stranger out of a railway carriage in Gide's *The Vatican Cellars*. Or Albert Camus's Caligula, for whom freedom is both absolute and absurd, a terrifying drive which 'wants to make the impossible possible' and which nothing in the world can assuage. Caligula in Camus's play regards the world as worthless, and sees freedom as the exhilarating release from it which this insight brings. Once you accept that you might just as well kill yourself, there are no limits to what is possible. Nothing can harm one who has given up on life already. True freedom means divesting yourself of the world, not engaging with it.

Even so, absolute liberty consumes itself, since to realize itself is to abolish itself. Like the crazed anarchist professor of Conrad's *The Secret Agent*, such freedom must be prepared to blow to pieces the world it wants to transform, and itself along with it. Stefan, the Faustian revolutionary of Camus's play *The Just*, claims that there are no limits to liberty; but he fails to see that it is just this lack of determination which renders it pointless. The anarchist revolutionary, like the tragic scapegoat, is the one who has strayed beyond the frontiers of the possible into a twilight region trapped somewhere between life and death, the human and the inhuman.

There are other senses in which reason and freedom are in conflict, familiar from Max Horkheimer and Theodor Adorno's *Dialectic of Enlightenment*. Modern freedom is the enemy of reason, since it reduces it to a mere tool of power in the conquest of Nature and the oppression of others. Even if knowledge of Nature and society exists for the ends of emancipation, as it does for Francis Bacon, the upshot of this is to set reason on the despotic throne once reserved for God, which is hardly a measure of unqualified progress. Reason is how the human subject imposes its ends on Nature; but it can do so only by simultaneously laying predatory hands upon itself, doing violence to its own sensuous, creaturely existence. The result is a subject who emerges from the act of individuating itself looking much like everyone else. As Jürgen Habermas comments: 'Reason itself destroys the humanity it first made possible'.[27] And if it destroys our freedom, it ruins our happiness too, which is now beleaguered from a number of directions. So it is that the great dishevelled outpouring of energy and desire which is the modern epoch ends up in an 'iron cage' of rationalization.

The phrase is Max Weber's,[28] himself a tragic philosopher who feared that all this mighty creation of the unbridled bourgeois will had led to a paralysis of the individual life and the threat of a new age of serfdom. Liberal values were now in jeopardy from the very social order which had given birth to them, and the elegiac Weber could see no escape from this contradiction. As with Marx, his critique is all the more persuasive because he was himself no anti-modern Jeremiah of the Heideggerian ilk. Rationalization was not simply to be deplored: if it obstructed individual freedom, it also helped to create the conditions for it. Weber's neo-Kantian separation of fact and value, the public and the private domains, is among other things a way of protecting the ethical sphere, with its high, heroic ideals, from a drearily administered world. In its own way, it is another version of the widening fissure between tragedy and the novel.

Freedom, then, would seem hard to reconcile with reason and happiness; but happiness would seem equally at odds with virtue, at least for some modern moralists. It is in this period that the lethal belief grows up that virtue and self-fulfilment, so closely entwined for Aristotle, Aquinas and Marx, are more or less antithetical. For Kant, as for a self-lacerating figure like Alissa in Gide's *Strait is the Gate*, an action is unlikely to be virtuous if it feels in the least pleasant. There is a class basis to this way of seeing. It is the petty-bourgeois roundhead, not the upper-class cavalier, who finds virtue an uphill struggle. The difference is dramatized in the clash between the two leading eighteenth-century English novelists, Richardson and Fielding. There is a patrician blitheness about the writing of a novelist like Fielding, or a moralist like the Earl of Shaftesbury, which is quite the reverse of tragic. Whereas the grim-minded middle classes are earnest, self-interested, sectarian and far too *au sérieux*, the aristocrat sees morality as an aesthetic matter, a question of playfulness, irony, *bonhomie*, benevolence, pleasurable fulfilment and a delight in the cosmos as an enchanting work of art.

Both viewpoints, curiously enough, are comic; but whereas the middle classes are bright-eyed and buoyant because they trust to teleology and instrumental reason, believing that one good thing can lead to an even finer one, the upper classes are sanguine because they are anti-teleological, holding that virtue is its own satisfaction and that the cosmos exists not for some instrumental purpose but, like some splendid symphony, for their own rapt contemplation. This is an anti-tragic vision, whereas middle-class progressivism accepts the reality of time, which is the medium of tragic breakdown, and the irrevocability of action, which can have tragic consequences. Besides, the world for the middle classes, who have to work for a living, is a recalcitrant sort of place, as it is not for the indolent who can afford their ludic ironies. Virtue for the middle class is not virtue unless you have sweated for it; for the upper class it is as spontaneous as one's taste in herbaceous borders.

For Shaftesbury as for Hutcheson, virtue springs not from some leaden imperative but from a natural affection for one's kind, affections which are also the chief source of our self-enjoyment.[29] Henry Fielding, despite regarding social life as mostly predatory, cultivates a similarly good-natured outlook, playing the ideal off against the empirical in order to satirize them both. Fielding both supports the innocent and sends them up. Indeed, satire is a well-trodden escape-route from tragedy, which is no doubt one reason for its popularity in a progressivist age. Satire gives vent to malice but in a way which belittles its target, a diminishing which by defusing your aggression prevents it from taking a tragic turn. Satire is thus both an outlet for a potentially tragic pugnacity and a protection against it. It is a convenient device if you want to savage an opponent without granting him too much status. For a hard-headed, virulently anti-metaphysical pragmatist like Swift, whose satiric diminishments in *Gulliver's Travels* take a literal turn, and who grew up in a society to which tragedy was hardly a stranger, the tragic mode would be far too inward, profound and portentous; it is an art of the surface which he desires. *A Modest Proposal* needs its satirical obliquity partly as a defence against its Anglo-Irish author's own rancorous aggression as a second-class colonialist; partly because the horror of the Irish situation, if not scrupulously externalized, would risk overloading the text; and partly because as a colonial, which is where the text's political sympathies partly lie, one learns fairly quickly the perils of candour. In Pope's *Dunciad*, by contrast, satire is moving towards the grand tragic vision.

Shaftesbury aestheticizes virtue, so that law and fulfilment, duty and pleasure, altruism and self-interest, freedom and responsibility pass fluently into each other to avert the possibility of tragic conflict. In Richardson, by contrast, virtue and happiness are ripped rudely apart. Both cases are surely correct. The sanguine Shaftesbury is right to reject the Kantian opposition of virtue and happiness, but he can do so partly because as a grandee he is too far removed from the rapacious world of a Clarissa, in which good conduct makes you vulnerable rather than triumphant. He is also right to think that virtue should be its own reward, that we should exercise mercy and compassion just for the sake of it rather than for any self-advantage. Yet he urges this case partly because as a nobleman he has no pressing need to busy himself with questions of social justice, whereas the petty-bourgeois Richardson understands that to expect Clarissa and her kind to be saintly for its own sake is to deny them justice. Clarissa *should* have won compensation for her woes, as Richardson's Pamela does, and it is the mark of a heartless society that she does not. It is all too easy for the patrician to poke supercilious fun at the middle class's obsession with utility. Fielding does the same, though as a magistrate he is closer to the social ground than Shaftesbury, and sends up the Earl's brand of deism or cosmic Toryism in the person of the odious Square in *Tom Jones*. He is enough of a gentleman himself to despise the utilitarians, while shrewd enough to see how it is social necessity which makes them what they are. Shaftesbury's ethic is right but politically premature. As long as there are Lovelaces around, virtue and happiness are unlikely to coincide, and sacrifice – foregoing happiness in the name of virtue – may prove tragically essential. Jane Austen thought much the same.

In Kant's *Critique of Judgement* the aesthetic proves anti-tragic in a rather different sense. It is what allows us to impute a purposiveness to the world, however hypothetically, and thus to indulge the utopian fantasy of a reality which is magically pliable to our touch, fitting our faculties as snugly as a glove. For a blessed moment, the thing in itself can also be a thing for us, turning its face benignly towards us, and reflecting back to us the structure of our subjectivity in an imaginary mirror-relation, without ceasing to be an object in its own right. The pleasure principle and the reality principle may thus unite. The blissful contemplation known as the aesthetic is the antidote to desire, that *perpetuum mobile* by which modernity is hag-ridden from Hobbes to Freud; for desire is heedless of the sensuously specific, seeking out the hollow at its heart and moving straight through it to pass indifferently onward. The scandal is that desire is now transcendence – that transcendence has indeed come down to earth, but this time as disincarnation rather than incarnation.

One of the great documents of this dissatisfaction is Baudelaire's *Les Fleurs du mal*, in which passion is intensified by its very unfulfilment. The aesthetic, by contrast, is the cherished moment when sensuous matter becomes the very language of spirit, and so the utopian resolution of all the notorious contradictions by which modernity is afflicted: form and content, universal and particular, freedom and necessity, state and civil society, concept and intuition, fact and value, nature and spirit, law and love. Most of which the Georg Lukács of *History and Class Consciousness*, in a gesture as breathtaking as it is reductive, traces to the commodity form. But it is just as breathtakingly reductive for the aesthetic to offer to resolve these antinomies. How remarkably convenient to have to hand this all-encompassing solution to modernity's ills, and how dispiriting that it is the aesthetic, of all marginal, coterie pursuits, which advances it!

If the work of art can perform this task, it is because its form or law is no arid abstraction, but simply the articulation of its sensuous particulars. The law is thus inscribed on the inside of the artefact, as indeed it is with the bourgeois subject. What can be called aesthetic in the former case can be called hegemonic in the latter. And this is a fruitful unity for an age torn between rationalism and empiricism, abstract law and the sensuous particular. In his *Discourse on Method*, René Descartes performs a cerebral equivalent of tragic *kenosis* or self-emptying, ridding himself experimentally of all knowledge derived from empirical – and thus fallible – sources such as custom, perception and convention. But within a few pages, this sacrificial self-abandonment has resulted in an ingenious reconstruction of classical theology from God and the soul downwards, now resting on solid *a priori* principles. The *tabula*, so to speak, was not *rasa* for very long; indeed it was never really *rasa* at all, since what Descartes's radical reduction uncovers is a mind already thinking and possessed of an idea of the deity. Everything is exactly as it was only more so, and something, *pace* Lear, has come of (almost) nothing.

Yet the sensory world is not entirely restored, since to know reality we must trust to our understanding rather than our senses. To possess the world conceptually thus means to lose it sensuously, grasping little more than an odourless, colourless spectre of the real thing. It is the mind, rather than the eye, that sees, as Descartes maintains in the second of his *Meditations*. The concept is the death of the thing. Yet empiricism simply inverts the dilemma, since the more vividly intimate one's experience, the less one can comprehend it. Things are at once intense and adrift, rather as in Virginia Woolf's fictional world. Experience is the fuzzy, hybrid domain which mediates between self and world and partakes ambiguously of both. As a ground, nothing could seem less controvertible, and nothing could be more slippery. If sensory experience is the touchstone of reality, then structure, design, causality, temporal identity and the like, all those schemas which might lend shape to the self, are no more than hypothetical inferences from the stuff of our sensations, like plot, time, character and narrative in Laurence Sterne's *Tristram Shandy*.

At the same time, the human subject itself is shattered to fragments, since nothing in our experience would intimate the existence of an abiding self. When we finally come exhilaratingly eyeball-to-eyeball with the world, then, we find both it and ourselves empty of substance. We are, to be sure, freed from tragic fate – but only because, for Hume at least, we must suspect causality of any sort. The price we pay for our liberty is contingency, which is never very far from absurdity. The self is philosophically dismantled at exactly the moment it is politically affirmed, reduced by empiricism to a random flux of sensation, by sentimentalism to an emotional intuition, to a set of mechanical reflexes by materialism, an impalpable spiritual substance by Descartes and an impenetrable enigma by Kant.

This failure to grasp the self, however, is nearer to the truth than it knows. Indeed, later modernity will argue that this void *is* the subject, this permanently lacking *être-pour-soi* which is shuttled from one signifier to another but can articulate itself fully in none of them. This, to be sure, is a creative kind of void or *néant*, one which keeps us perpetually on the move; but by this late point it is also hard to deny that subjectivity is now something of a tragic phenomenon in itself. From its early revolutionary vigour to its later listless disenchantment, the subject itself has clung faithfully to the trajectory of classical tragedy. Like the tragic hero, too, the bourgeoisie for the most part works its own destruction. Its labour mars what it does, and its very force entangles itself with strength, as Antony comments of another kind of self-undoing in *Antony and Cleopatra*. At the same time, again like the tragic hero, it is not entirely to blame for its fate: there are powerful political forces arrayed against it. And although it has fallen on hard times, it had at its zenith a visionary idealism and nobility of spirit to which its enemies pay homage, and which make its decline all the more bitter.

If uniting the universal and the particular is a problem for epistemology, so is it for ethics. The Marquis de Sade thought it a contradiction of liberal morality that all individuals should be treated as one, since this seemed to negate the very notion of the individual.[30] To be a moral individual, one must conform to universal laws which ignore one's individuality. For Sade, the question of how I am to act is simply side-stepped, since Kant and his ilk can only reply: just like everyone else. It is a contradiction endemic to liberalism – for to value the individual is to value every individual, a universalism which would then seem to threaten individuality. The individual, being that which eludes the universal, cannot be the object of a science. The most vital constituent of the world is beyond the scope of cognition. The epistemology of the Enlightenment excludes what it politically most prizes. This is why, in an era largely indifferent to artistic value, a special pseudo-scientific discourse – call it aesthetics or poetics – needs to be developed to deal with the unique particular. Adorno will later dub this discourse 'dialectical thought'. Yet even this threatens to give tongue to the particular only to negate it. The philosophy of Jacques Derrida is in one sense a belated version of this tragic Romanticism, but it is also a remedy for it. For nothing in deconstructive eyes is more common than difference, which in Derrida's hands accrues all the properties – subjectlessness, repetition, derivativeness, hybridity, exchangeability, 'bad' infinity and so on – which are the ruin of Romantic uniqueness; while at the same time the very idea of difference, in its originary, unthinkable, ubiquitous, *a priori*, quasi-transcendental nature, retains more than a trace of such Romantic absolutes. Difference splits the particular, and so is anti-aesthetic; but it does so in a way which unravels totality, a move which particularism applauds.

Nietzsche thought that tragedy needed myth, and that modernity had banished them both. But though this is true in one sense, it is false in another. It is true that a rationalized, administered world cannot easily accumulate the symbolic resources it needs to legitimize itself. Its own profane practices constantly deplete them. This, one assumes, is part of what Marx has in mind when he inquires sardonically whether Achilles is possible with powder and lead, the *Iliad* with the printing press, or song and saga with the printer's bar.[31] Yet religious mythology survives modernity, in however diminished a shape; and Horkheimer and Adorno claim in *Dialectic of Enlightenment* that Enlightenment in any case becomes its own mythology. For them, the fate which brought low the heroes of antiquity reappears in the modern world as logic. To which one might add that the gods stage a come-back in the form of Reason, providence in the shape of scientific determinism, and nemesis in the guise of heredity. Infinity lingers on as sublimity, and the traumatic horror at the heart of tragedy, still a metaphysical notion in the case of Schopenhauer's Will, will be translated by Jacques Lacan as the Real, which has all the force of the metaphysical but none of its status.

For Horkheimer and Adorno, the ego strives to shake itself free of Nature by dominating it on the outside and repressing it on the inside; but this divorce of Nature from reason simply allows it to run wild. The resurgence of mythology is then one example of 'the perpetuation of the blind coercion of nature within the self'.[32] It is enlightened reason itself which heralds the return of the dark gods, the progressive which ushers in the pagan. As Slavoj Žižek comments: 'the very chaotic violence of modern industrial life, dissolving traditional "civilized" structures, is directly experienced as the return of the primordial mythopoeic barbaric violence "repressed" by the armour of civilized customs'.[33] Meanwhile, the self is forced to renounce its own creaturely nature, locked in a grinding contradiction between Nature and Reason which for Horkheimer and Adorno is the secret of modern suffering. *Logos*, then, is not entirely the other of *mythos*. It cannot survive without its own symbolic fables and enabling fictions, or without inciting the tumultuous return of the so-called primitive. An absolute distinction between the two is itself mythical.

The dream of Schlegel, Schelling, Hölderlin, Nietzsche and Wagner is that myth will be reborn on an epic scale at the heart of the modern epoch. Only in this way will an atomized social order be furnished with the collective symbolic resources of which it is in need. Dionysus must return, countering a barren individualism with an ecstatic de-differentiation of the self, dissolving the autonomous subject back into its blissful pre-conscious union with Nature. Modernity is faced with something of a Hobson's choice here. Only by distancing ourselves from Nature can we confront it, fend-off its devastating threats to our existence, and

225

so secure the conditions of happiness; yet this severing of ourselves from Nature is also a painful affair, a self-inflicted wound in the psyche which will never heal. There is a seductive *promesse de bonheur* in the vision of sacrificing the autonomous ego for the pleasures of the undifferentiated. 'Tragedy', writes Yeats, 'must always be a drowning and breaking of the dykes that separate man from man, and . . . it is upon these dykes that comedy keeps house.'[34] Yet this archaic regression involves an abolition of the self, which will thus no longer be on hand to enjoy its pleasures. It is a spurious form of liberation, just as the autonomous ego is a Pyrrhic sort of victory. There is also false liberation in the way the Dionysian unites within itself knowledge, power and art, confounding the carefully distinguished spheres of modernity. This, too, offers an alluring image of happiness; but it also cuts the ground from under critique, which depends on a distinction between knowledge and power.

As truth in the modern era is increasingly pressed into the service of power, the world of myth, for which power and knowledge are at one, returns in the guise of instrumental reason. But myth can also be acclaimed as the home of all those free-wheeling energies and libidinal intensities that an instrumental rationality discards as so much waste-matter, from *Eros* and madness to art and the body. Myth and modernity are thus both adversaries and mirror-images. The latest wave of this Dionysian current is poststructuralism, which suspects that the idea of tragedy is bound up with a metaphysical humanism. So did Nietzsche, who preserved the idea of tragedy but gave it a post-humanist inflection. For him, it is possible to live joyfully, but to do so means sacrificing that last redoubt of the humanist subject, subjectivity itself. The modern subject stands in its own way, blocking its own light, and must be immolated in order to come into its own.

Jürgen Habermas writes of this paradox as 'the heightening of the subjective to the point of utter self-oblivion'.[35] It is, perhaps, the final irony of the bourgeois order: what impedes the evolution of humanity is Man. Or, to put it in less gnomic terms: the humanist subject, in the sense of the stable, self-identical, metaphysically grounded creature of bourgeois *ideology*, is now the obstacle to the ecstatic, inexhaustible energy of bourgeois *society*. If the two realms are at loggerheads, then Nietzsche's hair-raisingly radical solution is simply to abolish the former. Metaphysical foundations are a lie, no longer necessary, and in any case increasingly implausible; God is dead – indeed, it is we, actual bourgeois humanity, who have despatched him with our remorseless secularization – but we behave nostalgically as though he were still alive. If only we had the daring to relinquish our neurotic grip on this excess ontological baggage, we would truly be free.

But Nietzsche, who appreciates the blood and toil which went into the production of this magnificent, self-torturing humanist subject, does not underestimate the price of transcending it. 'Profoundest gratitude for that which morality has achieved hitherto', he writes in *The Will to Power*, 'but now it is only a burden which may become a fatality!'[36] Moral man, he comments in *The Wanderer and his Shadow*, 'has become milder, more spiritual, more joyful and more circumspect than any animal. But now he still suffers from having borne his chains too long'.[37] Nietzsche admires the humanist subject as a marvellously self-disciplining work of art, and as a sort of teleologist appreciates just how vital for the future its reign has been; but its historical hour has now struck. History demands not only a cruel dismembering of this moral subject, a case which Hegel or Schelling could well endorse, but a dismembering of the whole category of subjecthood itself, a liquidation of Man. And though this overcoming of the lethal principle of identity yields its own savage enjoyment, the obscene pleasure of the death drive, the joy remains tragic even so. The *jouissance* of self-dissolution is well worth the agony of it, but the agony is quite as real. For our latter-day post-humanists, by contrast, the sacrifice of this subject is no longer tragic, since what is being relinquished is no longer of especial value. The thought of its obsequies fills Michel Foucault with deep satisfaction, not dismay. Poststructuralism and postmodernism inherit this tragic strain of thought, but in a post-tragic spirit. Dionysus returns not as tragic sacrifice but as the infinite proliferation of play, power, pleasure, difference and desire as an end in itself. Nietzsche's aestheticizing of reality is re-echoed, but the violence and brutality needed to achieve it are thrust aside. Instead, tragic joy bifurcates into political pessimism on the one hand, and aesthetic or theoretical *jouissance* on the other.

If the subject of modernity stands in its own light, it scarcely needs remarking that it stands in that of others too. An individualist society is not supposed to be tragic, as no credo could be more buoyant; yet tragic is exactly what it is, since one individual's project is bound to obstruct another's. A society of free individuals sounds a fine ideal, but also has an ominously oxymoronic ring. How can one sustain a social order which consists of perpetual disorder? 'Elena', writes Turgenev in *On the Eve*, 'did not know that every man's happiness is founded on the unhappiness of another, that the comfort and advantage which he enjoy demands, as surely as a statue demands a pedestal, the discomfort and disadvantage of other people' (ch. 33).

This is the Hobbesian jungle of Jean-Paul Sartre's *Being and Nothingness*, in which, as soon as another human subject appears on the horizon, I feel my own freedom being sucked inexorably into its orbit, as my world dissolves, leaks away from me and finds itself reconstituted by and around the other. I am now conscious of myself as existing for someone else, an exteriority which I can never master and which reduces me to a mere helpless *être-en-soi* or cryptic object for the other's gaze. Kant's duality of freedom and objectivity has burgeoned into a full-blown tragic philosophy. Thomas Hardy's novels are marked by this phenomenological tension between one's vivid presence to oneself as an active, desiring subject, and a humiliated awareness of one's presence to others as a body to be sexually exploited, a spectral presence in their midst, or an anonymous member of the rural labouring classes. For the early Sartre, we experience the subjectivity of the other only in the destruction of our own. In this Cartesian world, one cannot be simultaneously subject and object for another, and nothing in the other's objectivity refers to his or her subjecthood. If Sartre had gone to school on this issue with his colleague Maurice Merleau-Ponty, he might have recognized that the human body is itself a signifier – that the whole notion of having to 'infer' or 'deduce' a subjective life lurking within it is as untenable as the idea that we 'infer' meanings from words. He might also have considered the implications of speaking, rather than gazing, as a medium of human encounter.

The self-fashioning of one, then, is imperilled by the self-inventions of others. For the Sartre of *Being and Nothingness*, my own life is reduced to mere background to yours, a stain on the transparency of your being-in-the-world. It is Hegel's deathly struggle of master and slave once more – though at least that fable involved a classically comic outcome, as the slave comes to have the ontological upper hand over the master. For Sartre's play *In Camera*, hell is other people, or at least a Parisian love triangle. Others are the means to your own identity, but also an impediment to it. To maintain one commitment is to betray another; every mutuality is refracted through the objectifying gaze of a third; and mutual torture is all that is left to remind you that you are still alive. For this current of late modernity, from August Strindberg onwards, relationship is now tragic in itself. To exercise your freedom is to damage someone else; so that the sadistic lesbian Inez of Sartre's drama, who can't survive without making others suffer, is simply this common condition lived out as a choice. Nor is there a way out of this vicious circle by abstaining from action, refusing to meddle with the autonomy of others. Henry James, E. M. Forster and their liberal confrères do not need telling that inactivity is always an intervention, that abstention can wreak quite as much havoc as agency.

The price of freedom, then, is an incompatibility of persons or goods; and to this extent tragedy would seem built into a pluralist or individualist culture. Indeed, into some non-pluralist cultures too, since Aristotle in the *Ethics* also sees goods as incommensurable. You can avoid collisions of competing goods only by suppressing the specificity of value, proposing some common yardstick or exchange value by which different kinds of excellence can be compared. But it is hard to see how you can weigh courage against patience, any more than you can balance duck soup against double glazing. Max Weber maintains that there are some fundamental, intractable conflicts of value which must simply be soberly confronted: 'the ultimately possible attitudes to life are irreconcilable, and hence their struggle can never be brought to a final conclusion'.[38] Rosalind Hursthouse argues likewise that whereas utilitarianism is tooled up to resolve moral dilemmas, virtue ethics accepts that there are situations in which you may act well but can still only emerge with dirty hands. Or you might resolve a dilemma, but still come out of it with your life indelibly the poorer.[39]

Perhaps the most renowned exponent of this quasi-tragic moral theory is Isaiah Berlin, who maintains that 'the world that we encounter in ordinary experience is one in which we are faced by choices equally absolute, the realization of some of which must inevitably mean the sacrifice of others'.[40] There is no single formula to harmonize the diverse ends of humanity, and tragedy in Berlin's view can thus never be entirely eliminated. One might complain with some justice that he himself was a mite predictable in his choices between absolutes, plumping with remarkable regularity for liberty rather than justice or equality. It may also be that these tragic deadlocks would loom less large in a political order in which such values were structurally more compatible. Berlin speaks at times of choosing between moral goods rather as one might vacillate between equally enticing brands of perfume; but socially speaking the cards are of course already stacked. Nor does he properly consider the question of who gets to define and debate these options in the first place. But he is right to see that what characterizes the moral order of modernity is our failure to agree even on the most fundamental questions. This is so flagrant a fact that we have forgotten to be surprised by it. We might well have expected to agree on essentials but diverge on particulars, but this is not so. There is absolutely no common view on why torturing people is wrong. And while such discord need not be tragic in itself, it is bound to breed conflicts which can slip rapidly in that direction.

Martha Nussbaum plays down the tragic potential of this pluralism, arguing that it is all part of the opulence and diversity of the good life.[41] So it is; but there are times when we might wish our lives poorer but happier. Diversity is not an absolute good, whatever the non-absolutists may think. Fewer goods is sometimes preferable to serious conflict between those one has, a case which the liberal is often loath to acknowledge. Nussbaum speaks of the desire to purchase 'neatness' by abolishing this heterogeneity, but it might also mean not being forced into invidious choices between competing goods. It is not a hankering for tidiness which leads one to such a view. Nussbaum remarks of Sophocles's *Antigone* that 'we are asked to see that a conflict-free life would be lacking in value and beauty next to a life in which it is possible for conflict to arise'.[42] This is a remarkably modern-day liberal reading of the work, as though one were to claim that the lesson of the *Iliad* is that the ancient world needed a United Nations Organization. Conflict-free lives may lack value and beauty, but they are at least lives, as opposed to those products of conflict known as corpses. Nussbaum shrewdly sees that any good worth pursuing is so partly because it is bounded off from other things and thus potentially at odds with them, but she seems rather sanguine about the possible outcome of such contentions.

One such tragic dilemma is staged by Thomas Otway's drama *Venice Preserv'd*, in which Jaffeir must either betray his friends or allow Venice to become a bloodbath. Chimena in Corneille's *Le Cid* is another such instance, torn between her love for Don Rodrigo and her outrage at the fact that he has slain her father. The eponymous hero of Corneille's *Cinna* is a traitor if he assassinates Caesar, but will lose the love of Emilia if he does not. The great tragedian of this condition, however, is Henrik Ibsen. Ibsen feels the imperative to fulfil oneself as an absolute law, so that the self-sacrificial Irena of *When We Dead Awaken* has committed 'self-murder – a mortal sin against myself'. As with D. H. Lawrence, you hold yourself in sacred trust, and Nora of *A Doll's House* must act on this merciless obligation to be oneself even if it means walking out on her children. Yet what if the result of reaching for one's own fulfilment is the crippling, betrayal and scapegoating of others, as so often in Ibsen? And what if the guilt which this engenders then weighs in on your self-realization to corrode it from the inside?

It is in this sense that Ibsen, for all his liberal agnosticism, is a firm believer in original sin. In the complex reciprocities of social life, there can be no creative action which is not infected at its roots by the damage it causes to others. August Strindberg, in pieces like *The Father* and *Easter*, is even more deeply gripped by this sense of the criminal debts which we all inherit, the obscure guilt which we incur by our destiny being woven into that of others. As in Gothic fiction, one's legacy is always a polluted one, both gift and poison. Raymond Williams speaks of the idea of inheritance in this kind of tragedy as 'tainted and terrifying'.[43] It is a condition which Ibsen usually dramatizes as a deadlock between past and present, as the contaminated origins of your present achievement, as in *Pillars of*

230

the Community, return to plague you, or as the struggle to clear away present falsehood in the name of the future strangles that future at birth. It is impossible to live without accruing debts, but to pay them or pass them over are often just as deadly. The ending of *Rosmersholm* and *The Master Builder*, in which affirmation and expiation, a capitulation to the past and a transcendence of it, are as finely balanced as at the close of Eliot's *The Mill on the Floss*, is then testimony to this tragic deadlock. Ibsen's characters, like John Gabriel Borkman or Irena and Rubek of *When We Dead Awaken*, often end up marooned in some limbo between life and death, present and past, submission and rebellion, jubilant affirmation and the guilt which debilitates it.

Truth and happiness in Ibsen are not easily compatible. Indeed, it could be that zealous, high-minded truth-tellers like Brand, Dr Stockmann in *An Enemy of the People* or Gregers Werle in *The Wild Duck* are simply mirror-images of the corrupt society they denounce, spiritual versions of the individualism which engendered this unsavoury state of affairs in the first place. In these unbending idealists, bourgeois society protests at the practical consequences of its own high-flown fantasies of freedom. The enemy of middle-class individualism turns out to be the conformist middle class. From being a dynamic force in social life, individualism has become a disdainful critique of it from an aloof distance. In Ibsen's Norway as in Stendhal's France, the middle-class order is still young enough to recall its noble aspirations, but old enough to have seen them turn sour. In any case, there is a fine line between necessary truth-telling and a stiff-necked priggishness blind to the virtues of expediency. Antigone may be right, but Creon has a point. Rosmer's emancipatory ideal is both lofty and dreary, and figures like Hedda Gabler or Hilde Wangel suggest that idealism can be quite as self-interested as the pragmatism it castigates. The truth may be just as deadly as deception.

Hedda Gabler admires Lövborg's courage to live his life in his own way, a callous idealizing of a career which ends in suicide. We are on the verge here of the modern cult of authenticity – the claim that what matters is less the content of one's life than its coherence and consistency. If an impulse springs straight from one's inner depths, then it is blasphemous to deny it, however pernicious the results of acting it out. D. H. Lawrence thought that this even applied to murder, and that most murderees were asking for it in any case. How we are to identify such authentic impulses, without public criteria which are themselves an affront to individual uniqueness, is another question. Our duty is no longer to the moral law but to our own spontaneous selfhood, which, rather like Dickens's Mr Pecksniff warming his hands at the fire, we must care for as tenderly as if it was someone else's. This, needless to say, is a theme much older than the twentieth century, indeed a staple of Romanticism; but in the era of late modernity it begins to emerge as a rather exotic sort of alternative ethics, not least in the guise of existentialism.

What matters for existentialism, as for the doting owner of some sickly cur, is not so much that what I have is sound as that it is mine. Like liberalism, it is thus a rather adolescent kind of ethics. For an objectivist morality, by contrast, it doesn't really matter who does it as long as it gets done. For the existentialist, my values are no more securely founded than yours, but at least I get to create them. That it is this proprietorship that matters, not the nature of the values themselves, follows logically from the situation. What sets me free to shape my own values is the fact that there are no given ones any longer; but since this is because the world is indifferent to value as such, it is bound to be just as unimpressed by those I fashion for myself. Like the existentialist Troilus of Shakespeare's *Troilus and Cressida*, we make things valuable by bestowing value on them, rather as someone might try to give a familiar word an outlandish meaning by staring hard at it while murmuring the new meaning over and over to themselves. Self-determination is thus finally drained of force: since there are no given ends or constraints, it is absolute, but for just the same reason it is absurd.

The aestheticist notion that what matters about a life is its coherent shape is close to the belief that value lies simply in not backing down, in a tenacious fidelity to your desire whatever its nature or outcome. Both cases are equally formalistic. As Goethe puts it in *Wilhelm Meister's Apprenticeship*: 'Anyone whom we can observe striving with all his powers to attain some goal, can be assured of our sympathy, whether we approve of the goal or not' (Book 2, ch. 1). The position is generous to the point of fatuity. Jean Genet holds a similar view, writing in his journal that 'acts must be carried through to their completion. Whatever their point of departure, the end will be beautiful. It is because an action has not been completed that it is vile.'[44] It is the kind of sublime absurdity to which only an intellectual could rise. We do not admire someone simply for striving with every sinew to blow up a high school, or reap aesthetic pleasure from a magnificently well-achieved act of child abuse. There is nothing admirable about commitment as such. The case is a curious travesty of Aristotle: we fear the outcome of the project, but feel for the unswerving determination which drives it.

Tragic characters on this view are those who remain loyal to an unconditional demand laid upon them, perhaps by themselves, in contrast with those less stalwart figures who climb down, back off or walk away. An example of the former is the fearfully authentic hero of John Arden's

Sergeant Musgrave's Dance, driven to an inhuman extreme in the name of humanity. An example of the latter is Lizzie of Sartre's *The Respectable Prostitute*, who backs off from helping an unjustly accused African-American in the southern states. Michael Kohlhaas, in Kleist's story of that name, lays waste whole towns because a couple of his horses have been ill-treated. The search for justice or exact equivalences can ironically breed a monstrous excess. Prometheus is another such intractable character, a role-model in his sullen constancy and indomitable will for the parodically heroic Satan of *Paradise Lost*. But the archetype of this sort of tragic hero is the bloody-minded Oedipus, with his obduracy and persistence, his epistemophiliac passion to lay bare his own origins. Indeed, all of Sophocles's heroes, as Bernard Knox points out in *The Heroic Temper*, are distinguished by a ferocious obstinacy of being, by their capacity to stay in some fundamental way unbroken even in the most terrible of circumstances. As Knox comments: 'there is something monstrous, more or other than human, in such inhuman stubbornness',[45] which is evident alike in Oedipus, Ajax, Antigone, Philoctetes, Electra and Heracles. These are figures who typically court disaster by their intransigence, driven by it to the margins of social life, cross-grained, incorruptible and solitarily self-sufficient.

Tragedy, so Jacques Lacan remarks in one of his seminars, is in the forefront of the experience of the psychoanalyst. The ethical injunction of psychoanalysis, so Lacan declares, is 'Do not give up on your desire!'[46] It is not empirical desires that Lacan has in mind; the slogan is not to be mistaken for a French translation of the American dream. For one thing, desire for psychoanalytic thought is a profoundly impersonal process which is deaf to meaning, which has its own sweet way with us, and which secretly cares for nothing but itself. Desire is nothing personal: it is an affliction which was lying in wait for us at the outset, a perversion into which we were plunged almost from birth. What makes us human subjects is this foreign body lodged inside us, which invades our flesh like a lethal virus and yet which, as Aquinas declares of God, is closer to us than we are to ourselves. Since desire for psychoanalytic thought is always bound up with death, a death which the lack at the heart of desire prefigures, not to give up on one's desire means to maintain, Heidegger-like, a constant relation to death, confronting the lack of being that one is. It means not to stuff that lack with imaginary objects but to grasp that it is what defines you, that death is what makes one's life real. This, then, which Lacan bluntly terms the reality of the human condition, is a tragic imperative, exhorting the subject to an affirmation which can arise only from embracing its own finitude. In this particular world, there are only ever Pyrrhic victories.

This is why for Lacan the heroine of psychoanalysis is Antigone, the one who refuses to give way, who in the words of the Duke of *Measure for Measure* is absolute for death, and who thus comes to symbolize the sublimity of desire. Antigone feels no guilt about her supposed transgression, which can only be seen by the ruling powers and local mores as madness or evil. She refuses to give way on what she regards as the laws of heaven, and allows this refusal to carry her to her death. The martyr is the one who raises some contingent object to the sublime status of the Thing, the enigmatic law or unconditional injunction of the ethical, and who values this more than life itself. As Slavoj Žižek remarks: 'Tragic dignity shows us how an ordinary fragile individual can summon the incredible strength and pay the highest price for his fidelity to the Thing . . . in the tragic predicament, the hero forfeits his earthly life for the Thing, so that his very defeat is his triumph, conferring sublime dignity on him'.[47]

It is not, then, as Hegel imagines, that law and desire in *Antigone* are at loggerheads, but that the sublimity of the moral law *is* Antigone's desire. Her loving fidelity to the Real rips through the symbolic order and moves unswervingly into death, which, as Creon sneers, is her 'god'. One might claim something of the same about the Abraham of Kierkegaard's *Fear and Trembling*, who remains doggedly faithful to his impossible desire that his son Isaac should live, a desire which does indeed turn out to be the law of heaven. Or there is the case of Jesus, a condemned political criminal who like Antigone refuses to identify the Lacanian Thing, the Real of the ethical, with the political chicanery around him ('My kingdom is not of this world'), and who is left clinging in darkness on the cross to a law of love which seems to have deserted him.

One can trace this motif of tragic intransigence all the way from *King Oedipus* to *Death of a Salesman*. One thinks, for example, of George Chapman's titanic, swashbuckling, supremely self-confident Byron or Busy D'Ambois, men passionately dedicated to their own self-realization and prepared to be baulked by nothing to attain it. Dauntless, wilful and fired by a boundless Marlovian ambition, these heroes stamp their mark on a world which in Senecan fashion they simultaneously despise. A. C. Bradley detects a certain monomania in Shakespeare's protagonists, 'a fatal tendency to identify the whole being with one interest, object, passion, or habit of mind'.[48] Few of Racine's characters understand the meaning of the word moderation. Corneille's Polyeucte is a martyr resolute for death who refuses to back down from this glory even for his beloved Pauline. What to him is unconditional commitment is to others insane pigheadedness. The incestuous Giovanni and Anabella of Ford's *'Tis Pity She's A Whore* create their own mutually validating world in defiance of moral convention, and advance proudly together into the absolutism of death. Ford's Perkin Warbeck, who speaks of being 'kings o'er death', has a similar unbending commitment to his own (illicit) cause as pretender to the throne of Henry VII, and meets his end with lip-curling contempt. The exasperated Dalila calls Samson 'implacable, more deaf / To prayers than wind and sea' in Milton's *Samson Agonistes*. There is more than a touch of Philoctetes about him.

These, then, are men and women to whom Conchubar's warning to Cuchulain in Yeats's *On Baile's Strand* applies: 'You mock at every reasonable hope, / And would have nothing, or impossible things'. They are versions of the Camusian rebel, who feels a spontaneous loyalty to values which he is prepared to defend whatever the risks. The non-compromiser is half in love with death, but can exploit this guilty desire for the ends of life. It is not, to be sure, much of a way to live; but the Freudian double-bind is that those who cannot tread this perilous path, but who compromise their desire, fall sick of neurosis, which is not much of a way to live either. Or you can have the worst of both worlds: the doctrine of tragic tenacity needs to recognize that you may compromise and still come to grief. Even so, it seems to some that in a modern society bereft of heroic goals, the only nobility left lies in the intensity of one's commitment, not in its content.

It is this, as we have seen, which the lawyer Alfieri in Arthur Miller's *A View from the Bridge* guardedly admires about the deluded Eddie Carbone:

> Most of the time now we settle for half and I like it better. But the truth is holy, and even as I know how wrong he was, and his death useless, I tremble, for I confess that something perversely pure calls to me from his memory – not purely good, but himself purely, for he allowed himself to be wholly known and for that I think I will love him more than all my sensible clients. And yet, it is better to settle for half – it must be. And so I mourn him – I admit it – with a certain . . . alarm. (Act 2)

It is a classic combination of pity and fear, which nonetheless sounds the authentic modernist note: being purely oneself is more daring and commendable than being merely good or merely right. There is an aesthetic beauty about existential integrity which trumps both knowledge and virtue. Tragedy permits us the vicarious satisfaction of indulging our devotion to death, but at the same time lays bare the hazards of this allegiance and recalls us to civic prudence. Even if we settle for half, then, we can still have it both ways in the theatre. There are times, as Miller's Willy Loman is wisely instructed, when a man simply has to walk away; but Loman can do this no more than he can fly, which is both his victory and his undoing. Modernism is in love with the extreme and excessive, which in their Dionysian style rip the veils of deception from late bourgeois life. But these are also forces which tear ordinary people apart while despising them in the process, and Alfieri is right to put in a word for the Apollonian.

By the time of Anton Chekhov, the more hopeful visions of modernity have declined into wistful, elegiac mood. This is ironic, since the wry bemusement of Chekhovian drama is among other things a reaction to the still-dawning modernization of Russia on the part of those whom this process is ousting. Even so, this bleak, befuddled response to a modernity still in the making finds its echo in the rather later modernity of Europe, as the landowners, rentiers, military officers and prosperous merchants of old Russia compose between them a structure of feeling – jaded, febrilely self-dramatizing, politically palsied – which the victims of late modernity have no difficulty in recognizing. This clutch of washed-up cracker-barrel philosophers, comically but also alarmingly idiosyncratic, are at once marooned with their private fantasies and pitched claustrophobically together, so that what we see in Raymond Williams's phrase is not deadlock but stalemate,[49] an interlocking of fantasies which is the nearest one can now come to social interaction. It is a drama of both intense isolation and shared sensibility.

Chekhov's dramas have the fascination of soap operas, in which nothing much happens but in which we take an inordinate interest in the daily trivia of amiable, off-beat characters. At times it is almost like a social realist version of Beckett, Beckett with the thickness of social texture restored, as characters conduct their extravagantly aimless lives in an atmosphere of tedium which is as infectious as typhoid. It is a world of spiked hopes and baulked ambitions just this side of surrealism, a perpetually subjunctive mood laced with saving illusions, desperate self-aggrandizements, random cries of pain. Some fatal lassitude has fastened upon the will but failed to extinguish desire. In this milieu of ennui and disenchantment, Ivanov can kill himself purely out of self-disgust, nauseated by the utter contingency of the world. If you can no longer hope for redemption, you can at least trust that there is some obscure teleology to your suffering, some benefit that the future will reap. In this sense, Chekhov's characters look upon themselves as transitional, displaced, ephemeral, in contrast to the self-absolutizing of some classical tragic figures. Tragedy thus modulates into tragic irony. All kinds of portentous diagnoses of the present are possible, but these speculations are part of the problem rather than the solution. And the form of the plays, with their symphonic orchestration of voices, overlapping digressions and lack of shapely plot or narrative direction, itself casts doubt on such dreams of purpose.

Thomas Hardy's Jude Fawley also views his own tragedy as transitional. It is not that working men like him will never break into higher education, just that he himself has tried to do so too early. Indeed, not long after the novel was published, Ruskin College, the trade-union establishment in Oxford, was founded. The failure which is absolute for Jude is historically relative, as he recognizes himself. This irony is staged in the novel's extraordinary final cameo, which like *Jude the Obscure* as a whole forms a kind of pivot between Victorianism and modernism. We have a stereotypical deathbed scene, with the dying, abandoned Jude whispering to himself passages from the Book of Job while into his window floats a medley of cheers from an Oxford boating ritual. But his room is also penetrated by the organ notes of a college concert, and, after he is dead, by the murmur of voices from an honorary degree ceremony across the road, which is also punctuated by some lusty cheering. What Chekhov smoothly orchestrates, blending disparate voices into complex unity, Hardy wrenches into tonal dissonance, playing Schoenberg to the Russian's langorous mood music.

The sounds which pierce the room where Jude is dying are random and diverse, fragments of disparate texts which could never be unified, snatches of carnival mingling with organ music and ceremonial rhetoric in an arbitrary *mélange* of sacred and profane, high and popular culture, the spontaneous and the scripted, which reflects Jude's own tragically fissured career. There are literally different languages in play here, since the discourse of the degree ceremony would be Latin. But there is no simplistic contrast of mass and elitist culture either, since the shouts of youthful exuberance from the river stem from the same context – Oxford University in celebratory mood – as the organ music, ringing of bells and solemn murmurings from the Sheldonian theatre. The carnivalesque is complicit with the elitist, as Jude is shut out by both festivity and solemnity, pleasure and knowledge.

Within this polyphony of idioms, Jude's melodramatic recitation from Job threatens to become just another piece of theatre, in line with the degree ceremony and the ritual competition of the college boats, with Jude playing the part of Job rather as some private citizen over the road is playing the august role of Vice-Chancellor. This deathbed cursing, as much a performative speech-act as the words which accompany the degree-bestowing across the street, risks becoming just as much a string of empty signifiers as a wave of cheers or a peal of bells, another contingent drift of noises on the air, which nobody but the novelist is in fact there to record. Jude's dying recitation, like much else in this realist novel so careless of orthodox realism, is a deliberately stagey gesture on Hardy's part, a textually self-conscious citing from sacred texts which Jude has ruined himself to gain access to. There is no attempt to naturalize this abrupt rhetorical outburst, which is no more realistically plausible than the story of Job itself. As Jude dies with a text on his lips, we are forcibly reminded by the sheer gratuitousness of this act, its calculatedly set-piece, overpitched quality, that we, too, are in a text. Even the interpolated 'Hurrahs!' in Jude's speech are a little too pat to be true.

The effect is reinforced by the contrast between the biblical language and the sparse, deliberately flattened prose in which the scene is couched. The scriptural language operates as a kind of alienation effect (Brecht exhorted his actors to 'quote' their parts), and the reader is forbidden to empathize with Jude's dying, not least by the fact that it is so arrestingly undwelt on. We are not allowed to attend his bedside; instead, the novel forces us out into the street to follow the meanderings and mild flirtations of Arabella, which means that like her we miss his actual death. The whole scene is at once calculatedly over-the-top and casually underplayed. We are held literally on the outside of Jude's dying, forced into reluctant complicity with the callousness of Arabella as we, like she, wander off in search of the source of the random sounds which enter Jude's room, thus leaving nobody, not even the narrator, to witness his death. Once he is dead, we are told in a few perfunctory jottings that his corpse was 'as straight as an arrow', but we are not allowed to look at his face. We have had no access to his feelings, just a set text. The tragedy, as with Aristotle, lies in the action, not in the sentiments. At one level, the scene is controlled by rather too emphatic a contrast between the sorrow of Jude's death and the joy surrounding it. But at another level nothing really comes together, one distraction dissolves into another, random sounds flare and fade, and the emotional centre of the scene quietly drops out and disappears while we are not looking. It is an aggressive parody of a Victorian deathbed scene. After producing this passage, Hardy ceased to write novels.

'We're all of us sentenced to solitary confinement inside our own selves, for life', remarks Val in Tennessee Williams's *Orpheus Descending*. It is one of the great clichés of late modernity, along with 'If only I could find the words', 'You've got to stop running from yourself', or 'Let us cease to dwell morbidly on the past and face the future with confidence'. The individualism of modernity, in which each of us is locked in his or her own sensory world, will find its surreal culmination in the avant-garde theatre of Beckett, Pirandello, Ionesco, Pinter and other exponents of miscommunication. Empiricism leads in the end to insanity, atomism to illusion. As the relativity of the senses is pressed to an extreme limit, it yields a world in which truth is just an interlocking of illusions, identity the ensemble of what others make of you, and sanity whatever consensus the majority has currently happened to hit on. As Shakespearian comedy had long ago suspected, a shared, consistent fantasy is in no way distinguishable from reality, and may well be just another name for it. Pirandello's *Henry IV* and *So It Is (If You Think So)* are classics of this epistemological relativism. But a world without shared meanings is a violent one, not just a Stoppardian sport: Henry ends the play, which is announced as a tragedy, by killing Belcredi, one of his 'courtiers'. For the Strindberg of *The Father*, the uncertain grounds of modern knowledge are figured in the metaphor of paternity, as the Captain's rabid epistemophilia only serves to convince him that one can never know for sure whether one's children are one's own, never lay bare the origins or foundations of reality.

What did the political left make of this condition? At its least inspired, the left reflected the crass progressivism of modernity on the one hand, and the mandarin gloom of modernism on the other. The revolutionary avant-gardes of the early twentieth century represented an audacious, imaginative riposte to capitalist modernity; yet they also gave a left-wing twist to its technological triumphalism, as some earlier forms of leftism had aped its evolutionary meliorism. Western Marxism, by contrast, for all its depth and originality, betrayed something of the gloom and *Angst* of modernism rather than the wide-eyed aspirations of modernity. There is a tragic quality to its reflections, as Perry Anderson has shown in *Considerations on Western Marxism*. A compound of high cultural melancholy, idealist displacement and historical pessimism, it had theoretical roots in such dubiously radical sources as Spinozist determinism, Kantian and Nietzschean thought, *Lebensphilosophie*, Weberian sociology, Italian idealism and Heideggerian existentialism. Adorno despaired both of the working class and the efficacy of instrumental reason, while Benjamin espoused a Messianic eschatology rather than a materialist theory of history. Lukács could increasingly find a solution to alienation only in the realist novel. Some members of the Frankfurt school tended to confuse capitalism with fascism, passed over the more positive aspects of modernity, and helped to reduce an emancipatory project to an academicist pursuit. In its patrician distaste for the popular, its wariness of economic analysis and gathering historical gloom, Western Marxism was at once a remarkably rich current of radicalism and a curiously conservative one.

As with the tragic protagonist, however, it was not entirely to blame. Like every other left-wing movement from the early twentieth century onwards, it was doomed to live under the shadow of Stalinism, which never ceased to blight it. Stalinism, not just in its Russian variety, was a reflection of one of the most abiding tragedies of the twentieth century: the fact that socialism proved least possible where it was most necessary. A vision of human emancipation which presupposed for its success all the precious fruits of modernity – material wealth, liberal traditions, a flourishing civic society, a skilled, educated populace – became instead the lodestar by which wretchedly impoverished nations bereft of such benefits sought to throw off their chains. Shunned by those well-heeled nations who might have smoothed their path to freedom, they marched their people into modernity at gun-point, with criminal consequences. One would not describe fascism as tragic in itself, whatever the destruction to which it gave birth. But Stalinism was tragedy of a classical kind, as the noble intentions of socialism were deflected into their opposites in that fatal inversion which Aristotle calls *peripeteia*.

Something of the mood of left modernism or Western Marxism has been bequeathed in our own day to poststructuralism, with its curious vein of libertarian pessimism. The spectre of an emancipatory project lingers on, but it would be the height of hubris to try to realize it. The most we can muster is a Marxism without a name, absolved from the crimes of its political forebears only at the cost of being politically and doctrinally vacuous, as free from such complicity as the blank page of the ideal *symboliste* poem. But while poststructuralism remains ensnared in high modernist melancholia, postmodernism seizes a chance to leap beyond the tragic by tapping into the diffuse, provisional, destabilizing forces of a post-metaphysical capitalism. Which is to say that if poststructuralism has not quite travelled beyond Adorno, postmodernism has yet to advance far beyond Nietzsche.

Chapter 9

Demons

If tragedy springs from the contradictions inherent in a situation – a large enough supposition, to be sure – then modernity is tragic in exactly this classical sense. It is the author of its own undoing, giving birth, as Marx sardonically put it, to its own gravedigger. The trope of capitalism is tragic irony, as the system needs for its own purposes to unleash forces which are able to take it over. To grasp this Janus-facedness of the modern epoch, however, requires the kind of dialectical approach which is these days in short supply. The vulgar postmodernism for which everything from 1500 onwards was an unmitigated disaster known as 'Enlighten-ment' leaves a little to be desired, forgetful as it is that some records of barbarism are also documents of civilization. But neither is it enough to claim that Enlightenment needs only to be democratized, feminized or dialogized to come into its own. Of contemporary theories, only Marxism insists that modernity has been a revolutionary advance in human welfare, and, with equal passion, that it has been one long nightmare of butchery and exploitation. No other thought seems capable of holding these two stories in tension, in the teeth of patrician nostalgia on the one hand, and crass progressivism or postmodern amnesia on the other. Yet it is the necessary relation between them which holds the key to modernity.

One of the bravest attempts to do so is Marshall Berman's classic work *All That Is Solid Melts Into Air*, for which 'to be modern is to find ourselves in an environment that promises adventure, power, joy, growth, trans-formation of ourselves and the world – and, at the same time, that threatens to destroy everything we have, everything we are'.[1] As Perry Anderson summarizes Berman's case:

> On the one hand, capitalism – in Marx's unforgettable phrase of the [*Com-munist*] *Manifesto*, which forms the leitmotif of Berman's book – tears down every ancestral confinement and feudal restriction, social immobility and

claustral tradition, in an immense clearing operation of cultural and customary debris across the globe. To that process corresponds a tremendous
emancipation of the possibility and sensibility of the individual self, now
increasingly released from the fixed social status and rigid role-hierarchy
of the pre-capitalist past, with its narrow morality and cramped imaginative range. On the other hand, as Marx emphasized, the very same onrush
of capitalist economic development also generates a brutally alienated and
atomized society, riven by callous economic exploitation and cold social
indifference, destructive of every cultural or political value whose potential it has itself brought into being. Likewise, on the psychological plane,
self-development in these conditions could only mean a profound disori-
entation and insecurity, frustration and despair, *concomitant with* – indeed
inseparable from – the sense of enlargement and exhilaration, the new
capacities and feelings, liberated at the same time.[2]

Modernity is both political democracy and global warfare, the possibility of feminism and the reality of women's degradation, the fact of
imperialism and the value of human commerce across frontiers. In a
move scandalous to the *ancien régimes*, it claims that freedom and respect
are rights from which no one should be excluded; it also forces its own
definitions of these values on humanity at large. Everything in such a
state, as Marx comments, seems pregnant with its opposite, so that irony,
oxymoron, chiasmus, ambivalence, aporia, seem the only suitable figures
for capturing its logic. Sources of wealth are turned into want, tech-
nologies which could emancipate human labour end up squeezing it dry,
and freedom twists by some uncanny logic into domination. In a stirring
piece of political theatre, modernity brings one absolutist state after
another to its knees, then installs the tyranny of capital in their place. It
is this bafflingly self-thwarting phenomenon which for some is the only
civilized future for the Nuer and Dinka, and for others is no more than
a bad dream of dominative reason from which, perhaps somewhere
around 1973, we began slowly to awaken in a redemptive reversal of
the Fall.

Capitalist modernity is indeed a Fall; but like all the most interesting
Falls it was one up rather than down, a freeing of human energy which
was also a binding of it. It is an object-lesson in the incestuous intimacy
of the death-dealing and the life-enhancing, and the myth which encodes
this duality most hauntingly for the modern period is the fable of Faust.[3]
The pact with Mephistopheles is the price we pay for progress. In *The
Communist Manifesto* Marx portrays the bourgeoisie as a sorcerer who con-
jures up forces beyond his control. Or as Byron expresses this diabolical
pact in his play *Cain*: 'Strange good, that must arise from out / Its deadly
opposite'. This is not so of the great bombastic tragic heroes of the Renais-

sance like Marlowe's Tamburlaine, whose conquests one is made to feel could last indefinitely, and whose cutting off is always a touch arbitrary. Their downfall is not ironic, a matter of destructive forces inherent in their aspiring. As Northrop Frye comments: 'the relation between [Tamburlaine's] hubris and his death is more casual than causal'.[4] The Faust story, by contrast, concerns the fact that the roots of our creativity are tainted – that civilization is rooted in the barbarism of exploitation, that culture needs to press the death instinct into its service, that remembrance demands oblivion, that beneath value and meaning lies the senseless, non-signifying materiality of Nature, the body and the unconscious drives.

Nature is the ground of our valuing but thereby transcends it, as Nietzsche's will to power is the transcendental source of all values but must therefore escape value-judgement itself. To be authentic, culture must immerse in the destructive element, acknowledge these things of darkness as its own, otherwise it will fall ill of the neurosis which springs from repression; but how is it to confess its roots in the non-rational without succumbing to a demonic irrationalism which might tear it apart? Karl Jaspers argues that 'when we are most highly successful we most truly fail',[5] thinking no doubt of the hubris which blinds us to the frailty from which any effective ethics or politics must take its cue. Yet how can we confess this failure without some morbid celebration of fiasco?

The question can be reposed in terms of aesthetics. How can spirit dip itself in the senses, as Schiller and the aesthetic tradition urge it to do, without falling prey to their mindless power; and how can spirit not hollow the senses out in its relentless pursuit of fulfilment? The dream of the aesthetic is to sensualize spirit with no loss of its transcendence; but this will prove a harder task than Schiller imagines in his *On the Aesthetic Education of Man*.[6] It leaves out the question of desire, which lies somewhere on the troubled frontier between body and spirit, and which is as blind to the sensuous particularity of its object as the most lofty abstraction. Reason and desire, so often contrasted as rivals, are in this sense partners in crime.

Transgression is what makes historical beings of us, which is why the Fall is a felicitous one.[7] Like the Lacanian Real, in this respect a psychoanalytic version of original sin, it is the flaw or blockage which makes things work. The myth of Prometheus teaches much the same wisdom. 'Sin is more fruitful than innocence', St Anselm declares, sailing close to the heterodox wind.[8] Without the dynamic which comes from trying to repair our condition and failing yet again, history would slide to a halt. Like the smaller Greek islands, Eden is alluring, but there is not enough to do. But a history of creative transgression is also the open possibility of overreaching and undoing ourselves. In being driven from Eden, we shift upwards from the relative security of biological life to the chronic precariousness of the labouring, linguistic creature. Milton's Satan tells Eve, falsely as it happens, that eating from the forbidden tree was how he learned to speak. Otherwise the notion of a *felix culpa* makes no sense, since if life in Eden is not that of pre-reflective animality, Rousseau's care-free but constricted state of nature, it is hard to see how expulsion from it can lead to higher things. According to the biblical myth, however, Adam and Eve are precisely such pre-reflective beings, still anterior to difference in their ignorance of good and evil. The doctrine of the Fall is thus a tragic one – not because its outcome may not prove to be benign, but because even if it does, it will have involved unimaginable waste and suffering.

It is possible to argue, then, that even if one's end is superior to one's origin, the cost of the journey is too high and it would have been preferable to stay put. If to achieve socialism means that every social order must be hauled through modernity's baptism of fire, as Mensheviks and others have taught, then this might well seem too high a price to pay. Or take the case of colonialism and imperialism. It is absurd to assume that no good whatsoever came of them. How could a phenomenon as complex, wide-reaching and persistent as colonialism have bred not a single positive effect? In Ireland, Britain's oldest colony, the metropolitan power actually dispossessed the Anglo-Irish landowning class at the end of the nineteenth century, handing the land instead to the rural tenantry. It also handed the Irish some of the linguistic, political and educational tools by which they would finally drive out their colonial masters. The period which followed the political union between Britain and Ireland, despite being punctuated by a horrendous famine, was on the whole one of economic advance, however inequitably. Postcolonial societies are certainly capable of economic development. And so on. The question which divides left and right is not whether any good ever came of colonialism, but whether what sporadic benefits it bestowed could ever have been enough to justify it. Even if they occasionally built schools and hospitals alongside their churches, brothels and military barracks, the colonialists should have stayed at home.

One should question the currently fashionable distaste for the very idea of social progress, then, a privileged scepticism if ever there was one, but not at the cost of a brutal teleologism. Kenyon in Nathaniel Hawthorne's *The Marble Faun* maintains that crime is a necessary transition to a higher state, whereas Hilda rejects this view as an obscene rationalization. For her, crime is just crime. This is not, if one may pull rank on Hilda, the Archangel Michael's view of the balance-sheet of good and evil at the end of Milton's *Paradise Lost*. He thinks it wonderful that so much good will eventually come of so much evil (though he has divine salvation in mind rather than international socialism), and compares it to God's original act of bringing creation out of darkness. But his author may not have been wholly of this opinion. Milton may well have believed that humanity would have done better to remain in Edenic bliss, but that, once the Fall had happened, it mercifully proved fortunate as well as fatal.

This is also an issue in the work of Jean-Jacques Rousseau, who considers in his non-primitivist way that the shift from Nature to culture was a move up and not down, one essential for our civility, but that even so the ills of civilization outweigh its assets. Science is ruining us, and progress is an illusion; it is humanity's supposed improvements which have plunged it into misery. The *Discourse on Inequality* sees property as bringing war, exploitation and class conflict in its wake, and the social contract as a fraud perpetrated by the rich on the poor to preserve their privileges. Civilization is a sickness, and the chief culprit is desire: 'The savage lives within himself; social man always lives outside himself; he knows how to live only in the opinion of others, and it is, so to speak, from their judgement alone that he derives the sense of his own existence'.[9] For this stern acolyte of self-dependence, it is the idea of the self as refracted through the Other in a complex symbolic order which is insupportable. Desire is what renders us eccentric to ourselves.

Like Marx, Rousseau sees that this dependency has a basis in material production, but for him it means a lamentable loss of freedom. Iron and wheat have civilized society and ruined the human race. On the other hand, the state of nature seems to be free of conflict only because it is free of relationship: individuals pursue their projects in mute isolation, bereft of work, home, language and kinship. It is an innocuous existence, but also an impoverished one; it cannot be said to be noble, since like Eden or early infancy it pre-dates moral distinctions altogether. Political virtue can thrive only in very simple societies, and humanity in more advanced social states is invariably corrupt; even so, there can be no duty, conscience or social relations outside such a condition. Humanity has a faculty for self-improvement built into its species-being, and the advance of society improves human reasoning; but civilized self-reflection, for Rousseau as for Nietzsche, is enfeebling as well as enriching. Civilization undoubtedly has its value, but this is a poor thing compared with its evils. The poor die of their needs and the rich of their excesses.

The transgression is thus originary, a structural necessity for our flourishing, and the snake had infiltrated the garden from the outset. In this sense, perhaps, the classical theorists of tragedy have a point: *hamartia* or

245

going awry is built into the action, not some external force which afflicts it, and one name for this perpetual missing of the mark is desire. Without this, there would be no history at all. There is a botching or bungling at the heart of the historical enterprise without which it cannot function, rather as civilization for Freud requires repression. Whatever can hit its mark must be structurally capable of deviating from it. 'A mistake crept in when we were made', Büchner's Danton reflects, 'there's something missing . . . How long are we mathematicians of the flesh in our hunt for the ever elusive x to continue to write our equations with the bleeding fragments of human limbs?'(Act 2).

There are a number of ways in which, Faust-like, virtue and its negation are interwoven. As Michael Hardt and Antonio Negri argue, 'the evil, barbarity, and licentiousness of the colonized Other are what make possible the goodness, civility, and propriety of the European Self'.[10] Virtue relies on its opposite to define itself. But this, as Milton sees and Hardt and Negri perhaps don't, can be a positive as well as insidious opposition. The Milton of the *Areopagitica* refuses with admirable puritan zeal to praise a craven, cloistered virtue, preferring one which defines itself in strenuous combat with vice.[11] The Dostoevsky of *Crime and Punishment* sees virtue and suffering as bound up in a different sense: those who suffer themselves are likely to be most sensitive to the suffering of others. Compassion presupposes pain. These are minor theodicies, suggestive or sophistical attempts to place evil in the context of good.

Thomas Mann's Naphta of *The Magic Mountain* does so in rather more flamboyant style, arguing that the normal is parasitic on the abnormal, that human beings have 'consciously and voluntarily descended into disease and madness, in search of knowledge which, acquired by fanaticism, would lead back to health'.[12] Adrian Leverkühn of Mann's *Doctor Faustus* is one who descends into disease and madness for the sake of knowledge, though not for the sake of others. Genius is a kind of illness, but its fruits can be made available to the healthy suburbanite, hence justifying this decadence. 'Thus from the horrible may perfection flower', as Gregorius reflects in Mann's *The Holy Sinner*. Leverkühn insists that the most revolutionary art has to make use of staleness, fatuity and cynical parody, of a sense of disgust and absurdity, rather than to speak out directly. In this sense, too, good is drawn out of evil, as vitality springs from Baudelairean ennui. T. S. Eliot's early poetry might exemplify the point.

Modernism is a reaction to boredom, banality, suburban staleness – but lacking much faith of its own it can undo this spiritual inertia only from the inside, by mordant scepticisms and elaborate intellectual parodies which seem to mimic the very qualities they abhor. Leverkühn's music is precisely of this kind, splendid but sterile, an 'intellectual mockery of art' which in its proud, nihilistic dissociation betrays the mark of the demonic. The demonic, or annihilating desire, is indifferent to the sensuous particular, which it seizes upon only to hollow out and surge on to the next; and Leverkühn's superb art, not to speak of his less-than-superb life, has just this anti-sensuous quality. In its pastiche-like character, his music can gain some semblance of autonomous life only by sucking animation from others. Plagued by a pervasive sense of unreality, Leverkühn asks why everything seems to him like a parody of itself.

Alternatively, as far as the complicity of good and evil goes, you can claim with Leverkühn that the line dividing culture and barbarism must always be drawn from within a particular culture, which is then bound to demonize its opposite. From the standpoint of order, all dissent appears demonic. The bohemian is how the artist looks to the burgher. To dissent from an entire social order, even a fascist one, is bound to look like madness from within the order itself. Then again, you can claim that evil must exist if human freedom is not to be infringed, a case pressed by the Marquis in Schiller's play *Don Carlos*: God, 'rather than lock away one speck of freedom, / Allows the ghastly armies of the devil / To swagger through the universe unhindered' (Act 3, sc. 10). Evil implies freedom in the sense that nobody can be damned against their will, which is why Adrian Leverkühn studies theology; it is important for his impending perdition that he knows just what he is turning down.

One of Adrian's theological mentors, Dr Schleppfuss, argues that since vice finds its fulfilment in defiling virtue, it enjoys a freedom to sin which is inherent in creation itself. Creation contains its own negation, since the act of bringing virtue into being necessarily implies the freedom to deface it. The devil is less the joker in the pack or floating signifier in the order of creation, than a structural component of it. If good would not be good without evil, and if God's greatest glory lies in his bringing the former out of the latter, then the two states of being are mutually dependent. In any case, the devil is as creative in his own perverse way as divine power can be destructive. He is also a deconstructionist, who in his conversation with Leverkühn resists too absolute an opposition of good and evil with the shopsoiled Romantic platitude that the artist is the brother of the madman and criminal. Michel Foucault would have got on famously with him. What is beguiling about the devil is that he is anti-bourgeois. But then so is the rhetoric of fascism.

The modern discourse which most vigorously rejects this tragic concomitance of good and evil is Romantic humanism. Marx himself, despite his dialectical judgement on capitalism, shares much of this outlook. It tends to look upon human powers as inherently creative, and to see nega-tion as whatever obstructs their free expression. Unlike William Blake, it can accept only with reluctance that desire secretes its own undoing, that there is a block or prohibition at its heart that drives it to devour itself. This is the tragic condition of Faust. 'The restless pleasure principle is what makes man Faustian', writes Norman O. Brown, 'and Faustian man is history-making man.'[13] Faust's desire is for infinite self-enrichment as an end in itself, which the actual is always likely to disappoint. Hence the embarrassingly trivial pursuits in which Marlowe's Faust finds himself embroiled. The more inflated one's desire, the more it devalues the empir-ical world where it seeks to fulfil itself, and so the more it must curve back on itself to become its own object, having no other goal worthy of it.[14] In the end, all that matches up to desire is desire itself.

If desire levels its various objects to so many hollow shells, it is because what it is really hankering after is itself, a consummation which it can achieve only in death. The dynamic within this insatiable quest for ful-filment is thus *Thanatos* or the death drive, which seeks to abolish history, wind the clock back and attain a homeostasis in which the ego will be free from harm. Death is the goal of life, not just its end. An alternative way of suspending history is to strive for an eternity of life rather than for death, which is what the demoniac hero of the finest Faustian work in English, Charles Maturin's novel *Melmoth the Wanderer*, is on the prowl for. For the Freud of *Beyond the Pleasure Principle*, it is a tendency implaca-bly hostile to history which generates historical time, committing human-ity to what Brown calls 'an unconscious quest for the past in the future' or a 'forward-moving *recherche du temps perdu*'.[15] What impels us forward, perversely, is an instinct to travel backward to Eden. It is the sorrowfully self-defeating condition portrayed at the end of Scott Fitzgerald's *The Great Gatsby*, as we row forward into the future beaten inexorably back by the current into the past.

Goethe's vein of humanism, with its belief in the harmonious, all-round realization of one's impulses, has the anti-tragic buoyancy of the early bourgeois epoch. This is one reason why his Faust can finally be redeemed, if only by what Erich Heller calls 'the feeble trick of a future tense'.[16] 'For Goethe', comments Georg Lukács, 'the tragic is no longer an ultimate principle.'[17] Nothing could deject Lukács more than that. In Part 2 of his great drama, Faust heroically rejects the tragic vision unveiled by the figure of Care of the eternal non-gratification of desire, trusting instead that those who never cease to strive will be saved. It is a slogan which could stand on the desk of any chief executive officer, and indeed Faust ends up as a kind of industrial entrepreneur, though perhaps more of a Saint-Simonian utopian planner than a capitalist. His project of subduing Nature involves misery, exploitation and even murder, but through this essential suffering a dynamic economy and authentic community will spring into being. It is a case, once more, of history moving by its bad side, of the Hegelian version of theodicy. The Faust legend is among other things about the life instincts or *Eros* seeking to press *Thanatos* or the death drive into their service, only to find themselves brought low by it. Indeed, this is pretty well the tragic vision of the later Freud. *Eros* tricks *Thanatos* out of its nefarious intentions by harnessing it to the task of conquering Nature; but in pursuing its own role in building civilization, *Eros* depletes its forces through sublimation and so lays itself open to the ravages of death.

Watching Goethe's Faust construct his dams and dykes to salvage land from the ocean, Mephistopheles murmurs in a cynical aside: 'And yet it's us you're working for' (Part 2, Act 5), meaning the forces of hell. His point is that the water-devil Neptune will reap sadistic pleasure from razing Faust's mighty edifices to the ground. The demonic is keen on creation, since it needs something to put its foot through. Yet Mephistopheles's words might also suggest how the desire to master Nature is aggressivity or the death drive turned outwards, and thus ironically complicit with the very chaos and nothingness it strives to overcome. Indeed, he himself makes the point that infinite creation involves endless annihilation. What is achieved is over and done with and thus negated, as good as never performed. Faustian man's unstaunchable passion for achievement is also an insatiable lust for nothingness; but by speaking of events as 'over' rather than obliterated, placing them in time rather than eternity, he conceals this negativity from himself. Mephistopheles, cynical but candid, mutters that he would rather speak of 'the Eternal Void'. The fact that desire *is* such a void is obliquely confessed in the angels' announcement that 'He who strives on and lives to strive / Can earn redemption still' (Part 2, Act 5). In a familiar capitalist chiasmus, life is for striving, not striving for life, not least because any particular achievement is bound to look paltry in the light of an eternity of longing. From this viewpoint, Faust and Mephistopheles come to much the same thing; it all depends on whether you call it infinite striving or infinite nothingness. Yet by being redeemed, Faust is allowed to outwit the death drive, coupling destruction to the business of creation without falling prey to it himself.

This was not the case with the German National Socialists. The great allegory of the Nazis' demonic cult of death is Thomas Mann's *Doctor Faustus*,[18] whose protagonist Leverkühn deliberately infects himself with venereal disease in order to heighten his creative powers. Nothing combines *Eros* and *Thanatos* more effectively than syphilis, or, for the contemporary world, AIDS. Leverkühn treats the disease as a kind of *pharmakos*, a poison which will act as an inspiration, which for the later Freud is true of the life instincts themselves. Polluting your bloodstream in order to compose magnificent music is *felix culpa* with a vengeance. But the question of sickness and cure is one which the novel poses on a more global scale. Liberal humanism, as championed by the novel's good-hearted narrator Zeitblom, looks a feebly Apollonian faith when confronted with a barbarously Dionysiac fascism; so should it make a devilish wager, play dice with Mephistopheles and ally itself with the revolutionary forces of modernism and socialism? Or would that simply be to oppose one form of collectivist, anti-humanist avant-gardism with another? Fascism is a radicalism of the right; and nobody is more revolutionary than the devil, who in this novel praises 'excess, paradox, the mystic passion, the utterly unbourgeois ideal' (p. 243).

Bourgeois humanism is an honourable but spineless critique of fascism, whereas revolutionary modernism, which as a critique of fascism has the advantage of cutting to the same Dionysian depths as it does, may for that very reason be collusive with it. In one sense, then, it is ironic that fascism bans modernist art. Both fascism and modernism are avant-garde yet atavistic, progressive and primitivist, technological and mythological together. Like fascism, modernism is, so to speak, a barbarism to the second power – one which comes after the culture of modernity, and so is well acquainted with the values it refuses, as Leverkühn must be acquainted with salvation if he is to be damned. But it is also a sophisticated savagery because, as Nietzsche dreamed, it raises all those unreflective energies to the level of a self-conscious cult of naivety, thus forging fresh bonds between folk and minority culture. An elitist populism, a contrived cult of folk wisdom and spontaneity, is another shared bond between fascism and modernism. But modernism is also a clean break with time, not just a clean break within it, which is part of its perilous appeal. As Zeitblom reflects, are not reaction and progress, past and future, old and new indistinguishable for both left and right, so that in the mirror-image relation between them can be seen something of a shared 'old–new world of revolutionary reaction' (p. 368)? The very old, after all, is what hasn't been tried for a long time, and so is the latest thing. If you want to leave modernity behind, you can always learn how to spurn it by looking to its own original act of breaking with the pre-modern, and so, by negating that negation, return to that archaic world.

Bourgeois humanism, derided by Leverkühn as 'false and flabby middle-class piety' (p. 490), is not only a rather toothless creed with which to combat fascism, but is actively in cahoots with it, as its idealism provides a convenient rationale for political brutality. Anyway, humanism is itself secretly indebted to the anarchic and archaic, tapping into these primitive energies in the act of sublimating them, and thus acts, as Zeitblom comments, as the 'propitiatory entrance of the dark and uncanny into the service of the gods' (p. 10). Science and enlightenment have their magical or mythical correlations. If humanism has gone soft, then it must return to its roots in Nature to become authentic. But either this will be, in classical style, a rational, idealized Nature of its own creation, in which case nothing has been achieved; or it will be actual Nature, Nature as rapacious and barbaric, in which case it is not clear how humanism can avoid the monstrous and mythological. Actual Nature has a fearful sublimity about it, not a humanistic beauty, diminishing the human in its unimaginable vastness.

But if liberal and fascist are uneasily allied, a similar criminal complicity might be claimed between fascism and avant-garde modernism. It is not clear, for example, whether modernism, which can launch a searching critique of humanism, can also deflate the pretensions of a dementedly idealizing fascism; or whether it is a twin of fascism in representing a similar headlong flight from freedom. The modernist artist actually chooses to be fettered by a stringent formal logic, making his destiny his choice; but is this a blow against the bogus freedom of fascism, or a mirror-image of its totalitarianism? Freedom, so Leverkühn advises Zeitblom, must now consist in subjecting oneself to law, system, coercion; but since this compulsion is self-imposed, it remains freedom even so. Kantian liberalism is thus summoned to justify autocracy. The highest freedom is to abnegate freedom, as Leverkühn does in delivering himself to the devil. Total organization is the new agenda in both art and social life. A discredited Romantic expressivism must now give way to a closed system in which freedom is no more than a random permutation, an accidental by-product of necessity. But since this system will also arbitrarily throw up quite traditional combinations, the avant-garde is in this sense too the archaic, the cutting-edge of cultural technology a regression to the occult. Rationality, pressed to an extreme parody of itself, becomes full-blown irrationalism.

Is culture healthier when it is free but ineffectual, or in its cultic, ritual state, which is ominously irrational but at least yoked to social ends? Should the left reinvent this ritual, pre-modern culture in the form of a politically organized art, or would this simply reflect the cultic fascism it is meant to oppose? Perhaps the autonomous art of modernity is just a transition between one state of unfreedom and another, between the traditionalist art of church and court and the propagandist art of the party. And if art may need to be revolutionized, the same goes for epistemology. Perhaps truth now needs to yield to the fruitful *falsum*, contemptuous of science and objectivity, and rationality to be redefined in terms of political interests rather than some spurious disinterestedness. In this novel it is the fascists who advocate this project, not, as it will be some decades later, the postmodernists. The devil himself is a devout Nietzschean, for whom truth is simply 'what uplifts you, what increases your feeling of power and might and domination' (p. 242). Zeitblom, for his part, believes that truth should be independent of community interests, and will serve the community all the better by being respected as such. The vanguardist programme to press truth and justice into the service of power, *doxa* and authority is in his eyes a reversion to medieval autocracy, which then has the impudence to brand liberalism itself as archaic and superannuated. But doctrines of objective truth and impartial justice are already going up in flames in the ruined cities of Europe.

Modernism is an 'inhuman' form, extremist, fetishizing technique, obsessive about correspondences, cruelly disciplined and empty of interiority; so that art, that acme of the humane, comes to have an unnervingly demonic quality about it, a transcendence not in the humanist sense but of the human as such. It is difficult to distinguish between a positive and a negative brand of anti-humanism, between a puncturing of false idealizings of humanity and a brutal contempt for the human as such. This is meant to be part of the difference between Birkin and Gerald Crich in D. H. Lawrence's *Women in Love*, though Birkin complicates the contrast by blending both forms of the creed. Is the emergence of the inhuman an auspicious beginning or a sterile dead end? Is it a clearing away of the rubble of liberal humanism for the birth of a better world, or does it herald the frightful emergence of some rough beast? Dissolution may be an essential prelude to new life, or the final apocalyptic collapse of human civilization. Several of the high modernists are intriguingly unsure which option to back, and several of them – Yeats, for example – hedge their bets on the question.

Form in modernist art is an inhuman force, imposing itself like a kind of fate. Expression can be wrested only from new arrangements of materials which, as in the case of language, are arbitrary and non-signifying in themselves. Non-meaning is the condition of meaning in art, signification and the unconscious. But if this is true, then the avant-garde regresses once more to the archaic, since myth, too, plucks meaning from a Nature which in itself is inexpressive. The demonic is another species of formalism, a pure dissociation of the intellect which for all its *froideur* is also savagely mocking, since even tragedy is bound to look farcical to those who are purely detached. Leverkühn is cerebral and satirical in equal measure. Yet the demonic is also the amorphous, the irruption of the purely chaotic and instinctual into the world of stable forms. The two states are logically related: once reason petrifies into formalism, the instinctual life lapses into sensationalism.

Doctor Faustus is an allegory of one of the greatest tragedies of the modern epoch, a work whose very existence testifies to the survival of at least some of the values it fears may have foundered. Yet despite its astonishingly synoptic vision, it passes over one highly relevant solution to the problems it addresses: socialism. Socialism is the form of avant-garde politics which, unlike modernism and its progeny, greets the great liberal-bourgeois heritage with acclaim as well as antagonism. It therefore brings together two currents of thought which *Doctor Faustus* can only see as implacably at odds. For Marx at least, there can be no durable socialism which is not firmly based on the revolutionary advances of the capitalist era. By the time Mann came to write, a good many socialist hopes had been dashed by the history of the Soviet Union, which had had no such heritage to build on. And this is doubtless one reason why his novel is silent on this question. Yet it was, ironically, a combined front of the Soviet Union and Western liberal democracies which finally rid the world of the Dionysian dementia which had broken out at the heart of Europe. Whatever Zeitblom's intellectual misgivings, fascism and communism proved in practice deadly foes, not terrible twins, and the latter played an heroic part in the defeat of the former.

The fact that the outcome of that struggle was positive, however, does not mean that the action was not a tragic one. We have only to think of Stalingrad. The same applies to Mann's novel. For the very last note of this courageous fiction is, most audaciously of all, one of hope. It is, to be sure, a hope as spectral and muted as the last trembling cello note of Leverkühn's great cantata, a mere vibrant ghost on the air or scarcely audible silence. If there is indeed hope, the narrator reflects, it can only be 'a hope beyond hopelessness', one which germinates out of the sheerly irredeemable; it cannot undo the dreadfulness of what has taken place. But it is from just such a tension between taking the full measure of despair, and refusing to acknowledge it as quite the last word, that the most fruitful tragic art is born.

The demonic is mysterious because it appears to be without cause. It is an apparently unmotivated malignancy, which delights in destruction for its own sake. Or, as the saying goes, just for the hell of it. It is hard to know quite why Iago feels so resentful of Othello. The witches of *Macbeth* reap no obvious profit from driving the protagonist to his doom. This kind of wickedness seems to be autotelic, having its grounds, ends and causes in itself. It thus joins a privileged, somewhat underpopulated class of objects, which includes God and art. It is enigmatic because it is brutely itself, not because it has the inscrutability of something too deep to fathom. As St Augustine remarks in the *Confessions* of his youthful debauchery, 'I had no motive for my wickedness except wickedness itself. It was foul, and I loved it.'[19]

For many commentators, the Holocaust would be the prime example of demonic evil. Part of its horror lies in its apparent pointlessness. Even if you had wanted to rid the world of Jews, you could have found some less unspeakable way of doing it. As Stangl, the ex-commandant of Treblinka, was asked later: 'Considering that you were going to kill them all . . . what was the point of the humiliations, the cruelties?' Or as Primo Levi inquires:

> Why go to the trouble of dragging them on to their trains, take them to die far away, after a senseless journey, die in Poland on the threshold of the gas chambers? In my convoy there were two dying ninety-year-old women, taken out of the Fossoli infirmary; one of them died en route, nursed in vain by her daughters. Would it not have been simpler, more 'economical', to let them die, or perhaps kill them in their beds, instead of adding their agony to the collective agony of the transport? One is truly led to think that, in the Third Reich, the best choice, the choice imposed from above, was the one that entailed the greatest amount of affliction, the greatest amount of waste, of physical and moral suffering. The 'enemy' must not only die, but must die in torment.[20]

One might point out banally enough that the Nazis indeed had a reason for killing Jews, namely the fact that they were Jews. They were killed because of their ethnicity. The mystery is why were they killed on that account. Stalin and Mao were respectively responsible for the deaths of millions of Russians and Chinese, but not because they were Russian or Chinese. Their deaths had some instrumental value in the eyes of the perpetrators. 'Wars are detestable', writes Levi, '[but] they are not gratuitous, their purpose is not to inflict suffering.' This, however, does not seem to be the case with the Holocaust. It is true that the extermination of Jewish people served among other things an ideological purpose. To unify the *Volk* by demonizing their frightful Other is by no means peculiar to Nazism. But you do not need to slaughter six million men and women in order to create an ideological bogeyman. As Immanuel Wallerstein points out, racists usually want to keep their victims alive in order to oppress them; they derive no practical advantage from destroying them.[21] Slavoj Žižek draws attention to those aspects of the Holocaust which seem like obscene jokes or tauntings – bands playing while camp inmates marched to work, the 'Arbeit macht frei!' slogan – and wonders whether the whole affair was not 'a cruel aesthetic joke accomplished just for the sake of it, and thus fitting the Kantian notion of "diabolical evil"'.[22]

Žižek is careful, however, to distinguish this case from the ideological propaganda which would see the Holocaust as a unique metaphysical mystery without analogue or explanation, an absolute ahistorical Evil beyond all comprehension. The Nazi camps are by no means the only example of this kind of evil, and part of the point of the present argument is that such evil is not in fact entirely beyond comprehension. 'Evil' means a particular kind of wickedness, one by which we distinguish, say, the Final Solution from the Great Train Robbery. It does not mean 'without material cause'. Nor does it necessarily involve a glamorous, Byronic spiritual elitism. Hannah Arendt pointed long ago to the sheer banality of Nazism.[23]

Stangl's own response to the question of why the Nazis felt a need for such cruelty is bluntly utilitarian: 'To condition those who were to be the material executors of the operation. To make it possible to do what they were doing.' As Levi comments on this response: 'before dying the victims must be degraded, so that the murderer will be less burdened by guilt'.[24] But Stangl's response obviously begs the question, since why were they doing what they were doing in the first place? And even if the Nazis had a purpose, were not the means they used to achieve it madly excessive? Levi himself remarks that the years of Hitler were characterized by 'a widespread useless violence, as an end in itself, with the sole purpose of creating pain, occasionally having a purpose, yet always redundant, always disproportionate to the purpose itself'.[25] His own language buckles under the strain of this enormity: this 'useless' violence had the 'sole purpose' of creating pain, yet 'occasionally [had] a purpose'; this purpose was 'redundant' but also 'disproportionate', which is not quite the same thing.

Yet the fundamental point surely stands. Logistically speaking, the Holocaust was counter-productive, tying down personnel, equipment and resources which might well have been used for the German war effort. And the Nazis could have benefited militarily from the practical skills of some of those they murdered. Levi points out that the SS probably did not make a profit from selling human hair from the camps to textile manufacturers; 'the outrage motive prevailed over the profit motive'.[26] Perhaps, as Geoffrey Wheatcroft suggests, 'the most difficult truth of all is that the Shoah [Holocaust] was meaningless'.[27] Karl Jaspers, writing under the shadow of Nazism, speaks of 'the delight in meaningless activity, in torturing and being tortured, in destruction for its own sake, in the raging hatred against the world and man complete with the raging hatred against one's own despised existence'.[28] It is as succinct a summary of the demonic as one could find.

Perhaps the reason for the genocide was the Nazis' desire for racial purity. But why did they desire that? There are no rational grounds for it, as there are for poisoning someone in order to lay your hands on her money. But there are, so to speak, irrational reasons for it. To see evil as unmotivated is not necessarily to regard it as inexplicable. People who destroy just for the hell of it are not exactly doing that. They tear apart strangers because they fear that they pose a threat to their own fullness of being, which is a reason of a kind. The group which threatens to negate their being must be annihilated because they signify the irruption of chaos and non-sense into their own world. They are a sign of the hollowness at the heart of one's own identity. Annihilating the other thus becomes the only way of convincing yourself that you exist. It allows you to forge an illusory identity from the act of fending off non-being. Only in the obscene enjoyment of dismembering others can you feel alive yourself. Evil is a self-undoing attempt to negate non-being by creating even more of the stuff around you.

This is why those in hell are said to revel in their own torment. They do so because only pain can persuade them they are alive. The demonic are those lost souls who can find release from the anguish of non-being only by destroying others, but who in doing so deplete themselves even further. Charles Maturin's doomed Melmoth in *Melmoth the Wanderer* knows a torment which 'seeks its wild and hopeless mitigation in the sufferings of others' (vol. 2, ch. 10), but is at the same time savagely hostile to anyone who would ease his agony. The demonic is like a drunk so ravaged by alcohol that he can gain a spot of illusory vitality only by stepping up his intake, which then shatters him so atrociously that he needs to consume still more. Those caught in this spiralling circle are in the grip of the death drive. The death drive is a wily way of trying to stay alive, a source of obscene enjoyment to which we cling for dear life, and are thus incapable of dying for real.

Hell is about finality, not perpetuity – the inability to break out of the lethal circuit of Law and desire and scramble back to life. *Pace* Sartre, it is precisely not other people. It is the condition of those whose destiny is to be stuck with themselves for all eternity, like some bar-room bore. It has the absurdity of utter solitude, since nothing which could happen to me alone could make any sense. The damned cannot relinquish their anguish because it is bound up with their delight, cannot escape the cruel sadism of the Law because this is just what they desire. This is why they are in despair. They are under the power of death already, but since this yields them gratification they can always fool themselves that they are vibrantly alive. And the fact that they find pleasure in self-destruction is what keeps them just this side of death.

The demonic, then, is the vampiric condition of the undead – the hellish state of those who cannot die because, like William Golding's Pincher Martin, they are really dead already but refuse to accept the fact. Evil may look alluring, and the devil may appear to have all the best tunes, but its brio is just tawdry melodrama. If virtue seems so unappetizing, it is partly because of the mixture of prudence, sexual obsession, self-repression and self-righteousness to which the middle classes have reduced it. It is tedious for Fielding, but not for Dante or Chaucer. For Thomas Aquinas, evil is an incapacity for life, and one should not be fooled by its flaming energy or seductive panache. 'A thing', Aquinas argues, 'has as much good as it has being', and evil is a deficiency of being.[29] Which is not to say that evil is unreal, any more than thirst or darkness are. A being which is not determined by some other being, so Aquinas considered, has life in the highest degree, which is why God is infinite vitality. Kierkegaard writes in *The Concept of Anxiety* of 'the dreadful emptiness and contentlessness of evil'.[30] 'The demonic', he comments, 'is the boring.'[31] In *The Sickness Unto Death* he portrays this as the condition of those who cling stubbornly to their despair and spit in the world's face for bringing them to this pass, those who refuse to be saved since it would relieve them of their delight in their rebellious rejection of the world.

The demonic is thus a kind of cosmic sulking. Comfort would be the undoing of such despairers, who like Pincher Martin wax most furious at the thought that eternity may have the insolence to deprive them of their misery. Such men and women are in rebellion against existence as such. The Satanic, declares Dostoevsky's Father Zosima in *The Brothers Karamazov*, 'demand that there be no God of life, that God destroy himself and all His creation. And they shall burn everlastingly in the flames of their own hatred, and long for death and for non-being. But death shall not be granted them' (Part 2, Book 6, ch. 3). An anarchist character in Joseph Conrad's *The Secret Agent* declares that he depends on death, which knows no restraint and cannot be attacked. Pure negation is invulnerable, since it cannot be destroyed; and if it resembles God in this, so it does in its lack of finitude. The demonic, like those who planned the death camps in Germany, detest the sheer fact of existence, symbolized for them in their Jewish, homosexual and other victims, because it reminds them of their own unbearable non-being. They have given way on their desire, finding its lack impossible to live with, and now seek to destroy non-being itself. Because they live only vicariously through the agonies of others, they cannot die because in a sense they are dead already, monstrous, Dracula-like travesties of the living. But the wicked also cannot die because they regard themselves as too precious to be extinguished. This is why Pincher Martin cannot accept the inconceivable scandal that, unknown to himself, he drowned on the first page of the novel.

The inverted mirror-image of evil, as we have seen already, is Creation. The two share in common their autotelic or just-for-the-hell-of-it character. From this viewpoint, Büchner's Danton is mistaken when he argues that 'anything created can never be grounded in itself' (*Danton's Death*, Act 3, sc. 1). Evil resembles the being whose pure existence it finds so scandalously offensive, in subsisting just as much for its own sake. As being has no end other than to be, so evil has no purpose other than to negate it. It is the fact that the Jew, woman, homosexual or foreigner exists, not what he or she actually does, which it finds so intolerable. Good, on the other hand, accepts and delights in being as such, not for any instrumental purpose. Once St Augustine turns from his debauched youth, he speaks of those who worship God with no reward save the joy that they derive from it. One can understand, then, why the devil was once an angel. The devil is a parody of God, not just his antithesis. Good and evil are on unnervingly intimate terms, and both of them bear more than a passing resemblance to the aesthetic. Nothing is supposed to exist for its own solitary self-delight as much as art, mocking our pathetic struggling for achievement. 'O self-born mockers of man's enterprise!' as Yeats exclaims of some icons. Yet evil mocks at our achievements too.

This uneasy complicity of good and evil can be observed in the case of children. Children are largely non-functional creatures – they don't work, for example – and it is not easy to say exactly what they are for. Perhaps this is one reason why an aesthete like Oscar Wilde found them so fascinating. But it may also be why Victorian Evangelicals found them so sinister, as indeed do some modern horror films, since anything which falls outside the realm of functionality seems to a utilitarian to fall outside the domain of morality too. The Victorians thus could not make up their mind whether children were angelic or demonic, Oliver Twists or Artful Dodgers. They are also, of course, sinister because they are uncanny, very like adults but not at all like them.

In much of his fiction, Milan Kundera sees the angelic as a bland, 'shitless' discourse of wide-eyed idealism and high-sounding sentiment. The angelic is full of moralistic rhetoric and edifying kitsch, allergic to doubt or irony. The angelic for Kundera are those who troop merrily forward into the future shouting 'Long live life!', all grins and cheers, beaming and cart-wheeling. They do not seem to realize that an advance into the future is a step towards death. The angelic is a hygienic disavowal of the unacceptable: it is, as Kundera puts it, the septic tank which the Gulag uses to dispose of its garbage. In the sphere of the angelic, the dictatorship of the heart reigns supreme, which is why men who put other people out of work wax sentimental about their own families. The official culture which today most exemplifies the angelic is surely that of the United States, ill at ease as it is with the negative, ironic, debunking or unhygienic. The angelic has too glazed a smile and too ready a handshake to appreciate the seed of truth in Seneca's comment in his play *Thyestes* that 'Pain is real, and everything else is merely a moment of respite, irrelevant. Scars are the only parts of the body to trust.'

Kundera also sees the angelic as a sphere in which there is too much meaning rather than too little. The kingdom of the angels is one in which everything is instantly, oppressively meaningful, in which no shadow of ambiguity can be tolerated. It is the up-beat world of official ideology, in which language comes to assume an authoritarian over-ripeness and everything is drearily legible and transparent. Kundera is thinking here mostly of the neo-Stalinism with which he grew up. Yet this world in which everything is glaringly on view, flattened and two-dimensional, is also one awash with rumour and innuendo, tell-tale traces, whispered treacheries. Nothing is ever quite what it appears to be, and calls for a constant labour of decipherment.

Kundera tells the story in *The Book of Laughter and Forgetting* of a Czech being sick in the centre of communist Prague. A fellow Czech wanders up, shakes his head and murmurs: 'I know just what you mean'. The joke here is that the second Czech reads as significant what is just a random event. Under communism, even throwing up must assume some instant symbolic value. Nothing can happen by accident. The extreme version of this state of mind is paranoia, in which the most casual scraps of reality conceal a grand narrative. One can never be quite sure in Kundera's Soviet-run Czechoslovakia whether a meaning is intended or not – whether there is some fateful significance in the late arrival of your spouse, the boss's failure to say good morning, that car which has been behind your own for the last ten miles.

The opposite of this condition for Kundera is the demonic, in which there is too little meaning rather than too much. There is a dim parallel here, perhaps, between Kundera's angelic and demonic, and Lacan's Symbolic and Real. If the angelic is too solemn about meaning, the demonic is too cynical. This, to be sure, can have its value. The demonic is the cackle of mocking laughter which deflates the pretensions of the angelic, puncturing its portentous world. It is the kind of amusement which springs from things being suddenly deprived of their familiar meanings, a sort of estrangement. It is the farcical subtext of *King Lear*, in which Lear cannot throw off his lendings because his button gets stuck, or Gloucester pitches himself dramatically off an imaginary Dover cliff only to end up grovelling on the ground. We find this vein of debunkery in the satyr play which accompanied the Greek performance of tragedy, as an essential deflation of tragic solemnity. In our own day, the demonic has reared its horned head once in the guise of poststructuralism, and has encountered the usual ambivalent response: is it a bracingly sceptical questioning of suburban pieties or a metaphysical nihilism? It is never easy to distinguish the claim that no meaning is absolute from the suggestion that there is no meaning at all.

The demonic is a momentary respite from the tyrannical legibility of things, a realm of lost innocence which pre-dates our calamitous fall into meaning. Like most realms of lost innocence, it is never far from the graveyard, and Kundera associates it with the death drive. The devil in Dostoevsky's *The Brothers Karamazov* tells Ivan Karamazov that his role is to act as a kind of friction or negativity in God's creation, a cross-grained factor which keeps it in existence and prevents it from withering of sheer boredom. Otherwise, he comments, the place would be far too angelic – 'nothing but Hosannas', in fact. The devil describes himself to Ivan as 'the x in an indeterminate equation', the 'requisite negativity' in the universe without which order would break out and put an end to everything (Part 4, Book 11, ch. 9). It is in something like these terms that Jacques Lacan characterizes the Real, that cross-grained, out-of-joint factor within the symbolic order which keeps it in business; and since the hard-core of the Real is the obscene enjoyment of the death drive, its linkage with the demonic is a typically imaginative stroke on Dostoevsky's part. In the hell of *Doctor Faustus*, torment is mixed with shameful pleasure, screechings of agony with groans of lust.

Angels can only see demons as cynics rather than sceptics; but though the demonic is the clowning which mocks the high and mighty, there is an implacable malice about it as well. As the devil of *Doctor Faustus* tells us, its laughter is a 'luciferian sardonic mood', a 'hellish merriment' of 'yelling, screeching, bawling, bleating, howling, piping . . . the mocking, exulting laughter of the Pit' (p. 378). Hell is a combination of suffering and derision. Revolted by the over-stuffed meaning of the angelic, the demonic keels over into nihilism, levelling all values to an amorphous shit. The Satanic cry 'Evil, be thou my good!' at least preserves moral distinctions in the act of inverting them, whereas the pure cynicism which Kundera has in mind does not. It cannot suppress a spasm of incredulous laughter at the gullibility of men and women, their pathetic eagerness to believe that their values are as solid as flat-irons. For the demonic, value is just a sham, which is why it seeks to demolish it. The demonic are exasperated beyond endurance by the bland, shitless angels, feeling the incurable itch to unmask their high-mindedness as bogus. But in doing so they come to jeer at meaning and value as such. The Iagos of this world cannot bear the ponderous, overblown rhetoric of the Othellos. They suspect that behind this pompous facade lurks some utter vacuity, some unimaginably dreadful non-being, and their sadistic delight is to expose it for what it is. This, outside the senior ranks of fascist organizations, is an extremely rare moral condition, though as the Holocaust demonstrates it is a contagious one too, which can come in epidemics. There is very little of it in tragic art. Disappointingly, Dante's hell is populated not by demoniacs but by a drearily predictable gang of traitors, lechers, gluttons, heretics, hypocrites and the like. The usual suspects, in short.

The demonic, then, is not so much opposed to value as unable to see the point of it, any more than a squirrel could grasp the point of algebraic topology. What it finds offensive is not this or that value, but the whole farcical business of value as such. This resolves an apparent contradiction, one which haunts both Sade and Baudelaire: evil needs value in order to exist, but at the same time does not believe in it. Baudelairean Satanism must surely be ironic, since how can you derive a *frisson* of wickedness from contravening moral codes which you know to be purely conventional anyway? The demonic, however, derives its *frisson* precisely from showing up value as purely conventional, not from a defiant belief in the reality of evil. Evil is the last thing it believes in, since this would involve granting credence to good. To be wicked is to share the same terms as the virtuous, whereas the demonic is infuriated by the delusion that anything could actually matter, good or bad. As Vladimir Nabokov's novel *Laughter in the Dark* comments of one of its less savoury characters: 'Perhaps the only real thing about him was his innate conviction that everything that had ever been created in the domain of art, science, or sentiment, was only a more or less clever trick'. Goethe's Mephistopheles, a spirit that 'endlessly denies', believes that 'all that comes to birth / Is fit for overthrow, as nothing worth' (Part 1, Faust's Study (i)).

What drives the demonic to sardonic fury is the obscene repleteness of human existence, its smug belief in its own solidity. This is why the Satanic have a secret pact à la Baudelaire with the bohemian artists, who likewise scoff at the stolid pomposity of the bourgeoisie. In deflating a world which calibrates value on a scrupulously nuanced scale, the demonic collapses these unique identities into the eternal sameness of shit, and thus ironically ends up with pure identity. In destroying the

unique aura of the angelic, it is stuck with an endless mechanical repro-
duction, for which the prototype in Kundera is the sexual orgy. There is
something uproariously comic about the supposed singularity of erotic
love endlessly repeated in a wilderness of mirrors. Yet the sight of
ungainly naked bodies crowded into a single space is also for Kundera an
image of the gas chamber. The unique is a fetish, to be sure, but a cynical
exchangeability of objects is no alternative. If bodies are interchangeable
for carnival, so are they for Nazism and Stalinism. We move on a hair-
thin line between clowning and cynicism, too much meaning and too
little, debunking and annihilating, shitlike sameness and fetishized difference. In classically comic style, our biological nature reminds us of
what we share in common, in contrast to the jealously fostered discrim-
inations of culture; but identity is also a form of death. In hell everything
is exactly, eternally the same. It is agonizing not because of all those
wickedly sharp toasting forks, but because it is intolerably boring. Hell is
not a torture chamber but a perpetual cocktail party.

The problem, then, is how to tread a line between too much meaning
and too little. It is a line we cross every time we open our mouths, since
there is always both too much and too little sense in what we say. Freud
saw non-meaning as lying at the root of meaning, yet meaning is also
excessive, as the signifier comes to suggest more than we intend. And
the meaning of what we say is thickened by the sheer act of saying it.
We live suspended between an excess of meaning and a deficiency of it,
both too angelic and too demonic, and these states are mirror-images of
each other. Societies, for example, need the angelic to plug the gap of the
demonic. In the sphere of the angelic or ideological, we affirm the unique
value of each individual: 'I am Willy Loman and you are Biff Loman!'
Yet in the realm of the market-place, these individuals are of a shitlike
sameness, indifferently exchangeable: 'Pop! I'm a dime a dozen, and so
are you!'

Evil, then, would seem to have two faces. On the one hand, there is
the desire to negate the negation – to annihilate that nameless, slimy stuff
(call it the Jew or the Muslim) which signifies one's own vacuity; on the
other hand, there is the drive to destroy that obscene fullness of being
which would deny its own lack of foundation. One might almost call
these angelic and demonic forms of evil – the former repressing its own
lack of being, the latter revelling in it. It is noteworthy that Nazism combines the two modes: it is laced with 'shitless' rhetoric, bogus vitalism,
puristic idealism and phony ontologies, but also glutted with sheer self-
consuming destructiveness.

There is a leftist equivalent of the demonic/angelic division. Left-
wingers tend to be either caustic, sceptical, debunking demons, or

affirmative, utopian, humanistic angels. The demons stress conflict, power, demystification, the falseness of positivity, the need for constant hermeneutical vigilance. The angels stress community, view conflict as necessary but regrettable, respect common meanings rather than scorn them as false consciousness, and see a just future as extending values already active in the present. Raymond Williams and Jürgen Habermas are angelic, whereas Michel Foucault and Jacques Derrida are demonic. It is a rare leftist who combines the two; Edward Thompson at his finest maintained a foot in both camps. Both brands of leftism are indispensable, but the tension between them is ineradicable. The demons overstress the discontinuity between present and future, whereas the angels are too evolutionary in this respect. The demons are too sceptical of the present, and the angels too tender for it.

The French have a certain proprietorial claim on the demonic. Trifling with others' feelings just for the deadly delight of the game is a preoccupation of Stendhal's protagonists as well as of *Les Liaisons dangereuses*, and a Satanic snarling breaks out again in the poetry of Baudelaire. There can be little doubt that the devil is a Parisian, though he has the odd German counterpart: Fritz von Moor in Schiller's *The Robbers* is a figure who deliberately opts for evil. Goetz, the powerfully complex protagonist of Sartre's play *Lucifer and the Lord*, is a German general who espouses evil for its own sake before turning to an equally aestheticist cult of good. It is a full-blown metaphysical drama at the heart of late modernity, though the fact that it is backdated to the Thirty Years War renders this rather more plausible. Goetz is a self-declared demoniac ('Don't you understand that Evil is my reason for living? . . . I do Evil for Evil's sake' (Act 1, sc. 2)), and decides to destroy a city just because everyone wants him to spare it. His use of violence is purely gratuitous, in contrast with the strategic violence of the popular leader Nasti, which the play endorses. Evil is an elitist affair: one does it because of its difficulty, prizing it for its extreme rarity.

Goetz has a horror of being loved, rather like Graham Greene's Pinky of *Brighton Rock* or Golding's Pincher Martin, whose response to God's offer of forgiveness is 'I shit on your love!' The demonic experiences love as a violent threat to its non-being, since it is a form of value and meaning, and Martin is finally pounded to pieces by the merciless 'black lightning' of God's love. It is this terrifying love which is traditionally known as the fire of hell. Like Goetz, Martin knows that the ultimate freedom is that God will never forgive him against his will, so that he has his Creator completely in his power. Goetz prizes evil because it is the only thing which God has left humanity to create, having created all the interesting stuff himself. 'Man', he remarks, 'is made to destroy man in himself, and to open himself like a female to the huge dark body of the night' (Act 3, sc. 9). The *Übermensch*, oddly, is also a eunuch, and the sexual coupling here is also the pleasure of the death drive. Since God doesn't prevent his massacres, Goetz speculates, he must implicitly approve of them, and evil-doers are the instruments he hides hypocriti-cally behind: 'Thank you, oh Lord, thank you very much. Thank you for the women violated, the children impaled, the men decapitated' (Act 1, sc. 3). Through him, Goetz believes, 'God is disgusted with himself', so perhaps the wicked are the instruments of divine masochism. Or perhaps God, being fullness of being itself, cannot grasp nothingness and thus is innocent. If God allows the innocent to suffer then he is in the hands of evil-doers, who must then be godlike themselves, so that evil is a mon-strous form of good.

Evil, as we have seen, is on terms with good, and the devil is a devout religious believer. 'Here we are face to face again', a reformed Goetz says to God, 'like in the good old days when I was doing evil' (Act 3, sc. 9). He enjoys hobnobbing with the high and mighty; God, he declares, is the only enemy worthy of his talents. It is logical, then, that once persuaded that evil is commonplace and good in short supply, Goetz should switch his allegiance to a cult of self-scourging sentimentalism, which is the best parody of Christian virtue he can muster. It is a self-vaunting kind of self-abasement, which turns out to be just as destructive of human life as his former evil. Goetz's altruism, like that of Shakespeare's Timon of Athens, is just a devious form of egoism. But at least, so he realizes later, he has remained consistently himself, true to his own terrible egoism, through these apparent shifts of loyalty: 'you remained faithful to yourself, faith-ful; nothing other than a bastard' (Act 3, sc. 10). Better an authentic bastard than a self-deceiving saint.

As Will Ladislaw counsels Dorothea Brooke in George Eliot's *Middle-march*, one should beware of a 'fanaticism of sympathy'. The obverse of the aestheticism of evil is a false utopia – the sentimental belief that the kingdom of heaven can be here and now – which is as scornful of instrumental action as evil itself. Both evil and false utopia are averse to politics, whereas the revolutionary Nasti holds that the only alternative to a false love is a militant hatred, and that the good society must pass through a violent struggle for justice if it is to be born at all. The evil and the spiritual elect are alike in disdaining utility: false prophets like Goetz, Nasti observes, declare that 'I shall do what I think is right, though the world perish' (Act 2, sc. 4). The Antigone who is a heroine for Lacan would be for Nasti a politically irresponsible egoist. Yet the alternative to this lordly contempt for consequences may be a political expediency which is prepared to clamber into the kingdom of freedom over a pile of corpses.

Goetz is really a left-bank bohemian gone horribly awry, and through him Sartre probes with commendable candour the flaws of his own faith. What Goetz really desires is to be neither good nor evil but 'inhuman', beyond the reach of bad faith and the conformism of the mob. In the end, he redeems himself by rejecting God and becoming a devout Sartrean existentialist, recognizing that his evil has presupposed God as much as his good. He now accepts responsibility for his own existence and fights alongside Nasti for the emancipation of humanity, an end which will involve butchery and ruthless calculation. His mirror-image in existentialist theatre is Albert Camus's monstrous Caligula, whose only happiness lies in scorn and malice – in 'the glorious isolation of the man who all his life long nurses and gloats over the joy ineffable of the unpunished murderer; the truthless logic that crushes out human lives . . . so as to perfect at last the utter loneliness that is my heart's desire' (Act 4). Like Goetz, Caligula is a grisly parody of the existentialist hero, exposing the creed's soft underbelly. If freedom is absolute and value arbitrary, and if what matters is authenticity rather than virtue, then why not simply ravage and destroy?

The tragic tensions of Sartre's drama are quite as much political as metaphysical. You cannot fight for justice without some regulative idea of a good beyond the present, yet how is the present not then to be sacrificed for it? The just society, as the utopianist recognizes, is an end in itself; yet how is it not to be undermined by the unavoidably instrumental, morally compromised action necessary to secure it? Those who struggle for such a world may therefore be the last people to exemplify its virtues, as Bertolt Brecht comments in his poem 'To Those Born Afterwards': 'Oh we who tried to prepare the ground for friendship / Could not ourselves be friendly'. Or as one of Camus's revolutionaries insists in *The Just*, 'There *is* a warmth in the world, but it is not for us' (Act 3). A working-class activist in Raymond Williams's novel *Second Generation* comments that 'the feelings we learn from the fighting disqualify us from the peace . . . We'd be the worst people, the worst possible people, in any good society' (ch. 18). In the end, Sartre's play solves this dilemma, which Williams rightly sees as tragic, by effectively equating the autotelism of good with the egoism of evil, writing both of them off in the name of revolutionary practice. And the two certainly have enough in common to make this a plausible move. But it is also a familiar rhetorical ploy: forget about starry-eyed utopias and attend to the material struggle. Yet one has only to ask what values that struggle is meant to promote, what means are permissible to it, or how such a case differs from pragmatism and utilitarianism, for the moral questions to return.

The demonic are those who destroy others for the fun of it, a gratifyingly rare condition. Valmont and the Marquise de Merteuil of Laclos's *Les Liasions dangereuses* are leading literary contenders for this status. Pechorin, the raffish protagonist of Lermontov's *A Hero of Our Time*, also belongs to this uncommon species, with his delight in injuring others, his use of them as mere fodder for his own ego. Like the devil, he is a disenchanted idealist, having once been full of youthful dreams. Shelley's Count Cenci, who reaps a sadistic pleasure from cruelty while devoutly believing in God, is another such diabolical figure. For Sade's cult of evil, the ultimate perversity would be the transgressing of transgression itself, the destruction of the sources of destruction. But since this is impossible, the demonic desire is bound to remain dissatisfied, which is one reason why Sade's extraordinarily monotonous texts rehearse one sexual permutation after another, with all the compulsive repetition of the death drive, in their search for the ultimate perversity. Yet as long as such perversity is intelligible, it cannot be ultimate at all. Doing injury to oneself and others is the only way one can triumph over a meaningless Nature, shucking off its constraints and entering the void where all is permissible and nothing matters.[32] But this, as Dostoevsky's Ivan Karamazov understands, is a perfectly futile freedom: if your transgression demonstrates that nothing matters, then this must include the act of transgressing. It has propaganda value only, as a useful weapon in a campaign to *épater le bourgeois*.

Rare though this state of mind is, a non-evil version of it is exceedingly commonplace – indeed, in the form of self-destruction or sadomasochism, is nothing other than the death drive, which for Freud is a 'daemonic' constituent of all human existence. Freud identifies a primary masochism at the core of the human subject, which is then extroverted as sadistic aggression. Turning this instinct outwards is necessary if the organism is not to destroy itself – indeed, not only necessary but constructive, since the death drive then fuses with a sublimated form of *Eros* to master Nature and fashion civilization. Destroying others is our escaperoute from annihilating ourselves.

This is true enough of the tormented theatre of August Strindberg. The relationship between Jean and Miss Julie, for example, represents an internecine power-struggle from which both partners reap perverse pleasure, detesting and despising each other in a way which fuels their obscene enjoyment. What is uncommon is the literal destruction of others for one's delight; the metaphorical version of this, for much modern thought, is known as human relationship. And not just for modern thought. Socrates remarks on the closeness of pain and pleasure, and speculates in Aesopian style that God may have fastened their heads together to stop their perpetual quarrelling.[33] If John Dryden's excellent tragedy *All for Love* is not as compelling as Shakespeare's *Antony and Cleopatra*, it is among other things because it lacks the latter play's complex sense of perversity, its joy in dissolution. Franco Moretti sees Jacobean tragedy as 'a world whose deepest desire is for oblivion',[34] in thrall to the *jouissance* of the death drive. The deeply perverse relationship of Beatrice and De Flores in Middleton's *The Changeling*, another mistress/servant liaison, prefigures *Miss Julie*, rather as Edward Albee's *Who's Afraid of Virginia Woolf?* repeats the play with a difference.

Strindberg writes in the preface to *Miss Julie* of how he finds 'the "joy of life" in life's cruel and mighty conflicts'. In *The Dance of Death* Alice and the Captain are locked in a similarly ambivalent relationship, unable to separate since their only gratification lies in each other's pain. The play describes them as 'in hell'. As the Lawyer remarks in *A Dream Play*: 'A life tormenting each other, then! One person's pleasure is the other's pain!' It is the closest one can now approach to what used to be known as a love-relationship. 'There is no longer any place in present-day civilized life', Freud comments gloomily, 'for a simple natural love between two human beings.'[35] It is not, however, simply a matter of tragedy showing us the interweaving of love and death on stage. The play evokes a similarly ambivalent response from its audience. In this sense, the compound of discomfort and fascination with which the spectators greet the action signifies the workings in them, too, of the death drive which they see acted out before them.

Politically speaking, a perverse joy in total wrecking is either the death cult of fascism, or the extreme brand of anarchism which marks Conrad's mad professor in *The Secret Agent*, who really wants to blow up time and matter themselves and start history again from scratch. His spiritual confrère is Souvarine, the haughty, puristic revolutionary of Zola's *Germinal*, who yearns to shake the whole world to pieces along with the despicable, politically compromised proletariat. There is a similar ultra-leftist absolutism about the Jesuitical Marxist Naphta of Thomas Mann's *The Magic Mountain*, as we shall see later. The jaded Danton in Büchner's drama also dreams of an orgasmic annihilation of matter, finding the world obscenely replete: 'Nothingness has killed itself, creation is its wound' (Act 3, sc. 7). Things are just flaws or irregularities in the pure perfection of nothingness, irksome blemishes on eternity. 'Better to take it easy *under* the earth', Danton remarks, 'than dash around on top getting corns.'

D. H. Lawrence's Birkin of *Women in Love*, who longs for humankind to pass away so that some less obnoxious product of the life-force may take its place, is another such exponent of the political death drive. Birkin is perversely attracted to the idea of ultimate dissolution and decay, symbolized in the novel by the African statuette. But the image of the moon in water which he tries to shatter with a stone inexorably reforms, just as tell-tale pieces of Stevie's exploded body in *The Secret Agent* survive the bomb blast at Greenwich Observatory, the still point of the turning world. Matter is not so easily eradicated, and like some ghastly science-fiction slime will come seeping over the edges of the abyss in which one attempts to sink it without trace. If the New Jerusalem is to be built, it can only be with the chipped, crumbling bricks that we have to hand. Even so, nothing seems more ecstatically creative than the idea of total destruction, which makes rather more palpable a difference to the world than fashioning a political state or a work of art. The politics of the death drive, from Georges Sorel and Patrick Pearse to W. B. Yeats and the apologists of fascism, sees violence as a purifying force, shocking a torpid suburban civilization into new life like the bolts of electricity which the mad scientist sends through his monster.

Love struggles against death, but involves an ecstatic abandonment of the self which is death's mirror-image.[36] Life, as Pasternak's Yury Zhivago writes tenderly in one of his poems, 'is only the dissolving / Of ourselves in all others / As though in gift to them'. Thomas Buddenbrook, at the end of Thomas Mann's novel, comes to realize in a moment of epiphany that 'death was a joy, so great, so deep that it could be dreamed of only in moments of revelation like the present. It was the return from an unspeakably painful wandering, the correction of a grave mistake, the loosening of chains, the opening of doors – it put right again a lamentable mischance' (Part 10, ch. 5). Life or *Eros* is the later Freud's term for this unspeakably painful wandering, which is no more than the crooked path taken by the ego in its hunt for the bliss of extinction. It is no wonder that we seek an exit from love, which in Plato's *Symposium* is a potentially tragic quest. Racine's Phèdre is literally dying of desire, and his Hippolytus speaks of love as the author of dreadful ruins and calamities. It is scarcely a surprise that the ego, after the injurious labour of separating itself from the world, should be tempted by the easeful, fearful joy of deliquescing into it once more.

'Most terrible, although most gentle, to mankind' is how Dionysus is portrayed in *The Bacchae*. As with Christ's 'Come unto me all you who labour and I will give you rest', the god in Euripides's play brings with him forgetfulness of self and a compassionate release from toil, not least for the poor. Since he is an indiscriminate force, the emancipation he promises has no respect for rank. For *Dialectic of Enlightenment*, 'the dread of losing the self and of abrogating together with the self the barrier between oneself and other life, the fear of death and destruction, is intimately associated with a promise of happiness which threatens civilization in every moment'.[37] This Dionysian drive, which for Nietzsche is exactly what tragedy celebrates, pre-empts death by self-destruction, so that at least our extinction comes to us in pleasurable if punitive form. Dionysus, as Nietzsche remarks in *The Birth of Tragedy*, is a horrible mixture of cruelty and sensuality. If the Dionysian is ecstasy and *jouissance*, it is also the obscene enjoyment of playing ball with bits of Pentheus's mangled body. Perhaps the finest Dionysian drama of the modern period is Kleist's *Penthesilia*, an extraordinary fusion of violence and eroticism, domination and subjection, tenderness and aggression, in which the Amazon heroine, who believes in kissing men with steel and hugging them to death, tears her lover Achilles apart with her teeth. It is scarcely suitable for family entertainment. Penthesilia speaks in one modern-day translation of a kiss and a bite being 'cheek by jowl', and regrets her savaging of Achilles as 'a slip of the tongue'.[38]

The Law is not in the least averse to our delight, so long as it is the pleasure we pluck from allowing its death-dealing force to shatter us erotically to pieces. It is tender for our fulfilment, ordering us to reap morbid gratification from destroying ourselves; and the more guilt this self-odium breeds in us, the more we clamour for the Law to chastise us and so deepen our pleasure. Like all effective authorities, the Law good-heartedly encourages the participation of its subjects. In admirably paternalist spirit, it wishes us to take a hand in the business of torturing ourselves, work all by ourselves, make it appear that our self-undoing is our own doing, so that it may accomplish its ends all the more successfully.

The martyr and the demoniac are sometimes hard to distinguish, since both are steadfast for death. Both see living in the shadow of death as the only authentic way of life. Indeed, if Freud is to be credited, this is where we live whether we like it or not; but the martyr and the demoniac both make their destiny their decision, actively appropriate what we less saintly or sinful types, the moral middle classes so to speak, must simply endure as a fatality. Rilke has this distinction in mind when he contrasts *der eigne Tod*, meaning a death which somehow grows out of your life and which you personally authenticate, with *der kleine Tod*, which is death as sheer biological event, arbitrarily cutting you off. There is a parallel with the distinction we have noted in the theory of tragedy between immanence and accident. Death is indeed something which just happens; but by anticipating it one can let it put meaning in perspective, which is the message of Calderon's *Life is a Dream*. Once you come to see how fleeting and hollow most achievement is, you can relinquish your neurotic grip on pomp and power, relish the present more intensively, and live the less deceived. By accepting one's finitude one can live provisionally, not fetishizing or overvaluing existence and thus free from tragic despondency. What is tragic fact for some can become moral value for others.

Humanity is 'the only living thing that conceives of death', as the philosophical Big Daddy remarks in Tennessee Williams's *Cat on a Hot Tin Roof*. Or, as Heidegger might put it with less of a southern twang, *Dasein* is the only mode of being which can put itself into question. To address the question of one's death is to allow something to come of nothing. The demonic is the living death of those who feed like vampires or scavengers on the ruin of others, those who long to be alive but can manage only this paltry parody of it. The opposite condition, which can look disconcertingly like it, is that of the martyr, who offers her death as a gift to the living. Even if this is beyond our means, or gratifyingly doesn't come up, we can disarm death by rehearsing it here and now in the self-bestowals of life. This is the stance towards death ('we die every moment') that St Paul recommends. For some, this rehearsal or pleasurable anticipation of death is known as tragedy. Hegel writes in the *Phenomenology* that 'Death . . . is of all things the most dreadful, and to hold fast to what is dead requires the greatest strength . . . But the life of Spirit is not the life that shrinks from death and keeps itself untouched by devastation, but rather the life that endures it and maintains itself in it.'[39] It is, to be sure, no simple matter to distinguish a morbid fetishism of death from this refusal to back down from the question of one's own finitude. One would not expect any clear distinction here in reality.

Perhaps the most distinguished piece of writing we have about *Eros* and *Thanatos* is Thomas Mann's *The Magic Mountain*,[40] a novel all about that mingling of frost and fire which is what it feels like to be a fever patient. England's rather less resplendent version of it is Lawrence's *Women in Love*, though Oscar Wilde's *Salomé* is also a relevant work. The novel's concerns can be summarized in the splendid Freudian slip of one of its characters, who demands that the *Erotica* be played at the graveside of a handsome young consumptive. Life itself, Mann's novel speculates, is perhaps no more than a 'fever of matter' (p. 275), and the fever of the consumptive has the hectic flush of a bogus vitality. Life may be a kind of sickness, a sort of feverish excitation of matter which is then neither quite matter nor spirit. If so, it can scarcely be tragic, but has the non-sadness of things 'which have to do with the body and only it' (p. 27). An invalid is all body, and thus an affront to the humanist affirmation of spirit.

Love is certainly a kind of disease, being the most perverse, unstable and error-prone of our instincts, and the sacred and profane aspects of it are as impossible to distinguish as matter and spirit. Conversely, disease in a certain psychosomatic reading of it may be love transformed, desire worn on the body as a decipherable symptom. The mountain air of the novel's Swiss sanatorium brings out consumption as well as curing it, being a *pharmakos* or homeopathic unity of health and poison. Indeed, the doctor who runs the place, Behrens, may even have the illness himself. As an 'ailing physician' he is thus a *pharmakos* himself, like the wounded surgeon of T. S. Eliot's *Four Quartets*. As Mynheer Peeperkorn observes in the novel, all substances are the vehicle of both life and death, all both medicinal and poisonous; indeed therapeutics and toxicology are to his mind one and the same. Hans Castorp, in an 'incestuous abomination', is inoculated with a serum prepared from his own blood. The clinic itself, which seems an aberration from the healthy flatlands below, is also a microcosm of their endemic sickness, as the novel ends with the carnage of the First World War. *The Magic Mountain* is thus the other of Mann's great war novels, a counterpart to *Doctor Faustus*. But if the clinic therefore has the typicality of a work of art, it also shares something of art's idle, privileged decadence, as a narcissistic enclosure in which emotions become dissolute and unstable, and states of mind extravagantly intensified. And the clinic is just as evasive about death, the secret at its heart, as the militaristic rhetoric of the world below.

For all his awkwardly well-intentioned averageness, the hero Hans Castorp has an early, orgasmic encounter with the death drive. For a precious moment, he tastes 'how it must feel to be finally relieved of the burden of a respectable life and made free of the infinite realms of shame'; and he shudders 'at the wild wave of sweetness which swept over him at the thought' (p. 81). The death instinct, at least, is resolutely anti-bourgeois, a form of politics in itself. Life and death, the novel reflects, are perhaps just different viewpoints on the same reality, as indeed are the organic and the psychoanalytic, the sacred and obscene, the subjective and objective or the intuitive and scientific. The frontiers between these forms of knowledge are as indeterminate as those between matter and spirit. Death is in one sense the very acme of objectivity, since it falls utterly beyond our experience, and in another sense the very kernel of the human subject.

Humanity is suspended undecidably between the affirmation and negation of life, which is to say in this novel between the enlightened liberal humanism of Settembrini, with his Wellsian brand of progressivist rationalism, and the irrationalist death-cult of Naphta. Setttembrini's vision is both generous and racist, cosmopolitan and Eurocentric; the communistic Naphta is politically radical in his scorn for bourgeois progressivism, but dismisses the creed from a neo-feudalist viewpoint and is violently in love with death. In his patrician pessimism, moral absolutism and contempt for Enlightenment, Naphta is a full-blooded modernist in Satanic revolt against the spirit of Settembrini's modernity. An exhausted liberal humanism must now yield ground to the inhuman, archaic, formalistic and occult. What is now obsolescent is progress itself, as the clinic, where hardly anyone seems to be cured, would suggest. If Settembrini's humanism affirms the ego and seeks to rationalize death, Naphta sacrifices the ego, finding as a Jesuit that his deepest delight lies in disciplined obedience, and thus stands forth as a symbol of *Thanatos*. 'All his thoughts are voluptuous, and stand under the aegis of death' (p. 412), as the oppressively normative Settembrini comments of him; and indeed Naphta ends by shooting himself. He is the pure spirit of tragedy as the traditionalists conceive it: ascetic, elitist, sacrificial, hierarchical, anti-rationalist, spiritually absolutist, hostile to modernity.

Both Naphta and Settembrini represent a kind of death in life, which is to say a deconstruction of the polarities they are respectively meant to signify. Settembrini celebrates life yet is dying; Naphta believes in living his life with all the absolutism, formal rigour and self-sacrificial zeal of death. Death in this novel, as in *Doctor Faustus*, is on the side of both ecstatic disintegration ('release, immensity, abandon, desire' (p. 496)), and rigorous formalism. The same is true of Mann's *Death in Venice*, in which the more you sublimate life into pure form as an artist, the more of a prey to deathly dissolution you become. The more reason represses the senses, the more riotously they clamour for attention. Art shields you from a knowledge of the abyss, but in doing so helps to tip you into it. The Apollonian seeks perfection, but since nothing is more purely unblemished than nothingness, it rejoins the very formless Dionysiac sublimity it is meant to ward off. The austerely self-disciplined Aschenbach of *Death in Venice* is gripped by a 'monstrous sweetness', a Dionysian lust for death, disease and nothingness; and this is an occupational hazard of the artist, who has to approach the spirit by way of the flesh, and so can always be seduced by it en route.

Naphta's Jesuitical asceticism issues logically if incongruously in an absolutist, dogmatic strain of socialism. He is that most perverse of figures, a Catholic Marxist, an oxymoronic type whom history throws up from time to time. But there is an alternative form of death-in-life which is to affirm the human non-hubristically, in the knowledge of its frailty and finitude. This tragic humanism, which reflects Mann's own outlook, accepts the disruptiveness of death as Settembrini does not, but refuses to make a fetish of it *à la* Naphta. Settembrini preaches a version of death-in-life, but only so as to gather death into the life of reason and so disarm its terrors. For him, to see death as an independent power, 'to feel drawn to it, to feel sympathy with it, is without any doubt at all the most ghastly aberration to which man is drawn' (p. 200). With his repressive cult of health and *sanitas*, for which disease is akin to depravity, Settembrini views a perversity common to all men and women as unutterably scandalous. He does not see that true deviancy would be *not* finding death unconsciously alluring. But Naphta's morbid embrace of death is equally unacceptable. 'The recklessness of death is in life, and it would not be life without it' (p. 496), as Hans Castorp comes to realize, but this shouldn't license a vulgar Nietzscheanism, as with those grotesque inmates of the clinic who dance themselves desperately into eternity, draining the beaker of life recklessly to the final drop and dying *in dulci jubilo*.

To be human is to be ailing, as the bourgeois humanist is reluctant to acknowledge, but this ailment lies close to the sources of our achievement. Life and death are not at loggerheads: on the contrary, only by bowing to our mortality can we live fulfilledly. In his great epiphany in the Alpine snow, Hans Castorp encounters a form of sublimity from which he learns 'the fearful pleasure of playing with forces so great that to approach them nearly is destruction' (p. 477). One could find worse accounts of the disposition of the audience of a tragedy. At the heart of his moving utopian vision of love and comradeship lurks an image of the Real, the ghastly cameo of the tearing of a child's flesh, the blood-sacrifice which underpins civilization. But perhaps, Hans reflects, the comradeship he has witnessed in his vision is as sweetly courteous as it is precisely because of its silent recognition of this horror. Hans clings fast to this revelation of the human as pitched between recklessness and reason, mystic community and windy individualism, and will henceforth refuse to let death have mastery over his thoughts. It is love, not reason, he recognizes, which is stronger than death, and from that alone can come the sweetness of civilization – but 'always in silent recognition of the blood-sacrifice' (p. 496). One must honour beauty and idealism, while knowing how much blood and suffering lie at their root. The hero of this great *Bildungsroman* has now matured, and will finally leave the sanatorium to fight on the plains below as a soldier, offering his life, however misguidedly in the historical circumstances, for the benefit of others.

Chapter 10

Thomas Mann's Hedgehog

Radicals tend to be wary of the argument that tragedy had religious origins. This is partly because they usually have crudely reactionary images of religion, partly because the argument is indeed deeply suspect, but also because the association of tragedy with cult, myth and ritual is a staple of conservative scholarship. Raymond Williams speaks for a whole current of left-wing critics when he doubts the value of seeing tragedy 'in a context, however rhetorically defined, of the turn of the year and the seasons, of the dying god, the tearing to pieces in sacrifice, and a spiritual rebirth'.[1] There are a few notable exceptions to this scepticism among radical ranks, not least the Marxist classicist George Thomson, whose *Aeschylus and Athens* qualifiedly endorses the case that tragedy derives from ritual. And Eva Figes, in a feminist study of the form, examines it in terms of tribal patriarchy.[2]

In general, however, it is easy to see why radicals should be so ill-disposed to this thesis, even if one leaves aside their aversion to religion. Talk of blood sacrifice, dying gods and fertility cults smacks of a naturalization of history, an opposing of the mythic to the rational and the cyclical to the historical, along with a dubious belief that suffering is an energizing, revitalizing part of human existence. In this latter respect, the road from the plains of Argos to the playing fields of Eton is not as circuitous as one might suspect. It is the cultural ambience of the Cambridge school of anthropology and *The Waste Land*, an unholy *mélange* of Nietzscheanism and high Anglicanism which values the cultic above the commonplace, the pre-modern over the modern, natural vitality against urban decadence. It is a world of slain heroes and risen redeemers which shades easily into the Grail and Arthurian legends, and from there to the more fey dimensions of Oxford medievalism. It does not seem to have much to do with *Juno and the Paycock*.

The idea of sacrifice seems particularly insidious, combining as it does a whiff of barbarism with a streak of self-abnegation. Sacrifice means relinquishing one's own desires in the service of a master's. It has unpleasant overtones of self-repression and self-laceration, of bogus appeals to tighten one's belt in the general interest. It is what women do for men, infantrymen do for generals, or what the working class are expected to do for the benefit of all. It suggests false asceticism, anthropological exoticism, ruling-class ploys. For Jacques Lacan, sacrifice is the inauthentic desire to fill in the lack of the Other, supply the gods with what they are missing, thus blocking the traumatic recognition that the Other is intrinsically incomplete. The end of psychoanalysis is to persuade us out of our guilty placating of the superego, and into an acknowledgement that it is the lack in the Other which supports our own being.

Yet the political left should never surrender a notion too easily to its opponents. Its task is to find a radical use for such concepts if it can, not to dismiss them out of hand in a fit of pleasurable self-righteousness. One should try to salvage even apparently unpropitious ideas, since as Walter Benjamin might have said, one never knows when they might come in handy. If he himself was able to give a revolutionary twist even to the notion of nostalgia, the idea of sacrifice might also be pressed all the way through to see whether it might emerge in some more promising context. Horkheimer and Adorno give the idea such a usable meaning in *Dialectic of Enlightenment*, whatever one thinks of their theses. The modern self is the product of sacrifice or internal renunciation, as we relinquish our sensuous unity with nature in a way which is both the root of civilization and the cause of irreparable self-damage. Anyway, since *tout commence en mystique et finit en politique*, it is necessary at this point in our argument to constellate two quite different moments of history in Benjaminian fashion, and trace an improbable itinerary from the fertility cult to political revolution.

Sacrifice can mean just what the left suspects it means. But it also means that there are times when something must be dismembered in order to be renewed. If a situation is dire enough, it must be broken to be repaired. It is just the same for individual lives – not that they should be violently extinguished, since such terror is a parody of sacrifice. As Robespierre sardonically remarks in Büchner's *Danton's Death*: '[Christ] redeemed them with his blood, I redeem them with their own . . . The revolution rejuvenates humanity by hacking it to pieces' (Act 1, sc. 6). Camus's play *The Just* also turns on the paradox of killing in order to create a peaceful society. It is rather that for political change to take root we must divest ourselves of our current identities, staked as they are on a false situation, and this demands a painful process of self-abandonment. It is not clear quite how this is to be done, since one would need a remarkably strong selfhood to be able to rid oneself of it. But the point is that the sacrificial victim which matters is not a goat or a foreigner, but ourselves.[3] Those who complain with good reason that theorists of tragedy are too sanguine in seeing destruction as creative might be less ready to protest when what has to come under the hammer is themselves. To demur might suggest rather too robust a faith in one's own righteousness.

Ritual sacrifice is a kind of message to the Other, asking anxiously if it is still there and has taken cognizance of one's existence. Since such recognition can never be assured, the act must be compulsively repeated. It traditionally involves propitiation, soothing the rancour of the gods with a burnt offering. The Yahweh of the Old Testament has occasional bouts of irritability over this practice, brusquely informing the Israelites that their burnt offerings stink in his nostrils, and demanding that they do something instead to protect the weak from the violence of the rich. 'I have had enough of burnt offerings of rams and the fat of fed beasts', he declares in a bilious assault on religion, 'Bring no more vain offerings; incense is an abomination to me . . . seek justice, correct oppression; defend the fatherless, plead for the widow' (Isaiah 1: 11, 17). Or in the Book of Amos: 'I hate, I despise your feasts . . . Even though you offer me your burnt offerings and cereal offerings, I shall not accept them . . . But let justice roll down like waters, and righteousness like an ever-flowing stream' (Amos 5: 21–4). The New Testament will dramatically invert the usual idea of sacrifice by making God himself the victim. But in general the value of ancient sacrifice lies in harnessing the power of the gods. Tragedy is in this sense a humanistic displacement of religion, since now the value which emerges from destruction is not so much that of the gods as of the victim herself. Indeed, the victim takes on a strange kind of divinity precisely by being taken apart. The only authentic power is one which springs from a transformation of weakness.

Walter Benjamin draws our attention to what he sees as a double meaning of tragic sacrifice – as an atonement or expiation which deflects divine wrath, but also as 'the representative deed in which new contents of the life of a people announce themselves'.[4] Sacrifice is the performative act which brings a new social order into being. As Simon Sparks puts it, 'tragic sacrifice is the site of a transformation from the order of the gods to that of the life of the community', and the hero marks 'the fissure between the two, the point of the violent passing over from one to the other'.[5] This, to be sure, is the way that the epistles of St Paul and the Letter to the Hebrews seem to understand Christ's sacrifice, as one which has rendered the old cultic kind of sacrifice redundant, relegated it to the antique order. As the author of Hebrews puts it: 'He entered once and for all into the Holy Place [of sacrifice], taking not the blood of goats and calves but his own blood' (Hebrews 9: 11).

This definitive consigning of ritual sacrifice to the past involves redefining it in ethical rather than cultic terms as a self-giving for others. The slain king becomes the suffering servant of others, a parody of a god or hero. This is why sacrifice is the act which grounds and maintains the community itself. As a mutual self-giving, it is no longer an esoteric ritual but the structure of sociality. This, however, is no new-fangled Christian invention; it is part of the Jewish Law. Mark puts into the mouth of a Jewish scribe who encounters Jesus the opinion that 'to love one's neighbour as oneself is much more than all whole burnt offerings and sacrifices' (Mark 12: 33). No pious Jew would disagree with that, despite Mark's grossly tendentious views of the Pharisees (actually the theological wing of the militantly anti-colonialist Zealots) as hard-hearted legalists. But this does not put paid to the business of sacrifice, since to establish justice and compassion will involve exactly that, in the shape of dismantling the old world to build it anew.

Most theory of tragedy is a hangover from the old days of cult, a version of antique ritual updated for modern consumption. Rather than finding the value of tragic sacrifice in ethical terms, it sees such destruction as somehow valuable in itself, thus regressing to notions of the fertilizing power released by the mutilated god. In this sense, it undoes the ethical reinterpretation of the natural which is central to the Judaic tradition. The Old Testament is among other things a record of Yahweh's unenviable struggle to persuade his people that he is not a nature god to be appeased or manipulated, but the god of freedom and justice. Ritual sacrifice continues, but its meaning has now to be grasped in this context, as the symbolic affirmation of a community in which cult takes second place to justice and liberation. And the crucial test of these values is what the Hebrew scriptures call the *anawim*, meaning the destitute and dispossessed. St Paul refers to them rather colourfully as 'the shit of the earth'. The *anawim* are the dregs and refuse of society, its tragic scapegoats. They are the flotsam and jetsam of history who do not need to abandon themselves to be remade, since they are lost to themselves already. And it is with them that Yahweh identifies. He will be known for what he is, in the words of Luke 1: 53, when you see the mighty cast down and the lower orders exalted, the hungry filled with good things and the rich sent away empty. The true sacrificial figure, the one which like the burnt offering will pass from profane to powerful, loss of life to fullness of it, is the propertyless and oppressed.

The scapegoat or *pharmakos* has a long history in tragic thought. Tragedy means 'goat song', but it might perhaps be better translated as 'scapegoat song'. It may be that Greek tragedy has some roots in animal sacrifice,[6] though the question is controversial. Pickard-Cambridge and Gerald Else think there is no evidence to suggest that the Greek theatre derives from ritual or religion, from hero cults, Eleusinian mysteries or indeed from the cult of Dionysus.[7] The origins of the art form are shadowy, and Georges Bataille describes it somewhat hyperbolically as 'the least explained of all the "mysteries" '.[8] If it is indeed a Dionysian form, it contains precious little allusion to the god. But the genetic issue aside, the figure of the scapegoat is clearly central to a certain strain of tragedy. At the annual rite of Thargelia in ancient Greece, the pollution accumulated by the city during the previous year was expelled by selecting for purification two *pharmakoi*, chosen from among the most destitute and deformed of the city, who were housed and maintained by the state and fed on certain special foods, then paraded through the streets, struck on the genitals, thrust out of town and in early times perhaps even put to death. One could be, so to speak, a professional *pharmakos*, as one cannot really be a professional martyr; but this is logical, since the whole point of the scapegoat is its anonymity, as a human being emptied of subjectivity and reduced to refuse or nothingness. When it comes to victimage, anyone will do. Or at least anyone of a suitably degraded status. Because being rescued from that status would demand a universal transformation, this desolate, abandoned figure is a negative sign of social totality.

The *pharmakos* is symbolically loaded with the guilt of the community, which is why it is selected from among the lowest of the low. It is then thrust out into the wilderness, the symbol of a traumatic horror which we dare not contemplate. Yet in thus representing the community and having the power to deliver it from its trespasses, it is an inverted image of the king, who is likewise a representative figure charged with the health of the *polis*. In the figure of the scapegoat, the borders between power and weakness, sacred and profane, central and peripheral, sickness and health, poison and cure, are accordingly blurred. The scapegoat is a holy terror, a 'guilty innocent'[9] like Prometheus, another outcast whose simultaneous theft and gift of fire recalls the doubleness of the *pharmakos*. As E. R. Dodds remarks, 'the *pharmakos* is neither innocent nor guilty',[10] inhabiting like the subjectively innocent but objectively polluted Oedipus some indeterminate zone between the two. Both ruler and scapegoat are free of the laws of the city, the former by being set above them and the latter by falling below them. To be sacred is to be marked out, set apart, and thus to resemble the criminal or outsider; human *pharmakoi* were sometimes recruited from the local gaols. The criminal has come into contact with the gods, however negatively, and thus retains something of that aura. As René Girard comments: 'Because the victim is sacred, it is criminal to kill him – but the victim is sacred only because he is killed'.[11]

The scapegoat incarnates dirt, deformity, madness and criminality, and rather like the insane of classical antiquity, it is both shunned and regarded with respectful awe. This unclean thing is a substitute for the people, and thus stands in a metaphorical relation to them; but it also acts as a displacement for their sins, and is in that sense metonymic. In burdening it with their guilt, the people at once acknowledge their frailty and disavow it, project it violently outside themselves in the slaying of the sacrificial victim or its expulsion beyond their political frontiers. The victim is thus both themselves and not themselves, both a thing of darkness they acknowledge as their own as well as a convenient object on which to off-load and disown their criminality. Both pity and fear, identity and otherness, are at stake. The scapegoat must be neither too foreign nor too familiar; it must be in Lacan's term *ex-time*, different enough to dread and loathe, yet enough of a mirror-image to be a credible point of displacement for one's sins. As such, it bears an oblique relation to the Freudian notion of the uncanny, another ambiguous phenomenon caught between life and death, the strange and the familiar.[12] It is a 'monstrous double',[13] as indeed is the word 'sacred' itself, which in Latin can mean both holy and accursed. The *pharmakos*, being both poison and cure,[14] symbol of both transgression and redemption, has a homeopathic doubleness rather like *catharsis*, which similarly provokes sickness in order to cure it.

Pity and fear reflect here alternative political agendas. To fear the scapegoat is to load it with whatever ails the *polis* and thrust it beyond its limits, so that the status quo may be purged and strengthened. Sacrifice in this sense is a consolidation, not a revolution. To pity the *pharmakos*, however, is to identify with it, and so to feel horror not of it but of the social order whose failure it signifies. The scapegoat, itself beyond speech and sociality, becomes a judgement on that order in its very being, embodying what it excludes, a sign of the humanity which it expels as so much poison. It is in this sense that it bears the seeds of revolutionary agency in its sheer passivity; for anything still active and engaged, however dissidently, would still be complicit with the *polis*, speaking its language and thus unable to put it into question as a whole. Only the silence of the scapegoat will do this.

Charles Segal writes that 'Greek tragedy . . . operates both within and beyond the limits of the *polis*, at the borders where polarities merge, definitions become unclear, the orderly composition of human institutions becomes ambiguous'.[15] The tragic hero in Segal's view demonstrates the necessity of order by infringing it, and so has a foot in both camps. And the drama itself is hybrid in this respect, releasing the forces of disorder within an artistic form which contains them. Tragedy breaks down the barriers between gods, humans and beasts; and the *pharmakos*, a human being thrust down to the depths of animal destitution yet thereby curiously sacred, combines something of all three species. The great *pharmakos* of Greek tragedy, as Segal recognizes, is Oedipus – in Adrian Poole's words, 'the paradigm of doubleness, monstrous but still familiar, and the same but two and different'.[16] As Francis Fergusson writes, 'The figure of Oedipus himself fills all the requirements of the scapegoat, the dismembered king or god-figure'.[17] But Antigone, described by Creon as derelict and abandoned, is another such incarnate ambiguity. As indeed is Philoctetes, that monstrous outcast from human society who is at once blessed and cursed, crippled and potent, fearful and pitiful. Marooned between life and death, he is a rotting human body which will nonetheless prove historically fertile.

The *pharmakos* is at once holy and terrifying, and thus has something of the dual structure of the sublime. But whereas the sublime beggars description by soaring above it, the scapegoat puts paid to speech by falling below it, slipping through the net of discourse into sheer brute ineffability. It is that which is cut off from language, about which there is absolutely nothing to be said – all those violently disfigured creatures who have strayed beyond the frontier of the human into some ghastly life-in-death limbo beyond it. Rebuffing the claims of the symbolic order, such creatures – or rather the Abrahams, Lears, Oedipuses and Antigones who represent them – inaugurate a revolutionary ethics by their death-dealing, heroically tenacious commitment to another order of truth altogether, a truth which discloses the negativity of the subject rather than legitimating a positive regime, and which figures for Jacques Lacan as the terrifying abyss of the Thing or the Real.[18] Such figures represent a truth which the system must suppress in order to function; yet since they therefore have the least investment in it of any social group, they also have the strange, hallowed power to transform it. They incarnate the inner contradictions of the social order, and so symbolize its failure in their own. The demonic see nothing in value but shit, whereas it is in shit that the revolutionary finds value. Holy shit, as they say. Evil finds its own lack of being unbearable, and seeks to plug this gap with the plundered lives of others. Rather than confronting this frightful abyss in itself, it is prepared to will the loathsome and excremental, the mad and meaningless. The rite of the *pharmakos*, by contrast, recognizes that non-being is the only path to true identity, and that to embrace this dissolution can be life-giving rather than annihilating.

Oedipus, as Poole remarks, is a doubled subject, as indeed is humanity in general, caught contradictorily between gods and beasts. The
theatre is itself an image of this dual condition, since gods there have
anyway to be represented by humans. The themes of incarnation and
hybridity, difference and identity, demi-gods and god-men, are built into
the theatrical apparatus itself. Humanity is a riddle, definable only by
paradox and aporia. It is open like the Sphinx's conundrum to conflicting readings, a question which is its own solution since it can be defined
only in terms of itself. Oedipus the decipherer of enigmas is himself an
enigma he cannot decipher.[19] The unknowable, the Kantian *noumenon*, is
humanity itself, constituted as it is by something which is centrally
missing. And this enigma in Sophocles's drama is also the riddling or
garbling of incest, which scrambles or telescopes the various stages of life
(youth/age, parent/child) which the sphinx's riddle lays out in sequence.
Incest erases boundaries, as does Oedipus's answer to the sphinx's query.
The human confounds categories just like the sphinx itself, composite of
bird, lion and woman.

But Oedipus is also dual because he is both Law and transgressor, *énon-
ciation* and *énoncé*, a split subject 'spoken' by the discourse of the Other
(the gods) in a way at odds with his conscious identity, receiving his true
selfhood back from that oracular Other in enigmatic form. With his usual
managerial efficiency, he is successful in ridding Thebes of its curse; it is
just that the curse turns out to be himself. Oedipus is *tyrannos*, meaning
a self-made king, proud of his self-dependence and forensic powers. Marrying your mother and becoming your own father is doubtless the nearest
you can come to being entirely self-generated. Yet something quite alien
acts and speaks in him, persisting as a riddling subtext within his speech,
decentring his imaginary selfhood and finally destroying him.

This is the true sense in which, as Freud suggests, Oedipus is all of us,
not because we are all potential parricides or aspiring mother-lovers. As
with the rest of us, there is a gap between his objective location in the
symbolic order and his imaginary idea of himself, between what he is for
the Other and what he is for himself. He is what he is – king, husband,
father – only by virtue of this separation. The truth of the ego does not
coincide with the truth of the subject, divided as they are by some fatal
slippage or opacity; but Oedipus will never be more estranged from
himself than when these two registers merge in the terrible light of recognition. To come to selfhood is to acknowledge your self-alienation, the
fact that subjectivity just is the process whereby the self constantly gives
itself the slip. Oedipus is both king of Thebes and stranger to the city,
both kinsman and exile. In being too intimate with the other, the wife-
mother or husband-father, you are blinded to your own being, since it

depends on distance and otherness for its constitution. Too much probing into the poisoned sources of your identity will put out your eyes.

Oedipus, as we have seen, is divided in his very name between knowledge and monstrosity – between *oida* ('know') and *oidieo* ('swell', 'be swollen'), referring to his wounded foot. There is a fissure in his name between the enlightened subject of cognition and the obscure trauma which brings it to birth. Simon Goldhill adds other possible word-plays on his name ('I don't know', 'I suppose', 'Know where'), observing that 'the name of the king is excessive, overdetermined in its excess'.[20] When you come to self-knowledge, you confront yourself as a piece of deformity. Oedipus believed that he was equated with the gods; but the Chorus has added up the total of the life of this man so talented in working out equivalences, and finds that it amounts to zero.[21] The swollen foot is the sign of a secret history of dependency upon others;[22] but it is an acknowledgement of these lowly dependencies and material affinities which prevents you from being a monster in the literal sense of a self-sufficient beast.

So it is that in casting himself out, Oedipus recognizes his own pollution and arrives at Colonus as the *pharmakos*, the reviled, unclean thing which will prove the city's salvation. Redemption lies in taking to oneself this obscene disfigurement of humanity, as Theseus welcomes the wounded king into his city. In doing so, he learns to pity what he fears. 'I come to offer you a gift – my tortured body – a sorry sight', Oedipus informs him, 'but there is value in it more than beauty'. Something has come of nothing, as the defiled body of the parricide is transformed into a sacred totem to protect the city. As the Chorus comments: 'Surely a just God's hand will raise him up again'. From identifying with the besmirched and contaminated, a great power for good is bound to flow.

It is in this sense that value and tragic suffering finally converge – not that destruction is an inherent good, but that when humanity reaches its nadir it becomes a symbol of everything that cries out for transformation, and so a negative image of that renewal. 'Am I made a man in this hour when I cease to be?' Oedipus wonders aloud when he arrives at Colonus. Such change can spring only from a full acknowledgement of the extremity of one's condition. If even *this* can be salvaged, then there is hope indeed; but unless the promise of redemption extends even to the flesh of those like Oedipus who are destitute and polluted, then it is ultimately worthless. In this sense, tragedy of this kind is itself a *pharmakos*, both gift and threat, power and weakness. 'Through tragedy', writes Adrian Poole, 'we recognize and refeel our sense of both the value and the futility of human life, or both its purposes and its emptiness.'[23]

This dual vision is marked in ancient Greece, with its sense of the human as both precious and precarious, its affirmation of culture along with the dark forces which threaten it with dissolution. Perhaps it is this tenacious Greek belief in civility on the one hand and the turbulent powers which ravage it on the other which lays the foundation for tragedy, as it does in the writings of the later Freud. Certainly Plato discerns something of this scapegoat-like ambiguity in the poet himself, a representative figure who must nevertheless be driven into exile. For Nietzsche and Romanticism later, the poet is both holy and accursed because as the bearer of a dreadful knowledge he peers into the foundations and finds instead a bottomless abyss. If the power to gaze unflinchingly into that depth makes him quasi-divine, the infinite emptiness of it makes him a signifier of nothingness.

The scapegoat represents a kind of death-in-life, and so is a more positive version of the living death of evil. Evil, which reaps a sham sort of vitality from destruction, is a parody of the martyr or sacrificial victim who plucks life from death. Slavoj Žižek writes of Oedipus that 'he has lived the "human condition" to the bitter end, realizing its most fundamental possibility; and for that very reason, he is in a way "no longer human", and turns into an inhuman monster, bound by no human laws or considerations'.[24] The monster is in this sense as lordly as the monarch. To press the human all the way through is to find the other-than-human installed at its heart. Oedipus, Žižek argues, is 'less than nothing, the embodiment of some unspeakable horror', one of those who like Lear have trespassed beyond the limits of humanity and entered that hellish realm of horror and psychosis which the ancient Greeks call *ate*. It is a liminal domain suspended between life and death, in which a human being 'encounters the death drive as the utmost limit of human experience, and pays the price by undergoing a radical "subjective destitution", by being reduced to an excremental remainder'.[25] In Christian terms it is Christ's descent into hell, sign of his solidarity with torment and despair.

Christ is one of many tragic scapegoats thrust beyond the city and sacrificially dismembered, reduced to a piece of butcher's meat in a savage parody of kingship. In St Paul's phrase, he is 'made sin' for our sake, and the gospel writers portray him as a type of the *anawim*. The protagonist of Graham Greene's *The End of the Affair* is embarrassed and disgusted by God's vulgar vulnerability, the way he lays himself so artlessly open to being hurt by human beings. In the Christian eucharist as in ancient sacrifice, symbolic identification with the *pharmakos* is not just a mental attitude or political predilection. It takes the scandalously literal form of actually eating the body of the scapegoat. In linking oneself with this abject animal, absorbing this nauseating piece of matter into one's flesh, one proclaims a solidarity with what the social order has rejected as so much shit. The cannibalism of the Catholic Mass is the latest version of the fertility cult.

Nobody actually eats King Lear, though this is one of the few mishaps not to befall him. No doubt someone would have got round to it, had the drama stretched to another act. One of the chief doublenesses of this play involves a conflict between bodiliness and consciousness – the former being the sign of our material species-life, what we share in common with the other beasts, and the latter signifying our potentially overweening desire. In banishing Cordelia, Lear cuts himself off from his own material life and the creative constraints of kinship, leaving his consciousness to consume itself in a void. In madness, the mind ranges impotently beyond the body's frontiers, able to destroy its very substance; Edgar tells us that he eats poisonous matter when seized by devils. Lear's own mind is so anguished that it numbs his body to the storm around him: 'When the mind's free / The body's delicate; this tempest in my mind / Doth from my senses take all feeling else, / Save what beats there' (Act 3, sc. 4). Gloucester, once blinded, will learn to 'see feelingly', allow his perceptions to be shaped by the constraining, commiserating body. As he is forced to 'smell his way to Dover', his body will become a mode of communication with the world less treacherous than the verbal trickery of his bastard son Edmund.

It is this arduous rediscovery of the body and material constraint which Lear must also be forced through: 'They told me I was everything; 'tis a lie – I am not ague-proof' (Act 4, sc. 6). He has, he remarks, 'smelt out' this truth, and by opening himself to his own finitude or cypher-like status he becomes in the play's complex calculus a determinate something rather than an illusory everything. *King Lear*, like several of Shakespeare's works, plays on 'all', 'nothing', 'something', 'everything' as recurrently as *King Oedipus* conjugates 'all', 'one', 'several', 'zero'. To know your own nothingness is to negate the negation and become an entity at once less grandiose and more definitive than some kingly 'all'. The Fool, 'Lear's shadow', knows in his Socratic way that the wise man is he who knows he knows nothing. Lear himself will be ruthlessly cut down from regal sovereignty to tragic scapegoat, left mad, naked, destitute, disfigured and betrayed. The hubristic fantasies which have to be hacked to the bone are in his case so extravagant that the process of purging them is one which he will not survive.

The play is not about the emergence of new life from this sacrificial self-divestment. It is rather about the fact that if such life is ever to labour through, as it does in the Last Comedies, it can only be as a result of such drastic self-abandonment. Edgar makes the point when he reflects that 'To be worst, / The lowest and most dejected thing of fortune, / Stands still in esperance, lives not in fear. / The lamentable change is from the best; / The worst returns to laughter' (Act 4, sc. 1). Or, as Ross declares in *Macbeth*, 'Things at the worst will cease, or else climb upward / To what they were before' (Act 4, sc. 2). If you can fall no further, then the only direction is up. To know the worst is to be free of fear. It is in this sense that the scapegoat is a foretaste of a less brutal world precisely in its dereliction. That this is so, however, is because of the extremity of the condition which needs transfiguring. It is not a good in itself, and it is tragic that it should be necessary. Otherwise one would be faced with a version of political catastrophism – the ultra-leftist heresy that the worse a political situation grows, the better it is for the forces of change.

What really numbs the body in this play is not madness but wealth. Too many material goods blunt your capacity for fellow-feeling, swaddling the senses from exposure to the indigence of others:

> Take physic, pomp;
> Expose thyself to feel what wretches feel,
> That thou mayest shake the superflux to them,
> And show the heavens more just . . . (Act 3, sc. 4)

> Let the superfluous and lust-dieted man
> That slaves your ordinance, that will not see
> Because he does not feel, feel your power quickly;
> So distribution should undo excess,
> And each man have enough. (Act 4, sc. 1)

Rarely have political economy and the physical senses been so intimately coupled, except perhaps in Marx's *Economic and Philosophical Manuscripts*. If we could divest ourselves of the abstract consciousness which comes from blunting the body with a surplus of goods, we would be able to feel on our pulses the misery of those dispossessed by our wealth, and be moved to shed our superfluity by sharing it with them, thus converting an injurious excess into a creative one. The play has thus argued its way up from the body to communism, as indeed does the young Marx. If you want to emancipate the senses, you have to alter social relations. *King Lear* is all about the ambiguities of superfluity, which in one sense lends humanity its value and in another sense offers to undo it. When Lear is insolently asked why he needs a retinue of knights, he responds:

O, reason not the need! Our basest beggars
Are in the poorest things superfluous.
Allow not nature more than nature needs,
Man's life is cheap as beasts. (Act 2, sc. 4)

There is no *reason* why men and women should delight in what is more than strictly necessary for their physical survival, a superfluity known as culture. It is, ironically, part of their natures to do so. It is constitutive of the human animal that its demand should outstrip its need. A capacity for gratuitously transgressing its material limits is actually built into its being. The supplement of culture is no mere superaddition to human nature, but is needed to fill a structural lack at its core. *King Lear* sees this, but it also sees that there is only a thin line between this creative kind of surplus and a destructive one. Forgiveness is a lavish overflowing of the measure, a refusal to calculate equivalences; but this sort of benign excess must be distinguished from Lear's hubris, the grotesquely inflated discourse of his daughters, or the foppishness of the overbred Oswald. Conversely, to be precise may be constructive, as Cordelia's dutiful exactitudes in the first scene of the play contrast with her sisters' self-interested hyperbole; but precision is also what we share with the other animals in all the worst ways, in the form of a ruthless utility for which the gratuitous is merely a waste, or an inability to be anything but true to one's pitiless nature. Self-fashioning has its virtues as well as its perils.

At the end of *King Lear* Edgar counsels us to 'Speak what we feel, not what we ought to say' (Act 5, sc. 3). It seems a trite enough tag with which to round off so mighty a drama. Yet the implications of this apparent banality ('Be sincere!') run right to the heart of the play's concerns. Speaking must be shaped by feeling – or, as Emmanuel Levinas might put it, the subject must be *subject*, open to the passivity of its senses, a creature of sentience and sensibility.[26] 'Only a being that eats can be for the other', Levinas remarks – or, in Simon Critchley's gloss, 'only such a being can know what it means to give its bread to the other from out of its own mouth'.[27] In the early scenes of *King Lear* this is exactly what Lear does not know; he has yet to be subjected, in every sense of the term. To acknowledge one's creatureliness is to recognize one's dependence. Human dependency is prior to freedom, and must provide the ground of it. 'In what must be the shortest refutation of Heidegger', Critchley comments, 'Levinas complains that *Dasein* is never hungry.'[28] Ethics for Levinas, as Critchley puts it, involves a 'corporeal obligation' to the other, as Lear has come to recognize by the time of his great 'naked wretches' speech. Alasdair MacIntyre speaks in his *Dependent Rational Animals* of our rationality as being part of our animality, not what distinguishes us from it. For much contemporary theorizing of the body, however, Edgar has his priorities the wrong way round. Bodiliness is not dependency but political autonomy, a somatic version of the self-determining subject; and it is not a question of shaping language to the sentient body, but of recognizing that the body is constructed by language.

The Judaeo-Christian tradition plucks an ethico-political meaning from the cyclical cult of sacrifice and seasonal round of fertility. Rather than leaving them behind as so much benighted paganism, it reads them in a fresh light. The natural now becomes a metaphor for the ethical and historical. But in doing so one must be careful not to *over*-humanize the natural, and so hubristically overshoot it. Perhaps this is the point of the *Oresteia*'s final incorporation of the holy, horrible Furies into the democratic settlement. You must not ethicize, politicize and historicize to the point where you forget about humanity's roots in a recalcitrant otherness which we share with stoats and asteroids. Modern-day left-historicisms have been largely deaf to this caveat. Tragedies like those of Oedipus and Lear thus retain a trace of the archaic as a kind of drag or ballast within the historical, a reminder that whatever our civilized achievements we remain an arbitrary outcropping of Nature, monstrous or amphibious animals who straddle two domains and will never be quite at home in either.

Perhaps one reason why there is no postmodern tragedy to speak of is that postmodernism, in its belief that culture goes all the way down, has repressed this difficult duality. It is true that there is no value or meaning without culture; but culture depends for its existence on material forces which have no meaning or value in themselves. This is the inhuman 'barbarism' which modernism detects at the root of civility; and the problem is how to acknowledge this darkness without being claimed by it, how to confess the fragility of culture without being duped by its foes. This is a tragic dilemma, not least for the ancient Greeks. The forces from which civic virtue has been laboriously wrested must not be allowed to wreck those values; but neither must that civility be allowed to sap the very energies which sustain it. It is hard to see how civilization is not to be sabotaged by the powers which hold it in place. But you can try, as with the ceremonial enshrining of the Eumenides, to propitiate these powers by turning their aggression outwards as a protection of the *polis*. Athena warns her people at the end of the *Oresteia* that they 'must never banish terror from the gates'. Sublimity has its political uses.

Postmodern theory tends to value the abject and marginal, which is one face of the *pharmakos*. But it is slow to recognize its other, more constructive aspect – its role in the building of a new social order, one based this time on the Real, on a mutual confession of finitude and frailty, rather than on fantasies of self-fashioning and endless pliability. For some postmodern thought, prejudiced as it is in its Romantic-libertarian way against social order as such, this would no doubt count as an 'appropriation' of the abject to the cause of a tyrannical new consensus. Indeed, in some postmodern eyes, 'tyrannical' and 'consensus' seem more or less synonymous, a fact which might come as a mighty surprise to those who toppled apartheid or Bulgarian neo-Stalinism.

The point, however, is not just to champion or sentimentalize this reviled, disgusting excrement of the current power-system, but to recognize in it the uncanny power to transform the system itself. Thrust out of the city, the scapegoat can turn this exile to advantage, building a new habitation beyond the walls. That which the builder has rejected as a *skandalon* or stumbling-block will become the cornerstone. Or as Marx puts it rather less biblically: 'A class must be formed . . . which is the dissolution of all classes, a sphere of society which has a universal character because its sufferings are universal, and which does not claim a *particular redress* because the wrong which is done to it is not a *particular* wrong but wrong in general'.[29] This conundrum of a class which is not a class, at once the supreme expression and final dissolution of class society as such, is suspended like the *pharmakos* between identity and non-identity, symbolic like the scapegoat of universal wrong and thus with the secret power to repair it. The process which Marx describes here is a classically tragic one.

Thomas Mann's *The Holy Sinner* contains an extraordinary parody of this condition. In this novel the *pharmakos* is represented not by the proletariat but by a hedgehog. Consumed with guilt, the incestuous Gregorius casts himself Oedipus-like out of human society, and in his search for a place of ultimate isolation ends up chained to a rock in the middle of a lake. Here he remains for seventeen years, his body gradually shrinking beneath the invasion of the elements until he comes to resemble 'a prickly, bristly moss-grown nature-thing' (ch. 24). Meanwhile, the Vatican is searching for a new pope, and learns in a vision that he is to be found chained to a rock in the wilderness. It is by this mildly improbable process that a furry, hedgehog-like creature becomes Pope Gregory the Great. Perhaps he would have done less harm had he stayed perched on his rock.

Gregorius becomes little more than a natural object in the course of his long penance; and there is a sense in which the *pharmakos* is the very paradigm of that nowadays much derided notion, objectivity. To strive for objectivity of judgement in fact demands a fair amount of courage, realism, openness, modesty, self-discipline and generosity of spirit; there is nothing in the least bloodless about it. But the true paradigm of objectivity is not epistemological but ethical. The model of objectivity is a selfless attention to another's needs. Sacrifice presses this to a dramatic extreme, converting the self into an object in the public realm, a self-for-others which in its sheer inert materiality, its utter inconsiderableness, reminds us by stark contrast of the arrogance of power and presumptuousness of desire. Clym Yeobright is brought to this condition at the end of Thomas Hardy's *The Return of the Native*, the curbing of his ambition symbolized by his loss of sight.

This is not a condition to rest in, as Thomas Mann's frozen hedgehog conspicuously does not. Passing one's life as an inert material object is hardly the last word in emancipation. Life as a frost-bitten mammal is scarcely the *summum bonum*. Objectivity, the self-for-others, is only a basis for freedom and well-being if it happens all round. If it is not reciprocal then it is simply the dismal condition we have now, in which some squander their lives in the name of pampering others. Only by a mutual recognition of finitude, frailty and material needs can such objectivity become the basis of an emancipated world. But the pathos of this condition is, so to speak, an object-lesson in how drastically out of hand desire has grown if, to purge it, we are in need of this savage cutting down to size. As the Duke of *Measure for Measure* comments, 'there is so great a fever on goodness that the dissolution of it must cure it' (Act 3, sc. 2). To transform the subject involves not wishing objectivity away, but pressing its implications all the way through. It is in this sense that there is an internal bond between virtue and materialism.

'Granted that disorder spoils pattern', writes the anthropologist Mary Douglas, 'it also provides the materials of pattern.'[30] It is this dialectical movement which much current radical thought overlooks. For some tribal cultures, so Douglas argues, dirt secretes a sacred power because it disrupts set categories. It is a destabilizing force which must be eliminated if order is to be maintained, so that 'reflection on dirt involves reflection on the relation of order to disorder, being to non-being, form to formlessness, life to death'.[31] As disorganized matter, stuff which is out of place, dirt represents a threat to the political structure, one associated with the amorphous, subversive power of the sacred. And this power can be felt especially on the margins and in the interstices of social life, at the ragged edges where it blends into chaos.

So far, there is nothing in the case to disturb a deconstructionist. But there is no simple opposition here between the power of the margins and the oppressiveness of the centre. For the intricately wrought social structures which define the identity of certain tribal peoples are also, so Douglas insists, expressions of sacred power. There is something sacred about collective meanings, as well as about the disruption of them. The non-institutionalized forces which lap up against the edges of society threaten to dissolve it to so much shapeless slime; but they also constructively question its categories. If these forces are encountered unflinchingly, they can be carried back into social life in a movement of renewal. 'That which is rejected is ploughed back for a renewal of life.'[32] Douglas comments on a ritual in which the most unclean animal is taken and eaten: 'By the mystery of that rite they recognize something of the fortuitous and conventional nature of the categories in whose mould they have their experience'.[33] 'When someone embraces freely the symbols of death', she observes, '. . . a great release of power for good is bound to follow.' Perhaps tragedy is not, after all, an experience confined to the West.

The effect of these rituals is no doubt for the most part conservative. In challenging its own categories, the system displays its resilience; in ploughing back what was rejected, it gains a new lease of life. Yet this need not be the only politics of dirt. Dirt is not a good in itself, any more than social order is. It becomes 'sacred' only when it refashions that order on the basis of what it shuts out. And this is a movement of both dissolution and reconstruction, the sacred as both structure and anti-structure, which is quite different from multicultural 'inclusiveness'. It is not a question of incorporating cast-off groups in ways which bolster the given system. On the contrary, it is a matter of grasping the excluded as a sign of what it is in that order which must be broken and remade at its very root.

This sacrificial rhythm is by no means definitive of tragedy as a whole. There are plenty of tragedies without scapegoats, ritual slaughter or turbulent transitions from death to life. And there are some in which this rhythm is present, but so faintly that it is hard to recognize. In Miller's *Death of a Salesman* what used to be the redemptive blood of the martyr takes the rather less exalted form of an insurance policy, which Willy Loman knows will benefit his family after his death. Even so, there would seem to be some family resemblances in this respect between ancient fertility ritual, the cult of the *pharmakos* and tragic art. Walter Benjamin's theory of tragedy is particularly relevant in this respect. Sacrifice for Benjamin is an act of liberation: through the death of the hero, the community comes to consciousness of its subjection to mythological forces. But history, the opposite of mythology in this respect, is for Benjamin by no means to be commended in its stead. On the contrary, *Trauerspiel* or German tragic drama is marked by a sense of the vacuousness of secular history, which is bleached of absolute value. Yet Benjamin has his own version of the *pharmakos*. For when this sluggish, faithless realm is pressed to an extreme, it can become a negative image of salvation. As Richard

Wolin puts it: 'only a perspective which was utterly convinced of the wretchedness, profanity, and insignificance of all natural, earthly existence was deemed capable [by *Trauerspiel*] of rising above the ruins of mere life and gaining access to the realm of salvation'.[34] The worst, once more, is the only place to start.

For Benjamin, then, it is as though history is so bankrupt that some salvific epiphany must inevitably be trembling on its brink. The destitution of history is a negative index of a redemption beyond it. The mounting heap of rubble which is historical life proclaims the need for a salvation which can arrive only with the devaluation of all worldly objects. Nature is fleeting and decaying, but this transience is itself a sign of the Messianic passing away of history itself. The sickness of history thus becomes, homeopathically, its own cure. The later Marxist Benjamin will find a similar kind of dialectical reversal in the commodity, an object so drained of immanent meaning that it is released for revolutionary new uses. Something of the same might be said of Georg Lukács's idea of the proletariat, which comes to emancipatory awareness of itself precisely by being degraded to an object. 'Such redemption as [*Trauerspiel*] knows', Benjamin writes, 'resides in the depths of this destiny (i.e. historical hopelessness) rather than in the fulfilment of a divine plan of salvation.'[35] Messianic time is thus the opposite of teleology: redemption is not what history immanently brings forth, but what arises from its ruins. Hope and history travel in different directions, as the former is thrown into relief by the bleakness of the latter. As Ernst Bloch reminds us in *The Principle of Hope*, even despair projects a future, even if it is one of nothingness.

Suspicions of the idea of sacrifice, however, are not dispelled so easily, not least when the protagonist of the action is a woman. Hester Prynne of Nathaniel Hawthorne's *The Scarlet Letter* is such a sacrificial victim, cast out of the community but soon to prove herself a holy sinner and a symbol of humanity to others. The scarlet letter she wears is a sign of capacity as well as transgression, signifying 'Able' as well as 'Adultery'. Publicly traduced herself, she is all the more capable of succouring others in dire straits, converting her polluted status into a source of power. Ejected from the moral structure of society, 'she had wandered, without rule or guidance, in a moral wilderness' (ch. 18), marooned in the liminal space of the classical scapegoat; but this is also an ambiguous form of emancipation, as the scarlet letter becomes 'her passport into regions where other women dared not tread'. She is to be sorrowed over, regarded with awe, yet revered as well. Along with the standard tragic responses of pity and terror, the *pharmakos* evokes one of reverence. Hester is outside the law, monstrous yet redemptive; and her repentant lover Arthur Dimmesdale will publicly declare his solidarity with this unclean victim before he dies. Nothing, to be sure, could be more stereo-typical than the woman as both revered and reviled; but Hester, pioneer of as yet uncharted regions, also sketches the lineaments of a form of life beyond patriarchal oppression.

Dostoevsky's fiction is no stranger to saintly, self-sacrificial women, or indeed to guiltless victims in general. Ivan Karamazov angrily rejects the idea of the scapegoat – that the innocent, especially children, have to suffer on others' behalf. Along with it, he spurns all teleological theories that suffering plays an essential part in evolutionary progress, as well as the hypothesis that we need evil in order to illuminate good. In refusing salvation in protest against such pious cant, he becomes himself a gen-uinely tragic figure. But the novels offer an alternative view of sacrifice. Alyosha Karamazov believes in an all-round scapegoating: everyone must take responsibility for everyone else, in which case victimization cancels all the way through, and a community of mutual guilt can be converted into one of mutual freedom and forgiveness. It is a Christian or existen-tial version of the *pharmakos*: you must assume the burden of another's guilt even though you are innocent yourself, thus becoming like the tragic scapegoat 'objectively' guilty, or in Pauline terms 'made sin' rather than plain sinful. Yet if this act is universalized, made reciprocal rather than unilateral, it can become the basis for mutual equality and accep-tance. A society of victors and victims can be turned into one of common responsibility. It is no longer a question of one individual suffering for all, as Dimitri Karamazov proposes he should do in a suspiciously ecsta-tic moment. Dostoevsky is well aware of the hair-thin line between martyrdom and masochism.

The distinction between true and false martyrdom can sometimes seem undecidable, as readers of the later Henry James do not need to be reminded. Is renunciation the ultimate selflessness, or the most deviously self-regarding act of all? Is Maggie Verver of *The Golden Bowl* a saintly altru-ist or a wicked schemer? At one point in the novel, she casts herself explic-itly in the role of scapegoat: her role, she reflects, is 'to charge herself with [peril] as the scapegoat of old, of whom she had once seen a terrible picture, had been charged with the sins of the people and had gone forth into the desert to sink under his burden and die' (Book 2, ch. 36). Maggie, however, does rather well in the end out of her victimage, which is what has led some critics to see it as less than altruistic.

Even so, the act of renunciation for James can have a luminous aes-thetic beauty about it, a disengagement from the squalid play of power and interest which to that extent resembles nothing quite so much as the act of writing itself. Art itself, for James as for Flaubert and Joyce, is a form of sacrifice, a priestly self-abnegation, as the writer pays with the paucity of his life for the prodigal fullness of his art. Something, in this respect, can come of nothing. James himself had enough money to live as little as possible and to practise instead that supreme mode of virtue known as literature. The modernist version of sacrifice is art. Such an exquisitely nuanced intelligence, existing entirely for its own sake, must buy its disinterestedness at the price of dissociation. In the end, there seemed nothing that Henry didn't know, but to be integral this knowledge had to be entirely impractical, utterly without exchange-value, as magnificently useless as the *acte gratuit* by which Milly Theale in *The Wings of the Dove* hands over her fortune to the lover who she knows has betrayed her.

Like Strether in *The Ambassadors*, James must emerge from the whole fatiguing business with clean hands, untainted by self-interest. One can only enter eternity with empty hands, and yet the abnegation this involves can look ominously like manipulation. It is hard to decide between the two, just as there is the slimmest of lines between aestheticization in the sense of living your life richly and beautifully, and aestheticization in the sense of fetishizing others as fine possessions. James's 'drawing-room tragedies', as Jeanette King aptly calls them,[36] see what is wrong with Kant's strict separation of the ethical and aesthetic, but what is right about it too. Virtue surely cannot be the gauche, unlovely affair which the utilitarians make of it; and in the practice of novel-writing above all, goodness and fineness can be momentarily reconciled, as an implicit critique of a society in which it's the fine who get the pleasure and the good who take the blame. But in the novels and stories themselves, as opposed to the act of producing them, goodness and fineness, the ethical and the aesthetic, are often enough at each other's throats, in the guise of America versus Europe, character against style, the syntax of the self versus its sensations. James understood how many innocent victims had to be sacrificed to pay for the civility he practised. His secretary Theodora Bosanquet writes of him that 'When he walked out of the refuge of his study and into the world and looked about him, he saw a place of torment, where creatures of prey perpetually thrust their claws into the quivering flesh of doomed, defenceless children of light'.[37]

Sacrifice can be a way of losing in order to win, appeasing Nature or the gods so as to get them on your side. In *Dialectic of Enlightenment* Horkheimer and Adorno see it as inherently deceitful, subjecting the gods to whom you sacrifice to the primacy of human ends. This may be true of a Fleda Vetch or a Maggie Verver, conducting themselves with such scrupulous selflessness that they attain their ends, or hope to, by the sheer stylish enchantment of their moral intelligence. In sacrifice, the masochistic pleasures of the death drive can also be turned outwards as aggression, which is then part of what you relish about the act. Self-oblation may be a transcendence of history, but it is also an historical act like any other, an abstention which has all the force of an intervention, and which may well leave others marooned with their burden of guilt and indebtedness. Perhaps that was the vindictive point of it all along, though one will never be entirely sure. James understands perfectly how surrendering power can be the supreme exercise of it – how a refusal to intervene in others' lives can be aestheticist irresponsibility as well as a liberal respect for autonomy; how you can persuade someone to fall in love with you by yielding up your life for them, while exacting vengeance for that sacrifice by no longer being there to return their passion. Perhaps this is what Milly Theale does to Densher; or perhaps she is a modern-day *pharmakos* who turns her victimage into victory, conjuring life from her death and plucking redemption from defeat. Like the final decision of the heroine of *Portrait of a Lady*, she could be seen as the exponent of a pure act, regardless of consequence, which both accepts and refuses, puts the agent entirely at stake, and in doing so transgresses the symbolic community of norms and expectations to inaugurate a new dispensation. For one lineage of thought from Kierkegaard to Lacan, such an act is the very paradigm of the ethical.

Life in death is the theme of Melville's *Moby-Dick*, centring as it does on a whaling industry which makes its living from slaughter on an ocean which is both life-bearing and entombing. The demonic Ahab's whole existence is a fanatical being-towards-death, just as his ivory leg is a piece of dead matter literally incorporated into his flesh and blood. In his remorseless pursuit of the white whale, he refuses to give up on his desire and is finally destroyed by his fidelity to this ghastly imperative. 'Thy thoughts have created a creature in thee' (ch. 44), Ishmael reflects, recognizing that desire is an alien wedge in one's being which obeys its own logic rather than yours. What Ahab desires is Moby-Dick, whose white-ness is a sign of holiness, of something 'sweet, and honorable, and sublime' (ch. 42), but also of an uncanny, abysmal nothingness which you can gaze upon only at the risk of blindness. Moby-Dick's colourless-ness is at once symbol of spiritual truth and an appalling image of the Real. Whether you see this creature as devil or archangel, we are told, depends much on your mood. Like the Real, the whale is at once pure negation and stumbling-block, a cypher which eternally eludes cognition but also a ravaging force for destruction. Its indefiniteness reminds the narrator of annihilation, of the 'heartless voids and immensities of the universe' (ch. 42), and the Satanic Ahab can see this sublimely unfathomable being only as vengeful and rapacious, marked by an 'inscrutable malice'.

It is certainly as the Law that Ahab views the whale, a beast both accursed and alluring. It deranges all zoological categories, and (as Aquinas says of God) can be defined only analogously. God himself is a sort of *pharmakos*, with one terrible and one loving face, rather as Quee-queg's tomahawk pipe can both brain his foes and soothe his soul. Or rather as a port in a storm is both welcome and perilous to a ship in dis-tress, 'her only friend her bitterest foe' (ch. 23). There is a similar ambiva-lence about the whaling industry, an unclean, death-dealing affair in itself which is nevertheless a vital source of civilization. Whalers, the narrator reminds us, are spurned, outcast souls, but it is on their labour that kings' coronations rest. The whaling community represents a rejected corner-stone. Ahab himself is a crazed demoniac transgressor, another of those tragic figures who has wandered beyond the frontiers of humanity into some hellish region in which, as he cries Miltonically, 'all loveliness is anguish to me' (ch. 37).

Melville's Billy Budd is a rather less subtle sort of scapegoat, with his Adamic innocence contrasted with Claggart's malevolence; but Bartleby of Melville's curious tale *Bartleby, the Scrivener* has some of the features of the traditional *pharmakos*. A proto-Beckettian figure bereft of hope, history or occupation, there is something of the traumatic, catatonic quality of the scapegoat in his unnerving habit of staring for hours at a wall, his inability to invest his world with meaning. Bartleby incarnates a kind of ultimate refusal ('I prefer not to' is his catchphrase), and in doing so manifests something of the perverse power of the powerless, dying in prison divested of human qualities yet for the same reason an infuriating enigma, a source of bafflement and frustration to his employer.

The *pharmakos*, then, is by no means a subject confined to classical antiquity. There are resonances of it today, for example, in the fiction of J. M. Coetzee. Yet historicists can scarcely feel at ease with the sugges-tion that polluted kings and ancient fertility cults might speak relevantly to the politics of our time. The blunt truth is, however, that they are a good deal more relevant than the politics of most present-day left-historicists. From Sydney to San Diego, today's cultural leftists have largely repudiated an earlier revolutionary zeal, settling eagerly or dispiritedly for some brand of pragmatism, liberal pluralism or social democracy. In a world of deepening poverty, widening inequality, enforced migration, ethnic warfare, social devastation, natural pillage and renewed military aggression, even the mildest dash of social democracy would be welcome enough. But it is risible to think that it would be sufficient. The structure of a world increasingly governed by the greed of transnational corporations is one which has to be broken in order to be repaired. If this is the lesson of the *pharmakos*, it is also the faith of political revolution.

In the current preoccupation with minorities, one vital insight is in danger of being obscured. The astonishing fact about global capitalism is that it is the *majority* who are dispossessed. There are, to be sure, degrees of dispossession, and shipyard workers are by no means destitute. But while the idea of a social order which excludes certain vilified minorities is familiar enough, and these expulsions are visibly on show, the mind-shaking truth of a class analysis is that social orders have always invisibly shut out the majority. This is so paradoxical a fact, as well as so impalpable a one, that we have failed to be sufficiently struck by it. It carries a double message: that a system entranced by success is in fact a miserable failure; and that there is more than enough of this failure for it to convert itself into power. The classical *pharmakos* can be thrust out of the city because its rulers have no need of it, other than as an object on which to off-load their collective guilt. It is also terrible to look on, too hideous to tolerate within one's walls. But the modern-day scapegoat is essential to the workings of the very *polis* which shuts it out. It is not a matter of a few hired beggars or gaolbirds, but of whole sweated, uprooted populations. The duality of power and weakness returns, but in a new configuration.

In this context, Lacan's 'Do not give up on your desire!' becomes a political injunction. It means 'Be steadfast for death': don't be fooled by 'life' as we have it, refuse to make do with the bogus and second-best, don't settle for that set of shabby fantasies known as reality, but cling to your faith that the deathly emptiness of the dispossessed is the only source from which a more jubilant, self-delighting existence can ultimately spring. And for that, the left needs a discourse rather more searching than pluralism or pragmatism. There can be no falling back on metaphysical dogmatism or foundationalist complacency. But if the language of critique is to match the depth and urgency of our political situation, neither can the left be content to remain caught within the repetitive round of its present cultural concerns.

Something of the same, ironically, can be said of the system itself. As the West's global ambitions grow increasingly more predatory, it will no doubt find itself increasingly less able to defend its operations by the culturalist or pragmatist formula 'This is just the kind of thing we happen to do'. What may work in philosophy departments proves rather less persuasive when Western capitalism is asked why it is busy poisoning the planet, breeding poverty and preparing once more for nuclear showdown. Pragmatist apologias for this agenda sound all the more feeble when one is up against antagonists like Islam, some of whose adherents, as the West might have noticed, have rather less of a problem with foundational or metaphysical claims. What is already challenging this pragmatism in the West is an ugly religious and political fundamentalism, which we can expect to see spread more widely. The last thing the left needs is its own version of that. But neither is it enough for it to peddle its own versions of a pragmatism which is in any case likely to be increasingly discredited.

We may leave Franz Kafka with the last word. At the end of *The Trial*, as he is about to be executed, Josef K. glimpses a vague movement in the top storey of a nearby house. 'The casement window flew open like a light flashing on; a human figure, faint and insubstantial at that distance and height, forced itself far out and stretched out its arms even further. Who was it? A friend? A good man? One who sympathized? One who wanted to help? Was it one person? Was it everybody?'

Notes

Introduction

1 Jonathan Dollimore, *Death, Desire and Loss in Western Culture* (London, 1998), p. xviii. There is, even so, much to be admired in this ambitious, wide-ranging, passionately serious study.

2 Francis Barker, *The Culture of Violence* (Manchester, 1993), p. 213. I cannot mention Francis Barker's work, much less take it to task, without registering my sorrow at the untimely death of this brilliant, trenchantly committed scholar, my friend and once my student.

3 Ibid., p. 233.

4 See Eric Hobsbawm, *Age of Extremes: The Short Twentieth Century 1914–1991* (London, 1994), p. 12.

5 See Miguel de Beistegui and Simon Sparks (eds), *Philosophy and Tragedy* (London, 2000).

6 For a superb, truly monumental study of this kind, see Walter Cohen, *Drama of a Nation* (Ithaca, NY, 1985).

7 See, for example, Terry Eagleton, *The Illusions of Postmodernism* (Oxford, 1996).

8 See Francis Mulhern, *Contemporary Marxist Literary Criticism* (London, 1992), p. 22.

9 T. W. Adorno, *Negative Dialectics* (London, 1973), p. 320.

10 See Sebastiano Timpanaro, *On Materialism* (London, 1975), chapter 1.

11 Ibid., p. 52.

1   A Theory in Ruins

1 Susanne K. Langer, *Feeling and Form* (London, 1953), p. 336.

2 Geoffrey Brereton, *Principles of Tragedy* (London, 1968), p. 5.

3 R. P. Draper, *Tragedy: Developments in Criticism* (London, 1980), p. 11.

4 Paul Allen, *Alan Ayckbourn: Grinning at the Edge* (London, 2001), p. 224.

5 Paul Ricoeur, *The Symbolism of Evil* (Boston, 1969), p. 221.

6   Leo Aylen, *Greek Tragedy and the Modern World* (London, 1964), p. 8.
7   Raymond Williams, *Modern Tragedy* (London, 1966), pp. 45–6.
8   Arthur Schopenhauer, *The World as Will and Representation* (New York, 1969), vol. 1, p. 254.
9   Horace, 'On the Art of Poetry', in *Classical Literary Criticism* (Harmondsworth, 1984), p. 87.
10 F. L. Lucas, *Serious Drama in Relation to Aristotle's Poetics* (London, 1966), p. 25.
11 John Orr, *Tragic Drama and Modern Society* (London, 1981), p. xii.
12 Richard Kuhns, *Tragedy, Contradiction and Repression* (Chicago and London, 1991), p. 76.
13 Walter Kaufmann, *Tragedy and Philosophy* (New York, 1968), p. 135.
14 For an excellent study of this topic, see Terence Cave, *Recognitions* (Oxford, 1988).
15 David Hume, *A Treatise of Human Nature* (London, 1985), p. 420.
16 Georg Simmel, *The Conflict in Modern Culture and Other Essays* (New York, 1968), p. 43.
17 A. C. Bradley, *Oxford Lectures on Poetry* (London, 1950), p. 381.
18 Oscar Mandel, *A Definition of Tragedy* (New York, 1961), p. 20.
19 Aylen, *Greek Tragedy and the Modern World*, p. 164.
20 Brereton, *Principles of Tragedy*, p. 20.
21 Mark Harris, *The Case for Tragedy* (London, 1932), p. 182. The book contains some rather questionable historical judgements. See its assertion that 'The middle ages had been a snug time' (p. 88).
22 John Holloway, *The Story of the Night* (London, 1961), p. 136.
23 Walter Kerr, *Tragedy and Comedy* (New York, 1968), p. 121.
24 Ibid., p. 128.
25 Ibid., pp. 274 and 279.
26 Dorothea Krook, *Elements of Tragedy* (New Haven, CT and London, 1969).
27 I. A. Richards, *Principles of Literary Criticism* (London, 1963), p. 247.
28 Northrop Frye, *Anatomy of Criticism: Four Essays* (Princeton, NJ, 1957), p. 38.
29 See George Steiner, *The Death of Tragedy* (London, 1961), p. 324.
30 Williams, *Modern Tragedy*, p. 189.
31 See Murray Krieger, *The Tragic Vision* (Chicago and London, 1960). It is ironic that Krieger's conservative view of tragedy comes rather close to that of Timothy Reiss's radical one, which we shall be examining a little later. It is just that what Krieger approves, Reiss condemns. Reiss's book, even so, is by far the more intricate and illuminating.
32 Brereton, *Principles of Tragedy*, p. 5.
33 Adrian Poole, *Tragedy: Shakespeare and the Greek Example* (Oxford, 1987), p. 65.
34 See Alasdair MacIntyre, *After Virtue* (London, 1981), pp. 1–5.
35 I am indebted for much of my knowledge of tragedy in this period to Henry Ansgar Kelly's formidably erudite *Ideas and Forms of Tragedy* (Cambridge, 1993).
36 Ibid., p. 7.

37 Johann Wolfgang von Goethe, *Wilhelm Meister's Apprenticeship* (Princeton, NJ, 1989), p. 14.

38 Ibid., p. 12.

39 Gerald Else, *The Origin and Early Form of Greek Tragedy* (Cambridge, MA, 1965), p. 70.

40 Ibid., p. 89.

41 W. McNeile Dixon, *Tragedy* (London, 1924), p. 5.

42 Franco Moretti, *Signs Taken For Wonders* (London, 1983), p. 55.

43 C. S. Lewis, *Experiments in Criticism* (London, 1961), p. 78.

44 A. C. Bradley, *Shakespearian Tragedy* (London, 1904), p. 3.

45 Ulrich Simon, *Pity and Terror: Christianity and Tragedy* (London, 1989), p. 37.

46 Williams, *Modern Tragedy*, p. 62.

47 Brereton, *Principles of Tragedy*, p. 18.

48 H. A. Mason, *The Tragic Plane* (Oxford, 1985), p. 24.

49 John S. Smart, 'Tragedy', *Essays and Studies* (Oxford, 1922), vol. 8.

50 Karl Jaspers, *Tragedy Is Not Enough* (London, 1953), pp. 75–6.

51 Maud Bodkin, *Archetypal Patterns in Poetry* (London, 1934), p. 21.

52 Smart, 'Tragedy', p. 36.

53 Williams, *Modern Tragedy*, p. 46.

54 Roland Galle, 'The Disjunction of the Tragic: Hegel and Nietzsche', in N. Georgopoulos (ed.), *Tragedy and Philosophy* (London, 1963), p. 39.

55 See Simon Sparks, 'Fatalities', in Miguel de Beistegui and Simon Sparks (eds), *Philosophy and Tragedy* (London and New York, 2000), p. 200.

56 See also Simon Crictchley, *Ethics–Politics–Subjectivity* (London, 1999), chapter 10.

57 Michelle Gellrich, *Tragedy and Theory: The Problem of Conflict since Aristotle* (Princeton, NJ, 1988), p. 7.

58 For an evaluation of these aspects in early-modern English tragedy, see Jonathan Dollimore, *Radical Tragedy* (London, 1989).

59 See Louis Althusser, 'Letter on Art to Andre Daspre', in *Lenin and Philosophy* (London, 1971), pp. 203–4.

60 See Pierre Macherey, *A Theory of Literary Production* (London, 1978).

61 Timothy Reiss, *Tragedy and Truth* (New Haven, CT and London, 1980), p. 6.

62 Ibid., p. 36.

63 Ibid., p. 284.

64 See T. R. Henn, *The Harvest of Tragedy* (London, 1956), p. 65: 'The crux of tragedy is the place of evil and suffering in the world'. However questionable, it is a case re-echoed by several other critics.

65 Williams, *Modern Tragedy*, p. 45.

2 The Value of Agony

1 See Ovid, *Tristia ex Ponto* (Cambridge, MA, 1996), p. 83.

2 The *Guardian*, February 15, 2001.

3　Clayton Koelb, ' "Tragedy" as an Evaluative Term', *Comparative Literature Studies*, vol. 9, no. 1 (March, 1974), p. 72.

4　Philippe Lacoue-Labarthe, 'On the Sublime', in *Postmodernism: ICA Documents 4* (London, 1986).

5　See *Waiting for Godot*'s comment on the fact that one of the Calvary thieves was saved: 'It's a reasonable percentage'.

6　Kenneth Allott (ed.), *Poems of Matthew Arnold* (London, 1965), p. 656.

7　Plato, *The Republic* (London, 1987), p. 81.

8　W. B. Yeats (ed.), *The Oxford Book of Modern Verse* (Oxford, 1936), p. xxxiv.

9　Quoted in Jeanette King, *Tragedy in the Victorian Novel* (Cambridge, 1978), p. 3.

10　Geoffrey Brereton, *Principles of Tragedy* (London, 1968), p. 130.

11　Dorothea Krook, *Elements of Tragedy* (New Haven, CT and London, 1969), p. 116.

12　Ibid., p. 239.

13　D. D. Raphael, *The Paradox of Tragedy* (London, 1960), p. 27.

14　Quoted by Raymond Williams, *Modern Tragedy* (London, 1966), p. 116.

15　Richard Wagner, 'Cultural Decadence of the Nineteenth Century', in Albert Goldman and Evert Sprinchorn (eds), *Wagner on Music and Drama* (London, 1977), p. 63.

16　Gilbert Murray, *The Classical Tradition in Poetry* (Cambridge, MA, 1930), p. 66.

17　I. A. Richards, *Principles of Literary Criticism* (London, 1963), pp. 247 and 246.

18　Miguel de Unamuno, *The Tragic Sense of Life* (London, 1921), pp. 17 and 45.

19　Claude Schumacher (ed.), *Artaud on Theatre* (London, 1989), p. 117.

20　Christopher Caudwell, *Illusion and Reality* (London, 1937), p. 297.

21　W. MacNeile Dixon, *Tragedy* (London, 1924), p. 111. The book is rather ambiguously dedicated to 'The Lovers of Great Men and their Speculations'.

22　William James, *Pragmatism and Other Writings* (London, 2000), p. 129.

23　Williams, *Modern Tragedy*, p. 55.

24　Ibid., p. 55 (my italics).

25　A. C. Bradley, *Shakespearian Tragedy* (London, 1904), p. 15.

26　Andrew McNeillie (ed.), *The Essays of Virginia Woolf* (London, 1994), vol. 4, p. 42.

27　F. W. J. Schelling, *The Philosophy of Art* (Minneapolis, MN, 1989), p. 89.

28　Franco Moretti, *Signs Taken For Wonders* (London, 1983), p. 49.

29　Friedrich Holderlin, *Essays and Letters on Theory* (Albany, NY, 1988), p. 85.

30　T. R. Henn, *The Harvest of Tragedy* (London, 1956), p. 288.

31　MacNeile Dixon, *Tragedy*, p. 145.

32　F. L. Lucas, *Tragedy: Serious Drama in Relation to Aristotle's Poetics* (London, 1966), p. 79.

33　Oliver Taplin, 'Emotion and Meaning in Greek Tragedy', in Erich Segal (ed.), *Oxford Readings in Greek Tragedy* (Oxford, 1983), p. 12.

34　Walter Stein, *Criticism as Dialogue* (Cambridge, 1969), pp. 160–1.

35　Walter Kerr, *Tragedy and Comedy* (New York, 1968), p. 130.

36　Walter Kaufmann, *Tragedy and Philosophy* (New York, 1968), p. 182.

37 Ibid., p. 81.
38 A. O. Rorty (ed.), Introduction, *Essays on Aristotle's Poetics* (Princeton, NJ, 1992), p. 18.
39 Ibid., p. 85.
40 John Jones, *On Aristotle and Greek Tragedy* (London, 1962), p. 170.
41 R. P. Draper, *Tragedy: Developments in Criticism* (London, 1980), p. 34.
42 George Steiner, *The Death of Tragedy* (London, 1961), p. 10.
43 For Hebbel's theories, see Mary Garland, *Hebbel's Prose Tragedies* (Cambridge, 1973).
44 E. R. Dodds, 'On Misunderstanding the *Oedipus Rex*', in Erich Segal (ed.), *Oxford Readings in Greek Tragedy* (Oxford, 1983), p. 187.
45 Roy Morrell, 'The Psychology of Tragic Pleasure', *Essays in Criticism* vol. 6 (1965), p. 26.
46 Jonathan Lear, 'Katharsis', in A. O. Rorty (ed.), *Essays on Aristotle's Poetics* (Princeton, NJ, 1992), p. 335.
47 Quoted in Susan Sontag (ed.), *A Barthes Reader* (London, 1982), p. 67.
48 Marcel Proust, *Three Dialogues* (London, 1965), p. 125.
49 King, *Tragedy in the Victorian Novel*, p. 16.
50 Leo Aylen, *Greek Tragedy and the Modern World* (London, 1964), p. 161.
51 Harold Schweizer, 'Tragedy', in Michael Payne (ed.), *A Dictionary of Cultural and Critical Theory* (Oxford, 1996), p. 537.
52 Kerr, *Tragedy and Comedy*, p. 140.
53 Henry Ansgar Kelly, *Ideas and Forms of Tragedy* (Cambridge, 1993), p. 222.
54 Blaise Pascal, *Pensées* (London, 1995), p. 106.
55 Una Ellis-Fermor, *The Frontiers of Drama* (London, 1945), pp. 17–18.
56 Chu Kwang-Tsien, *The Psychology of Tragedy* (Strasbourg, 1933), p. 236.
57 Oscar Mandel, *A Definition of Tragedy* (New York, 1961), pp. 113–14.
58 Northrop Frye, *Anatomy of Criticism* (Princeton, NJ, 1957), p. 42.
59 Charles Taylor, *The Sources of the Self* (Cambridge, 1989), Part 3.
60 Stein, *Criticism as Dialogue*, p. 147.
61 Søren Kierkegaard, *The Sickness Unto Death* (London, 1989), p. 133.

3   From Hegel to Beckett

1 G. W. F. Hegel, *The Phenomenology of Spirit* (Oxford, 1977), p. 19.
2 Rodolphe Gasché, 'Self-dissolving Seriousness', in Miguel de Beistegui and Simon Sparks (eds), *Philosophy and Tragedy* (London and New York, 2000), p. 39.
3 Peter Szondi, *On Textual Understanding and Other Essays* (Manchester, 1986), pp. 54–5.
4 De Beistegui and Sparks, *Philosophy and Tragedy*, p. 28.
5 G. W. F. Hegel, *The Philosophy of Fine Art* (London, 1920), p. 321.
6 See A. C. Bradley, 'Hegel's Theory of Tragedy', in *Oxford Lectures on Poetry* (London, 1950).

7   Hegel, *The Phenomenology of Spirit*, p. 444.

8   Søren Kierkegaard, *Fear and Trembling* (Harmondsworth, 1985), p. 52.

9   Ibid., p. 50.

10 Ibid., p. 89.

11 Ibid., p. 103.

12 George Steiner, *The Death of Tragedy* (London, 1961), p. 194.

13 Jean-François Lyotard, 'Adorno as the Devil', *Telos* no. 19 (spring, 1974), translation amended.

14 Blaise Pascal, *Pensées* (London, 1995), p. 187.

15 For an excellent analysis of Eliot on these lines, see Graham Martin, 'Language and Belief in Eliot's Poetry', in Graham Martin (ed.), *Eliot in Perspective* (London, 1970).

16 Søren Kierkegaard, *The Sickness Unto Death* (London, 1989), p. 88.

17 Ibid., p. 107.

18 Theodor W. Adorno, *Kierkegaard: Construction of the Aesthetic* (Minneapolis, 1989), p. 16. A Kierkegaardian ethics of a kind has recently been revived by Jacques Derrida. See his *The Gift of Death* (Chicago, 1995), which argues that ethical decisions are at once necessary and 'impossible', falling outside all knowledge and convention and made in relation to an utterly impenetrable otherness. One can only hope that he is not on the jury when one's case comes up in court.

19 The point is made by Roland Galle in his essay 'The Disjunction of the Tragic: Hegel and Nietzsche', in N. Georgeopoulos (ed.), *Tragedy and Philosophy* (London, 1993).

20 Raymond Williams, *Modern Tragedy* (London, 1966), p. 51.

21 Erich Heller, *The Disinherited Mind* (London, 1952), p. 131.

22 See ibid., p. 161.

23 Northrop Frye, *Anatomy of Criticism: Four Essays* (Princeton, NJ, 1957), p. 237.

24 Williams, *Modern Tragedy*, p. 83.

25 Ibid., p. 77. It is worth remarking that Williams's use of the term 'revolution' in 1966, before the resurgence of revolutionary notions a few years later and in the context of a British New Left which did not habitually speak in such terms, is very striking. Nor was he discussing the phenomenon of violence at second hand, having fought as a tank commander in the Second World War. He himself was committed as far as possible to non-violent political change, a point which he makes in his study.

26 Ibid., p. 171.

27 Ibid., p. 82.

28 See Maud Bodkin, *Archetypal Patterns in Poetry* (London, 1934), p. 23.

29 Karl Jaspers, *Tragedy Is Not Enough* (London, 1953), p. 41.

30 Ibid., p. 74.

31 Ibid., pp. 27 and 36.

32 Ibid., p. 41.

33 Georg Lukács, *Soul and Form* (London, 1974), p. 158.

34 Ibid., p. 162.

35 Jonathan Dollimore, *Radical Tragedy* (London, 1989), p. xxi.
36 Adrian Poole, *Tragedy: Shakespeare and the Greek Example* (Oxford, 1987), p. 12.
37 René Girard, *Violence and the Sacred* (Baltimore and London, 1977), p. 292.
38 Walter Kaufmann, *Tragedy and Philosophy* (New York, 1968), p. 363.
39 Poole, *Tragedy: Shakespeare and the Greek Example*, p. 2.
40 Ibid., p. 2.
41 Bertolt Brecht, *The Messingkauf Dialogues* (London, 1965), p. 47.
42 It is interesting, even so, that there is very little tragic literature in this historically disrupted nation.
43 F. R. Leavis, *The Common Pursuit* (London, 1962), p. 152.
44 Jean-François Lyotard, 'The Other's Rights', in Obrad Savic (ed.), *The Politics of Human Rights* (London, 1999), p. 186.
45 Quoted in Poole, *Tragedy: Shakespeare and the Greek Example*, p. 10.
46 John Snyder, *Prospects of Power* (Kentucky, 1991), p. 30.
47 For a general account of his thought, see my *The Ideology of the Aesthetic* (Oxford, 1990), chapter 6.
48 Arthur Schopenhauer, *The World as Will and Representation* (New York, 1969), vol. 1, p. 253.
49 Susanne K. Langer, *Feeling and Form* (London, 1953), pp. 333–4 and 354.
50 See C. Andrew Gerstle, 'The Concept of Tragedy in Japanese Drama', *Japan Review* no. 1 (1990). I am grateful for this information about Chinese, Indian and Japanese culture to Professor Glen Dudbridge, Professor Richard Gombrich and Dr Brian Powell of the University of Oxford.
51 J. Florio (ed.), *The Essays of Montaigne* (New York, 1933), p. 1012.
52 Christopher Norris, *William Empson and the Philosophy of Literary Criticism* (London, 1978), p. 86.
53 Blaise Pascal, *Pensées* (London, 1995), p. 6.
54 Simon Critchley, *Ethics–Politics–Subjectivity* (London, 1999), p. 230.
55 Ibid., p. 235.
56 William Empson, *Some Versions of Pastoral* (London, 1966), p. 114.
57 Slavoj Žižek, *Did Somebody Say Totalitarianism?* (London, 2001), p. 179.
58 Michael Wilding sees Samson in Milton's *Samson Agonistes* as another flawed, old-style hero, public and military rather than private and pacific. See his 'Regaining the Radical Milton', in Stephen Knight and Michael Wilding (eds), *The Radical Reader* (Glebe, Australia, 1977).
59 See Rolf Tiedemann and Hermann Schweppenhauser (eds), *Walter Benjamin: Gesammelte Schriften* (Frankfurt am Main, 1966), vol. 1, p. 583.
60 Jaspers, *Tragedy Is Not Enough*, pp. 99 and 100.
61 Ibid., p. 101.

4   Heroes

1 Dorothea Krook, *Elements of Tragedy* (New Haven, CT and London, 1969), pp. 78–9.

2   Bruno Snell, *The Discovery of the Mind* (Oxford, 1953), p. 99.

3   See John Jones, *On Aristotle and Greek Tragedy* (London, 1962), chapter 1.

4   See Humphrey House, *Aristotle's Poetics* (London, 1964), p. 94.

5   Bernard Knox, *The Heroic Temper* (Berkeley and Los Angeles, 1954), pp. 2–3.

6   Northrop Frye, *Anatomy of Criticism: Four Essays* (Princeton, NJ, 1957), p. 208.

7   H. D. F. Kitto, *Form and Meaning in Drama* (London, 1956), pp. 201–2.

8   Rosalind Hursthouse, *On Virtue Ethics* (Oxford, 1999), p. 28.

9   Aryeh Kosman, 'Acting: Drama as the Mimesis of Praxis', in A. O. Rorty (ed.), *Essays on Aristotle's Poetics* (Princeton, NJ, 1992), p. 66.

10 Martha C. Nussbaum, 'Tragedy and Self-Sufficiency: Plato and Aristotle on Fear and Pity', in A. O. Rorty (ed.), *Essays on Aristotle's Poetics* (Princeton, NJ, 1992).

11 E. F. Watling, *Sophocles: Electra and Other Plays* (London, 1953), p. 10.

12 Thomas Rymer, *The Tragedies of the Last Age* (1678, reprinted Cambridge, 1972), pp. 98–9. See also his *A Short View of Tragedy* (London, 1693).

13 David Hume, *A Treatise of Human Nature* (London, 1985), p. 418.

14 Duncan Wu (ed.), *The Selected Works of William Hazlitt* (London, 1998), vol. 1, p. 126.

15 David Farrell Krell, 'A Small Number of Houses', in Miguel de Beistegui and Simon Sparks (eds), *Philosophy and Tragedy* (London and New York, 2000), p. 91.

16 Pierre Corneille, *Writings on the Theatre*, ed. H. T. Barnwell (Oxford, 1965), p. 29.

17 Chu Kwang-Tsien, *The Psychology of Tragedy* (Strasbourg, 1933), p. 80.

18 Elder Olson, *Tragedy and the Theory of Drama* (Detroit, 1961), p. 243.

19 Ibid., 245.

20 Richard Steele, *The Spectator* no. 290 (1 February 1712).

21 Jean-Jacques Rousseau, *Lettre a d'Alembert sur les spectacles* (Paris, 1939), p. 89.

22 Raymond Williams, *Modern Tragedy* (London, 1966), p. 50. For accounts of domestic tragedy, see Henry H. Adams, *English Domestic or Homiletic Tragedy 1575–1642* (New York, 1943), and E. Bernbaum, *The Drama of Sensibility* (Cambridge, MA, 1925).

23 Georg Lukács, *Soul and Form* (London, 1974), p. 67.

24 Quoted in Walter Benjamin, *The Origin of German Tragic Drama* (London, 1977), p. 102.

25 George Steiner, *The Death of Tragedy* (London, 1961), p. 241.

26 Ibid., p. 194.

27 A. Paolucci and H. Paolucci (eds), *Hegel on Tragedy* (New York, 1962), p. 50.

28 T. W. Adorno, *Aesthetic Theory* (London, 1984), p. 341.

29 Horace, 'On the Art of Poetry', in T. S. Dorsch (ed.), *Classical Literary Criticism* (Harmondsworth, 1965), p. 87.

30 Werner Jaeger, *Paideia: The Ideals of Greek Culture* (Oxford, 1945), p. 252.

31 Williams, *Modern Tragedy*, p. 13.

32 Steiner, *The Death of Tragedy*, p. 243.

33 Ibid., pp. 291 and 128.
34 Friedrich Nietzsche, *Human All Too Human* (London, 1956), section 23.
35 D. H. Lawrence, *Phoenix* vol. 1 (London, 1955), p. 180.
36 Quoted in Alessandro Manzoni, *The Betrothed*, translated by Archibald Colquhoun (London, 1959), p. xii.
37 See Jeanette King, *Tragedy in the Victorian Novel* (Cambridge, 1978), p. 12.
38 Introduction to *Anton Chekhov: Plays* (London, 1959), p. 19.
39 Arthur Schopenhauer, *The World as Will and Representation* (New York, 1969), vol. 1, p. 254.
40 N. Georgopoulos, in Georgopoulos (ed.), *Tragedy and Philosophy* (London, 1963), p. 108.
41 S. Robb, *Balzac* (London, 1994), p. 330.
42 John Orr, *Tragic Drama and Modern Society* (London, 1981), p. xviii.
43 *Arthur Miller: Collected Plays* (London, 1961), p. 32.
44 Ibid., p. 35.

5   Freedom, Fate and Justice

1   Susanne K. Langer, *Feeling and Form* (London, 1953), p. 333.
2   Quoted in Miguel de Beistegui and Simon Sparks, *Philosophy and Tragedy* (London and New York, 2000), p. 63.
3   William Desmond, *Perplexity and Ultimacy* (Albany, NY, 1995), p. 53.
4   Paul Ricoeur, *The Symbolism of Evil* (Boston, 1969), p. 221.
5   Oscar Mandel, *A Definition of Tragedy* (New York, 1961), p. 104.
6   Walter Benjamin, 'Fate and Character', in *One-Way Street and Other Essays* (London, 1979), p. 127.
7   Simon Critchley, *Ethics–Politics–Subjectivity* (London, 1999), p. 225.
8   Northrop Frye, *Anatomy of Criticism: Four Essays* (Princeton, NJ, 1957), p. 208.
9   Geoffrey Brereton, *Principles of Tragedy* (London, 1968), p. 8.
10 See Max Scheler, *Le phénomène de tragedie* (Paris, 1952).
11 J.-P. Vernant and P. Vidal-Naquet, *Tragedy and Myth in Ancient Greece* (Brighton, 1981), p. 4.
12 See Peter Dews, *Logics of Disintegration* (London, 1987), p. 62.
13 Quoted by Robert J. C. Young, *Postcolonialism: An Historical Introduction* (Oxford, 2001), p. 38.
14 Dews, *Logics of Disintegration*, p. 21.
15 See John Jones, *On Aristotle and Greek Tragedy* (London, 1962), p. 209.
16 Oliver Taplin, 'Emotion and Meaning in Greek Tragedy', in Erich Segal (ed.), *Oxford Readings in Greek Tragedy* (Oxford, 1983), pp. 6–7.
17 See Martin Heidegger, *Being and Time* (Oxford, 1962), p. 289.
18 For an excellent treatment of this topic, see Peter Osborne, *The Politics of Time* (London, 1995), chapter 3. Osborne rightly points out that Heidegger largely dissociates being-towards-death and being-with-others, and illuminatingly suggests how these two ontological registers can be drawn together. But in

exploring their psychoanalytical relation he passes over the ethical link between them, evident in the Pauline sense of self-giving as a proleptic dying.

19 Niccolo Machiavelli, *The Discourses* (London, 1970), p. 234.
20 See Ernst Cassirer, *Kant's Life and Thought* (New Haven, CT and London, 1981), pp. 246–7.
21 Fredric Jameson, *The Political Unconscious* (Ithaca, NY and London, 1981), p. 101.
22 Fredric Jameson, *Marxism and Form* (Princeton, NJ, 1971), p. 177.
23 See de Beistegui and Sparks, *Philosophy and Tragedy*, p. 1.
24 Critchley, *Ethics–Politics–Subjectivity*, p. 219.
25 Mandel, *A Definition of Tragedy*, p. 61.
26 T. W. Adorno, *Negative Dialectics* (London, 1973), p. 365.
27 F. W. J. Schelling, *The Philosophy of Art* (Minneapolis, MN, 1989), p. 249.
28 See Ralph W. Ewton Jr., *The Literary Theories of Schlegel* (The Hague, 1972), pp. 91–2.
29 D. D. Raphael, *The Paradox of Tragedy* (London, 1960), p. 25.
30 See Ricoeur, *The Symbolism of Evil*, p. 221.
31 See ibid., p. 218.
32 W. B. Yeats (ed.), *The Oxford Book of Modern Verse* (Oxford, 1936), p. xxxiv.
33 Georg Lukács, *Soul and Form* (London, 1974), p. 155.
34 Mandel, *A Definition of Tragedy*, p. 94.
35 Cleanth Brooks (ed.), *Tragic Themes in Western Literature* (New Haven, CT and London, 1955), p. 5.
36 Ibid., p. 5.
37 Raymond Williams, *Modern Tragedy* (London, 1966), p. 49.
38 Slavoj Žižek, *Did Somebody Say Totalitarianism?* (London, 2001), p. 15.
39 Williams, *Modern Tragedy*, p. 75.
40 Bertolt Brecht, *Writings on Theatre* (London, 1973), pp. 87 and 78.
41 Ibid., p. 30.
42 William James, *Pragmatism and Other Writings* (London, 2000), p. 50.
43 A. Paolucci and H. Paolucci (eds), *Hegel on Tragedy* (New York, 1962), p. 71.
44 Patrick Roberts, *The Psychology of Tragic Drama* (London and Boston, 1975).
45 Henri Peyre, 'The Tragedy of Passion: Racine's *Phèdre*', in Cleanth Brooks (ed.), *Tragic Themes in Western Literature* (New Haven, CT and London, 1955).
46 Frank Kermode, *An Appetite for Poetry* (London, 1990), p. 69.
47 Frye, *Anatomy of Criticism*, p. 214.
48 A. C. Bradley, *Shakespearian Tragedy* (London, 1904; reprinted 1985), p. 16.
49 Ibid., p. 20 (my italics).
50 Ibid., pp. 22–3.
51 Karl Jaspers, *Tragedy Is Not Enough* (London, 1934), p. 98.
52 Ibid., p. 27.
53 Ibid., p. 28.
54 Ibid.
55 S. H. Butcher, *A Theory of Poetry and Fine Arts* (New York, 1951), p. 312.

56 Leo Aylen, *Greek Tragedy and the Modern World* (London, 1964), pp. 151–2.

57 Quoted by Mandel, *A Definition of Tragedy*, p. 72.

58 H. D. F. Kitto, *Greek Tragedy* (London, 1939), p. 147.

59 Ibid., p. 141.

60 A. J. A. Waldock, *Sophocles the Dramatist* (Cambridge, 1951), p. 157.

61 Richard B. Sewell, *The Vision of Tragedy* (New Haven, CT, 1959), p. 48.

62 Kitto, *Greek Tragedy*, p. 235.

63 T. R. Henn, *The Harvest of Tragedy* (London, 1956), p. 41.

64 E. R. Dodds, in N. Georgopoulos (ed.), *Tragedy and Philosophy* (London, 1963), p. 180.

65 Much of Lessing's most interesting reflections on tragedy can be found in his *Hamburgische Dramaturgie* (1767–8).

66 George Steiner, *The Death of Tragedy* (London, 1961), p. 4.

67 I. A. Richards, *Principles of Literary Criticism* (London, 1963), p. 247.

68 Ibid., p. 246.

69 Lukács, *Soul and Form*, p. 158.

70 Frye, *Anatomy of Criticism*, p. 41.

71 Sadhan Kumar Ghosh, *Tragedy* (Calcutta and London, n.d.), p. 8.

72 Philip Sidney, *An Apology for Poetry* (London, 1986), p. 22.

73 Earl of Shaftesbury, *Characteristics*, ed. J. M. Robertson (London, 1900), vol. 1.

74 R. P. Draper, *Tragedy: Developments in Criticism* (London, 1980), p. 34.

75 For Addison's reflections on tragedy, see *The Spectator* no. 40 (16 April 1711) and no. 548 (28 November 1712).

76 Rosalind Hursthouse, *On Virtue Ethics* (Oxford, 1999), p. 185.

77 Arthur Schopenhauer, *The World as Will and Representation* (New York, 1969), vol. 2, p. 435.

78 See John Dennis, *The Advancement and Reformation of Modern Poetry* (London, 1701).

79 Jean-Jacques Rousseau, *Lettre a d'Alembert sur les spectacles* (Paris, 1939), p. 83.

80 Quoted in Walter Kerr, *Tragedy and Comedy* (New York, 1968), p. 135.

81 J.-P. Vernant and P. Vidal-Naquet, *Tragedy and Myth in Ancient Greece* (Brighton, 1981), p. 9.

82 Moses Finley, *The Ancient Greeks* (Harmondsworth, 1966), p. 105.

83 Martha Nussbaum, *Love's Knowledge* (New York and Oxford, 1990), p. 15.

84 Frye, *Anatomy of Criticism*, p. 37.

85 Williams, *Modern Tragedy*, p. 54.

86 See Perry Anderson, 'Modernity and Revolution', *New Left Review* no. 144 (March/April, 1984).

87 See Franco Moretti, 'The Great Eclipse', in *Signs Taken For Wonders* (London, 1983).

88 See S. S. Prawer, *Karl Marx and World Literature* (Oxford, 1976), p. 222.

89 I have developed these comments in *Shakespeare* (Oxford, 1986).

90 Williams, *Modern Tragedy*, p. 17.

91 See the translators' note to Franz Kafka, *The Castle* (Harmondsworth, 1962), p. 7.
92 Franco Moretti, *The Way of the World* (London, 1987), p. 166.
93 See Slavoj Žižek, *Did Somebody Say Totalitarianism?*, p. 100.
94 A. C. Bradley, *Oxford Lectures on Poetry* (New York, 1955), p. 191.
95 I discuss these ideas of Burke in more detail in my *Heathcliff and the Great Hunger* (London, 1995), ch. 2.
96 Walter Benjamin, *The Origin of German Tragic Drama* (London, 1977), p. 114.

6 Pity, Fear and Pleasure

1 See Plato, *The Republic* (London, 1987), pp. 374–7.
2 The meaning of this doctrine has proved deeply controversial, and I am assuming a particular, reasonably popular interpretation of it here without arguing for it. Gerald F. Else, in his magisterial study of Aristotle's *Poetics*, adopts the now rather unfashionable case that *catharsis* does not refer to the spectators at all. See his *Aristotle's Poetics: The Argument* (Cambridge, MA, 1957), pp. 224–32.
3 Douglas Bush (ed.), *John Milton: Poetical Works* (London, 1966), p. 517.
4 Philippe Lacoue-Labarthe, 'On the Sublime', *Postmodernism: ICA Documents 4* (London, 1986), p. 9.
5 See Edmund Burke, *Philosophical Inquiry into the Origin of our Ideas of the Sublime and the Beautiful*, in *The Works of Edmund Burke* (London, 1906), vol. 1, pp. 95 and 102.
6 Walter Kaufmann, *Tragedy and Philosophy* (New York, 1968), p. 50.
7 F. L. Lucas, *Serious Drama in Relation to Aristotle's Poetics* (London, 1966), p. 50.
8 See Friedrich Nietzsche, *Human All Too Human* (Edinburgh and London, 1909), vol. 1, p. 191.
9 See Martha Nussbaum, *The Fragility of Goodness* (Cambridge, 1986), p. 384.
10 See J. G. Robertson, *Lessing's Dramatic Theory* (Cambridge, 1939), p. 362.
11 David Hume, *A Treatise of Human Nature* (London, 1985), p. 417.
12 Oscar Mandel, *A Definition of Tragedy* (New York, 1961), p. 90.
13 Miguel de Beistegui and Simon Sparks (eds), *Philosophy and Tragedy* (London and New York, 2000), p. 13.
14 Thomas Hobbes, *English Works*, ed. Sir William Molesworth (London, 1890), vol. 4, p. 44. I have omitted Hobbes's frequent italicizations from the quotation.
15 Amartya Sen, 'Rational Fools: A Critique of the Behavioral Foundations of Economic Theory', *Philosophy and Public Affairs* no. 6, 1977.
16 Henri Bergson, *Time and Free Will* (London, 1971), p. 19.
17 Hume, *A Treatise of Human Nature*, p. 424.
18 For an account of Hutcheson, see my *Heathcliff and the Great Hunger* (London, 1995), chapter 3.

19   See, for example, his *An Inquiry Concerning the Original of our Ideas of Virtue and Moral Good*, reprinted in L. A. Selby-Bigge, *British Moralists* (London, 1897). See also his *Short Introduction to Moral Philosophy* (Glasgow, 1747), *An Essay on the Nature and Conduct of the Passions and Affections* (Glasgow, 1769), and *A System of Moral Philosophy* (London, 1755).

20   Hume, *A Treatise of Human Nature*, p. 432.

21   Ibid., p. 437.

22   Jean-Jacques Rousseau, *A Discourse on Inequality* (London, 1984), p. 100.

23   Samuel Beckett, *Proust* (London, 1931), p. 29.

24   Raymond Williams, *Modern Tragedy* (London, 1966), p. 92.

25   I have written more fully on eighteenth-century benevolence and sentimentalism in *Crazy John and the Bishop* (Cork, 1998), chapter 3.

26   Mandel, *A Definition of Tragedy*, p. 68.

27   Williams, *Modern Tragedy*, p. 27.

28   *The Confessions of St Augustine* (London, 1963), p. 201.

29   Sir William Molesworth (ed.), *The English Works of Thomas Hobbes* (London, 1839), vol. 7, p. 73.

30   I. A. Richards, *Principles of Literary Criticism* (London, 1963), p. 245.

31   Roland Barthes, in Susan Sontag (ed.), *A Barthes Reader* (London, 1982), pp. 175–6.

32   Franco Moretti, *Signs Taken For Wonders* (London, 1983), p. 74.

33   Blaise Pascal, *Pensées* (London, 1995), p. 194.

34   I do not mean that this is literally a solution to the so-called naturalistic fallacy. To be that, one would have to show that there was something in our material situation which made it automatically desirable that it should be kept going.

35   A. O. Rorty (ed.), *Essays on Aristotle's Poetics* (Princeton, NJ, 1992), p. 16.

36   Philip Sidney, *An Apology for Poetry* (London, 1986), p. 22.

37   Edmund Burke, *A Philosophical Enquiry into the Origin of our Ideas of the Sublime and Beautiful* (London, 1958), p. 46.

38   Ibid., p. 45.

39   Ibid., p. 46.

40   Franco Moretti, *The Way of the World* (London, 1987), p. 127.

41   See Earl Wasserman, 'The Pleasures of Tragedy', *English Literary History*, vol. 14, no. 4 (1947), pp. 288–90.

42   Earl of Shaftesbury, *Characteristics*, ed. J. M. Robertson (London, 1900), vol. 1, p. 297.

43   A. D. Nuttall, *Why Does Tragedy Give Pleasure?* (Oxford, 1996), p. 74.

44   Plato, *The Last Days of Socrates* (London, 1993), p. 113.

45   Sigmund Freud, 'Mourning and Melancholia', in *Sigmund Freud: On Metapsychology* (Harmondsworth, 1984), p. 425.

46   Northrop Frye, *Anatomy of Criticism: Four Essays* (Princeton, NJ, 1957), p. 94.

47   Oscar Mandel, *A Definition of Tragedy*, pp. 74–5.

48   D. D. Raphael, *The Paradox of Tragedy* (London, 1960), p. 36.

49 Friedrich Nietzsche, *The Genealogy of Morals*, in Walter Kaufmann (ed.), *Basic Writings of Nietzsche* (New York, 1968), p. 503 (translation amended).
50 *The Poems of Matthew Arnold*, ed. Kenneth Allott (London, 1965), p. 592.
51 For a psychoanalytical study of tragedy, see André Green, *The Tragic Effect* (Cambridge, 1969).
52 Slavoj Žižek, *Did Somebody Say Totalitarianism?* (London, 2001), p. 87.
53 The concept crops up in much of Žižek's work, but for two particularly relevant texts, see *The Ticklish Subject* (London, 1999) and *The Fragile Absolute* (London, 2000).
54 *The Confessions of St Augustine*, p. 71.

7 Tragedy and the Novel

1 Quoted in Jeanette King, *Tragedy in the Victorian Novel* (Cambridge, 1978), p. 36.
2 George Steiner, *The Death of Tragedy* (London, 1960), p. 118.
3 Henri Peyre, in Cleanth Brooks (ed.), *Tragic Themes in Western Literature* (New Haven, CT and London, 1955), p. 77.
4 Thomas Mann, *Reflections of a Nonpolitical Man* (New York, 1983), p. 218.
5 Franco Moretti, *The Way of the World* (London, 1987), p. 55.
6 Ibid., p. 11.
7 Ibid., p. 64.
8 Ibid., p. 105.
9 Quoted ibid., p. 102.
10 John Orr, *Tragic Drama and Modern Society* (London, 1981), p. xvii.
11 M. M. Bakhtin, *Collected Works*, ed. S. G. Bocharov and L. A. Gogotishvili (Moscow, 1996), vol. 5, p. 463, n.1. I am grateful to Ken Hirschkop for drawing my attention to this passage.
12 Quoted in Ken Hirschkop, *Mikhail Bakhtin: An Aesthetic for Democracy* (Oxford, 1999), p. 182.
13 Quoted ibid., p. 183.
14 One of the great modern instances of the genre is Thomas Mann's *Confessions of Felix Krull*.
15 See Declan Kiberd, *Irish Classics* (London, 2000), p. 258.
16 Moretti, *The Way of the World*, p. 12.
17 Rüdiger Bittner, 'One Action', in A. O. Rorty (ed.), *New Essays on Aristotle's Poetics* (Princeton, NJ, 1992), p. 109.
18 Henri Lefebvre, *Critique of Everyday Life* (London and New York, 1991), pp. 130, 264.
19 Erich Auerbach, *Mimesis: The Representation of Reality in Western Literature* (Princeton, NJ, 1953), p. 444.
20 Ibid., p. 491.
21 John Synder, *Prospects of Power* (Kentucky, 1991), p. 90.

22 Henry James, *The Tragic Muse* (London, 1921), vol. 1, p. 59.

23 Moretti, *The Way of the World*, p. 25.

24 For excellent accounts of Lukács's text, see J. M. Bernstein, *Philosophy and the Novel* (Brighton, 1984), chapter 2, and Fredric Jameson, *Marxism and Form* (Princeton, NJ, 1971), chapter 3.

25 Karl Beckson (ed.), *Oscar Wilde: The Critical Heritage* (London, 1970), p. 244.

26 Quoted in Galin Tihanov, *The Master and the Slave* (Oxford, 2000), p. 279.

27 Franco Moretti, 'The Spell of Indecision', *New Left Review* no. 64 (July–August, 1987), p. 27.

28 Raymond Williams, *Modern Tragedy* (London, 1966), p. 58.

29 See John Carroll (ed.), *Selected Letters of Samuel Richardson* (Oxford, 1964), p. 108.

30 John Kerrigan, *Revenge Tragedy* (Cambridge, 1989), p. 218. For a fuller treatment of the novel, see my *The Rape of Clarissa* (Oxford, 1982).

31 John S. Smart, 'Tragedy', *Essays and Studies*, vol. 8 (Oxford, 1922), p. 15.

8 Tragedy and Modernity

1 Spinoza, *Ethics* (London, 2000), p. 187.

2 Ibid., p. 25.

3 Ibid., p. 187.

4 The concept of modernity is not unproblematic. See, for example, Perry Anderson, 'Modernity and Revolution', *New Left Review* no. 144 (March–April 1984), and Peter Osborne, 'Modernity is a Qualitative, Not a Chronological Category', *New Left Review* no. 192 (March–April 1992).

5 See, for example, his *Tractatus Theologico-Politicus*, especially chapter 20.

6 George Steiner, *The Death of Tragedy* (London, 1961), p. 88.

7 For a thoughtful account of this tradition, see Francis Mulhern, *Culture / Metaculture* (London, 2000), Part 1.

8 Georg Simmel, 'On the Concept and Tragedy of Culture', in K. Peter Etzkorn (ed.), *Georg Simmel: The Conflict in Modern Culture and Other Essays* (New York, 1968), p. 46.

9 See Galin Tihanov, *The Master and the Slave* (Oxford, 2000), ch. 5.

10 Georg Lukács, *Soul and Form* (London, 1973), p. 154.

11 See Lucien Goldmann, *Immanuel Kant* (London, 1971).

12 Frank Kermode, *An Appetite for Poetry* (London, 1990), pp. 77–8.

13 David Hume, *A Treatise of Human Nature* (London, 1985), pp. 315–16.

14 Ibid., pp. 311–12.

15 Claude Rawson, *God, Gulliver, and Genocide* (New York, 2001), p. 38.

16 Blaise Pascal, *Pensées* (London, 1995), p. 16.

17 Ibid., p. 62.

18 Ibid., p. 29.

19 Ibid., p. 32.

20 Ibid., p. 34.

21 Ibid., p. 34.

22 Ibid., p. 54.

23 Albrecht Wellmer, *The Persistence of Modernity* (Cambridge, 1991), p. 113.

24 Bernard O'Donoghue, 'The Faultline', in *Here Nor There* (London, 1999), p. 7.

25 Niccolo Machiavelli, *Discourses* (London, 1970), p. 268.

26 Quoted by J. H. Whitfield, *Giacomo Leopardi* (Oxford, 1954), p. 159.

27 Jürgen Habermas, *The Philosophical Discourse of Modernity* (Cambridge, 1987), p. 110.

28 See Max Weber, *The Protestant Ethic and the Spirit of Capitalism* (London, 1989), p. 181. See also W. G. Runciman, *A Critique of Max Weber's Philosophy of Social Science* (Cambridge, 1972), and Wolfgang J. Mommsen, *The Political and Social Theory of Max Weber* (Cambridge, 1989).

29 See Anthony Ashley Cooper, 3rd Earl of Shaftesbury, *Characterisks*, ed. J. M. Robertson (London, 1900), vol. 1.

30 For a relevant study, see Roland Barthes, *Sade–Fourier–Loyola* (London, 1977).

31 Karl Marx, *Grundrisse* (Harmondsworth, 1973), p. 111.

32 Peter Dews, *Logics of Disintegration* (London, 1987), p. 139.

33 Slavoj Žižek, *Did Somebody Say Totalitarianism?* (London, 2001), p. 38.

34 W. B. Yeats, 'The Tragic Theatre', in *Essays of W. B. Yeats* (London, 1924), p. 296.

35 Ibid., p. 93.

36 Friedrich Nietzsche, *The Will to Power* (New York, 1968), p. 404.

37 Quoted by Richard Schacht, *Nietzsche* (London, 1983), p. 370.

38 *Max Weber: Essays in Sociology*, ed. H. H. Gerth and C. Wright Mills (London, 1991), p. 152.

39 Rosalind Hursthouse, *On Virtue Ethics* (Oxford, 1999), ch. 3.

40 Isaiah Berlin, *Four Essays on Liberty* (Oxford, 1969), p. 168.

41 Martha Nussbaum, *Love's Knowledge* (New York and Oxford, 1990), p. 60.

42 Martha Nussbaum, *The Fragility of Goodness* (Cambridge, 1987), p. 81.

43 Raymond Williams, *Modern Tragedy* (London, 1966), p. 107.

44 Jean Genet, *The Thief's Journal* (Harmondsworth, 1967), p. 112.

45 Bernard M. W. Knox, *The Heroic Temper* (Berkeley and Los Angeles, 1964), p. 57.

46 See Jacques Lacan, *Seminaire* no. 7 (Paris, 1986), pp. 362–8.

47 Žižek, *Did Somebody Say Totalitarianism?* p. 81.

48 A. C. Bradley, *Shakespearian Tragedy* (London, 1904), p. 13.

49 See Raymond Williams, *Drama from Ibsen to Brecht* (London, 1968), p. 107.

9 Demons

1 Marshall Berman, *All That Is Solid Melts Into Air* (London, 1982), p. 15.

2 Perry Anderson, 'Modernity and Revolution', *New Left Review* no. 144 (March–April 1984), p. 98.

3   For a wide-ranging account of the Faust myth, see Harry Redner, *In the Beginning was the Deed* (Berkeley and Los Angeles, 1982). See also George Lukács, *Goethe and his Age* (London, 1968), chapter 7.

4   Northrop Frye, *Anatomy of Criticism: Four Essays* (Princeton, NJ, 1957), p. 283.

5   Karl Jaspers, *Tragedy Is Not Enough* (London, 1934), p. 95.

6   See Terry Eagleton, *The Ideology of the Aesthetic* (Oxford, 1990), chapter 4.

7   On the subject of the fortunate Fall, see Herbert Weisinger, *Tragedy and the Paradox of the Fortunate Fall* (London, 1953), which traces the idea back to early mythology.

8   Quoted in Arthur O. Lovejoy, *Essays in the History of Ideas* (Baltimore, MD, 1948), p. 288.

9   Jean-Jacques Rousseau, *A Discourse on Inequality* (London, 1984), p. 136.

10 Michael Hardt and Antonio Negri, *Empire* (Cambridge, MA and London, 2000), p. 127.

11 See *The Works of John Milton* (New York, 1931), vol. 4, p. 311.

12 Thomas Mann, *The Magic Mountain* (Harmondsworth, 1962), p. 466.

13 Norman O. Brown, *Life Against Death* (London, 1959), p. 87.

14 For an excellent treatment of Goethe's *Faust*, see Franco Moretti, *Modern Epic* (London, 1996), Part 1.

15 Ibid., pp. 88 and 89.

16 Erich Heller, *The Disinherited Mind* (London, 1952), p. 59.

17 Georg Lukács, *Goethe and his Age* (London, 1968), pp. 169–70.

18 Thomas Mann, *Doctor Faustus* (London, 1996). All subsequent references to this work are given in parentheses after quotations.

19 St Augustine, *Confessions* (London, 1963), p. 62 (translation amended). A notably uneven collection of essays on evil is to be found in Joan Copjec (ed.), *Radical Evil* (London, 1996). For Immanuel Kant, such demonic evil – flouting the moral law just for the sake of it – would be unintelligible. To be a person at all for Kant is to be conscious, however dimly, of the claims of morality; and a being which had no sense of these claims could not be said to be acting rationally, and hence would not be *acting* at all. Evil for Kant must be done freely, which presupposes some kind of commitment to reason. I owe this point to Peter Dews.

20 Primo Levi, *The Drowned and the Saved* (London, 1988), p. 96.

21 Immanuel Wallerstein, 'The Uses of Racism', *London Review of Books* vol. 22, no. 10 (May 2000).

22 Slavoj Žižek, *Did Somebody Say Totalitarianism?* (London, 2001), pp. 63–4.

23 See Hannah Arendt, *Eichmann in Jerusalem: A Report on the Banality of Evil* (New York, 1965).

24 Levi, *The Drowned and the Saved*, p. 101.

25 Ibid., p. 83.

26 Ibid., p. 100.

27 Geoffrey Wheatcroft, 'Horrors Beyond Tragedy', *Times Literary Supplement* (9 June 2000).

28 Jaspers, *Tragedy Is Not Enough*, p. 101.

29 *Thomas Aquinas: Selected Writings* (London, 1998), p. 567.
30 Søren Kierkegaard, *The Concept of Anxiety* (Princeton, NJ, 1980), p. 133.
31 Ibid., p. 132.
32 For a valuable philosophical account, see Timo Airaksinen, *The Philosophy of the Marquis de Sade* (London, 1991).
33 Plato, *The Last Days of Socrates* (London, 1993), pp. 110 and 112.
34 Franco Moretti, *Signs Taken For Wonders* (London, 1983), p. 81.
35 Sigmund Freud, *Civilization and Its Discontents* (London, 1930), p. 77n.
36 For an impressively wide-ranging study of this theme, see Jonathan Dollimore, *Death, Desire and Loss in Western Culture* (London, 1998).
37 Max Horkheimer and Theodor Adorno, *Dialectic of Enlightenment* (London, 1979), p. 33.
38 See the translation of the play by Martin Greenberg in *Heinrich von Kleist: Five Plays* (New Haven, CT and London, 1988).
39 G. W. F. Hegel, *The Phenomenology of Spirit* (Oxford, 1977), p. 19.
40 Thomas Mann, *The Magic Mountain* (Harmondsworth, 1962). All subsequent references to this text are given in parentheses after quotations.

10   Thomas Mann's Hedgehog

1 Raymond Williams, *Modern Tragedy* (London, 1966), p. 44.
2 See Eva Figes, *Tragedy and Social Evolution* (London, 1976).
3 For attitudes in classical antiquity to outsiders, see Edith Hall, *Inventing the Barbarian* (Oxford, 1989).
4 Walter Benjamin, *The Origin of German Tragic Drama* (London, 1977), p. 107.
5 Simon Sparks, in Miguel de Beistegui and Simon Sparks (eds), *Philosophy and Tragedy* (London, 2000), p. 203.
6 See, for example, W. Buckert, 'Greek Tragedy and Sacrificial Ritual', *Greek, Roman and Byzantine Studies* no. 7 (1966). Francis Fergusson's *The Idea of a Theater* (Princeton, NJ, 1949, p. 26) assumes that tragedy has its origins in fertility cults. John Holloway traces what he sees as a pattern of ritual scape-goating in Shakespeare in *The Story of the Night* (London, 1961).
7 See A. W. Pickard-Cambridge, *Dithyramb, Tragedy and Comedy* (Oxford, 1927) and Gerald F. Else, *The Origin and Early Form of Greek Tragedy* (Cambridge, MA, 1967). A similar case is argued by H. D. F. Kitto, *Form and Meaning in Drama* (London, 1956), p. 219, and by Oliver Taplin in 'Emotion and Meaning in Greek Tragedy' in E. Segal (ed.), *Oxford Readings in Greek Tragedy* (Oxford, 1983), p. 4. The classic case for tragedy as deriving from Dionysian ritual is famously advanced in Jane Ellen Harrison, *Themis: A Study of the Social Origins of Greek Religion* (Cambridge, 1927), which includes a celebrated excursus by the classical scholar Gilbert Murray on supposedly ritual forms in Greek tragedy.
8 Georges Bataille, *Visions of Excess: Selected Writings, 1927–1939*, ed. Allan Stoekl (Minneapolis, MN, 1985), p. 218.
9 The phrase is Paul Ricoeur's in *The Symbolism of Evil* (Boston, 1969), p. 225.

10 E. R. Dodds, *The Greeks and the Irrational* (Berkeley and Los Angeles, 1951), p. 41.

11 René Girard, *Violence and the Sacred* (Baltimore, MD and London, 1977), p. 1.

12 See 'The Uncanny', in J. Strachey (ed.), *The Standard Edition of the Psychological Works of Sigmund Freud* (London, 1955), vol. 17.

13 Ibid., p. 271.

14 See Jacques Derrida, 'Plato's Pharmacy', *Dissemination* (London, 1981). Derrida gives only a brief account in this essay of the scapegoat, concerned as he chiefly is with writing as ambiguously poison and cure, death and life. William Righter's essay 'Fool and "Pharmakon"', in C. Norris and N. Mapp (eds), *William Empson: The Critical Achievement* (Cambridge, 1993), is concerned with both terms as examples of Empson's 'complex words' but overlooks the substantive link between them.

15 Charles Segal, *Tragedy and Civilisation* (Cambridge, MA, 1981), pp. 45–6.

16 Adrian Poole, *Shakespeare and the Greek Example* (Oxford, 1987), p. 106.

17 Fergusson, *The Idea of a Theater*, p. 27.

18 For Lacan's discussion of these questions, see in particular his *Seminar VII: On the Ethics of Psychoanalysis* (New York, 1992).

19 For a fuller interpretation along these lines, see J.-P. Vernant, 'Ambiguity and Reversal: On the Enigmatic Structure of *Oedipus Rex*', in E. Segal (ed.), *Oxford Readings in Greek Tragedy* (Oxford, 1983).

20 Simon Goldhill, *Reading Greek Tragedy* (Cambridge, 1986), p. 217.

21 I am indebted here to the work of Bernard Knox, especially *The Heroic Temper* (Berkeley and Los Angeles, 1954), and his article on Oedipus reprinted in R. P. Draper (ed.), *Tragedy: Developments in Criticism* (London, 1980).

22 A. D. Nuttall considers that Greek poetry is obsessed with feet (personal communication).

23 Poole, *Shakespeare and the Greek Example*, p. 239.

24 Slavoj Žižek, *The Ticklish Subject* (London, 1999), p. 156.

25 Ibid., p. 161.

26 I follow here Simon Critchley's discussion of Levinas in his *Ethics–Politics–Subjectivity* (London, 1999), p. 63ff.

27 Ibid., p. 64.

28 Ibid.

29 Karl Marx, 'Contribution to the Critique of Hegel's Philosophy of Right', in T. Bottomore (ed.), *Karl Marx: Early Writings* (London, 1963), p. 58.

30 Mary Douglas, *Purity and Danger* (London, 1966), p. 94.

31 Ibid., p. 5.

32 Ibid., p. 167.

33 Ibid., p. 170.

34 Richard Wolin, *Walter Benjamin: An Aesthetic of Redemption* (New York, 1982), p. 52.

35 Benjamin, *The Origin of German Tragic Drama*, p. 81.

36 Jeanette King, *Tragedy in the Victorian Novel* (Cambridge, 1978), p. 10.

37 Henry James, *The Wings of the Dove*, ed. Peter Brooks (Oxford, 1998), p. xi.

Index